the new vegetable & fruit garden book

r. milton carleton

Henry Regnery Company • Chicago

Library of Congress Cataloging in Publication Data

Carleton, R. Milton.
    The new vegetable and fruit garden book.

    Includes index.
    1. Vegetable gardening.   2. Fruit-culture.
3. Agriculture—Handbooks, manuals, etc.
I Title.
SB321.C27   1976   635   75-32963
ISBN 0-8092-8132-5
ISBN 0-8092-8075-2 pbk.

Published by Henry Regnery Company
    180 North Michigan Avenue, Chicago, Illinois 60601
Manufactured in the United States of America
Library of Congress Catalog Card Number: 75-32963
International Standard Book Number: 0-8092-8132-5 (cloth)
                                    0-8092-8075-2 (paper)

Published simultaneously in Canada by
Beaverbooks
953 Dillingham Road
Pickering, Ontario L1W 1Z7
Canada

Contents

Introduction
Growing for the Table:
A New Approach   vii

I   **Vegetable Crops**

1   Why Hybrid Vegetables?   1

2   Tomatoes and Relatives   6

3   Greens: Grandma's Garden
       Sass Updated   29

4   Vine Crops   55

5   Peas and Beans   71

6   Sweet Corn as a Garden Crop   82

7   Bulb Crops   88

8   Root Crops: Summer
       and Winter   94

9   Potatoes and Sweet Potatoes   103

10   The Gardener's Spice
       Cabinet—Herbs   109

11   Perennial Food Crops   123

12   Do Vegetables Cross-Pollinate?   132

II   **Home-Grown Fruits**

13   Growing Fruits and Nuts
        at Home   139

14   The Strawberry   144

15   Grapes for Table and Wine   157

16   The Brambles or Cane Fruits   168

17   Gooseberries and Currants   178

18   Blueberries as a Home Fruit Crop   183

19   The Stone Fruits:
        Peaches, Plums and Cherries   190

20   Tree Fruits: Apples and Pears   203

21   Pruning: Discipline for Plants   224

22   Little-Grown Fruiting
        Trees and Shrubs   235

23   Nuts as a Food Crop   239

24   Subtropical Fruits   244

III   **Materials and Methods in the Garden**

25   Control of Insects
        and Diseases   259

26   Where Can You Garden?   266

27   Planning How Much to Plant   271

28   Fertilizers: Are They
        "Plant Foods"?   276

29   Soil: A Basic "Stuff" of Life   287

30   Tools and Other Equipment   300

31   Hotbeds, Cold Frames, and Cloches   311

32   The Many Reasons for Mulching   319

33   Storing Vegetables for
        Winter Use   327

IV   **The Modern Homesteader**

34   Facing Up to Modern
        Homesteading   337

35   Tools and Materials
         for Homesteaders   344
36   Meat Sources for Homesteaders
         and Suburbanites   351
37   Triticale—A Homesteaders' Grain   371
38   A Bible for Survival Farmers
         (a note on *Mother Earth News*)   373
     Index   375

Introduction

Growing for the Table:

A New Approach

A common failing of all too many books written by starry-eyed advocates of some cause or other is that they gloss over the difficulties that might result from following what they recommend. I must confess to this practice in my past efforts to persuade readers to grow vegetables just outside the kitchen door. The time has come to make amends.

Suddenly what is described as a world food crisis has created a need to discuss the pros and cons of home food production without exaggeration. Extravagant claims have been made for possible savings, even from the office of the president. In a situation charged with a sense of panic and disaster, such statements can be a disservice to millions of Americans already disturbed by rising prices and shortages of staple vegetables on the market, not to mention alarmist news of crop failures and mass starvation—starvation that even food-rich America is powerless to prevent.

Looming largest in the eyes of millions of Americans are prices for both fresh and processed foods that have zoomed over 500 percent for some items, and that may go even higher. Is the sensible answer to grow food F.O.B. the kitchen door? My purpose is to supply the facts needed to answer that question. Although I have written on food production in several of my sixteen books, old answers will not do today.

Formerly the most important reason for growing your own vegetables was quality—succulence, superior flavor, and better nutrition. While quality is still important, saving money and perhaps even supplying food for survival may be more vital. What has not been stressed in home gardening is the significant change in present-day varieties. A whole battery of modern hybrid vegetables now allows even the inexperienced home gardener to grow varieties that mature earlier, produce more edible food from the same space, are free from once devastating diseases, and make better use of fertilizers and soil moisture. Nor do these hybrid varieties call for any sacrifice of quality. Because they mature faster they are more succulent, more tender. Spraying for disease and insect control has been reduced to a point where gardening is a pleasure, not a constant war against old-time pests.

Another way in which this book will break new ground is in recognizing the importance of a 20th century phenomenon—the desire of millions to escape the city for what they feel will be a peaceful, happy existence far from noisy streets. Migration from urban to rural homes during the past decade has already swelled to such proportions that, in many states, prices of abandoned farm and marginal agricultural land now are as high as for high-grade crop land ten years ago. In the spring, summer, and fall of 1974, I found that hundreds upon hundreds of families had taken this step with little or no knowledge of what it involved.

Where this book can be of service to these present-day homesteaders is in discussing crops that serve two purposes—food for the table and for livestock and poultry—as well as meat and grain crops that provide a well-rounded diet.

My intention is to neither urge nor discourage those contemplating a flight from the city. Everyone must decide whether such a move is an escape to paradise or utter folly. The escapees with whom I have talked fall into two groups: those who struggle just to keep their heads above water financially, and those engaged in the senseless effort to keep up with the Joneses. Both groups are equally weary, and an increasing number are motivated by an uneasy fear of what might happen to our cities or even to our culture.

In 1974 and 1975, I was asked a number of times about warnings by a leading economist, who was predicting riots and anarchy in American cities. There were rumors that the FBI had a program for training city police departments for riot duty. To counter a breakdown of law and order, if and when it comes, a Canadian economist gave the following advice:

> Don't panic, but consider the following course of action if matters grow worse. Buy a small farm, or even a larger one if land is cheap, remote enough from giant cities so that hungry mobs and racial conflicts will pass you by. Grow all the food you possibly can. Stockpile such staples as coffee, tea, spices and salt you cannot produce. Buy and store materials and manufactured products needed for survival in quantities large enough to last for a long period. Find ways to become independent of petroleum, electricity and other outside sources of energy. Be prepared to sit out riots and panics that lie ahead, in hopes that some miracle may bring about better social and economic order. The sooner you buy that farm, the less it will cost and it might substitute as a summer home or a trip to Europe or South America.

A surprising development in the flight to the country, is the proliferation of magazines for the new homesteader, three in the state of Maine alone. Some of these paint rosy pictures of transitions from city chaos to country calm, but in others there have been grim stories of failures and disappointments.

For anyone whose night life has been no more strenuous than watching "All in the Family" or "The FBI" on television, sitting up in a dark barn by the light of an oil lamp, watching a sick pig, can be traumatic. For those who are determined to make the move, the section on Modern Homesteading presents facts and ideas that will make the transition easier and more satisfying.

Those who are able to make the move are, of course, only a small percentage of those who should consider growing food at home—urban and suburban families who number in the tens of millions. Having served on national and state food garden committees, I am familiar with both the possibilities and the limitations of emergency gardens. Disturbing to me are the claims for huge savings parroted on radio and TV and by the press. Even the president (obviously relying on information supplied him by agricultural experts) issued such a statement, quoting a figure that my experience tells me is beyond the reach of 95 out of 100 amateur gardeners.

True, a substantial return can be had from dollars spent on a home vegetable garden but largely because the gardener himself contributes the largest item of expense in commercial vegetable production—his own time and labor. To find out how successful the first big year of the present interest in home food production had been, I phoned and wrote to more than 100 authorities in the field—old friends among extension workers, garden editors, seedsmen, and some of the country's outstanding amateur gardeners. To learn still more, I agreed to teach an adult education course in home vegetable gardening. All this told me that millions upon millions of Americans are rushing into growing food at home without such basic knowledge as what varieties to plant, how plants grow, and which materials they will need.

What was particularly disturbing to me was a lack of appreciation of the role of hybrid vegetables, which can not only save gardeners hours of work but increase production per square foot, particularly important in small city gardens. I also found that there was a shortage in seeds. By May, many seedsmen faced bare bins and had to draw on seed stocks reserved for producing the next year's crop. Demand in some areas actually exceeded that during World War II. The story was the same for fertilizers, which were in critical supply because practically all of America's plant food is based on petroleum. Tools and working gear were similarly in short supply.

Even with the advance knowledge from 1974, the story was repeated in 1975, since, in the case of seeds, at least two years are needed to grow practically all crops; three years in the case of crops such as beets and cabbage, of which seeds are produced on second-year plants.

In late June, before the canning season had even begun, jars and closures were sold out in many areas, and in some instances small dealers received not a single jar all season.

In the face of this disorder the record of accomplishment was amazingly good. Of those gardening for the first time, an estimated 15 percent failed to produce enough vegetables to pay for their seeds and other costs. Part of this failure was the result of widespread drought. The record would have been better had someone told these neophyte gardeners that more than 90 percent of the elements used by plants is water; at least they could have prepared for sprinkling or irrigation. Other failures were due to disease and insect infestation, too much shade, and lack of fertility.

Those familiar with conventional garden books will notice several omissions in the present volume. Pictures will be scarce, in spite of the fact that customary practice is to cram in all the illustrations possible. Although pictures sell books, I have found that they are all but useless in helping a home gardener do his job; and they add to the cost of a book. Illustrations have been kept to a minimum, and line drawings have been used because they are easier to understand than a blurry photograph of some plant.

Nor will you find plans for gardens taking up space in these pages. When I served on state and national Victory Garden committees during World War II, I saw thousands upon thousands of such charts distributed, but I cannot recall a single garden based on them.

In 1974 and 1975, nearly 85 percent of all home gardens paid back all costs. Many who only broke even were still delighted because they ate better vegetables than they had ever tasted before, and others spoke of the pleasure of sharing their surplus vegetables with friends. Practically all were planning to garden again.

It is with a hope that I can help both those gardening for the first time, and those whose enthusiasm has not been stifled by failure, that I present a new approach to savings, succulence and possibly survival.

R. Milton Carleton

I

Vegetable Crops

1

Why Hybrid Vegetables?

For years I have argued for the preservation of old-time home garden vegetables for use in home gardens rather than tough, tasteless commercial varieties, which were listed for amateur use in most seed catalogs.

I am still convinced that many commercial varieties are not suitable for home gardens. There is, for example, the description of Danish Ballhead cabbage when it was first introduced, which read "Here is a cabbage so firm and so solid that it could be *kicked* to market and would still arrive in salable condition."

Salable it might be, but even before that treatment, hardly edible. The way a vegetable stands up in shipment is not the only difference between market varieties and those a home gardener should plant. A commercial grower wants a variety that is a "cropper," one that reaches maturity all at once, allowing the whole field to be harvested and the soil worked up for another crop. When such a variety is planted in a home garden, it might mature half a bushel of snap beans in a day or two but stop producing almost overnight.

Commercial varieties are strong on color: Shoppers buy with their eyes. Home gardeners can grow a snap bean such as Con-

1

tender, which is light green in color and has short, curved pods—less attractive than a market bean but superior in flavor and in length of harvest. Add disease resistance and early maturity for a perfect trouble-free home garden bean.

Within the past decade we have come into a whole new era of vegetable breeding—the production of hundreds of so-called hybrid vegetables. Although the work was done to produce commercial varieties, hybrid techniques have produced many varieties that fit the needs of the home gardener even better than choice old-time vegetables that lacked resistance to diseases and insects. Too, because of their greater vigor, these new hybrids produce earlier crops. Quick growth in turn means tenderness and flavor that equals or excels those of most old-time favorites.

Unfortunately these hybrids have not caught on quickly. Home gardeners still demand Ponderosa, Marglobe, Rutgers and John Baer tomatoes, first because they know them, and second because price tags on packets of hybrid seeds are often three to four times as high and just as often contain about one-fourth as many seeds.

Although I admit a cost of ten to twenty times greater for seed seems unreasonable, hybrids are practically all hand-pollinated and costly to produce. Passing up their advantages, however, can be penny-wise and pound-foolish.

A good example of the advantages of hybrids can be seen from the case of two neighbors who asked for my recommendation of a "good cucumber." I recommended to both that they plant Gemini 7 because it was free from disease, would bear earlier, and would produce at least twice as many cucumbers. One man took my advice, even though he paid 75¢ a packet for 30 seeds. His neighbor objected to the price and picked up a packet of Improved Long Green at a supermarket for 29¢.

The seed of Gemini 7 showed above ground a full week before Improved Long Green, a direct indication of hybrid vigor. It raced along and set fruits a full two weeks earlier. This was because Gemini vines are gynoecious; that is, they produce only female flowers. Since all fruits come from female flowers, gynoecious vines produce cucumbers sooner, and more of them. Even more advantageous, they are practically seedless.

As a result the man who used this variety picked not only the first cucumbers, but twice as many. His vines showed no trace of scab, mosaic, anthracnose or wilt—diseases that killed the Long Green variety just as the vines were coming into full bearing. Although there was a 46¢ difference in the cost of seeds, hybrids showed a profit of nearly $50 (at market prices) over production by Long Green. Even counting only those actually eaten and pickled for later use, the difference was over $20.

In the early days of hybrid vegetables, I was not too enthusiastic about them, largely because hybrid corn, the first available to home gardeners, lacked the flavor of older open pollinated varieties. Those who still feel that this is true will be jolted out of that notion with their first taste of Silver Queen Hybrid, with flavor no old-time corn can match. Add to that the fact that hybrids are immune to Stewart's disease, which infects old-time varieties, and any reason advanced for planting such museum pieces as original Country Gentlemen and Golden Bantam seems a bit silly.

Unfortunately when hastily reading a catalog or looking over a seed rack in a supermarket, one seldom encounters these tremendous advantages of hybrid vegetables. Usually the hybrids are omitted entirely from rack displays because their high price hinders sales. Although such racks do serve the casual buyer, reading catalogs carefully and searching out these supervarieties will be the most important step a home gardener can take in squeezing out all possible production.

Because only a reading of mail-order catalogs will locate sources for these better varieties, it would be a disservice to readers if I did not list them. In doing so I must apologize to many honest, reliable firms whose catalogs I may not have received. The following firms do list one or more of those I mention. They are all firms whose seeds I have grown and found true to description and of satisfactory germination:

Burpee Seeds, 300 Park Ave., Warminster, PA 18974 (General List) also Clinton, Iowa 52732

Farmer Seed & Nursery Co., Faribault, MN 55021 (Hardy northern vars.)

Jos. Harris Seed Co., Moreton Farm, Rochester, NY 14624

(General list)

H. G. Hastings Co., Box 44088, Atlanta, GA 30336 (Southern vars.)

Kitazawa Seed Co., 356 Taylor St., San Jose, CA 95110 (Oriental seeds)

Le Jardin du Gourmet, Ramsey, NJ (Shallots & European seeds)

Thompson & Morgan, Inc., P.O. Box 24, 401 Kennedy Blvd., Somerdale, NJ 08083 (Many English vars.)

Twilley Seed Co., Salisbury, MD 21801 (Some special vars. for the South)

Stokes Seeds, Inc., Box 548, Buffalo, NY 14240; and St. Catherines, Ontario, Canada.

Vesey Seed Ltd., York, P.E.I., Canada (Cold-resistant varieties)

One important fact to remember: Although seed houses tend to handle varieties adapted to their region, the idea that they grow all their seeds locally is not true nowadays. Instead these are grown by specialists in areas where certain crops grow to best advantage, as, for example, the highly specialized production of vine crops by the wholesale firm of Petoseed Co., Inc., in Saticoy, California. A majority of the cucumber, tomato, squash, and melon seeds sold in the United States originate with this one firm.

This is to the advantage of the gardener, since it insures him, in many crops, of a better quality seed than can be grown locally.

Nowadays seed catalog houses are finding printing and mailing costs so high that they are limiting the number they print. Be sure to write early for your copy. This is a pleasant task for the week between Christmas and New Year's Day.

As soon as that catalog arrives, make out your order and plan the garden for the coming season. Lately shortages have been common. Hybrid vegetables in particular are affected because they require hand labor and because it is difficult to build up the foundation stocks necessary to produce them.

A final word: If you are still undecided about paying the higher prices for hybrid vegetable seed, perhaps the following directions for preventing early blight, late blight, and Alternaria diseases ·with a well-known insecticide on open-pollinated tomatoes may help in making up your mind that hybrids are worth more than they cost: "Begin when disease threatens and repeat at seven- to ten-day intervals, or as often as necessary to maintain control. Under severe conditions shorten the spray interval."

2

Tomatoes and Relatives

No matter how you pronounce its name—toe-may-toe, toe-mah-toe or toe-matt-o—the tomato is without question America's favorite home garden crop. In many ways it deserves the honor because no other vegetable is more accommodating. It will survive in a wide range of soils and climate, producing abundantly until frost in spite of insect pests and diseases that would destroy other vegetables.

Yet it does present problems that can baffle beginning gardeners. Fortunately most gardeners set out more plants than are needed and so wind up with more tomatoes than they can eat. They could get along with fewer plants with less work in less space by understanding what the tomato's needs are.

The tomato has simple but specific requirements. These essentials are seven hours of direct sunshine, definite temperature limits, and plenty of space around each plant. Perhaps the least understood of these needs is that for a definite temperature range. The seedlings are tough, so long as frost does not occur. When they are ready to bloom, however, any thermometer reading below 55 degrees will cause them to shed all unopened buds as well as any flowers that have not been pollinated. The same is true of temperatures that are too high. If the thermometer stays above 76 degrees for several nights in a row, or if daytime readings reach 90 degrees or more, flower buds are also shed.

Unfavorable temperatures do not affect green fruits that are already set, which accounts for ripe tomatoes that are produced even though spells of heat or cold occur.

Tomatoes like free air movement around the plants; yet if there is no space for them in an open garden, they can be grown in unconventional ways—as vines on a fence, or as pot plants in tubs on a terrace, or in an oversized hanging basket (say one about a foot in diameter). For hanging baskets small fruited varieties such as Sugar Lump or Gardener's Delight are sensational when their long trusses of fruits are ripe.

A striking example of the adaptability of tomatoes to unusual cultural methods is the garbage-can tomato tower developed by the Sierra Chemical Company, Milpitas, California 95035. It calls for a plastic garbage can with drainage holes bored in it, an artificial soil mixture, a supporting trellis and Sierra's Green-Green slow release fertilizer. Explicit directions can be had from Sierra at their Milpitas address.

In the open garden, tomatoes will thrive sprawling on a straw or plastic mulch, trained to stakes or growing in cages made out of farm fencing or chicken wire. There are also bush types that grow upright without any supports.

Tomatoes are not fussy as to soil so long as it is well drained but will still hold moisture and is reasonably fertile. They enjoy well-decayed organic matter in the soil but fresh decaying matter on the surface of soil is a source of disease. Although they will grow in soils as acid as 5.5, they prefer a sweeter soil, up to a pH of 6.9. No single food crop the home gardener grows can produce more than a tomato plant, given the right conditions. A single plant occupying less than five square feet of space can produce as much as 100 pounds of ripe fruit in a growing season. I have seen a single specimen of the variety Giant Tree, trained on a trellis, produce more than four bushels of fruit, about half of them over one pound in weight. The trellis was 15 feet tall, and top fruits had to be picked from a ladder.

The amazing fact about the ease with which tomatoes can be grown is that no other crop in the home garden is attacked by as many diseases. Yet a beginning gardener can buy transplants about which he knows nothing and that may already be infected with disease and still produce better tomatoes than he can buy on the market. Is it any wonder that this is America's favorite home-grown food crop?

Tomato Growing Not Always a "Piece of Cake"

If you are content to lose some of your crop to disease and still gather all the tomatoes you can eat, the following description of some of the ills that can cut production can be skipped. If, however, your space is limited and you need every possible fruit in return for your efforts, yields can be increased from 100 percent to 500 percent by avoiding trouble.

In the past, catalogs for home gardeners kept quiet about tomato diseases, largely because nothing could be done about them. As one pathologist stated the problem a few years ago, "Once a plant has a disease, all you can do is hold a post mortem to find out why it died. Plant diseases cannot be cured; they can only be prevented." Although this is no longer strictly true, it does emphasize the importance of starting with healthy plants and keeping them healthy. Prevent disease rather than try to cure it by spraying. One exception is a new chemical called Benlate, containing benomyl, a systemic fungicide developed by du Pont that can actually invade a tomato plant and kill disease organisms.

Chemicals are wonderful when you need them, but it is cheaper to start with healthy seedlings and to give them tender, loving care. Don't expect to rush into a garden center or greenhouse about the middle of May and buy healthy, sturdy transplants. Although conscientious growers take precautions against infecting seedlings, there is no way you can tell by looking whether they are free from tobacco mosaic, early blight, or other diseases.

Of all tomato ills tobacco mosaic is the most harmful; it is caused by a virus passed on to the plants by anyone who smokes or chews tobacco. This virus is one of the toughest disease agents known. It has survived heating to as high as 300 degrees. Alcohol can't kill it. It can live for weeks on doorknobs, wooden flats, and water taps. Older plants do not gain resistance to it. If the gardener smokes he can transmit tobacco mosaic to his plants in tying or pruning.

Modern detergents cannot kill the virus, although soap and water can. Always wash your hands if you are a smoker before handling tomato plants. Big greenhouses where tomato transplants are grown usually have tubs containing a solution of trisodium phosphate for this purpose.

The sure way to avoid mosaic infection is to grow your own seedlings. If you smoke wash with soap and water before touching them. Or you can sow seed right in the garden where plants can grow without transplanting. About this technique, more later.

Infected plants do not develop signs of mosaic until warm weather occurs. The first sign will be leaves that are mottled light and dark green, changing to yellow and light green as the plants mature. Infected foliage twists as it grows and resembles that of ferns.

Many diseases can be transmitted by bacteria or spores from soil splashed onto foliage by rain or a strong stream from a hose. Among these diseases are fusarium, botrytis, and verticillium wilts. A clean mulch of straw or plastic helps prevent infection. Although mulches of lawn clippings have been used by millions of gardeners without trouble, in cool damp weather such a mulch can be a source of trouble. If the garden is shaded for part of the day, mildew in particular can be a serious problem since mildew organisms thrive in fresh lawn clippings.

If a green cover crop is plowed under to improve soil tilth, be sure it is completely covered, with no tufts of rotting vegetation sticking above the surface. When such a crop is used, it should be sprinkled with a fertilizer before turning under, to speed up decomposition.

The biggest boost to tomato growing, however, can be credited to vegetable plant breeders. They have given us plants resistant to or tolerant of three of the most important tomato ills—fusarium wilt, verticillium wilt, and nematodes. Nematodes are not a disease but hairlike worms, barely visible to the eye. They bore into roots to feed, not only doing direct harm, but opening the way for infection by diseases.

Today catalogs list many outstanding varieties that are identified by the initials VFN, indicating that they are resistant to all three of these troubles. There are many more resistant only to verticillium and fusarium, indicated by the initials VF. In the North, nematodes are not as serious, so these VF varieties are usually highly productive. In the South, VFN varieties should be given preference. Because Southern conditions favor disease, many varieties have been produced with multiple resistance or tolerance to problems such as leaf mold, grey wall, grey leaf spot, and alternaria. Two varieties of unusual value to home gardeners in the South, because of such resistance, are Manalucie and Hastings Red Chief Hybrid, described later.

Cultural Controls

A planting in an area that lies in shade for much of the morning, even if it does receive six hours of full sunshine later in the day, is much more likely to be hit by disease than one that receives some sunlight all day long. Sunshine is a powerful bactericide and fungicide. Use it by planting tomatoes in the sunniest area in the garden and by giving them more space so that the sun can reach the soil around them. Sunshine is particularly useful in preventing mildew because it dries off foliage, which kills mildew spores.

A condition that is not a true disease but can be controlled by good culture, is bud drop. This is a problem that garden editors hear about when spring has been late and cool, with night temperatures below 55 degrees. It comes up again in July and August, when the culprit is summer heat. To prevent bud drop hormones can be sprayed on the unopened buds to stop the formation of a cutting-off layer between the bud and stem. The brand with the widest distribution is called Blossom Set. If your spring arrives late, another answer is to grow varieties such as Cold Set and Spring Set, which will tolerate temperatures as low as 48 to 50 degrees without shedding buds.

Another cause of poor fruit set is a lack of pollination. Tomatoes are self-pollinating, but they depend on wind to shake the plant enough so that pollen will loosen and fall on the pistil. In greenhouses electric vibrators are used. Tomato plants out of doors usually have no trouble with pollination, but in gardens in closed-in areas, as in some fenced backyards, the weather of July and August may be too calm for proper loosening of the pollen. In gardens surrounded by hedges, buildings, and walls, an occasional shaking of staked and caged tomatoes can help.

Blossom end rot is a disturbing condition that looks like a true disease but is actually a physiological condition in which the free end of tomato fruits turns a sooty black. Plant physiologists are not sure what causes this condition, but they do know that two cultural steps can help to prevent it. A soil high in calcium is one requirement. The other is avoiding fluctuations in soil moisture. A soil that is alternately dry and wet causes cracking of the fruit so that black mold can enter.

Toward fall, production tends to decrease because older plants produce fewer flowers but younger plants continue to bloom and set fruit. If extra space is available, as where earlier crops have been harvested, set out a second crop of tomatoes to provide fruit for canning, freezing, and for table use. I root such plants from healthy vines of the old crop. Rooted suckers will have more vigor than the plants from which they were taken.

Weeds as a Source of Disease

Weeds not only pass on harmful organisms but also shelter insects that enable such organisms to survive over winter. Cucumber mosaic is an example. It lives over in milkweed, pokeweed, wild cucumbers, and ground cherry. It is spread to tomatoes by aphids that have fed on such weeds. Of the 114 or more diseases known to infect tomatoes, many are carried over from year to year in this way.

It has been my experience that when tomatoes are started indoors, the transplants are best kept there a week or two longer than is usually recommended. The reason is simple: Aphids that carry disease hatch out much earlier than do their natural enemies such as the praying mantis, lady bugs, and ichneumid flies. If these plants are set out a little later, when such predators are active, they will reduce aphid populations enough so that transmitted diseases are less serious.

Sensitivity to 2,4-D

Soon after the introduction of 2,4-D as a lawn weed killer, complaints of curling shoots on tomato plants became common. At first this curling or epinasty was blamed on cucumber mosaic, but later it was found to be caused by 2,4-D. Tomato plants were so sensitive to this chemical that they were used to detect it in laboratory research. Often spraying at a distance of a mile or more would cause the typical epinasty.

Two conditions were found to be responsible. One was volatility. Early formulations of 2,4-D were highly volatile, even at low temperatures. Newer forms are less volatile, so that no gaseous vapor is released to cause trouble. The other cause was drift. If high pressure was used in spraying and if the opening in the nozzle was small, spraying gave off extremely fine particles, almost like an aerosol bomb, that could be carried for long distances on the wind. You cannot, of course, control someone in your neighborhood who is spraying, but if you are treating your own surroundings use a nozzle with a larger opening so that the 2,4-D solution comes out in droplets instead of a mist, and use low pressure in the spray tank.

Direct Seeding of Tomatoes

Sowing tomato seed where the plants are to grow and fruit is a surprising idea to those who have been brainwashed into believing that tomatoes *must* be transplanted. In the tomato's native home, in the uplands of South America, there was no one to perform this act for it. Today hundreds of thousands of acres are direct-seeded every year to produce commercial crops for processing.

Tomato seeds are quite hardy, as can be proved in almost any garden where they were grown the year before. Unless all ripe fruits were cleaned up (as they should be) the previous fall, volunteer seedlings will appear all over the area. When such volunteers are allowed to grow and produce fruit, they are usually much healthier than plants grown indoors and transplanted, and they will usually continue to produce well right up until frost.

When sowing directly you will probably want to start some very early varieties indoors for your first taste of home-grown tomatoes; when moved outdoors, these should have green fruits already set if they are to beat the direct-sown main crop. I have had direct-sown plants produce fruits several days ahead of regular transplants.

Seed can be sown as soon as the soil is workable. Although it will not germinate in cold soil, it will not rot but will lie dormant until favorable conditions for growth occur. Perhaps this conditioning in cold soil has something to do with the extra vigor of direct-seeded plants.

Growing Transplants Indoors

Although I am a firm believer in growing your own seedlings for transplanting, I do not recommend doing so unless conditions are right. All too often gardeners try to do this in a room where the light is not right and where the air is too dry and hot. As a result the seedlings are thin and spindly, and they take weeks to recover.

Keys to good growth and germination are light and temperature. Unfortunately the eye is a poor instrument for measuring available light. Even a room that looks bright enough can be too dark to grow seedlings that will survive and thrive. To test whether you have enough sunshine lay a sheet of white paper on the windowsill on a day when the sun is moderately bright, perhaps with a thin overcast of clouds. The shadow of your hand on the paper should be sharp and distinct at noon, with no fuzzy edges. If not, better grow seedlings completely by artificial light.

Even if this test is satisfactory, still another element must be considered: Light has several "dimensions," of which intensity is only one. Equally important is duration or day length. Will it be long enough at the time seedlings are being grown? Over most of the area north of the Ohio River, tender plants such as tomatoes, peppers, and eggplant should be sown indoors about March 15, unless larger plants with green fruit are wanted; in that case March 1 is none too soon.

About that date the shadow of your hand on the sheet of white paper should cast a fairly sharp shadow, perhaps with a slightly fuzzy outline at 8:00 AM (standard time; an hour later daylight time). Since seedlings should have at least a 12-hour day, and since the sun goes down before 8:00 PM, you will need to provide extra artificial light to supplement the sun. An ordinary incandescent bulb is satisfactory. A 60-watt bulb suspended three feet above the seedlings will light an area about three by three feet. If the area is larger use more bulbs. A reflector increases efficiency.

Fluorescent tubes can also be used for supplemental lighting, but since their radiation "projects" poorly, they must be suspended within six inches of the seedlings. They are, however, the best energy source for growing entirely under artificial light. (See section on growing under lights later in this chapter.)

Conditions indoors are seldom ideal for growing seedlings. Natural soil can bring in diseases that are more devastating indoors. Nowadays most specialists use an artificial soil mixture for growing transplants. About the easiest mixture for the home gardener to put together is made up of half peat moss and half clean sand—by volume, not by weight. Thoroughly wetted but drained, so that it contains no free water, this mixture makes a perfect medium for root growth. If possible make the mixture a week before you are ready to sow seeds. The peat moss will gradually soak up moisture, even that clinging to the sand grains, so that the mixture may have to be wetted again before use.

Ready-to-use soil mixes are available, usually with fertilizer added. I prefer one that contains no fertilizer because it is usually a quickly available chemical type that will be exhausted before transplanting time. If a fertilizer is included in the soil mix it should be a slow-release type that contains a full range of the major and minor elements needed. About the only one I have been able to discover is the Green-Green product of Sierra Chemical Co., but this is so sparsely distributed that you may have to write the company at Milpitas, California.

What you will probably find more convenient is using a regular house plant fertilizer in solution, but at one-fourth the strength recommended by the manufacturer. Use this whenever you water. Because the sand-peat mixture drains well, any excess will drain off, avoiding the danger of overfeeding. However, before any feeding will be needed, the seedlings should develop true leaves. The two first "leaves" that appear are not leaves but cotyledons, parts of the seed that contain enough food to support seedlings until they can start making their own.

If space permits grow seedlings in individual containers big enough to hold them until ready to set out. Digging a seedling out of a flat and moving it into a pot may be necessary if space is limited, but this does set it back. In individual pots plant three seeds in each and cut away all but the strongest as soon as true leaves are formed. Notice that word *cut*. Pulling the extra seedlings disturbs roots on the one that is left. If possible use at least two-and-a-half-inch pots, three-inch pots if space allows.

For individual containers where space is limited, I like Kys Kubes, which are blocks made of compressed peat in which roots grow beautifully. I have grown tomatoes and geraniums to a height of ten inches in such cubes, and they were still vigorous when set out. These cubes contain fertilizer, but transplants should be watered with a liquid plant food when set out-of-doors because the fertilizer will be exhausted by that time.

If you must grow in a flat and transplant directly into the garden without spacing out in individual pots, do space seeds far enough apart so that each seedling can be lifted without disturbing its neighbors too much. Two inches apart is about right.

Peat-fiber pots that you fill with a soil mixture are good, but only if used properly. One drawback is that if they are planted with the rim sticking above the surface of the surrounding soil, the lip acts like a wick and sucks moisture from the soil at a critical time, just as the seedlings need to become established. Drying out around roots at this time can set back transplants two to three weeks.

When using the sand-peat mixture, plastic pots grow excellent plants because this mix drains well. If, however, soil is used there is a danger of over-watering in plastic containers. The lightweight foam plastic cups used for coffee make excellent containers for growing transplants, but be sure to punch a hole for drainage and, again, watch out for overwatering.

Growing under Lights

Where no sunny window is available, good transplants can be grown entirely under fluorescent tubes. Here it is necessary to consider another "dimension" of light—that of color or spectrum. Plants do not see light in the way the eye does. Only three segments of the solar spectrum affect growth substantially, although other colors do have minor effects. Any fluorescent tube should be strong in a narrow band of blue, a wider band of bright red and another of a dull red known as far-red. Incandescent bulbs are lacking in blue and contain yellow, which is wasted on plants, although they are rich in red. Conventional fluorescents—daylight, blue white and warm white—are extremely low in red. They can be used in combination with incandescent bulbs, but this calls for two separate circuits. Also incandescent bulbs often raise temperatures too high.

The combination I prefer is a fixture that holds four tubes. Two of these are Sylvania's Standard Gro Lux and two are Sylvania's Wide Spectrum Gro Lux. The latter is rich in red, and the standard type is rich in blue.

The wide spectrum type is not generally carried by dealers, in which case ten-watt incandescents, spaced about a foot apart along the tubes, can be used with Standard Gro Lux. With this combination, blue-white fluorescents can be substituted for Standard Gro Lux with only a small drop in efficiency.

Flats or pots seeded with tomatoes and placed under any of these combinations of light tubes for a 14- to 16-hour day should produce healthy seedlings as fast or even faster than those grown with some direct sunshine. One element that needs to be watched is temperature. Tomato seed germination is best in an alternating temperature of 55 degrees at night and 80 to 95 degrees during the day. This is difficult to provide indoors, but usually the cooling off at night and warming up when the lights go on will provide enough alteration in temperature.

Once true leaves have formed, try to keep temperatures

under the lights to about 65 degrees, even if this means ventilation to cool the air.

As mentioned previously in discussing aphid-borne diseases, don't be in a rush to set out tomato transplants. If they cannot be kept in good condition indoors any longer, set them outdoors, but use Hotkaps or similar plant protectors to keep them warm and protected against aphids.

Tomato Types and Varieties

Unfortunately most seed catalogs fail to describe the difference between types of tomatoes. One is called determinate, which in the past was called dwarf or bush. Today these names are no longer accurate. Plant breeders have been making so many crosses that today not all determinate types are dwarf. The thing that distinguishes them from the other or indeterminate type is their habit of growth. A determinate tomato does not keep growing indefinitely at the tip; instead, when it reaches a certain height, it stops growing and no more fruit forms. It seldom produces suckers and then only on varieties that have been crossed with an indeterminate type. It develops flower buds between each leaf or, at the most, between every two leaves. These factors mean that it produces all of its fruits early in the season. Because of interbreeding there is some variation from this pattern, but it is well not to depend on any determinate variety for tomatoes later than August.

Indeterminate varieties, on the other hand, keep growing at the tip and do not stop setting fruit until stopped by the coming of frosts. They produce flower clusters between every third or fourth leaf. A few varieties, such as Giant Tree and Triple Crop, climb so strongly that if trained on a trellis they can grow as tall as 15 feet. Where the leaf stem joins the main stalk, indeterminate varieties produce suckers or side branches. These suckers are the subject of sharp arguments among home gardeners. To prune or desucker, or to allow plants to grow without pruning, has caused almost as many arguments as a presidential election.

Perhaps the most common way of growing both determinate and indeterminate tomatoes is to allow them to sprawl naturally as vines on the ground. Although this does have some drawbacks because it causes some loss of fruits, the loss is more than offset in the saving in labor. A mulch of clean straw or black plastic will eliminate much of the loss by rotting where tomatoes touch the soil.

Tying plants to a stake and removing the suckers are worthwhile only if space is at a premium. While the production per plant is less by this method, the production by the square foot is higher.

A compromise, which will be discussed in detail later, is to grow them in wire cages.

Tomatoes vary in ways other than growth habit. Size of fruits can range from those as big as a gooseberry or currant to huge platters six to eight inches across, weighing as much as two pounds. In selecting for size remember: The larger the fruit the longer it takes to mature. For this reason, where space permits, about two plants of a determinate variety should be planted for each member of the family, to provide tomatoes until the giant types ripen.

Another variation is in color. Most tomatoes are a scarlet red. Unfortunately color names used in various catalogs are far from accurate. Bright red usually means scarlet. There are so-called pink varieties. When the pink is dark, it should be called crimson, but this term is also misused.

In modern hybrids most of the old-time high acid flavor of scarlet tomatoes has been modified. Even so, some people still cannot eat scarlet tomatoes because they are too acid. They prefer the pink or crimson varieties, one reason why old-time Ponderosa still sells. White varieties are too insipid to be worth considering. This cannot be said of yellow, golden, or orange tomatoes, which are beautiful when served with scarlet varieties.

In the following listing VFN identifies varieties resistant to verticillium wilt, fusarium wilt and nematodes. Maturity dates are the number of days needed to ripen the first fruits from the time seedlings are transplanted outdoors. Cold weather can delay ripening by several days, even weeks if a cold spell knocks off flower buds.

Large Fruited Varieties

Although huge tomatoes are spectacular and often delicious, main crop varieties on which commercial growers depend are much more reliable and, nowadays, so improved in quality through hybrid breeding that they are far more desirable for the beginner.

Giant Tree and *Triple Crop:* 90 days. These two "climbing" varieties have already been described except for fruit. They are, of course, indeterminate and produce individual fruits, deep pink in color, that often measure six inches across. Although not rated as disease resistant, I have never seen a badly infected vine of either variety.

Big Boy: 80 days. The first of the large-fruited hybrids, this is still a delicious scarlet tomato, with individual fruits weighing from ten ounces to a pound. Not listed as VF, but vigorous and usually does well. Indeterminate.

Beefmaster. VN: 65 days. Fruits scarlet with excellent flavor, weighing up to two pounds each. Although slightly irregular at times, this is an outstanding variety. A much better tomato than the one known as Beefsteak. A true hybrid, with hybrid vigor. Indeterminate.

Better Boy Hybrid. VFN: 72 days. Scarlet fruits up to one-and-a-half pounds each, with real tomato flavor. As many as 250 fruits to one plant. Indeterminate.

Ultra Boy. VFN: 74 days. Some claim that this is the earliest of the big scarlet hybrids, but Beefmaster beat it by several days for me. Has high disease resistance and keeps bearing until killed by frost. Indeterminate.

Ponderosa: 82 days. To not list this old-time giant pink tomato would be to incur the wrath of millions of gardeners. Even when infected it keeps on bearing huge, rough fruits weighing up to one-and-a-half pounds. Twilley lists an improved variety not quite as lumpy as the original variety. Indeterminate.

Golden Sunray: 85 days. The only golden variety with some degree of disease resistance. Perhaps the most solid slicing variety with a mild flavor I have ever grown. Indeterminate.

Standard Size Tomatoes (up to ten ounces)

Except for Manalucie, there are a number of outstanding new hybrids that incorporate disease resistance and excellent flavor, but they are much alike. You won't go wrong picking Manapol, Fantastic, Supersonic, or Heinz 1350.

Manalucie should be given special mention for its resistance to more diseases than any other variety—especially in the South, where many of these diseases cause serious losses. Hastings Red Chief Hybrid also has shown remarkable resistance.

All of the above are scarlet indeterminate varieties, with fruits weighing up to ten ounces.

Coldset: 70 days. A determinate variety with blood red or deep scarlet fruits, slightly more acid than most. Its one advantage is that it can be seeded in soil as cold as 50 degrees. Fruits five to six ounces.

Jetfire. VF: 62 days. A determinate variety for early use, with scarlet fruits seven to seven and a half ounces. Good flavor. One of the best early varieties. Springset is much like it.

Starfire: 65 days. Excellent flavor for an early variety. Fruits weigh up to eight ounces, scarlet. Determinate plant.

New Yorker: 62 days. Resistant to verticillium. Determinate, scarlet fruits about six ounces. Good flavor for an early tomato. Cold tolerant.

Bonus. VFN: 78 days. Semi-determinate. Excellent flavored eight ounce, fruits, scarlet.

Spring Giant. VF: 70 days. The name is somewhat deceptive since fruits are not really giant but average six to eight ounces. Determinate. Bearing season is short, but if you want early fruits this is a heavy producer. It is the leading early variety for the South. Does well except along the Canadian border. Scarlet fruits, excellent flavor.

Tomatoes for Container Culture

The fact that the past decade has seen a number of varieties suitable for container and pot culture is evidence that plant breeders are waking up to the importance of home gardening. Except that they do qualify as flavorsome additions to normal table fare, they are relatively unimportant; perhaps they justify their existence as conversation pieces. The Sierra Chemical's tomato tower might be an exception: One individual hopes to break all records for the number of tomatoes from a single plant with this gadget.

Artificial soil mixtures have made container gardening much more practical and less likely to fail.

Among the large number of varieties bred especially for container growing are many that are much superior in flavor to the older small-fruited varieties, such as plum, cherry, pear, and peach varieties, most of which lacked sweetness and had tough skins. Others bear fruits of fair size, as, for example, Pixie, which produces tomatoes nearly two inches in diameter, and Patio Pick, with slightly larger fruits.

Tiny Tim: 55 days. The plants are compact, less than ten inches tall and a prolific producer of bright scarlet fruits larger than a cherry tomato.

Small Fry Hybrid: 55 days. Plant is spreading rather than tall, 12 inches high with a 30-inch spread. A good hanging basket variety. One-inch bright scarlet fruits with superior flavor. Not limited to container growing; excellent in smaller outdoor gardens.

Pixie: 52 days. This is a 2-inch diameter tomato with a big flavor. Grows about fifteen inches tall. Produces long trusses of meaty tomatoes, bright scarlet. Needs to be staked if grown in a pot or larger container.

Presto: 60 days. Another variety with true tomato flavor in its fruits, about the size of a silver dollar. Two-foot vines will need staking if container grown.

Gardener's Delight: 65 days. One of the sweetest of all tomatoes; practically drips sugar. Scarlet fruits about the size of a Ping-Pong ball. Vines 24 inches tall need staking. An English variety available in the U.S.A. from Thompson & Morgan's branch in Somerdale, NJ.

Sugar Lump: 60 days. An American version of Gardener's Delight.

Patio Hybrid: 55 days. Produces an abundance of fruits somewhat larger than the other varieties in this group; bright scarlet. Vines grow up to 30 inches tall and need staking. Not suitable in pots smaller than ten to twelve inches in diameter, but great in planters.

Culture

What should be emphasized is that while all the varieties mentioned are recommended for container growing, they are equally adapted to outdoor culture where small-fruited tomatoes are wanted for salads and appetizers.

When container grown, artificial soil mixtures should be used along with liquid fertilizers. Any good houseplant fertilizer can be used, but it should be diluted to one-fourth the manufacturer's recommendation and applied in place of normal watering every time the soil needs more water.

Just because the plants are being grown in containers does not change the one requirement for growing good tomatoes—they must still have at least six hours of direct sunshine.

Paste Tomatoes

Although varieties in this group were bred especially for canning as condensed tomato paste, they are also desirable when canned for use as stewed tomatoes. They are much less watery when canned than full-sized varieties and hold their shape in cooking. Their fruits are plum-shaped, about two inches in diameter by three and a half inches long, thick and meaty. All are bright scarlet.

Roma. VF: 76 days. Valuable for its disease resistance and unusually high yields. A better tomato than the original Roma.

Veeroma. VF: 72 days. In the H.J. Heinz trials this was the top-rated variety.

Rex Chico: 70 days. Bright color and heavier yields than Chico Grande, its parent variety. Best for the South because of resistance to grey leaf spot and wilt.

Outdoor Culture of Tomatoes

As already mentioned, avoid mixing fresh organic matter with tomato soils. But if a cover crop is used for soil improvement, be sure it is thoroughly covered and is treated with an application of fertilizer to speed up decay. Tomatoes like plenty of well-rotted compost in the soil. Although they can be grown on shallow soils they prefer a deep root run. On shallow soils keeping them moist can cause trouble with blossom end rot.

Fertilizers need to be well balanced and preferably not too high in nitrogen. Inexperienced gardeners often use leftover lawn fertilizers that are high in nitrogen and low in potash, only to find that their plants are running to vine and are not flowering well. A basic rule of plant nutrition that has been overlooked even in modern lawn fertilizers is that any fertilizer product should have at least half as much potash as its nitrogen content. Actually since nitrogen is highly soluble and runs off before plants can use most of it, it should be applied in larger amounts. Potash is quite stable and remains available.

In soils that have been supplied with organic matter from time to time, tomatoes can get along well enough on an application of about 20 pounds per thousand square feet of a good mixed fertilizer in early spring, plowed under with whatever compost, sewage sludge, or other organic matter you can spare. In new gardens, on land that has not been cultivated for some time, a second application along the row, at about the same rate and when green fruits have formed, will mean a bigger crop. The advantages of slow-release fertilizers are discussed later. They are particularly valuable for tomatoes that bear for long periods.

The disease called blossom end rot, which causes the free end of the tomatoes to turn black, has been traced in some cases to a lack of calcium. If your garden has ever been affected with blossom end rot, try applying about five pounds of ground limestone along a 100-foot row. This condition is not a disease but a physiological defect: The rotting comes in after the fruits crack from a lack of calcium. Another factor is a soil that is alternately wet and dry. Try to keep the soil uniformly damp, which is easier in soils in good tilth—deep and rich.

Spacing depends on how you want to grow your crop. If the vines are allowed to sprawl on top of a clean mulch, indeterminate vines should stand about three feet apart in the row, with four feet between rows. Determinate vines, 30 inches apart in rows three feet apart. Where space is at a premium, tying the vines to stakes will allow spacing as close as 18 inches by three feet. Yields will be slightly better if staked vines are spaced two feet apart in the row, but wider spacing might mean less chance of disease.

Set stakes at the time of transplanting. If you try to drive stakes after the plants have made some growth, you may injure roots. Some diseases need only the broken end of a root to enter the plant and cause trouble.

If permanent woods, such as cedar, redwood, or cypress, can be had, these are worth using since they will last for years. Otherwise use what wood is available and soak the lower end in a solution of pentachlorophenol (usually sold as Penta), a wood preservative. Do this at least a month before using the stakes, since the oil in Penta solution needs to be absorbed or it will injure plants. An even better material is copper naphthenate, usually sold by dealers in greenhouse supplies. It is nontoxic to plants.

As the vine grows, tie it to the stake, leaving the tip free to grow upward. Suckers will grow from the place where leaf stems join the main stalk. Allow the lowest sucker to grow without pruning, but pinch out the rest except for those that grow from just below a flower cluster. These suckers produce food that will nourish the cluster just above them. Allow them to produce three or four leaves, then nip off the rest of the shoot.

While all flower clusters are nipped out until about the middle of July, the lowest sucker is allowed to grow without pruning. It is to serve as a top renewal when the original main stem begins to lose vigor. When this lower sucker has formed green fruits after July 15, cut out the old main stem. A few of the older plants can be left for later renewal so fruit production won't be interrupted. Tying material is important. Don't use the type with a wire imbedded in paper: The paper disintegrates and the wire cuts into the stem. The traditional tying material is raffia, but it is a nuisance to untangle. Soft cord is better, but don't overlook discarded nylon hose cut into strips. Any soft old cloth will do, however.

One bit of advice to smokers: Don't grow staked tomatoes. Sooner or later you will forget and work on the vines without washing and pass on tobacco mosaic.

A type of trained plant that is much easier to manage, with less work, is one grown in a cage made of chicken wire or large-mesh farm fencing. A cage two feet across and three feet high can be made of a piece of poultry wire six feet, six inches long bent into a circle. Spaced three feet apart in the row and three feet between rows, such cages allow the vines to scramble up the wire and hold the fruits off the soil. They are placed over the transplants as soon as they are set out. Winds will blow the cages, so anchor them with loops of stiff wire bent into hairpins. A wire coat hanger will make three such pins, but for safety you will need four for each cage.

A precaution in transplanting anything, from a delicate lettuce seedling to a mature tree, is to make the soil around the roots as much like the rest of the garden as possible. Otherwise roots sometimes have a hard time spreading into the surrounding soil, especially those of a seedling transplanted from rich potting soil into heavy clay loam. The hole should be about six to eight inches deep. If you have some, put a handful of compost in the bottom of the hole.

Don't use dry fertilizer in the planting hole. If you can find it, use a liquid starter solution (a highly soluble fertilizer dissolved in water—a sort of a plant tonic to help the seedling recover from the shock of transplanting).

One advantage in growing in cages is that, on chilly nights, a sleeve of plastic can be slipped over the cage to protect it. This can save flower buds already formed if temperatures drop below 50 to 55 degrees. It may sound like more work than it is worth, but to the true gardener this is a labor of love.

Most insecticide manufacturers now blend a mixture of insecticides and fungicides that should protect plants against insects and diseases that attack tomatoes, eggplant, and peppers. This will not protect against the virus diseases and blossom end rot already mentioned, but it is worthwhile if maximum yields are wanted. Even if you do not use such a preparation, you will probably produce more tomatoes than you can eat unless the garden is unusually small.

A mistaken idea prevalent among gardeners is that removing foliage exposes the fruits to the sun and ensures riper tomatoes. Actually this does more harm than good. Exposed fruits suffer sun scald, a dull tan toughening of the skin. In catalogs some varieties are recommended because their heavy foliage provides a good cover for ripening fruits.

If at all possible, fruits should be allowed to ripen fully on the vine. Those brought indoors and ripened in a sunny window never develop a true tomato flavor. Just before a killing frost don't waste time bringing in grass-green fruits to ripen: Only those that show signs of turning color (even if only from dark to light green) are worth saving. But don't expect these artificially ripened fruits to taste like real tomatoes. Instead try freezing fully ripened tomatoes for winter use. They can be frozen with slight loss of flavor. Peel them, using only fully ripe fruits—those that are still firm. Dip into boiling water until the peel loosens, then into ice water. Wrap in Saran, Glad Wrap, or similar thin plastic and freeze as quickly as possible. When these are thawed, they will at least taste better than the steam ripened product sold during the winter as tomatoes.

Tomato Relatives: Peppers and Eggplant
(with a salute to okra as well)

Eggplant
Except for its need for a much longer growing season and its high sensitivity to cold, the eggplant needs about the same treatment as the tomato. This crop should not be attempted in upper New England or in the Pacific Northwest. It is particularly suited to Southeastern United States, except that special controls are needed for certain well-established pests peculiar to the eggplant. Local farm bureaus can advise on permitted chemicals for spraying eggplant flea beetle, eggplant lace bug and eggplant tortoise beetle. The laws regulating insecticides keep changing almost from month to month, so no recommendation here would be of much use.

Modern varieties offer some resistance to diseases. Some of those available are Stokes Hybrid, Early Hybrid, T.S. Cross Hybrid, and Florida Market.

Follow the directions given for growing tomatoes indoors for eggplant as well, except that eggplant should be started about two weeks earlier and growing temperature should be about five to ten degrees higher.

In the open garden, space modern hybrid varieties three feet apart in the row, with four feet between rows. Although the plants do not occupy that much space, they need room between them for aeration and for spraying for flea beetles and other insects. Unless soil temperatures are above 65 degrees, do not attempt direct sowing of eggplant. Be sure that the season is long enough to mature the fruits.

Peppers

Duplicate the directions for eggplant, but space the plants 18 inches apart in the row, with 30 inches between rows.

Since peppers, as a rule, need more time to mature fruits, earliness is important north of the Ohio River. Perhaps the earliest red sweet pepper available is Earliest Red Sweet offered by Stokes Seeds of Buffalo. The plants are small and can be planted 12 inches apart in the row, in rows 24 inches apart. Production is not too heavy, so if you plan to make pickle relish or use large quantities in other ways, better plant a double row. If the weather is warm it begins to bear 55 days after transplanting. For most areas the California Wonder type is the most popular. It is heavy, meaty, and a reliable producer. It can be used either green or allowed to ripen to a rich scarlet.

Okra

Although okra is not a true tomato relative, its culture is so like that of the tomato that almost the only thing left to talk about is spacing. Plants should stand a foot apart for dwarf varieties and 18 inches to 24 inches apart for the taller types. Rows three feet apart are adequate, if anyone wants more than a single row of okra.

Harvesting needs special mention; the pods must be gathered every day once they reach edible size. Although some varieties produce pods as long as six inches, these will be much better harvested when half that length. Don't harvest in advance for the table: Okra loses flavor as rapidly as sweet corn. Any overmature pods should be cut off and thrown on the compost pile, since the plants quit producing if these ripen seed.

Clemson Spineless: This variety is almost smooth, with only slight ridges, and lacks the spines that occur on the pods of some varieties. Pods are up to seven inches long, rich green in color.

Plants are four feet tall. Needs two full months of hot weather.

Emerald: Another smooth podded variety without spines, very rich dark green color. Three-foot plants with six-inch pods. Developed by Campbell Soup Company, and excellent for canning.

Perkins Mammoth: An early variety popular in the North and in southern Canada. Pods are distinctly ribbed and grow as long as eight inches on plants four to five feet tall. A heavy producer for those who want plenty of okra.

White Velvet: Although I have searched through some 20 catalogs, I can find no present-day listing of this old variety. White-podded okra seems to have been dropped in favor of vitamin-rich green varieties.

Red Okra: Pods are purplish red in color, borne on a plant with foliage of the same color. Pods turn green when cooked. Allowed to mature, they are a rich brown, mottled in black and can be dried for use in flower arrangements as well as for food.

Spineless Green Velvet: Round, spineless pods seven inches long. Tall plants.

Drying Okra. In the United States okra is used almost entirely in soups and stews to add a gelatinous richness. In many parts of Europe and in Turkey, the pods are dried for winter use. Turkey ships tons of dried pods to the United States to supply the winter needs of ethnic groups.

Although the flavor differs from the fresh-cooked pod, dried okra soaked for an hour before cooking is a highly acceptable winter vegetable. To dry cut pods with a fairly long stem. Thread a needle with cotton twine, knotted at one end, and thread the twine through the pod stem. The pods should be separated so that they do not touch. They should be gathered on a sunny afternoon, so they will be thoroughly dry on the surface.

Hang the strings in a dry, airy, but dark, place (an attic or upper-story closet). If exposed to light the pods will lose their color; drying in the dark keeps them green.

3

Greens: Grandma's Garden Sass Updated

      The role of green vegetables as a source of vitamin A has been parroted by every food columnist in America and so needs no further mention here. What does need to be said is that to satisfy your need for green stuff, your pocketbook is going to be hit harder and harder.

Here is where your biggest savings can be effected by home-grown food. Even the smallest pocket-handkerchief city garden should concentrate on greens.

Types of Green Vegetables

Although specialists in commercial vegetable culture separate members of the cabbage family from other garden crops served as cooked vegetables, in the following descriptions I am simplifying matters by dividing green stuff into two general groups—salad crops, which are usually eaten without cooking, and potherbs. The term *potherbs* means only cooked greens, not vegetables that are used primarily for flavor alone. The phrase *cole crops* refers to members of the cabbage family such as cauliflower, kale, collards, and broccoli.

Salad Crops

Alfalfa Seed

To the uninitiated, sprouted alfalfa seed might sound like cattle fodder, but, surprisingly enough, the sprouts have a clean, fresh flavor that reminds one of garden peas. It is a natural vitamin pill, rich in vitamins A, B, B complex, E, G, and K, plus many essential minerals and amino acids. However, to include these nutrient elements the seed must be sprouted in sunshine so that chlorophyll (the green coloring matter in plants) can be formed.

Seeds can be purchased from dealers in farm supplies and occasionally at garden centers. Health food stores also sell them, but at a highly inflated price.

To sprout them begin by rinsing in a solution of a tablespoonful of Purex or Clorox in a quart of water. Allow the seeds to soak for not more than two minutes before rinsing in clean tap water. This prevents formation of mold during the sprouting process. Drain and spread two layers of damp paper towels on a platter. Cover the seeds on the platter with a thin plastic, such as Saran or similar food wrap. The trick is to keep the seed moist but not soaking wet. If a mist stops forming on the plastic add more water, but don't *float* the seed. The sprouts will develop chlorophyll and turn green; if keeping them moist for five days (the length of time needed before they can be eaten) is too much of a chore, they can be kept in a Mason jar for that length of time. Use the type of lid that comes in two parts. Discard the tight seal and substitute a piece of clean cheesecloth so air can move in and out of the jar. When grown in a Mason jar, not all of the sprouts will turn green.

Main use of the sprouts is in salads mixed with other green, leafy vegetables. However, they can be eaten in a sandwich, added to stews with meats, or served separately as a green vegetable. This is one salading that can be had at any time of year.

Asparagus

Covered under Perennial Crops, but here because of its use as a delicious salad with mayonnaise or French dressing.

Bean Sprouts

Used like alfalfa seed and sprouted in the same way. An essential ingredient in egg foo young and many chop suey dishes. The mung bean is sold by many seed houses and is the traditional variety used by the Chinese. However, seeds of *edible* soybeans such as Kanrich and Early Green Bush can also be sprouted, but not field varieties, which have an oily, weedy taste. There are, however, some who like this flavor.

Beans, Green Bush
Cooked green bush beans with French dressing and chopped onion make a delicious salad.

Beets
Culture is described under Root Crops. Pickled red beets are considered a salad. There are both white and golden beets that can be used as a substitute for celeriac, which many find difficult to grow and prepare. Boil them with celery seed until tender and the flavor will be like that of celeriac and usually much more tender.

Broccoli
Culture given under potherbs, but cold, boiled broccoli served with an herb-flavored mayonnaise is a delicious salad.

Brussels Sprouts
At my club (Cliff Dwellers in Chicago) the chef served boiled sprouts in a rather vinegary French dressing. When served on a buffet, they disappear before any of the conventional salads. See potherbs for the culture of Brussels sprouts.

Cabbage
Although it belongs under potherbs, perhaps more cabbage is used in coleslaw as a salad than winds up in the pot as sauerkraut or in company with corned beef. The quality of slaw can be greatly improved by using the right varieties.

Cauliflower
Another potherb that arrives on the table as a salad.

Celeriac
This "knob celery," as it is called by some, is much easier to grow

than regular celery and can be stored over winter in ordinary root cellars. Unfortunately while the flavor is like that of celery, the rough, knobby roots leave much to be desired. Name of the leading variety, Large Smooth Prague, is ironic: The root is about as smooth as a fiber doormat. In spite of the howls of the cook when it is to be peeled, celeriac is a delightful dish in midwinter, boiled and served with thinly sliced onions in an oil-and-vinegar dressing as a salad.

Like celery, celeriac demands a long season of growth, and rich, moist soil. Because of the long season it needs to mature (100 days) it is usually started indoors. When planting out, the tiny swelling above the root should be just at the surface. As the bulb develops it should sit on the soil like a duck on water. Any side shoots or surface roots that develop should be snipped off. As light frosts threaten, if the bulb has not developed fully, earth can be drawn around the bulb for a week or two. The labor required might seem excessive, but the luxury of a celery flavor in midwinter will repay you.

Celery

One of the more difficult crops for the home gardener, but less so since the ritual of blanching has gone out of style. Today's green celery varieties have more flavor. Celery is fussy as to temperature. Although it dislikes hot weather, if subjected to temperatures below 65 degrees when germinating and during early seedling growth, celery will bolt to seed and be worthless on the table. Because of the long growing season (100 days or over) it must be started early indoors. It likes a soil high in organic matter (most commercial crops are grown on muck) both in the seedling stage and when planted out in the garden.

Seed requires as long as three weeks to germinate, during which time it cannot be allowed to dry out.

In Northeastern United States it should not be set out before June 1. South of the Ohio River, its poor growth during hot weather makes it an inferior home garden crop. Celery is both a heavy feeder and a heavy drinker (in the wild it is a swamp plant). A rich garden loam is best unless you garden on muck, on which soil this should be one of your best crops. Celery needs to be fed with a complete liquid fertilizer about every two weeks.

Or if the soil is fertilized with a complete slow-release fertilizer such as Osmocote or Green-Green, this should carry it through until harvest. This must be used at twice the rate usually recommended for the vegetable garden. Dried blood or fish emulsion can be used in the organic garden.

Growing blanched celery is not recommended in a home garden because of the space needed and the difficulty of preventing rot.

Celtuce

Sometimes said to be a cross between lettuce and celery, but this is an improbable combination at best. It seems to be a type of lettuce that produces a pointed central stalk that is similar to the texture and flavor of water chestnuts. This stalk can be sliced thin and used in salads. When quite young the leaves can be used in place of lettuce, but soon become too tough. They are good cooked like spinach at this stage. Culture of celtuce is the same as for lettuce.

Chicory

In the United States this name is applied mainly to Witloof chicory, a root vegetable that is forced in winter to produce a shoot shaped like a dunce cap. In Europe this vegetable is usually called French endive. Magdeburgh chicory is a root crop used as a coffee substitute. Stokes Seeds is the only firm still listing it, as far as I can find. It belongs with salad crops since it is also forced like Witloof, but the leaves are allowed to spread out and do not form a head. Both types are blanched in the dark and are used as salading.

The roots for forcing are grown like parsnips in the open garden. They need 100 days or more to mature. In fall they are dug and stored as close to 32 degrees as possible, usually in damp sand, until wanted for forcing. A deep box is used, usually about a foot deep. In the case of Witloof, roots are cut to a uniform length (about six inches unless they are unusually big) and stood root to root upright in the box. Damp sand is poured over them, covering them completely. Magdeburgh is planted with the top at soil level exposed to air.

Standard practice for Witloof is to keep pouring in the sand until the box is filled to within an inch of the top. It is then moved into a warmer place where the temperature is at least 65 degrees, where it is kept damp until the roots produce a shoot that breaks through five inches of sand. If this shoot is then cut as close to the root as is feasible, a new shoot may be produced from the same root. The heads of Witloof form one of the true luxury vegetables the home gardener can produce. However, the flavor of Magdeburgh is identical and much easier to force. About the only reason for growing Witloof is that the heads sell at a higher price.

Chinese Cabbage

This is not a cabbage, although it belongs to the same family, the brassicas. It is actually a type of mustard that forms a head, sometimes long and pointed, but in many fine varieties it looks like an egg-shaped cabbage. Why this delicious vegetable is not more widely grown is a mystery. One count against it is that it cannot be seeded until July 1 in any part of the United States. If sown before this date it will not form a head but will shoot up a seed stalk instead. All too often gardeners ignore directions to sow late, and the crop is a failure.

It is not served as a cooked vegetable to any extent, yet as a cooked vegetable it is superior in flavor to the mustards used so widely in the South. It survives quite cold temperatures and as far north as parts of Georgia, Mississippi, and Alabama, can be relied upon for salad greens for most of the winter.

It is not fussy as to soils. Allow plenty of room between plants since they can grow as large as some cabbages. Use ten-inch spacing for the upright varieties such as Michili and eighteen inches for the shorter oval type.

Varieties of Chinese Cabbage. Michili: This is practically the only variety offered in most catalogs. Heads are about 18 inches tall and when trimmed of outer leaves at harvest time, measure about four inches through. Quality is high, but this variety does not store as well as the shorter Wong Bok type (stout egg-shaped head). Pei Tsai is similar to Michili.

Springtime and *Early Hybrid G:* Two varieties that are offered by

American seedsmen, which are supposed to produce solid heads if planted early. In my tests both are more resistant to shooting to seed, but if planted before June 10 will produce a flower stalk before they can be harvested for storage. My best luck has been with Early Hybrid G, which produces heads weighing up to five pounds. Both these varieties are of the Wong Bok type, which stores better than Michili.

All types of Chinese cabbage are self-blanching. Cabbage insects—imported cabbage butterfly and aphids—attack this crop. See Control of Insects and Diseases.

Corn Salad

To be limited to this rather tasteless green salading all winter long would be tiresome, but as an occasional change from stored cabbage, chicory, and endive, it is worth growing. In milder climates it can be sown in fall in rows 18 inches apart and covered with straw. Some gardeners blanch a few feet of row by covering it with black plastic and replacing the straw over this for a couple of weeks, but corn salad is also eaten green or cooked as a potherb. It is useless as a crop in warm weather. Over most of Northeastern U.S. it is seeded in September for winter use, a month later in the South. A spring crop can be sown as soon as the soil can be worked in spring, but the production season is short. In France corn salad is mixed with cut, raw celery and cooked beets in the famous *Salade Lorette.*

Cress

So-called garden cress is a European plant of the mustard family, which can be seeded as early in spring as the soil is workable. It should have a rich soil because rapid growth is needed to produce a tender salading. It is better flavored than corn salad but is not good in hot weather. Chopped fine, with a touch of salt, it makes a delightful sandwich filling. Children love it as a garden project: They can begin harvesting seedlings in about 15 days after sowing.

Cucumber

Described under Vine Crops but an important salad vegetable.

Dandelion

To speak of deliberately sowing this pernicious weed as a crop seems odd, yet until you have tasted the thick-leaved variety cultivated by the French, you cannot appreciate how good it can be. The flavor is improved if the leaves are tied together or covered to blanch them, in which form they belong among the salad crops. Green leaves can be cooked. Sow seed in late summer to produce mature plants the following spring, or seed in the open as soon as the soil can be cultivated. Allow 10 to 12 inches between plants. Keep flowers cut off to prevent dandelion from becoming a weed. Incidentally dandelion is about the highest in vitamin A of any vegetable you can grow.

Endive

This is a choice salading that is often given up by many after one or two years. They sow it in early spring only to find at maturity it is so bitter as to be unpalatable. Too, when they try to blanch it, it rots. The bitterness can be avoided by planting the right variety. This is Rose Ribbed or Ruffec. If you can't find seed of this variety, sold usually by those catering to the Italian market around New York City, wait to sow curly endive in midsummer (there is not too much choice between curly varieties). When seeded in July or early August in the North or grown as a winter crop in the South, it matures in cooler weather and develops a delightful flavor that adds interest to a mixed salad. The outer green leaves are tough in salad but can be cooked like spinach. To blanch, tie the outer leaves over the center on a dry, sunny day. Any trace of moisture in the heart will cause rot. Covering with a carton or a box big enough to cover a section of row also works. To provide room for blanching allow at least a foot between plants in the row.

Endive is not too fussy as to soil, but it does like a light feeding with a liquid fertilizer about halfway through growth. Or use about a pound of a good, mixed, dry plant food along a 25-foot row, watered in at once.

Escarole or Batavian endive is liked by more people than the curly type. Some find the prickly leaves of curly endive hard to eat. I have never found anyone who objected to the varieties Full

Heart Bavarian or Florida Deep Heart. These are called escarole to distinguish from the prickly leaved varieties. The leaf edges are wavy instead of crisp and when blanched form one of the best of salad vegetables. Although the heart blanches without special treatment, tying or covering as for the curly type produces a gourmet product worth the extra effort. Like the curly type these varieties should be given at least a foot of space between rows. July and August sowing is best, but don't pass up the chance to produce a summer crop by sowing early in spring. Because of the heat, blanching is difficult, but I have used plywood boxes painted with white or aluminum paint to reflect heat. Removing the boxes for an hour or so after dark may mean extra work, but this cooling period does produce a better-flavored plant.

Lettuce

No one can deny the value of lettuce as a salad crop. Unfortunately it is so easy to grow and use that it can become monotonous. Except for an occasional all-lettuce salad, it should be used mainly as an ingredient in a mixed salad in which it serves as a foil for other flavors.

Lettuce is available in several forms, unfortunately most often in the cellulose-filled head lettuce type beloved of chainstore buyers. There are perhaps times when a crisp wedge of some variety of lettuce, such as Great Lakes or New York Imperial, is acceptable if served with a first-rate French dressing, but when compared with a butterhead variety of the superb quality of Buttercrunch or Butter King, crisp head lettuce isn't in the running. If, however, the diet is low in fiber, as some nutritionists claim, then the head lettuce or crisp head varieties do provide bulk. The true butterheads, such as the two just mentioned, along with Bibb are the choice of every knowledgeable gourmet. These have more or less displaced the older butterheads, such as Big Boston, although the latter is still preferred in New England markets. Buttercrunch is now pushing Bibb out of the running, at least in home gardens. It is easier to grow, is not affected by summer heat and has thick, crisp, but tender, leaves in a buttery, loose head. Butter King is an intermediate variety between Bibb and White Boston, twice the size of the latter, with a fuller, more rounded, flavor.

Loose-leaf varieties, such as Grand Rapids and Black Seeded Simpson, are now being replaced in the home garden by Salad Bowl, an amazing lettuce that grows into a round bowl-shaped plant, too loose to call a true head and combining some of the qualities of both butterhead and loose-leaf varieties. Maturing in 45 days from seed, it is worth planting even when the main crop is Buttercrunch, which matures in 75 days.

Whether the variety Matchless (also called Deer Tongue) is a leaf lettuce or a loose head is a question of maturity. Picked young, it is perhaps the best-flavored of the leaf type. Allowed to form a loose head, it is crisp, delicious, and desirable in every way. Before the introduction of Buttercrunch, it was my favorite lettuce.

Although it would be easy to forget Cos lettuce, to do so would bring down on my head the wrath of devoted worshipers of this type of salading. Certainly it is crisp and the flavor is a unique sweet freshness, but the ribs are often tougher than a hard, firm head lettuce is at maturity. There is little choice of variety in the United States: White Paris Cos is about the only one offered. It is self-closing and blanches beautifully. Cos lettuce will not be missed if you grow Buttercrunch and add a spoonful of sugar to the dressing used.

Lettuce will grow well on soils ranging from clay loam to sandy loams and muck. It is fussy about pH: best crops are produced in the range of 6.0 to 6.6. On muck soils it needs more potash and phosphorus than such soils contain. If available a good potato fertilizer (low in nitrogen but higher in phosphorus and potash—improves lettuce growth on all types of soil.

Lettuce is sometimes started indoors for early crops, but better practice is to sow directly in the garden, using Salad Bowl for an early crop. In my experience transplanted lettuce takes several weeks to recover from transplanting.

One problem is that lettuce does not like heat when germinating; in fact, will not sprout at all if soil temperatures are 80 degrees or above. This makes successive plantings in late June or early July difficult. Seed for these plantings should be mixed with damp peat moss and sand (a 50-50 mixture of these by volume) and stored in a refrigerator for four or five days and planted immediately after the fifth day. The chilling starts germination, which will continue after sowing if the row is left sprayed with the coldest water possible for a week afterward. This treatment is all but essential in the South, where late crops should not be seeded until early August.

Spacing of modern lettuce varieties should be wider than for old-timers. Allow 10 to 12 inches between plants. Lettuce competes poorly with weeds; frequent shallow cultivation is needed.

Mustard

Although the large-leaved mustards used as potherbs in the South are sometimes used as salads, white mustard sprouted indoors and eaten when five or six days old is the major use of this crop. In England one commercial greenhouse sprouts a mixture of mustard and garden cress, turning out thousands of packages daily covered with thin plastic. The owner told a friend of mine that he felt he could sell 100 million packets a year if he could expand his capacity.

The process is surprisingly simple. I have used seed of white mustard (it is often labeled *yellow* mustard) from a chain store, sold in the spice department, and found it perfectly satisfactory. Since chain-store turnover is rapid, it does not have much chance to lose germination. Fill a shallow tray with vermiculite or clean sand. A good container is the flat polystyrene plastic tray used by butchers for displaying pre-packaged meats. Or use the miniature tubs in which soft margarine is packed. Wet the sand or vermiculite until saturated, then tilt the tray to get rid of excess moisture. Rinse the seed and sow thinly (about 10 to 15 seeds per square inch) all over the surface of the tray. Set in a light window, wait four or five days, and the tiny seedlings are ready to harvest. Cut off just above the soil and use as sandwich filling or to add flavor to a mixed salad. Mustard can also be sprouted by the method recommended for alfalfa seed.

Melons

Discussed under Vine Crops. For use as salads, form into melon balls with a ball scoop. In summer a gourmet's treat is a salad made of a mixture of muskmelon, watermelon, and drained, canned grapefruit sections in a sweet oil-and-vinegar dressing. Three parts olive oil, one part vinegar or lemon juice, and a level teaspoon of sugar with a dash of salt is perfect as the dressing.

Melon balls can be frozen for winter use (be sure to drain off all juice before freezing) and can be combined with fresh grapefruit sections, served in half an avocado.

Onion

Culture is described under Bulb Crops. Both green and dried onions can be used discreetly in salads. Shallots are, of course, the ingredient favored by gourmets. Southern gardeners can raise the tasty but mild Italian Bottle onion for salad use. Now Northern gardeners can grow a similar red variety called Hamburger Red, fully as mild as its Southern cousin.

Onion sets, on which most gardeners relied for green onions, will probably disappear completely from American seed catalogs. Land used for sets will return just as much money per acre in other crops and demand about one-tenth the labor that sets require. As a result seed houses are finding it more and more difficult to find growers. Some are importing sets from England and Europe, which all but prices them out of the market. This means that the gardener will have to grow his own from seed. See culture under Bulb Crops. Fortunately not too many sets are needed to supply scallions for salads. This is a vegetable that must be used with a delicate hand.

Radish

Although a minor crop and of limited use in salads, the radish appears on practically every home garden seed list. It is about the earliest crop that can be harvested and is a useful seed to mix with that of slow-germinating crops, such as carrots and parsley. As a quick germinator radish seedlings mark the row and are harvested before the companion crop needs the space.

My favorite variety is Burpee White, which has a true radish flavor, yet lacks the unpleasant bite of other varieties. It is particularly good in salads. If you insist on radishes being red,

Cherry Belle and Crimson Giant are almost as good as Burpee White.

Many years ago the late Harry O'Brien, well known as the Plain Dirt Gardener, told me he no longer grew radishes but instead used white turnips when they were not more than an inch and a half in diameter. In the past two years I have followed the same practice, largely because of the new fine-grained turnips introduced by two Japanese firms. One is Tokyo Cross, an All-American Award winner, which at one and a half inches is crisp, tender, and mild in flavor. The other is a variety not yet introduced, but too good to hold back, from the firm of Sakata. If anything it is better than Tokyo Cross in that it can grow to a diameter of three to four inches and will still be as tender as butter. Tentative name of the sample I grew was Tokyo Market Express. Watch for it: It should be one of the best vegetables in a decade, not only in salads, but cooked in other ways. Even our dog enjoyed this turnip.

Spinach

This name covers a number of different green leafy vegetables that can be used in salads. Their culture is covered under potherbs. Regular spinach is a tricky crop for many. It hates hot weather. In the South and as far north as Virginia, it can be grown as a winter crop, allowing the gardener to snip off leaves during warm spells for use in salads. In the North it can only be grown by seeding as early as the soil can be worked, or seeded in late August to produce a late fall crop.

Don't overlook New Zealand spinach, Malabar spinach, and tampala as material for salads. Not everyone likes the spinach tribe when used in salads, while others swear by anything resembling spinach. Even Swiss chard is often tossed into the salad bowl.

Tomato

Discussed at length in a separate chapter, the tomato is a basic ingredient in salads but can be improved in that role by better selection of varieties. For one thing a tomato that is full of wet seeds (a "slop of pips" as the great George Bunyard described it.

to me) is a poor addition to a salad. The seeds add nothing to its flavor and the pulp surrounding the seeds changes the taste of the dressing. I saw how this could be overcome while on a visit to France. A housewife preparing tomatoes for a salad carefully scraped out the seed and pulp, using only the solid cell walls. Improvement in flavor of that salad was amazing.

One unfortunate development in American tomato production is the increased growing of small-fruited varieties for the market that are sour, with a somewhat green taste instead of a true, rich tomato flavor. A variety that should be used instead is Sugar Lump, which produces long strings of bite-sized tomatoes with a sweet, rich flavor that puts older varieties in the shade. Another of the same quality is Gardener's Delight from England, offered in the United States by Thompson & Morgan through their new branch in New Jersey.

Turnip
See comments above in the description of radishes.

Watercress
No other cress has quite the flavor of watercress. It does not need running water to grow, although it is easier to propagate in a clean stream. The subsistence farmer usually has a creek or outflow from a spring where it will thrive. It can also be grown in a puddle of rich soil by allowing water to drip out of a tap at a slow rate, which allows the soil to take it up as fast as it drips. If not allowed to dry out, it can also be grown in a greenhouse bench or cold frame. It can be started from seed, or from pieces of the stems. It roots readily from every joint.

Where it is available only in spring, summer, and fall, it can be frozen for use in winter, when it will turn a drab salad of commercial lettuce into a gourmet's delight.

Potherbs
Too many Americans remember the garden sass of their childhood with anything but pleasure. Cabbage with salty corned beef or mustard greens with a chunk of salt pork boiling away for hours on top of the stove do not evoke memories they care to

perpetuate. Even today, when I think of watery spinach as I knew it years ago, I must force myself to include that crop on my seed list, knowing that when it is properly prepared it can be good.

Today's knowledge of nutrition has outmoded grandmother's daylong boiling of garden sass and allows us to enjoy green vegetables or potherbs as tasty, healthful foods we can grow outside the kitchen door.

Beets

Although their major use is as a root crop, their tops are a rich source of vitamin A. To throw them away is to waste most of the food value of beets. A three-and-a-half ounce serving contains 12,000 units of A, while the roots provide only 70 units for the same size serving. One reason why beet greens are not too well liked is that they are overcooked. They are best when pulled early in the season while thinning the row. This is always necessary because beet "seeds" are actually fruits that contain three or four seeds. If the thinnings have tiny beets attached, about three-eighths inch to one-half inch in diameter, so much the better; they add to the flavor. Six pints of tops after cooking will serve four or five people. Tail any small beets. Put about a pint of water in the bottom of a kettle, add the beet tops, and bring to a boil. Test to see that the greens are tender after six or seven minutes. Never boil longer than 15 minutes. Add butter or margarine and salt to taste. (Although serving them with Hollandaise seems extravagant, try it—you'll like it.) A poached egg per person can be used to top beet greens. Some cooks add vinegar or lemon juice, but since beet tops contain oxalic acid, they are usually tart enough.

So far no hybrid beets have been introduced, but modern varieties are much superior to those of a generation ago. See under Root Crops for varietal selections.

Broccoli

Even though none of the leaves of broccoli are eaten, it is classed as a green vegetable because the edible portion, actually the flower head, is green and is prepared by boiling like other greens. That is why it has more vitamin C than any other green crop except Brussels sprouts, another vegetable where the flower within the sprout is also eaten. Flowers are richer in vitamin C than leaves. For an early crop broccoli should be started indoors in March north of the Ohio River; late February farther south. Transplant out-of-doors in late April or early May in the North, two weeks earlier in the South. Like other cole crops, broccoli is not too fussy as to soil except that sandy loams warm up earlier in spring, and, if there is a choice, early broccoli should go on such a soil. This is a crop that likes cool weather, as do all cole crops. In the South it is grown largely as a fall and early winter crop, although some venturesome souls do attempt to sneak in a small row in spring. Around Norfolk, Virginia, growers set out plants in July, which are harvested in October, November, or December. Broccoli is a long season plant that needs about 70 to 100 days to produce a crop.

After the main head is cut most varieties produce smaller heads on side shoots. Because of the long season needed to mature broccoli, the plants should be encouraged to produce sprouts to prolong the season. Space the plants 24 inches to 30 with short seasons Green Mountain is a good variety, maturing in 85 days. It is slow to bolt, so not all heads need to be gathered at once. For late fall harvest Waltham 29 is a good choice inches apart to allow room for side shoots to grow. For regions but should be planted no earlier than June 1, since it is strictly a fall variety.

The earliest of all broccolis is Green Comet, which produces a single central head in 60 to 70 days. It produces a good crop of side shoots later in the season. However, it is what commercial growers call a cropper, producing most of its heads at the same time. Another hybrid is Cleopatra, a 75-day variety with large central heads, followed by abundant side shoots. This variety is more drought and cold resistant than others.

The biggest problem with broccoli is aphid infestation. Cabbage loopers are also hard to control without chemicals. Malathion for aphids and Sevin or Methoxychlor for loopers work well. Organic gardeners can use a biological control, Bacillus thuringensis (see chapter on Control of Insects and Diseases), but this calls for several sprays and is not cheap.

Always cut broccoli heads before they show a trace of yellow blossoms. If the crop matures too fast, heads will keep in the refreshener pan of a refrigerator for a week to ten days.

Brussels Sprouts

Another cole crop, and one that dislikes hot weather. It is all but worthless in Midwestern and Southern summer heat but south of the Ohio River, it can be set out about August 1, to mature in October and November. The plants can tolerate light freezes, which also improve the flavor of the sprouts. In areas with cool nights this crop can be grown in summer for early fall harvest. For home gardeners the best variety is Jade Cross Hybrid, which produces twice as many sprouts as an open-pollinated variety such as Long Island Improved. See broccoli for insect problems.

Allow 18 inches to 24 inches between plants. About September 10 to 15, pinch out the growing tip to stimulate growth and development of sprouts at the top of the stalk. Sprouts improve in flavor with light freezes. Brussels sprouts are the highest in vitamin C of any potherb but lower in vitamin A.

Cabbage

In pre-refrigerator days, food on the farm table during winter months consisted largely of salt pork, cabbage, potatoes, and corned beef. In spite of the way cabbage was boiled to death by hours on a stove, it still did provide traces of vitamins. Unfortunately some of the distaste for cabbage, a remnant of that too familiar use in grandmother's day, has lingered to downgrade it. What could be a delightful addition to the menu, both summer and winter, is often passed up when planting the home garden.

In one way this is a reflection of prices for commercial cabbage. Because it is one of the cheapest vegetables available and one that occupies considerable space in the home garden, it should not be grown at home if space is limited.

Nutritional values of cabbage have been overemphasized. In a three-and-a-half ounce serving, it contributes 50 units of vitamin A, 20 of vitamin B, and 12 of vitamin C. In the same size serving of Chinese cabbage there will be 2,000 units of A, 25 of B, and 40 of C. Since Chinese cabbage occupies less space and can be stored almost as long as cabbage, it seems a better use of garden space.

Nonetheless forgetting nutritional value in season when other greens are plentiful, young cabbage from the garden can be a real treat. The idea is to avoid the bullet-hard commercial varieties and plant only those with superior flavor.

In the United States perhaps the best-flavored early cabbage available is Jersey Wakefield. This is not a ball of green cellulose, but a cabbage with a pointed head and with a real cabbage flavor. It is sometimes listed as Jersey Queen, a variety that is resistant to a cabbage disease called yellows. Of late, catalogs have changed this name to Jersey Wakefield Resistant. If you live in an area where temperatures in summer stay in the 80s day after day, plant only yellows-resistant varieties.

Another old-time pointed head cabbage with superior flavor is Greyhound, an English variety available only from Thompson & Morgan in the United States. It is even earlier than Jersey Wakefield. Seedlings transplanted in the open garden about August 15 will produce tasty heads for late fall use in the Northeast area of the United States. In the South a September planting should provide cabbage as late as Christmas in a normal winter. It is not yellows-resistant, however.

For those who are not too fond of strong cabbage flavor, the Savoy varieties, with crinkled foliage and heads that are never really hard, are worth growing. Almost any Savoy variety is worth growing, although Savoy King, an All-America Award Winner, is much more productive than open pollinated varieties. Unfortunately no Savoy cabbage is yellows-resistant.

Cabbage for winter storage is of value largely for those with large suburban gardens and for subsistence farmers. This use has been shrinking every year for the past three decades. Today most winter cabbage is shipped in fresh from the South and Southwest rather than from storage in the North. At the same time there are many who would find it economical to store this crop along with other vegetables. They will have trouble finding varieties, however. Two catalogs I consulted to see if they listed such varieties as Late Flat Dutch and Danish Ballhead did not list a single storage variety. Those who want to store cabbage might find listings of Premium Flat Dutch, Penn State Ballhead, All Seasons, etc.

One reason why cabbage should be of interest to subsistence farmers is its value as a green feed for winter use with poultry and other livestock.

Red cabbage is a minor crop, yet should be included in larger gardens for variety. Mammoth Red Rock is a heavy producer with good flavor and a fairly good keeper. It matures in 90 days from transplanting. Red Acre, maturing in 85 days, is another good variety. Red Acre Yellows Tolerant should be grown in warmer climates. Red Danish is also yellows-resistant and perhaps the best for late storage. It is a 92-day variety.

Garden magazines carry ads for Southern-grown cabbage transplants, which are supposed to give the gardener an early start with this crop. Unfortunately most of these have been grown in the open field or in cool greenhouses where temperatures fell to below 40 degrees. When cabbage and other cole crops are exposed to such low temperatures, this causes some plants to produce flower stalks and go to seed prematurely. Add to this the lack of information on disease in such plants and the home gardener is better off growing his own, if he has the necessary conditions.

Cabbage is a heavy feeder but is not fussy as to whether fertility is supplied by organic matter or chemical fertilizers. It will grow on anything from sandy loams and muck to clay loams.

A common mistake made is in assuming that because cabbage is able to survive light freezes and cold weather, this is good for it. Actually this produces hard, fibrous plants that are not only tough when eaten but are smaller and grow slowly. Do not set cabbage plants out in the open until after the frost-free date. Growing seedlings indoors should follow the recommendations for handling tomato transplants. You may lose a few days in earliness, but the cabbage you harvest will be better. In the North seedlings for fall and winter cabbage are set out about June 15 to July 15. Spacing depends on the variety. Early Jersey

Wakefield and other very early varieties should be planted about 12 to 15 inches apart in the row. Large Flat Dutch and other late varieties need two feet between plants.

Root knot is not a serious disease in the North, but in the South it can be devastating. It is caused by nematodes burrowing into the root, causing irregular knots or swellings. The only real cure is soil fumigation. Rotation reduces the nematode population but is impractical in the limited space of a home garden, where the worms can be carried on shoes from one part of the garden to another. Heavy applications of organic matter help: Predatory nematodes that feed on their kin propagate in it. Also there are ring fungi that eat nematodes and need organic matter to propagate. Club root is caused by a slime fungus that invades the root. Liming the soil to a pH of 7.5 is the best, if not the only, control. Other cabbage diseases are not serious if clean cultivation and the use of only well-decayed organic matter is practiced.

Cauliflower

Of little value nutritionally (it has the lowest vitamin content of any other crop) cauliflower is grown mostly to add variety to the diet. The edible portion is the white tender head or "curd." It needs the same culture as cabbage but is much more sensitive to heat. It grows well only in areas with cool weather, such as northern New England, upper Michigan and Wisconsin, and the Pacific Northwest. Elsewhere it is grown only as a late fall or winter crop.

Cauliflower produces good heads only when grown slowly over a long season. For summer culture it should be started indoors in March, so it can take advantage of cool spring weather. It can tolerate light spring frosts, but these do not improve quality. Set out about a week before the usual frost-free date but cover with newspaper if an unseasonably late frost occurs. Transplants should not be older than six weeks when set out. Space 18 to 24 inches in the row. For a fall crop in the North seed can be sown directly in the garden in late July, but if used as a succession crop, it can be started a week or two earlier in a flat and transplanted.

Soil type is not too important, but pH is. Best pH is 6.4 to 6.9.

If a slow-release fertilizer was not applied when soil was prepared, apply a good mixed vegetable fertilizer at the rate recommended by the manufacturer. A second application along the row when the curd begins to form will mean bigger heads. Leaves should be brought over the curd and tied when the curd is the size of a tennis ball. Be sure it is dry. Foliage should form a cap that will shed rain. For those who don't want to fuss with blanching, the foliage on a new variety from Michigan State pulls itself over the curd when it is about six to eight inches in diameter. If larger heads are wanted, tying will be needed. Another variety, Early Purple Head or its improvement, Royal Purple, needs no blanching. Purple at first, when cooked these two varieties will turn an attractive light green instead of white. When you get used to this color, it is an improvement. Personally I have never liked the washed-out look of the white curd of cauliflower. The flavor of Early Purple Head is identical to conventional varieties.

There are so many varieties called Snowball in commerce that the name becomes confusing. Most are a safe bet for growing in cauliflower country. One that offers a slight degree of tolerance to heat is the All-America Award winner of 1969—Snow King Hybrid. As is typical of hybrid varieties, it is resistant to various cauliflower diseases. In my experience it matures heads 50 days after setting out transplants, which makes it close to the earliest variety in commerce. Where cabbage yellows occur, grow only Snowball varieties; they have some resistance.

Chard, Swiss

A beet that does not form a root, Swiss chard is identical in value to beet leaves already mentioned. It differs from beet foliage in one way; some varieties have a slightly earthy odor to which many gardeners object. Because it is such a valuable source of greens, I have experimented with it and find that by mixing Swiss chard with New Zealand spinach, both are improved. New Zealand spinach contains oxalic acid, which gives it a flat-sour taste. When combined with Swiss chard the two slightly unpleasant flavors seem to offset each other. At our home we prefer the mixture to the best conventional spinach.

Swiss chard seed should be sown a week or two before the last killing frost in spring. All too often the plants are allowed to grow without thinning. Since it is a beet, the seed is actually a fruit with several seeds in it and so no matter how far apart they are sown, the row must be thinned to space out the plants. They should stand at least six inches apart.

Lucullus is the most widely grown variety because of its broad, thick stems. The stems are often cooked in the manner of asparagus but are rather insipid unless dressed with a savory sauce. They are delicious with hollandaise, but then what isn't? A novel way to serve them is as chard rib fritters, just breaded and fried. The varieties Large White Rib and Fordhook Giant are much like Lucullus. Rhubard chard has beet-red stalks; the novel color does not seem to affect the flavor.

Collards

Scorned by damned Yankees, collards are beloved of Southern gardeners. Southerners are the gainers in nutrition, since collards are high in vitamin A, 7,000 units in a 3½-oz. serving. This is one cole crop that does not object to summer heat. It produces a crop of fleshy leaves that are cooked as green "sass." If not boiled to death it can be tasty. The plants are tolerant of low temperatures, as low as 15 degrees above. Exposure to cold improves the flavor. Growth is much like Brussels sprouts with the same culture. Collards are tolerant of poorer soil than other cole crops.

Fennel

Florence fennel is a cultivated variety of wild herb that is grown for the swollen bulbous stems. It has a distinctive anise flavor. Sometimes called bulb celery, it can be eaten like celery. It is particularly tasty as an appetizer, stuffed with a sharp cheese spread. The leaves can be used in flavoring (see under The Gardener's Spice Cabinet—Herbs).

Sow out of doors after the soil has warmed up (it prefers a rich, loamy soil and is not worth growing on clay loams). When the seedlings can be handled, thin to eight inches apart. Save the thinnings for use as a herb (delicious in fish sauces). When bulbs begin to form, draw earth up around them to blanch the bulbs.

About the only variety is Mammoth, if any varietal name is given. Fennel is usually listed among herbs in catalogs.

Kale

Kale is another vegetable that has had a bad press. I have known gardeners who grew it for use of its striking blue-green foliage in flower arrangements, but who have never tasted it. When properly cooked, it is as good as spinach and, to some tastes, better. After light frosts a mixture of kale and Swiss chard is particularly welcome.

As far north as Norfolk, Virginia, kale is hardy in winter and provides a green vegetable the following spring. With protection it often survives along the south shore of Lake Erie. Seed directly in the garden in early spring, and again in mid-July. The latter planting will provide tender leaves in late fall and early winter.

Its vitamin A content is high—9,000 units in a three-and-a-half ounce serving—more than double that of leaf lettuce. Young leaves can be served like lettuce as a salad.

Vates is the best variety sold in the United States. Unlike some varieties it does not turn yellow in fall but retains its clear blue-green color for use in garnishing and in flower arrangements. A ten-foot row should provide all the foliage needed by the average family. Space plants about a foot apart.

Kohlrabi

I was tempted to discuss this oddball vegetable under Root Crops or omit it entirely, until memory reminded me of the protests that poured into one seed house when it was left out of its catalog. Once a kohlrabi fan, always a kohlrabi fan. I suspect that those who grow it have learned what a delectable vegetable it can be if treated properly. The edible portion is a bulb-like swelling above ground level that resembles a light-green turnip. If harvested when this swelling is less than three inches in diameter, it can be sliced thin and either eaten as a relish with a touch of salt, or added to salads. The flavor is crisp and pungent, something like that of a turnip, but more delicate.

I realize that this attempt to describe a flavor (always difficult) sounds contradictory, yet this is a vegetable that can be delightful if well grown. It can also be cut into cubes and boiled in the same way as turnips and served with melted butter or an herb-flavored sauce.

Where kohlrabies have acquired a bad name is in allowing them to grow to the size of a softball before harvesting. Never allow them to get much bigger than two-and-a-half inches in diameter. They need to be grown quickly, which means early sowing since they don't like summer heat. A fall crop can be planted in late August as a catch crop if you liked the flavor of the spring planting. There are only two varieties offered in American catalogs—Early White Vienna and Early Purple Vienna.

Mustard

The broad-leaved mustards are grown mostly in the South, where one gardener calls them "Rebel spinach." Except for its attractiveness to the harlequin bug, it has few enemies. Sevin will control the bug, only serious in the South. The tender leaves are more sprightly than spinach or chard when cooked. If the flavor seems too sharp alone, try mustard blended with other green leafy vegetables. Sow a week or two before the frost-free date: Seeds are hardy. Plants should stand ten inches apart after thinning. Use the thinnings for greens. Varieties do not vary too much except that the variety Tendergreen is less pungent and closer to spinach in flavor. Make successive sowings if you like the flavor of the thinnings.

Orach

Formerly listed in catalogs as mountain spinach or orache, this is a species of Atriplex. It is an annual that often self-sows. The leaves are cooked like spinach when gathered from young plants. Seeds can be sown as early as the soil is workable. I have written several specialists, but no one seems to list it any more. It is worth growing if you can find it; the flavor of the young foliage is excellent. If it is at home in your garden, it will self-sow and perpetuate itself.

Sorrel

If your soil is acid, you probably won't want to sow this: It is a pernicious weed. If it has already invaded, lime most of the garden, but save a small patch of this for sorrel soup. The variety sold by French seed houses is a little less acid and with thicker leaves. If you have a hankering for this vegetable, I would recommend writing some French seed house for their seed of it.

Spinach

The ordinary garden variety of spinach can be a delectable dish in the hands of a good cook, or a limp-dishrag sort of a mess as often prepared. Few American home gardeners grow it unless they happen to live in a climate that is cool in summer or one warm enough to allow it to survive in winter. From a production standpoint only garden peas waste more effort and produce less food than does spinach. It dislikes heat, does not produce heavy yields per square foot of space and is likely to shoot to seed before it can be harvested. Yet spinach enthusiasts rave about its delicate flavor and point to its lofty content of vitamin A—14,000 units in a three-and-a-half ounce serving.

If you are willing to give it TLC for its scant return, by all means plant a variety such as Bloomsdale Long Standing or America that will not rapidly shoot to seed. There are hybrid varieties, but seed is not too plentiful. One such variety is Early Smooth Hybrid #8. It is resistant to certain spinach diseases. In warmer parts of the South, spinach is grown as a winter crop, sowing the seed from September to January. In the North it is usually planted in August for harvesting up to Thanksgiving Day.

Spinach is not particular as to soil as long as it is fairly rich and not acid. Seed is sown where it is to grow. In commercial production it is not thinned, but in the home garden, gathering excess plants so those left to grow are about five inches apart is not too hard. Use the thinnings for early greens.

The only serious pests are aphids, controlled by Malathion. New Zealand spinach has already been mentioned in discussing

Swiss chard. It has one requirement that is often overlooked, resulting in poor germination. Because it is sensitive to the least touch of frost, and because it thrives in hot weather, gardeners assume that it is semitropical and wait to plant it until the soil is warm. Actually the seed is fully winter hardy (it self-sows for me in Maine) and will not germinate if seeded in warm soil. Plant it as early as your soil can be turned over. Plant the seeds three feet apart to give the long vines a chance to run. New Zealand spinach can be frozen for winter use.

Malabar spinach should be treated as a warm weather crop, sowing the seed after the frost-free date or when apple trees are in full bloom. It thrives in ordinary soils. If space is limited, it is happy growing as a vine on a fence. It keeps growing in weather too hot for the garden type of spinach. A valuable substitute for spinach as a summer crop in the South.

4

Vine Crops

Winter Squash

Please, dear reader, don't skip the following lines, but hear me out. Although you may honestly feel that winter squash is only fit for cattle feed, that opinion will change if you can only taste the real thing.

Properly grown, stored and cooked, winter squash is not only a gourmet's delight, but one of the most valuable foods that can be stored at home.

R.M.C.

A recent survey of American food preferences rated winter squash near the bottom of the list, below liver and kidneys, which once suffered that ignominy. This dislike for a valuable and delicious food can be easily understood when judged by the flavor and texture as it is usually served.

The green, weedy flavor of squash harvested too early and the soupy mess served as cooked squash are enough to turn anyone with taste against it. Although to speak ill of any Hubbard squash is to offend thousands of New Englanders who were weaned on that noble vegetable, it is this very strain that is responsible for much of today's resistance to growing, storing, and eating it. It matures late, which often scares the gardener

55

into harvesting it too soon when early frosts are predicted. North of the Ohio River any squash cut from the vine before October 1 will hardly be fit to eat. Unripe Hubbard matures slowly and retains its unpleasant weedy flavor longer than other varieties. Is it any wonder that millions of Americans scorn a vegetable that is a gourmet treat when properly harvested and stored?

The introduction of two varieties—Butternut and Buttercup—have done much to change the unfavorable status of winter squash. When allowed to mature on the vine before harvesting, both these varieties will equal or surpass the finest sweet potatoes or yams in flavor. Used instead of pumpkin in Thanksgiving pies, they have gained new respect for that traditional dessert. In addition to providing superior flavor as pie filling, their smaller size means less waste in preparation and no bulky unused pumpkin to fill the refrigerator. Far from being unpleasant when immature, small fruits of Butternut can be used as summer squash. The flavor is like that of a perfect ear of sweet corn.

These two varieties stand out because they mature earlier than do Hubbard squashes and similar slow-ripening types. This means that some of their stored starches have been converted to fruit sugar, with an improvement in flavor. Although I would rate Buttercup as a slight favorite over Butternut, weight watchers should be warned against its seductions. Its delightful meat is an irresistible invitation to add butter and gravy to realize the sapor of the combination. Although Butternut is not quite as dry as Buttercup, if it is baked instead of boiled or steamed, it is not hurt by similar treatment and makes a marvelous substitute for potatoes during cold winter months.

There are, of course, other squashes than these two favorites, a number of which were lost in the shuffle because of the unfavorable reaction to unripe Hubbard. There is Gold Nugget, for example, a recent All-America Award winner. That award alone is significant: A vegetable as low in acceptance as winter squash had little chance of winning, yet it did. One thing in its favor is its bush habit, which means it takes less space in small gardens. It can be planted in rows with the plants spaced only a foot apart. Its deep orange flesh is unusually thick, dry, and will keep most of the winter in storage. The small fruits are just right for individual servings. A heavy bearer, there should be plenty of them from a 25-foot row in the garden.

Another bush winter squash is Table King, an Acorn variety. To my taste it is not up to Gold Nugget in flavor, but those who prefer Hubbard types may like it better. Too, there is a bush version of the vining Buttercup, identical except for slightly smaller fruits, which for small families is an advantage. It is called Emerald.

A novelty squash that will go far in adding variety to the diet is a "gee-whiz" vegetable that can help you outdo your friends and neighbors. Called Vegetable Spaghetti, it is far from new but has been revived recently with the demand for greater food production in home gardens. I had all but forgotten this squash until the managing director of Thompson & Morgan sent me a package as a novelty they planned to offer through their American branch.

This squash produces an egg-shaped fruit about eight pounds in weight and buff-ivory in color. Under good growing conditions a single vine can produce six or seven fruits. When these lose the tint of green that marks the unripe squash, they are ready for use. Actually in our experiments in cooking this variety, several were gathered before fully ripened and cooked in the same way as recommended for the mature fruits. When opened, the inside was a mass of greenish spaghetti, which made perfect green noodles, a new use. When the *mature* fruits are boiled, the long fibers inside look exactly like spaghetti, mild in flavor and perfect as a base for various meat and cheese sauces. This is a vegetable that promises to improve the quality and variety of those we can store for winter use. It is a vining squash, unfortunately not for small gardens.

Although I have been a bit rough on Hubbard, this by no means affects the status of that variety as an important winter vegetable. There are growers in New England, for example, who appreciate the need for late harvesting and who can grow the variety Blue Hubbard to perfection. Except for its size it is as valuable a vegetable as can be grown in larger gardens. Production by weight is the heaviest of any winter squash, an important consideration when space must be used to the limit. This advantage is offset by the ungainly size, which means that all of a squash is seldom used.

In planning the garden, space needed for growing vining varieties eliminates them from consideration in gardens of less than 1,500 to 2,000 square feet. A single vine occupies as much as 20 square feet. Bush varieties need from one-fourth to one-half this space, which means the use of Gold Nugget, Table King, or Emerald where space is limited.

One plus for Butternut is its immunity from attack by squash borers. All other varieties mentioned will be attacked in areas where the borer occurs. Chemical controls have been less than effective in attacking this pest. Fortunately there is a new way to protect both winter and summer squash. The trouble starts with a moth that lays an egg at the base of the stem, just an inch or so above the ground. The female moth is conditioned to fly under the leaves to reach this point, apparently guided by the shadow at the base of the stem.

Entomologists figured that if this spot were lighted, this would confuse the moth in her efforts to lay her egg. They laid aluminum foil under the leaves to reflect the sky. As they expected the moth was so confused that it never did find the target and the vines remained free of borers. In repeating this experiment I actually observed borer moths flying upside down, confused into thinking the reflection from the aluminum foil was the sky. The foil need only cover about a foot on either side of the stem to be effective.

Winter Squash Culture

Squashes are cucurbits, related to melons, cucumbers, and pumpkins, all of which do best in high-organic soils. Organic gardeners should find squashes particularly attractive since no other crop prefers soils so rich in compost. If no other space is available to grow them, try sowing a few seeds right in the compost pile. Production will amaze you. If enough compost is available to cover an area where squashes are to grow, you won't need fertilizer.

Although I have mentioned planting on a compost pile, I should warn neophyte gardeners against taking an old saying too literally. Any vegetable garden book written in the past half century has mentioned growing vine crops in "hills." I remember my first garden (at the age of eight) in which I took this recommendation as gospel and built mounds a foot high, where I planted cucumbers. Although I managed to keep the vines alive by almost daily watering, they certainly did not thrive.

When the books say "hill," think of a hole instead. By that I mean don't picture sowing vine crop seeds in a hole several inches deep, but imagine them as planted in a shallow basin perhaps an inch lower than the surrounding soil. This basin collects water when it rains. Vine crops love soil moisture. This means, however, that they must have good drainage or their fragile roots will rot. Again, added compost will help.

One problem is that vine crops cannot stand transplanting. Those fragile roots are so brittle that any attempt to dig them will end in failure. There is a way, however, that they can be started indoors. There are containers that can be used to grow plants of squash (of cucumbers and melons as well), which can be planted pot and all without disturbing the roots. The old-time Fertil-Pot made of compressed cattle manure was one of the best for all vine crops, but it is difficult to find nowadays. It has been replaced to a large degree by the newer peat-fiber pots, which need extra feeding to keep the vine seedlings growing well. The four-inch-square size needed for all vine crops is hard to find. Of late years I have been substituting the one-pint plastic baskets in which strawberries are sold. I line these with live sphagnum moss to keep the soil from washing away and fill them with well-rotted compost. Dried sphagnum will do nearly as well, although live sphagnum does contain growth-stimulating substances, if you can find it. For directions for growing plants under lights, see the chapter on Tomatoes.

The only difference is that instead of a two-month period for growing a tomato from seeding to transplanting, don't try to grow any vine crop indoors for a longer period than 40 days. They make such rampant growth that the vines are hard to handle if allowed more time. Wait until apple trees bloom if planting seed directly outdoors.

A disconcerting pattern of growth in practically all squashes is that at first they produce only male flowers. Since these do not set fruits the anxious gardener is disturbed, thinking something is wrong. Male flowers can be identified by examining the stem just under the blossom. Female flowers produce a small swelling (the fruit-to-be), but the stem of male blossoms is the same in diameter through its full length.

Squash pollen is heavy and does not fly from male to female flowers but must be carried by bees. If the weather is wet and stormy, bees are inactive. Sometimes this delays fruit set for as much as a week or two.

Insect Pests

Other than the squash borer the only other serious pest is the squash bug. It is a bad customer that injects a toxic substance as it feeds. This causes a disease known as Anasa wilt, which blackens new growth on old vines and can kill immature plants. The best control is clean housekeeping. Destroy anything that offers any shelter to wintering-over bugs. About the time squash vines begin to run, female squash bugs lay brownish eggs on the foliage that hatch in about two weeks into green nymphs (immature bugs with red heads that turn a dull white as they pass from one stage of growth to another). Fortunately there is only one generation a year; so if the vines are watched and are dusted or sprayed as soon as the eggs are hatched, this pest can be eliminated for the rest of the growing season. Use pyrethrum-rotenone dusts or ground sabadilla. All three materials are of vegetable origin and so should be acceptable even to organic gardeners. Sabadilla is probably the best control but is hard to find. Methoxychlor or Diazinon are safe chemical sprays or dusts.

Never use sulfur in any form on vine crops: It burns them severely.

Winter Storage

This is a highly important step in producing winter squash, since practically all use made of it comes after harvest. The more carefully the fruits are handled at this time, the better they will keep. Treat them like eggs. Just because squashes have tough outer skins, don't think they can be thrown carelessly into a bin. If you use a wheelbarrow in gathering them, it will even pay to line it with an old quilt or rug. A single bruise can cause rot that will spoil a squash in a matter of a few weeks. Properly handled they should keep all winter. Use winter squash as a substitute for potatoes; they contain 100 times as much vitamin A.

When you are harvesting, you may find dozens of small fruits of Butternut, say up to three inches in length. These immature squashes should not be wasted; they can be cooked in the same way as summer squash. The flavor is a treat; it is like that of the most delicate sweet corn.

The best storage temperature for mature squash is between 45 and 50 degrees, with a relative humidity of 70 percent but not too much higher. Too dry and squashes shrivel. Too moist and they may rot. Don't pile them in storage. Space them out singly on the shelf. I find that if the shelves are covered with clean excelsior this helps prevent injury.

For those planning to do subsistence farming, there are additional reasons why both squashes and pumpkins should be included among the crops they grow. All species of domestic animals kept for meat and eggs thrive on them during the winter when feed costs are highest and green feed hard to provide. Special plantings for this purpose can be made of varieties that produce more and bigger fruits than those for table use. For example, Howden's field pumpkin, introduced by Harris, has thick flesh much better in flavor than old-time pumpkins. It is high in sugar and also high in energy. The fruits are heavy and keep unusually well. If table squashes run short, baked or fried pumpkin from this variety is not the worst dish you can serve.

Another squash worth growing for animal feed, but with value on the table, is Golden Delicious. It was developed for use in processed baby foods and has an unusually high vitamin C content. The flesh is a rich orange and helps give egg yolks a deeper color when fed to laying hens. For heavy production Blue Hubbard is hard to beat.

Summing Up

To recap the pros and cons of winter squash: A highly nutritious starchy vegetable, even higher in vitamin A than canned or frozen spinach and exactly 100 times richer in that vitamin than white potatoes. Poor flavor if picked too soon, but when fully ripe, an improvement on pumpkins, yams, and sweet potatoes. Not difficult to store. Two serious insect enemies, but both readily controlled. Vine type a hog for space; even the bush type may be too much for smaller gardens. A valuable animal feed crop.

Summer Squash

Here is another vegetable that has suffered from a bad past. Not a little of the poor opinion of English cooking held by many is due to the tasteless boiled Vegetable Marrow favored by gardeners on the tight little isle. Equally innocuous were the yellow summer crookneck squashes of the early 20th Century on this side of the pond.

Childhood memories of the latter dish for years kept me from tasting summer squash until forced to rate some varieties of zucchini for flavor. I do not claim that plain boiled zucchini is too much better than old-time yellow crookneck, but because it came out of a culinary tradition that knew how to use it as a base for delectable sauces, it has become a chef's triumph.

Although I have no intention of writing a cookbook, here is one vegetable that is so dependent upon the chef to prepare it properly, I must give my favorite zucchini recipe. In the first place, if this squash is allowed to grow much longer than four inches, it loses most of its delicate flavor. Cut young fruits in half lengthwise and boil them until the opaque pale green flesh turns a translucent green (about five minutes). Next spread them on a broiler pan or cookie sheet and sprinkle with bread crumbs and grated cheese. Italian cheese, such as Romano or Parmesan, is best, but old cheddar, allowed to dry out a bit, will do. No need to remove the peeling on young zucchini; it adds to flavor.

Place the zucchini halves, cheese side up, under a broiler until the cheese is browned. Served with broiled bacon, this is a dish fit for any table.

Catalogs list dozens of varieties of zucchini, including a couple with yellow skins. Unfortunately the yellow varieties remind me of my childhood dislike, so I no longer grow these. The so-called golden varieties I have tried have been poor producers. Speaking of production, don't waste time growing anything but hybrid varieties of zucchini. One summer I ran tests on summer squash including both open-pollinated and hybrid varieties, 23 in all. In not one case did production from the open pollinated varieties equal that from the hybrids.

Although there are slight differences in these hybrids, they are not great enough to work too hard finding a specific variety. If you can find it, Clarita is highly female, which means that it produces more fruits than those that also produce male flowers. I rate its flavor a shade above all others. Unfortunately it is not widely distributed. The fruits are slightly gray green, much like Grezini, another quality hybrid. Ambassador, Chefini, Aristocrat, Elite, and President are all good hybrid varieties worth growing.

In the past I have said unpleasant things about the wishy-washy taste of the old White Bush Scallop summer squash, which I ranked with England's vegetable marrow as flavorless, dull table fodder. I am now ready to recant. For two years I have been growing new varieties of this old-timer—varieties such as Patty Pan Hybrid and St. Pat Scallop Hybrid. The improvement in flavor has been astonishing. Some of the gain in flavor comes from an improvement in harvesting. Instead of waiting until the fruits are big, with a tough, hard rind, I now harvest them when about the size of a silver dollar.

To produce enough for harvesting at this immature stage, at least a 25-foot row had to be planted, not practical in a small garden. Perhaps the most important improvement in flavor had nothing to do with the fruits but was a culinary discovery. When boiled until tender, they should be served in Hollandaise sauce. Except for those who own a blender, this tour de force of master chefs has been too difficult to attempt. Here is help for you. If this book does nothing more than teach you how to make Hollandaise easily, it will perhaps be worthwhile.

I discovered this method by accident. My wife hated making Hollandaise because it would curdle about two out of three tries. Once when she was out shopping, I decided to try my hand at it.

By mistake I started with a cold skillet that had been hanging in a 40-degree temperature. Into it I put a quarter-pound stick of margarine, two egg yolks, and two teaspoons of lemon juice, and over a slow fire, started to stir. When all the ingredients had melted, I added a dash of salt. Not a sign of curdling.

My horrified wife came home, heard what I had done and hardly dared look. We were both astonished when this unorthodox Hollandaise was the equal of any we had ever tasted. Since that time we always start with a cold skillet and don't have failures, except for one thing. Not all types of margarine will do. Better stick to butter to be safe. Margarines are concocted nowadays out of everything from whale blubber to vegetable oil and not all of them work. Of course, if you own a blender, you have no problem: It makes superb Hollandaise. However it is made, try it with the baby fruits of white scallop squash. Superb.

For those who sigh for the yellow summer squashes of their youth, modern hybrid varieties are available that are much more prolific, healthier, earlier, and have skin so tender it need not be removed but adds flavor to the cooked squash. Some of these are Seneca Prolific, Golden Girl, Gold Bar, and Baby Straightneck.

Summer Squash Culture

Soil, growing conditions, and insect pests are the same as for winter squash. When starting plants indoors for an early crop, plant at the same time as for winter squash, a month before the frost-free date in your area. Seed outdoors when apple trees bloom, no sooner.

Cucumbers

In contrast to the relative freedom of squash from insect pests and diseases, the cucumber would qualify as a vegetable hypochondriac. Here is one crop where the home gardener must give thanks for the work of modern plant breeders. A search of seed catalogs shows that older open-pollinated varieties have all but disappeared from commerce. The reason? Modern hybrids have been bred for resistance to practically every major disease attacking cucumbers. These include scab, mosaic, downy mildew, powdery mildew, angular leaf spot, anthracnose, and gummosis.

Among slicing varieties for table use, four varieties are outstanding—Shamrock, Victory, Gemini 7, and Sweet Slice. All are resistant or tolerant of all diseases except gummosis, largely a problem with forcing cucumbers in the greenhouse. Of these my favorite is Sweet Slice, a delicious variety completely without bitterness. It is of the so-called burpless type and can be eaten without distress by those who have trouble with other cucumbers.

All four of these varieties are distinguished for another desirable quality. They are gynoecious, which is just a fancy way to say that they produce only female flowers. In addition to increasing the number of places on the vines where fruits can form, this also reduces the number of seeds in those fruits. The increase in yield is greatest early in the season, because gynoecious varieties do not produce male flowers. Other cucumbers produce male flowers first, which reduces early fruiting.

There are even pickling varieties that are gynoecious. They are Mariner, Green Pak, and Crusader. Two others that are not all-female are Pioneer and Salty, but all the pickling varieties mentioned have high disease resistance.

Cucumbers are even more sensitive to cold than are squashes. Don't set out plants that were started indoors until the last petals have fallen from the apple trees. The same holds for sowing seed directly in the garden. Unlike squash plants, which can survive cool weather early, chilling a cucumber seedling early in its growth is thought to contribute to bitter fruits.

Except for these precautions, soil and culture for cucumbers are the same as for squash.

Melons

Because they are fruits that can be grown as annuals, melons of all kinds are especially welcome in the home food garden. Those who will grow them for the first time are in for a treat. During the past few decades relatively few people in America have ever tasted the superb flavor of a melon that was left on the vine until fully ripe. The skill of plant breeders in developing melons that had remarkably sweet fruits even when far from ripe, has fooled many into thinking that those sold on the market had a true melon flavor.

Unfortunately this sweetness did not have with it the more important elements of sweetness—esters and other volatile substances that develop only as the flesh in the fruit mellows and turns soft. The finest flavored muskmelon in the world, if picked before full maturity, still tastes like a gourd in spite of sweetness bred into it to fool the customers.

If these same varieties are allowed to ripen, the result is a melon so superior to the commercial product that the two seem like different fruits entirely.

Modern hybrid varieties are not markedly superior to many old-time melons in flavor, but in disease resistance and vigor, today's varieties have made it possible for anyone, not only the experienced amateur and the commercial grower, to grow good melons.

There are so many fine varieties that any one you pick will be a treat. Here are a few names found in modern catalogs: Harper Hybrid (my nomination for the best in flavor), Granite State (very early-maturing in northern New England), Saticoy (a rival for Harper Hybrid in flavor), Mainerock Hybrid (another variety for Northern areas), Burpee Hybrid (rated tops in sweetness by many), and Ambrosia (which I have tasted only once, perhaps a bit too early in the season—the flesh was quite firm).

Although many recall the flavor of old-time melons when fully ripe (as I remember Emerald Gem with nostalgia) they can grow these newer varieties with confidence that they will gain more than they have lost in greater disease resistance, increased plant vigor, earlier maturity, and more melons per vine. An example is Charentais, a famous old French variety, grown for generations both in the open garden and in greenhouses. It is closer to the true cantaloupe melon than the American muskmelon and has a distinctive flavor relished by connoisseurs. It is difficult to grow because of sensitivity to mildew.

Now there are two varieties of this epicurean delight—Chaca #1 and Oval Chaca. Both are highly resistant to mildew as well as to fusarium wilt.

For variety you may want to grow other melons as well as the muskmelon type. The one most commonly available is the Honey Dew melon, brought to the United States in the last decade of the 19th Century by the late J.C. Vaughan. The smooth ivory-colored skin and pale-green flesh are known to millions of Americans, but as sold in the market, this choice melon, which should taste like nectar, is more likely to resemble a potato in flavor. When this is in season I always look on the marked-down counter, hoping to find a Honey Dew that the produce man has decided is too ripe to be a first-class melon.

This is not a melon for Northern gardens. Unless an early start can be made by sowing seed in a cold frame, I do not recommend trying to grow it north of the Ohio River. It needs at least 115 to 120 days of weather above 65 degrees to produce a crop of ripe melons. At its best it is marvelous, but it is subject to disease and is temperamental in growth.

Honey Mist is an early-maturing version of Honey Dew, but it does need about 95 days of warm weather. It does have some hybrid vigor and is worth growing as far north as a line drawn from Chicago to New York.

If it were not for the delights of extending the melon season into early winter, Casaba melons wouldn't be grown that much. Granted the flavor lacks something of the rich, fruity aroma of a well-ripened muskmelon or the delectable winelike flavor of a perfectly ripened Honey Dew, but to sit down at Christmastime to a fully ripened Casaba melon that has been properly stored is a memorable gastronomic event. Again you must live south of the Ohio River to enjoy this temperamental fruit, unless you know of a quality greengrocer who stocks it.

The story is different in the case of the Crenshaw melon. Early Hybrid Crenshaw (currently offered only by Burpee Seeds) can be grown up to the Chicago–New York line and well into southern Michigan and the Golden Triangle of Ontario, Canada. It has the same distinctive flavor and thick salmon-pink flesh of the more temperamental and less hardy earlier Crenshaw melon.

Watermelon

Say watermelon to most Americans and the name conjures up a memory of picnics with that symbol of summer floating around in a tub of ice. In past years watermelon has been almost a monopoly of Southern growers, with commercial production carried on not much farther north than Iowa. Today there are watermelon varieties that will ripen as far north as Maine.

Since plant breeders have given us true hybrids, many of the former problems with disease have been minimized. Unfortunately most of these hybrid melons are too large in size for day-to-day use, with fruits that weigh from 20 to 65 pounds. Where space can be spared for their 12-foot-long vines, these big melons can be used fresh and what is left can be frozen as melon balls, perhaps mixed with cantaloupe. The larger sizes are not reliable north of the Ohio River. Among the best are Crimson Sweet, which produces melons up to 25 pounds, Calhoun Grey, averaging about 23 pounds, but under ideal conditions producing fruits that weigh up to 60 pounds, Top Yield, a 20-pounder, and Jubilee, with fruits up to 40 pounds.

Seedless watermelons have caught the public fancy and it is a pleasure to eat them without squirting seeds, but extra care is needed in growing. The seed is expensive and must be produced by a cross of a variety that will produce viable seeds, but that will, in turn, set fruits that do not have seeds. Triple Sweet and Seedless Hybrid 313 are superior to open-pollinated Seedless Watermelon.

Seeds of seedless watermelon (how peculiar that sounds!) must have high heat to germinate (85 degrees for three days in a row). Begin about 40 days before apple trees drop their petals. This means you must gamble on averages and guess when that date will be. If you have to keep started plants indoors for much longer than you planned, they grow so long as to be almost unmanageable.

If this happens you are probably better off setting them where they are to grow and protecting them with the plant protectors sold in most garden centers. The best answer is to start seedless watermelons in an electric hotbed, and let them grow out of the frame after the heat is turned off and the sash removed.

Among the smaller ice box watermelons that weigh up to eight and ten pounds, is an interesting All-America Award melon with yellow flesh called Yellow Baby. It originated in Taiwan. Although no special claims are made for disease resistance in this variety, it has been healthy wherever I have seen it growing. Many Oriental vegetables seem to have resistance because of the conditions under which crops are grown in Asia. The flavor is delightful and the color attractive.

Maturing in 86 days from seed, Yellow Baby can be grown in cooler areas such as northern New England but if a long season of production is wanted should be started indoors as recommended for seedless varieties.

Sugar Baby and Sugar Doll Hybrid are two red-fleshed icebox varieties that are much like Yellow Baby and delightful to serve with it. These varieties do not take as much space as do their giant relatives. Anyone who has struggled to find room in a refrigerator for a 25-pound melon will welcome those less opulent fruits.

Chayote

In the South the chayote is used as a substitute for potatoes. Its fruits, however, cannot be stored for any length of time. In addition to being served as a substitute for potatoes, the fruits are pared, cut into thick slices and boiled until tender and served with butter or with cream sauce. They can also be baked with cheese, pickled, or made into a salad much like potato salad.

Although rarely seen much farther north than Charleston, South Carolina, the chayote can be grown as an annual as far north as Washington, D.C. It belongs to the same family as squashes and melons, but is a true perennial. In tropical countries it produces large tubers, which are eaten as well as the fruits. In certain areas of the South, such as around New Orleans, Savannah, and Columbia, South Carolina, it has been grown for generations. It is known by various names, such as vegetable pear, squash potato, mirliton, and mango squash.

It thrives on the same types of soil as do other squashes and melons. Usually it is grown as a vine. In the United States it seldom grows longer than 12 feet. It can be trained on a trellis where space is limited.

The entire fruit is planted, with the thick end sloping slightly downward and with the smaller end barely exposed. It is difficult to grow without compost and thrives on organic matter. Light applications of liquid fertilizer from time to time will increase yields. Usually a single vine will produce all the fruits one family can consume.

It is attacked by the same insects as cucumbers and squashes. Once established the vines can be carried over (in the Southern regions where it has been grown) by mulching heavily with straw or other suitable material.

One reason for trying to protect vines over winter is that if good fruits were produced the previous season, the old vines can be depended upon for palatable chayotes. They do not always come true from seed, varying from those with no pronounced seed and without fiber to those that have a tough, hard seed coat with fibers running throughout the flesh.

One reason they might be a desirable crop for subsistence farmers is that livestock will eat the vines, which make good fodder. Hogs are particularly fond of any surplus fruits.

5

Peas and Beans

In a recent survey of vegetable gardening, except for tomatoes more people grew snap beans than any other crop. Although many wanted to grow peas, less than half those polled in the survey had grown them or were planning to do so.

This is a reflection of the ease with which beans are grown and the difficulties many have with peas. Too, it also means that peas as usually grown do not yield heavily enough to pay for the space they take. At the same time, in discussing horticultural crops, peas and beans are usually grouped together, largely because they need similar culture.

Both dislike acid soils but will grow well in any type soil from a light sandy loam to a fairly heavy clay so long as it has a pH above 6.0. Both dislike droughts. The only fertilizers both are likely to need are phosphorus and potash, since they are legumes and can extract most of their own nitrogen from the air.

Beans

Snap Beans
The low-growing plant we used to call bush string beans is no

71

more. It has been bred out of existence by specialists who have all but created the perfect food plant. To many, elimination of the string was the most outstanding accomplishment in breeding, but this was far less significant than what was done to produce a healthier, more vigorous plant.

In my youth anyone who would walk through the bean patch in the morning was considered a fool. Every packet of bean seed contained a warning that this would cause anthracnose to spread from plant to plant, which could cause a crop failure. Today, although it is still wise to keep out of the bean patch until foliage is dry, modern varieties are available that are fairly resistant to infection by anthracnose as well as several formerly dangerous diseases.

Other improvements in beans include much earlier maturity, improved flavor, and much heavier yields. But you should read catalogs carefully for clues to changes developed by breeders that are not to the advantage of the home gardener. As I have already pointed out, no one is breeding for home gardeners anymore: He must accept varieties that are high in quality but lack some growth factor needed by the commercial grower and so are saved for amateur use. The big goal in growing beans today is to produce the perfect bean for machine harvesting. This means the grower wants a variety that will mature every bean on the same day so that he can go over the field with a mechanical harvester, gather all the beans, plow under the vines, and plant a succession crop.

If the home gardener were to plant a variety such as Spartan Arrow, Provider, or Harvester, he would find himself without beans until the day all the pods matured at once. For a day or two he would be up to his ears in beans but then would have none for the rest of summer. Look for such phrases as "home market variety" or "long picking season." Avoid any varieties described as "concentrated set."

Green Bush Snap Beans

These come in two types, the flat podded varieties and those with round or oval pods. There are not too many flat pods. The newest and perhaps the best is an All-America Award Winner, Green Crop. It is a heavier producer than Roma, or Bush Romano, but a shade less flavorful. The flat pod varieties tend to make bigger plants than those with round pods and should be spaced six to eight inches apart in the row.

Today's descendants of the original Tendergreen round pod variety are all quality beans. You can plant any of these with confidence. They include such outstanding varieties as Tenderpod, Tendercrop, Improved Tendergreen, and Tenderette.

Another development in bush beans has been the introduction of bush varieties of the famous Blue Lake pole bean, which comes into bearing sooner than its parent. Bush Blue Lake 274 is one of these, particularly desirable because its production is spread over a much longer period than most bush beans. While the pods of these new Blue Lake varieties are not quite as straight and smooth as most modern market beans, this means nothing in the pot when you grow your own. Give these varieties a little extra room in the row, as for bush flat types.

Two varieties with special advantages for some purposes are Contender and Royalty. Contender was about the first of the new generation of beans, with the advantage of producing the earliest pods of any. They are not straight, but the slight curve in the pods is no disadvantage in a home garden variety. They are thick, oval, tender, and are borne freely. If you want an early bean to grow before pole beans mature, Contender is the one to plant.

All bush beans should be replanted every two weeks until mid-August, if pole beans are not grown to succeed the first crop.

Royalty is interesting both for its color and its history. The pods are a rich bright purple in color that turns to green when boiled. This makes it ideal for freezing, since as soon as the color change takes place, it is blanched and ready to freeze. For fresh use it is tender, full-flavored, and one of the best beans you can plant.

It is a descendant of one of the great beans of the past called Blue Coco, a French pole bean planted in France for nearly 200 years. The original pole variety is still in French catalogs, but I have been unable to find it in the United States for the past two decades.

Among bush beans sent to me for trial by Thompson & Morgan was an amazingly early flat podded green bean called Limelight. Listed as maturing in 38 days, I actually picked a full crop in 40 days. It was fully as good as bush Romano in flavor. However, it is a "cropper" and matures all its pods at once. This is a bean for the gardener with plenty of space who can afford to give it room so he can enjoy an early picking.

A delightful new variety from Burpee in my 1975 trials was Greensleeves. The perfectly round, slim, long pods match the name. It matured 14 days after Limelight. It is a perfect bean for home canning, with white seeds that do not discolor the canned product. Also tops for freezing.

Wax Snap Beans

Although not as popular as green beans, wax snap beans are preferred by some gourmets for their tender, delicate flavor. Although not my cup of tea, I like them if the delicate flavor is pepped up a bit by the addition of some herb or spice to give it more zest. For example, when served with a cream sauce the sauce itself can be improved with a touch of any number of flavors, or the sauce can be poured over the beans and sprinkled with nutmeg or paprika. In Germany beans are usually flavored with summer savory. An old-time favorite is Kinghorn Wax, best where bean mosaic is not a problem. Cherokee Wax is resistant to mosaic and a quality bean. Perhaps the best-flavored of all wax beans is Eastern Butterwax, which is also preferred by many for freezing.

Pole Beans, Green and Wax

There are good reasons for relying on pole beans for a main crop, even though you may have to plant a variety, such as Contender for early production. Pole beans will produce far more per square foot than bush varieties and will continue to do so until frost if maturing pods are kept picked. They are also economical of space, since production per square foot is much higher than from bush varieties. The one drawback is the difficulty of finding poles in urban and suburban areas. Buying lumber is expensive since the poles usually rot at the ends and only last a year or two. The GroNet described in the chapter on tools makes pole bean production much easier. Except in cool climates, avoid using chicken wire as a support; bean vines are quite delicate and will burn when the wire gets hot.

Kentucky Wonder Pole Bean is probably the most widely grown variety of all in the United States. How much of this is because many gardeners believe it is the only pole variety, or because they really prefer the flavor, is difficult to say. That Kentucky Wonder does have a strong "beany" flavor cannot be denied. When picked young this variety has both tenderness and flavor, but of all beans widely planted today, it loses quality faster at maturity than any other. It can be had in both green and wax varieties, but the latter does not have the beany taste of the original.

There are better varieties if they are left to mature. The standard against which experts compare all others is Blue Lake, about the only pole bean grown commercially. Its quality and heavy production justify the heavy investment in poles needed when it is grown for the canning trade. Although the new bush varieties of Blue Lake are high in quality, to get the true flavor of this famous variety it should be grown as a pole crop. It is tops for canning and freezing.

A pole bean not to discount is Romano, a flat-podded green Italian variety that many consider the acme of bean flavor. A similar wax pole bean is Burpee Golden, which is also flat podded. It has an unusual habit of growth. It first sets a crop as a bush bean, then sends up runners that climb. It is a perfect variety for small gardens where space is not available for both types of beans.

A pole bean that is well worth watching is the 1975 introduction Crusader. Perhaps the name comes from the tremendously long scimitar-shaped pods, 20 inches long and curved. I planted this without much faith, but it proved to be the best pole bean in my test plot. The beans, even at maturity, were tender, yet meaty and full of flavor. The vines would be an addition to a flower garden because of their brilliant scarlet flowers that contrast vividly with bright green foliage. A true runner bean, it needs tall, tall poles (it reached the top of eight-foot poles and then hung over in my garden).

Soybeans

These are attracting a great deal of attention among beginning gardeners who are told that they are a valuable source of protein to replace meat in the diet. Nutritionally this is a sound assumption, since the protein in soybeans is complete. That is, it provides all of the amino acids that the body cannot manufacture by itself. There is, however, another consideration, that of appetite appeal. Most people would be willing to eat a soybean meal once or twice a week, but as a steady diet would refuse to do so unless in extreme need.

My recommendation would be that you try soybeans on a small scale, developing your own ways to serve them and if they have appetite appeal, increase your planting in future years.

Many of those who have been disappointed with soybeans as a food tried them by buying field varieties grown for industrial processing. Most of these were selected by farmers because of their high oil content, valuable for industrial use. They are much less palatable than varieties selected and bred for food.

Varieties for growing in home gardens are not widely distributed. Many of those that were cataloged some 30 to 40 years ago were dropped from cultivation because they would flower and bear pods in only a narrow band of country. (They were highly sensitive to day-length variations.) Today only one variety is offered generally, Kanrich, but Verde (best adapted south of Philadelphia) and Early Green Bush (does well in northern U.S. and southern Canada) also are offered by one or two firms.

Soybeans are not too fussy about soil but it must be warm when seed is planted. Space plants three to four inches apart in a row. Most edible soybean rows are 30 inches apart.

Soybeans need a long season to mature and occupy the soil for the full season. They are ready to harvest for winter use when the leaves turn yellow. Left too long, they may shatter. Harvesting is a chore because there are only two or three seeds in each pod (a plant will produce as many as 50 pods). When opening the green pod for shell beans, there is no easy way to do the job. I find that the easiest way to get the beans out of the pod is to cut off the unfilled end of the pod with shears, then to run a knife along the edge of the pod to open it. Some cooks partially boil the pods before shelling.

Fava Bean

Also called English Broad Bean. Unlike most beans, this is a crop that must be seeded as early in spring as the soil can be worked. It thrives in cool weather. It is primarily a crop for New England, southern Canada, upper Michigan and Wisconsin and the Pacific Northwest. It stands light frost and can be grown as a winter crop along the Gulf Coast and parts of Texas. Elsewhere the foliage burns in hot weather.

If given proper conditions, broad beans are heavy producers. The beans are borne in pods about seven inches long, about five to seven to a pod and resemble lima beans. The flavor is a blend of that of peas and beans. They are used strictly as shell beans since the pods are inedible.

The worst drawback is the black aphid that seems to be drawn to this plant like flies to honey. Regular spraying with Malathion is the best way to keep the vines free of aphids.

In cool climates broad beans are easier to grow than lima beans and substitute for them in the diet, both as fresh shell beans and dried.

Cowpeas

In southern states, the cowpea is usually called a pea and if necessary to refer to the plant grown as peas in the North, this is always mentioned as *English* pea. Seeds of cowpeas are used both as green shell beans (they are actually a bean rather than a pea) and in dried form. Two crops can be grown in most seasons in the South. Purple Hull, one of the leading varieties is white with a purple eye when young but turns purple when mature. It has excellent flavor. A newer variety that is widely adapted is Mississippi Silver. Both varieties can be grown as far north as southern Illinois, Ohio, and Indiana. I have even seen them grown in warm spots in southern Michigan on sandy soils with fair success, always by transplanted Southerners yearning for a mess of black-eyed peas. They cannot be sown successfully until soil temperatures reach 70 degrees. Brown Crowder and White Crowder peas are similar in flavor and culture.

Dry Shell Beans

From Boston to Mexico the shell bean in some form or other is a basic food for millions. The species used will vary. In the diet high protein at low cost is the lure. Boston's famous baked beans are usually prepared from varieties of field beans that do not do too well in gardens. Fortunately, White Marrowfat is a larger, tastier bean that does well in home gardens and is better for baking. It is easier to shell than the familiar pea bean. Red kidney beans are good baked, boiled, and in soups. They are a familiar dish on the Swedish smorgasbord, as well as in many Spanish and Mexican dishes. They are no harder to grow than other beans.

Horticultural beans, both French Horticultural and Dwarf Horticultural are shelled when dry and cooked (often with salt pork) as a winter dish. My personal memory of this dish is not too favorable, but it certainly should stick to the ribs on a cold day. The variety French Horticultural is usually grown as a bush bean but produces lots of runners. Although it is not usually staked, I have grown it with boughs of trees (apple-tree prunings) stuck between plants in the row. This allowed the runners to climb (perhaps scramble would be a better word) and kept the crop off the ground. The brushed part of the row produced at least one-third more beans than did the row allowed to crawl on the ground. When young, horticultural beans can be used as snap beans or fresh green shell beans.

Bush Lima Beans

This is a crop that has suffered from a mistaken idea that so-called baby limas are superior to the large seeded type. As a result home gardeners growing the baby type found the flavor just so-so and forgot about limas for future gardens. Without question the best-flavored lima bean and the easiest to grow north of the Ohio River is Fordhook 242. It was produced by the U.S. Department of Agriculture to give gardeners a lima bean that would not shed its flower buds easily in summer heat, yet would be more tolerant of chilly weather than older varieties. Since this variety is offered by practically every seedsman, no other recommendation is made among large-seeded varieties.

For those who feel that the baby lima is more desirable, Henderson's Bush is as good as any and widely available. If you can locate it in catalogs, a variety that is halfway between the large seeded and the baby lima type is Dixie Butterpea. Its beans are almost round, white, and richly delicious.

North of the Ohio River it is a waste of time to plant any lima bean before June 1 to 10. I have tried and the seed usually rots.

Pole Lima Beans

These are hardly worth planting in the North: They take so long to mature that frost usually catches the vines about the time the first pods are ready to harvest. King of the Garden is so high in quality and is so widely offered that no other recommendation is needed. So far, no hybrid lima beans, either pole or bush, have been introduced.

Carolina or Sieva lima fits into a special niche in the bean family. It is the Southern equivalent of the northern bush shell bean, such as White Marrowfat. Although a pole bean that can be eaten fresh, it is grown in quantity to produce small, smooth white beans to dry for winter use. The quality is much better than bush baby limas. It can also be used as a fresh shell bean eaten when it is a pale green in color, but after it has reached full size.

Bean Plants as Hay

Although the foliage and stems of bean plants are high in nitrogen and make good organic matter to plow under, subsistence farmers who keep any kind of livestock should consider drying them to use as hay. Often, soybeans are harvested when the pods are only half-mature for that purpose. The stems of snap beans are tough, but livestock will pick over the plants and get nourishment out of them. Afterward the trampled stems mixed with manure are valuable compost material. Rabbits and chickens also enjoy this type of fodder.

Peas

Garden peas are not a crop that succeeds too well in areas with hot, dry summers. *Cool* and *damp* are words that apply with particular emphasis here. Day after day of 90-degree weather when the plants are in bloom means few or no pods will form. In spite of this difficulty millions of gardeners are tempted to grow them because they know only their own peas, cooked within an hour or two of picking, will allow them to enjoy the marvelous flavor of this vegetable. Peas are like sweet corn: Within less than a day after harvesting, the sugar they contain has begun to change to starch and the flavor is lost.

Fortunately today's vegetable breeders have given us a variety that will allow a much wider area to enjoy this gourmet crop. It is called Wando and was developed by the U.S.D.A. to give growers in southeastern United States a pea they could plant early in spring, even when the weather turned hot in May. Wando is the only variety to plant unless your night temperatures do not climb much above 60 degrees and unless day readings stay well below 90. In this case Lincoln or Green Arrow are more productive.

The one drawback to Wando is that its 30-inch vine is not tall enough to bear as many pods as are needed to give the family several pickings. This is a weakness of all peas—they are gluttons for space. My own answer is to grow the variety Alderman (also called Improved Telephone), which grows four to five feet tall and produces five times as many pods as a dwarf variety, such as Little Marvel. Growing Alderman has one disadvantage in that it must be staked. The new Gro Net promises to make this excellent variety easier to grow.

Probably the sweetest of all peas is Lincoln, which also has 30-inch vines and should be grown on brush. Next to it in quality is a new pea from England called Green Arrow. It can be allowed to sprawl since its vines seldom grow more than 24 inches long. Its pods are amazing, nearly five inches long and jammed with nine to eleven peas. It is the heaviest producer of any generally available variety, except for Alderman.

A new pea from Thompson & Morgan, which in a first-year test was fully as sweet as Lincoln and grows to the same height, is Gloriosa. It is a cropper, maturing all its pods at once, but what glorious eating they are for that one picking!

For decades Little Marvel has been the favorite very early pea. Today it is surpassed by Sparkle, which is about three days earlier and, if anything, a better pea. Just two days later than Little

Marvel is Frosty, a 28-inch variety that produces almost twice the crop. The quality is equally good.

Over most of northeastern United States, peas are usually planted about the first week in April. The tradition of sowing on St. Patrick's Day was fine when the old smooth-seeded variety, Alaska, was commonly grown, but it is so poor in quality that it is no longer sold. Modern wrinkled-seeded varieties are less hardy. If, however, March is warm, it pays to take a chance and plant at least a partial row. Nowadays most pea seed is chemically treated to prevent disease and will survive in cold soil for two or three weeks if spring is late.

Even organic gardeners would do well to use treated seed. The chemical used is Captan, a mild fungicide. If untreated seed is used, planting may be delayed so much that a profitable crop will be impossible.

Pea Vines

Subsistence farmers might investigate the possibility of growing extra vines for making pea vine silage. This is a standard fodder in the canning region of Wisconsin, a by-product of the pea harvest.

Inoculation

Although most soils where beans have been grown in past years contain bacteria that enable them to extract nitrogen directly from the air, unless you are sure they are present, it is best to use an artificial culture on the seed (available in garden shops). Be sure it is marked clearly for the type of bean (or pea) you are growing.

6

Sweet Corn

as a Garden Crop

Perhaps the most important question about sweet corn is whether or not you should use your garden space to grow it. No other crop, unless it be vining varieties of winter squash, is as extravagant a user of that space. Unless the harvest can be canned or frozen, sweet corn is a luxury to be enjoyed in summer and early fall. In the space occupied by enough corn stalks to provide ears for a family of four, from the earliest varieties until killing frost, that same family could grow enough of the following crops to let them enjoy fresh vegetables on the table over an even longer period—tomatoes, summer squash, beans, cucumbers, radishes, endive, onions, beets, carrots, lettuce, peppers, parsley, and cabbage.

In spite of having to give up all this, thousands of home gardeners with small plots, say 15 feet by 20 feet, willingly plant sweet corn instead. They feel that their enjoyment of the special flavor of ears harvested a few minutes before they are cooked is worth the sacrifice.

So much has been made of the loss of flavor in sweet corn following harvest that this problem needs to be brought into focus. Conversion of sugar into starch is rapid until total sugar has decreased about 62 percent and sucrose about 70 percent. The higher the temperature the more rapidly this takes place. If you must harvest corn ahead of cooking for the table, storing it in the refrigerator can cut sugar loss as much as 75 percent.

The introduction of the extra sweet and supersweet varieties that originated at the University of Illinois was a triumph of plant breeding and marvelous for the commercial trucker who wants all the sweetness he can get in corn for the market.

What the home gardener does not realize, however, is that this gain in sweetness is made at the loss of all-over taste because the sugar has replaced other volatile substances that make for a well-rounded flavor.

The home gardener does not need the slower flavor loss of extra-sweet varieties, since with the pot already boiling, corn can be picked, husked, and in the pot within a few minutes.

The new extra-sweet varieties do have a place in home gardens south of the Ohio River. Here temperatures are high at the time corn is ready to harvest and sugar loss right in the ear is high. Corn matures so rapidly at high temperatures that it is difficult to catch it at just the right stage, and extra-sweet varieties allow more of a margin. However, the theory that corn grown in the North has a higher sugar content is not true. In one test South Carolina corn had the highest sugar, while that from Connecticut was lowest.

Sweet Corn Culture

Perhaps no crop grown in America can be produced on a wider variety of soils. Sweet corn is not fertilized as heavily in commercial production as is field corn. On richer soils, often the only fertilizer used is superphosphate, but the usual application of a mixed fertilizer before tilling should give a somewhat better crop. The old-time method of adding a handful of manure or fertilizer under each hill is not only unnecessary but has been found harmful in dry seasons.

If you want to beat your neighbor to the first corn of the season, or if you yearn for that first ear before normal harvest, sweet corn can be started indoors. This should not be done more than four weeks before outdoor planting time. If you can find them, the best units for starting corn are three-inch-square peat-fiber pots. Although I have pointed out the weaknesses of peat-fiber pots, this is about the only container available that can be set out without disturbing the roots. We once were able to use a pot made of compressed cow manure that was perfect for starting corn, but this seems to have vanished from the market.

Plant three kernels in each pot, cutting out the two extra seedlings as soon as the one to be left seems to be growing well. Started corn can be set out when the danger from frost is past, usually when apple trees are in bloom.

In planting corn, spacing is much more important than with other vegetables. It is pollinated by wind and if planted in a long single line, pollen may not blow from stalk to stalk. Best spacing is not less than four short rows side by side.

Planting distances from hill to hill are about two feet by three feet for smaller, shorter varieties and three and one half feet by three and one half feet for taller, late varieties. When planted in hills (hill meaning a cluster of stalks rather than an actual mound) several seeds are sown in a hill and thinned to three or four stalks. Sweet corn can also be grown as single stalks in rows spaced eight to twelve inches apart in the row.

In planning the garden, subsistence farmers would do well to allow for planting extra rows of sweet corn for cattle, hog, and poultry feed. Although production is usually much lower than from field corn varieties, the feeding value is much higher. For this purpose late varieties with bigger ears should be grown.

Up to a decade or so ago, open-pollinated varieties were preferred in home gardens. Not only were hybrid sweet corns less tasty, but they were so uniform in maturity that the gardener would have to eat furiously for a day or two to use all the ears that would mature at once. Instead, present-day hybrids have as long a picking season as old-time varieties.

Today the corn I consider the finest of all for the home garden is Silver Queen, a hybrid variety that produces big, well-filled ears on seven-foot stalks. Its one drawback is that it needs three months from seed to maturity, but as a maincrop sweet corn, it is close to perfect. Practically as good, but two weeks earlier, is

Seneca Chief, a yellow variety, which is otherwise very similar.

For those who want to grow the new supersweet varieties, Illini chief is the best midseason variety. One difficulty with these varieties is that they must be planted at a distance from other corns since pollen from less sugary varieties can spoil their flavor. Corn is unique in that pollination can affect the ears of the same season. With some 100 excellent hybrids available on the market for home garden use, it would take a brave man to try to pick out more than those I have already named. The one fact to emphasize is that the day of open-pollination is over. The resistance of hybrids to one disease alone, Stewart's disease, would make their choice necessary. Now that they have been improved in the length of harvest and in flavor, only hybrids need be planted.

One precaution in reading catalog descriptions is to avoid any varieties recommended for shipping and commercial marketing.

Among very early corns, one I have found particularly desirable is Polar Vee, a corn that, even in cold springs, can be depended upon to produce mature six-inch long ears for Fourth of July picnics. The one precaution is that, even if planted with other corns, it should be grown side by side in at least four rows. It produces pollen so early that other varieties cannot pollinate it. An All-America Winner among early sweet corns is Extra Early Super Sweet, which is about ten days later than Polar Vee.

One trick for those who want to produce the earliest corn in the neighborhood is to buy more seed than you need and sort out all the largest kernels for planting. Although the stalks grown from small kernels are as productive as large ones, the latter will produce ears from three to five days sooner.

Programming the sweet corn harvest can be done in two ways. Perhaps the one that calls for the least work is to sow all varieties—very early, early, midseason, and late at the same time. If the maturity dates given in catalogs are used as a guide, this is highly satisfactory. Many experienced gardeners, however, like to plant in succession about two weeks apart. This has one weakness. A variety such as Silver Queen could only be planted once in regions with short growing seasons, since a late planting would be caught by frost before the ears on a second crop would be ready. If succession planting is practiced, late varieties should be dropped from the later sowings.

A common practice in the past has been the removal of suckers. Suckers are shoots that arise from around the base of the main stalk. The theory behind this practice was that if the plant did not have to produce suckers there would be more nourishment for the ears. As explained under fertilizers, the raw materials that come up from the soil are not food but raw materials for manufacturing food. Since suckers rarely bear ears, what nourishment they draw from the soil is elaborated into starches and sugars and returned to be used by the ears. Instead of using elaborated foods, they produce it. Removing suckers does more harm than good.

Perhaps the most difficult problem in corn culture is knowing when to harvest. Flavor is at its peak in the milk stage when the kernel bleeds when cut but is just about to turn starchy. Sugar increases up to this point, after which starch replaces moisture and the kernel turns harder. This is called the dough stage.

Early varieties of corn pass from milk to dough stage more rapidly than do late varieties. It is better to err on the side of immaturity than to pick too late. The color of the silk is a partial clue, particularly in varieties with yellow kernels. When this begins to turn from light green to brown, most varieties are at their best. Feeling the tip of the ear (in varieties that always fill to the tip) is a sign used by many experienced gardeners.

In the end, learning the right time for harvesting is an art that can only be perfected by trial and error.

Subsistence farmers should realize the value of cornstalks. Used as bedding under livestock, they absorb urine and manure, after which they make valuable material for the compost pile. If cut as soon as the ears have been gathered, they make excellent feed. A highly effective winter shelter I saw in Maine was made from cornstalks held between field fencing with a pole roof, also covered with cornstalks and on top of that, tar paper held down by more farm fencing.

One trick with surplus ears of sweet corn is to let them grow to full maturity, full of starch, and dry them for winter use. If not fed to poultry or hogs, they will make the tastiest cornmeal you have ever eaten. Farm supply houses can usually supply hand-operated gristmills, but in our house we find that making the meal in a Waring blender just before it is needed, beats all other methods of grinding it.

Popcorn

Popcorn is not a true food crop, yet many home gardeners enjoy growing and eating it. Culture is the same as for sweet corn. Hull-less varieties are a big improvement on old-time hard-hull popcorn.

The best way to keep the ears is to strip back the husks but not to remove them completely. Tie the husks with a string and then hang the stripped ears in chains. Suspended in a big attic they should pop well all winter long.

7

Bulb Crops

Although the edible parts of the onion family grow underground, they are not true root crops, since the bulb is actually a modified stem. In recent years the most important member of this family has become more important as a home garden crop because of high prices on the market. When onions cost more than oranges or apples, it's time to grow them at home! Unfortunately this comes at a time when commercial production of onion sets is being abandoned in favor of crops that require far less hand labor and are more profitable to the grower under present world conditions.

Onions

All onion crops prefer lighter loam soils. If clay loam is the only soil available, it is a waste of time to try to grow onions unless plenty of very well-rotted organic matter can be used to lighten it. A pH of 6.0 to 6.5 is preferred, which means that ground limestone could be used to lighten a clay loam if it is acid, as so many clay soils are. Onions are fairly heavy feeders; so an application of about three pounds of a vegetable fertilizer to 100 feet of row is desirable, with an additional side dressing of half that amount when the bulbs begin to swell.

Now that onion sets are high-priced and difficult to find even if you are willing to pay the price, either onions must be grown from seed, or Southern-grown onion *plants* can be substituted for sets. Some dealers are importing sets from England and Europe, which may present some problems, since onions are sensitive to day length and varieties that are adapted abroad would be likely to shoot to seed if planted in the South.

In the South the safest practice would be to stick to Hybrid Spanish or Bermuda onion plants, widely available from seed dealers. These are almost as expensive as sets. They are sold by the bunch, which is a variable unit of measure. Seeds of Spanish or Bermuda onions are sown in late fall in Texas, where they grow slowly all winter long. In spring the seedlings are harvested by grabbing a handful without any particular measure. If the field laborer has a big hand, a bunch may contain as many as 100 seedlings, but if his or her hand is small, there might be only 50.

These same plants can be shipped North and are available in garden centers and through mail-order seed houses. The one disadvantage to using plants is that there is little variety, only a choice between white and yellow types.

Because they have been grown out-of-doors all winter, onion plants have been hardened off and can be set out even if light frosts might occur afterwards. Because they will produce unusually large bulbs if conditions are favorable, allow five or six inches between plants in the row. Sets should be planted about four inches apart as they make smaller bulbs.

Starting from seeds may not be as easy as planting sets or transplants but has one advantage—you can select the variety that best fits your tastes and growing conditions. For example, the acme of onion quality is probably the Italian Red or Bottle onion with a delicate, mild flavor that is found in no other variety. If you live in the South you can grow this, provided you can locate seed. In the North the quality of this outstanding variety was formerly denied to home gardeners except as mature onions purchased on the market. It is highly sensitive to day length and will not bulb up much north of the Mississippi-Tennessee line.

Now a similar onion only slightly more pungent is Hamburger, a red onion that will only bulb up in the North. For Southerners who want a pungent onion, Red Creole is a variety that is widely adapted in their region. In the North, Red Wethersfield is the choice for strong onion flavor.

Northern gardeners are particularly fortunate in having available more than 20 varieties of true hybrid yellow onions adapted to their part of the country. Any one of these would be superior to old-time varieties, such as Yellow Globe or Ebenezer. Although the Sweet Spanish type will bulb up both in the South and the North, it should only be grown if you do not plan to store them for winter: They are poorer keepers than the yellow hybrids.

Since most onions require three months or more to mature from seed, an early start indoors is needed. This means starting by March 1 for Spanish types, (earlier near the Ohio River), by March 15 for yellow Northern varieties. Transplant into permanent position when apple tree buds show color.

For summer bulbs where no storage is planned, any of the yellow hybrid varieties can be seeded directly in the garden about a week before the last frost in spring.

Onions for storage should be examined about September 1 to see how many of the tops have fallen over. If more than 10 percent have done so, bending over the rest will hasten ripening of the bulbs. The idea is not to snap off the leaves but to put a kink in them to check the flow of sap. Before harvesting, outer skins of bulbs should be showing signs of drying: if green they are easily injured.

In ordering onion seed, keep in mind that any left over after the current year's crop has been planted can be used for producing your own sets for the following season's planting. No one can deny the convenience of growing your own. The seed is sown in a band about six inches wide with the individual seeds almost touching each other. The idea is to crowd them so they will not grow too big. Even with this spacing some will grow too big. Any set more than three-quarters of an inch in diameter should be used for pickling: Small sets will not shoot to seed when planted but larger sets will. Any set one inch or more in diameter is of no use for planting the following spring.

Sets are dug when tops begin to shrivel and stored in flat slatted trays to dry. Topping is not necessary since the thin foliage soon shrivels. Store the same as for large bulbs.

If special seed is purchased for growing sets, the varieties Stuttgardt and Ebenezer are best. Both will mature from sets as high-quality medium-sized onions that keep unusually well in storage.

There is a special use for any sets larger than one inch in diameter. Late in fall, just before the soil crusts over, these can be planted in the open garden with about an inch of soil over the tip. These will start growing in early spring, long before you can get in the garden to plant sets, and will produce the first crop of the year. They must be used quickly, since if left too long they will go to seed.

Shallots

The fact that as many as 1,000 cars of shallots are shipped out of Louisiana annually is an indication that the flavor value of this mild-flavored onion is known in the United States. All of this production, however, goes to fancy restaurant and hotel trade. It is an ingredient in many dishes concocted by professional chefs, but shallots are almost impossible to find in consumer markets. Although shallots are rarely listed in American catalogs, a firm that specializes in supplying gardeners with them is Le Jardin du Gourmet of Ramsey, New Jersey. (This firm also has a stock of another chef's secret ingredient, Rocambole, which is sometimes called Spanish shallots, a mild-flavored garlic that provides a touch of garlic flavor without polluting the atmosphere). H.G. Hastings Co. of Atlanta, Georgia offers *white* shallots.

Shallots can be grown in any loose soil supplied with well-rotted organic matter. They are hardy and can be planted as soon as the soil is workable. In the South they are left in the ground and gathered as needed during the winter. In the North they can be planted in late fall and mulched with straw or hay. The bulbs are sometimes delivered to you in clusters containing three or four cloves. These should be divided before planting.

Although pulling them and using in the same way as green

onions might seem extravagant, when needed for some special dish this can be done. In Louisiana, when grown for the restaurant and hotel trade, the summer crop is hilled up to blanch the leaves at the base. I remember with nostalgia a breakfast I once had with the late Dr. Miller of Louisiana State University, at which he served me country bacon and fried potatoes cooked with fresh green shallots, a gourmet dish worthy of the finest French chef.

Rocambole

Although this is sometimes called Spanish garlic, it is actually Danish in origin. The original name was Rocken Bolle, Danish for rock onion. Transported to France this became Rocambole. In addition it is also known as Spanish garlic and Spanish shallots. It is grown in exactly the same way as shallots. The bulbs are like those of true garlic. They should be broken up into individual cloves for planting.

The flavor is that of a mild garlic. If you have ever been tempted to try James Beard's recipe for chicken with 40 cloves of garlic, you would surely enjoy it, but you probably would be socially unacceptable afterwards. With Rocambole instead of true garlic, the flavor would be there but not the odor.

Garlic

Since this calls for the same treatment as both shallots and Rocambole, it is best to mention it on the same page, if not in the same breath.

Leek

This is not a crop for the careless gardener. It requires good culture in a very deep, rich soil. Because of the long growing season (from 90 to 130 days), in the North it must be started indoors. The seedlings are unimpressive at first and do not give any hint of the thick, fleshy stems they can produce. Plant seed indoors in late February or early March and set out as soon as the soil is workable.

Because the lower part of the leaves (usually a straight stalk about five inches long) should be blanched, seedlings should be set in a trench about that deep. As they grow, dirt will wash into the trench. When the leaves begin to spread out and are above ground level, fill in the trench. If this is done before the leaves are above ground level, soil will work into the stalk and cause rotting.

In Europe leeks are left in the garden over winter, hilled up with earth in colder climates. In America this is not a common practice. The limited supplies of leeks that do appear on the winter market are shipped in from the South.

Not all varieties are suitable for wintering-over. Among the best are Odin, Conqueror, Giant Musselburgh, Elephant, and Unique.

Although leeks are eaten fresh in the same way as green onions, they are at their best when cooked. Cream of leek soup is delicious. A famous dish in Scotland is cock-a-leekie soup, in which ancient roosters are combined with leeks that make even the winter climate of Glasgow acceptable as a human habitation.

8

Root Crops:
Summer and Winter

Although root crops are important for winter use, anyone who has enjoyed a young carrot or a beet the size of a golf ball in midsummer, will testify that they have as much flavor as any other vegetable you can grow in a home garden. When stored for winter use they probably represent a saving of as many dollars as do salad and potherbs in summer. Although relatively low in vitamin value, they are unusually well balanced in A, B, B complex, and C. Too, they rank high in mineral content.

One of the major problems with all root crops is soil. If your soil is a stiff clay, they are hardly worth planting. When a carrot or a parsnip tries to corkscrew its way into hard clay loam, it develops tough fiber. The more fiber, the poorer the flavor. Nor should large amounts of fresh organic matter be worked into such a soil in an effort to prepare it for root crops. Unless they are well-rotted, manures or green manure cover crops cause roots to fork, which also causes toughness.

Subsistence farmers or others who might have to rely on root crops throughout a long winter should be warned of one weakness of this dependence: After long storage some loss of vitamin content is inevitable. To offset this grow sprouted alfalfa seed, sprouted mustard, or lettuce in a window box.

Practically all root crops are attacked by wire worms and other soil pests. Pretreatment before planting with chlordane, Diazinon, or heptachlor is essential where these pests are severe. For some reason wire worms do not cause trouble in the South, but north of the Ohio River they can be devastating. Follow directions on packages when using any insecticide.

Beets

Although the seed is hardy, beets should not be planted out-of-doors until buds on apple trees are showing color. If seedlings are exposed to cold early in growth they are apt to go to seed, in which case, no bulbous root will develop. Although spacing the individual seeds three inches to four inches apart takes more time than dribbling them into a furrow, this will save more time later. Beet seeds are actually fruits containing three or four true seeds. As a result, when they grow, several plants will appear bunched together. The extra plants should be removed as soon as all seem well established, taking care that the one that is left is not disturbed too much. This is difficult to do, but if you take the precaution of firming the soil around it as soon as the others have been pulled, it will usually thrive. Some dealers offer beet seed, which contains only a single seed, so when they grow no thinning is necessary if spaced out when planting. However, of the three beets of this type I have tried, none had the quality of other new varieties I grew for comparison.

If I had to restrict myself to only a single variety of beet, that would be Long Season or Winter Keeper. The mature root is nothing to look at—rough and big, but no other beet I know, unless it be Pacemaker, can touch it for flavor. What is more important, it keeps this delectable flavor all winter long. When cut it is a deep ruby red with practically no zoning. It takes a full three months to mature for storage but can be pulled earlier for use before it reaches full size.

The tops are a light green, not red. Many prefer green foliage for potherbs. It is usually planted in late June or early July to mature about October 1 for storage. For an early variety the hybrid Pacemaker is a choice beet. Although it has a sugar beet in its ancestry, the color is a deep, rich red. It is one of the sweetest of all beets. It does not get as tough as other early beets.

Formanova and Cylindra are varieties that were developed for processing. Both are cylindrical in shape, from five to eight inches long. They can be cut into a number of uniform slices. Although developed originally for commercial use, they are of high quality and remain tender and sweet much longer than older varieties. For canned pickled beets they are even better than Winter Keeper because the slices are smaller and more uniform in size.

Ruby Queen is a very early beet of high quality, which would be a good variety to precede Pacemaker if more than one beet is grown. The various Detroit varieties are good standard beets that can always be relied upon to produce well with high quality if harvested early. They tend to grow fibrous if allowed to grow too long.

Do not rely on a spring planting for roots for winter storage. Even Winter Keeper is best if a second planting is made in late May or early June, for harvest in early October. Beets for an early crop can be started indoors, planting out in May.

Carrots

As usually served this can be a dull vegetable. If prepared by a good cook, it can be a gourmet's delight. Glazed carrots with mint or other herbs can be delicious. Carrot and orange marmalade made by the recipe in the Boston Cooking School Cook Book need not take a back seat to anything England can offer.

Of late there has been a fad for tiny fingerling carrots, which are all right as a novelty, but for anyone who is trying to get the most out of garden space, these yield too little for the effort they take. Grow them if you wish, but depend on full-sized varieties for enough to eat. Actually many of the baby carrots sold commercially are not of miniature varieties but are the thinnings from rows of larger types. I have seen bags of these small carrots that were obviously thinned from rows of Royal Chantenay (grown widely for baby food production) or Spartan Bonus (another processing variety).

Any carrot bearing the word *Nantes* as part of its name can be relied upon to be sweet, tender, and far above the quality of the long, spikelike commercial varieties, such as the many Gold Pak types. Nantes varieties are best for spring sowing. For winter storage Royal Chantenay is the variety I prefer. Touchon is a Nantes variety of high quality for the spring crop. A new Nantes hybrid of superb quality is Pioneer. Because it is a hybrid, it germinates faster and matures quickly, which makes for tenderness.

Carrot seed should be planted as early in spring as the soil can be worked for the summer crop. North of the Ohio River, the fall crop for storage should be planted about June 15, no later. The thinnings from this planting will provide carrots for the table for late summer and early fall use. Because carrot seed germinates very slowly, mix radish seed with it when sowing, say about 20 percent of radish to 80 percent carrot by volume. The radishes will have been harvested long before the carrots need the room.

Carrots should be thinned to allow about an inch between plants for Nantes varieties, about an inch and a half for Royal Chantenay.

Mangels

Unless you are interested in subsistence farming or keep backyard poultry, you may want to skip this paragraph. Those who raise sheep, cattle, poultry, and hogs should consider growing mangels as winter feed. No other crop can produce more succulent fodder, as much as 40 tons to the acre on good soil. Grow as a row crop, sowing the seed as early as the soil can be worked. Space the plants 10 to 12 inches apart: The roots grow big. Seed is usually available from farm supply dealers rather than those handling garden seed. There are crosses between Mangels and sugar beets that do not produce quite as much feed but that livestock seem to like as a change. Plant a little of each.

Do not rely on these succulent plants for all the feed needed by your meat supply. Some grain will be needed, but the culture of these crops will be discussed under subsistence farming.

Parsley

The plant discussed here is not the leaf form, but Hamburg Rooted Parsley, grown mostly as a flavoring root for soups and stews. The culture for this form is like that for the leaf type except that the roots, which grow about five inches long, are dug in fall and stored in damp sand for use where a strong parsley flavor is wanted. Although the foliage can be used for flavoring in place of regular parsley, the flavor is inferior. If you do not have facilities for freezing leaf parsley, the Hamburg Rooted type is a good way to enjoy the flavor in winter, which is definitely superior to that of dried parsley.

Parsnip

This is another vegetable that rated low on the totem pole in a survey of food preferences. Although not disliked quite as much as liver, it ranked far below carrots and beets. Why should this be so in a nation where sweetness is akin to goodness in the popular taste? True, a parsnip harvested before it has been sub- jected to chilling does taste like an inferior turnip, but once cold has converted its rich store of starch into sugar, the parsnip is a truly great vegetable. To enjoy it at its best, it must be grown at home. It is not grown widely as a commercial crop because it occupies the soil for an entire growing season, and so is not as profitable as carrots or beets, which can be cropped twice a year, even oftener in the South.

This is one crop that simply must have a deep, rich, loamy soil. A common fault is forking in heavy or rocky soils. In England, where perfect specimens for shows are the ideal of every exhi- bitor, double-digging of the soil to a depth of two feet in pre- paration for growing parsnips is not unknown. Because they occupy the row for an entire season, the use of slow-release fer- tilizers is a must. If the only fertilizer available is a slow-release 20-10-5, be sure to use some additional source of potash such as wood ashes, or muriate, or sulfate of potash. Even better, if they can be found, are Green-Green and Osmocote.

Seed is planted where it is to grow: Seedlings do not trans- plant well. Parsnip seed does not retain its germination for much more than one winter. In my experience, seed contained in packets sold in seed racks is often bad, two times out of three. If you order seed early, by all means keep it in the refrigerator until planting time. Plant soon after the ground is available, mixing about 20 percent by volume of radish seed with it. Germination is slow and erratic. A crop of radishes for the table can be harvested before parsnip seedlings will need the space. Weeding is particularly important with this crop because parsnips are weak growers at first and cannot compete with weeds.

By far the finest of all parsnips is Harris Model, which is smoother and whiter than any other variety I have grown, and with a superior flavor. For cooler areas All America matures early and is close to Harris Model in quality. Hollow Crown Improved is about the same as All America, but in some soils produces a smoother root.

A common impression is that parsnips must be frozen to turn sweet, which is why this crop is left in the garden through the winter and dug during thaws. This is not at all necessary and the bother of wading through snow and mud to dig parsnips can be avoided if they can be stored in damp sand where the temperature can be held below 40 degrees. The starch-to-sugar conversion begins at this temperature, but takes place faster as the temperature drops to 34 degrees. In short, if it can be stored a degree or two above freezing, you are in fat city, as the youngsters say.

Peanuts

In the South this is more of a field crop than one to grow in gardens. For damyankees who want to grow this as a novelty, it is important to remember that as harvested, peanuts are hardly edible and need to be roasted for a full hour in an oven at 300 degrees. They must not be planted until the soil is warm, say after the apple trees have dropped their petals. They must have a light soil since the nuts are formed on runners that start above ground, then turn and burrow below the surface. Shell the nuts (there are two in a single shell). Set them about four inches apart in the row, an inch below the surface. Dig before frost and hang up in a dry warm place to cure. The vines make peanut hay, a nourishing stock feed.

Early Spanish is the only variety suitable for growing north of the Ohio River.

Radish

Although of limited food value and devoid of vitamins, radishes are grown by practically every gardener. These are the spring and early summer types, which are also sown late in August for a fall crop. In the United States and Canada little attention is given to winter radishes, which in parts of Europe and in China and Japan are an important item in the winter menu.

Radishes are hardy and the first crop should be sown as early as soil can be worked in the North. In the South they can be grown as a winter crop. Successive sowings can be made every two weeks. Unless the family is large, anything more than ten feet of row devoted to this crop is space wasted.

The only spring radish I grow is Burpee White, which is the epitome of radish flavor, without a trace of bite if not allowed to get overgrown. If red radishes are wanted, Cherry Belle or Crimson Giant are almost as good as Burpee White.

If a long row of radishes is grown, particularly the winter types, the foliage can be cooked like spinach, boiled for less than ten minutes. In France this dish is served with sour cream.

The huge Chinese and Japanese winter radishes are milder in flavor and slightly more nutritious than the spring types. Chinese Rose and Chinese White grow to about six inches long and up to four inches in diameter. The roots are mild, crisp, and tasty. Much more pungent is Round Black Spanish with globe-shaped roots about four inches in diameter. The skin is black but the flesh is pungent and white. It lasts in storage a month or so longer than the Chinese types.

A new type of radish from Japan is Minowase Summer Cross. Sown in early spring it matures in early summer. The roots are 18 to 24 inches long, crisp and tender with a clean, biteless flavor. Obviously a rich, deep loam is needed to grow them. They remain in good condition for about six weeks. They can be seeded again in July for a fall crop. In Japan the earlier open-pollinated Minowase radish was a staple market cross, but it is erratic in growth and would bolt to seed unless conditions were just right. The new hybrid is offered only by Thompson &

Morgan in the United States, but it will probably become widely distributed when its special qualities are known. The Japanese originator also has an earlier variety, Minowase Spring Cross, but this has not yet been offered in American catalogs.

There is every reason to expect these two varieties to replace the so-called Bavarian or Strassbourgh beer radish.

Rutabaga

Most nongardeners know this only as yellow turnip. In England it is known as "Swedes," probably because in Sweden it is a food staple for winter use. Because the flavor is quite strong, the Swedes usually serve it mashed, mixed with white potatoes. The next day, leftovers of this dish are made into cakes exactly like potato cakes and fried. Americans will find this a welcome change from plain potatoes.

The rutabaga is similar in appearance to an over-sized yellow turnip, but the flesh is much firmer. Because it does not like hot weather, it is grown principally in the North where nights are cool. However, it should not be sown until night temperatures do not get cooler than 55 degrees; otherwise it will bolt to seed. It needs four to six weeks longer to reach harvesting size than do turnips and usually occupies the row for an entire season.

This can be an important crop for the subsistence farmer, who should grow it for feeding livestock and poultry, as well as for the table. It stores well and retains its flavor and food value better than most stored root crops.

Allow about ten inches between plants in the row. As a field crop, allow 24 inches between rows. The tops are sometimes cooked for greens, but the leaves are tougher than those of turnips and stronger in flavor. Livestock will eat them, however, and are often turned loose in the field to eat them before the roots are harvested. Unfortunately, they will often cause strong flavors in milk.

Salsify

Sometimes called vegetable oyster, this root crop is worth growing for frying in rounds, which do resemble oysters in flavor.

This is not a crop for stony, stiff, or heavily manured soils, which tend to produce forked roots of little value. Even in a deep, rich, light soil, the roots are rough and have to be scrubbed before cooking to remove hair roots. They should be cooked without peeling to preserve their delicate flavor. After cooking they can be peeled and served fried or scalloped. The extra care is worthwhile in a flavor found in no other crop that can be stored for winter use. Culture is the same as for parsnips with plants thinned to stand three inches apart in the row.

Scorzonera

This is often listed as Black Salsify and requires the same culture except that plants should stand four inches apart in the row. Soak in water overnight to remove the bitter taste and boil. Do not peel until after boiling. During the Middle Ages it was used as a medicine for digestive ills and is still considered easy to digest. It is cooked in the same way as salsify and often considered finer in flavor.

Turnip

The introduction of new hybrid varieties of turnip, principally from Japan, has substantially increased the popularity of this vegetable. Turnips have always been a cool season crop, grown largely in early spring or late fall in the North, as a winter crop in the South. For a fall and winter crop in the North, a variety such as Tokyo Cross should be sown about 45 days before the date of the first killing frost in autumn. In spring sow as early as the soil can be worked. In the South, Purple Top Milan is usually sown about a month before fall frosts occur, so the seedlings can become established before freezes check growth. When grown only for greens, Shoigon is a favorite variety. Just Right Hybrid has fine flavor in both roots and leaves.

Tokyo Cross is usually harvested when less than two inches in diameter, but will not get pithy if allowed to grow to five to six inches. If thinned to two inches apart early, plants will be spaced out by harvesting so that the plants left will have room to grow to large size for winter storage.

9

Potatoes and Sweet Potatoes

There are plenty of reasons given why you should not try to grow potatoes in a home garden. The people who advise home gardeners have persuasive arguments against doing so, which have been sound in the past. Today, warned by food experts from all over the world, we are told that the food crisis, which began late in 1973, was not a flash in the pan. Instead an ever-shrinking supply of food will be a way of life. How does that affect the desirability of growing potatoes in your personal food garden?

First the arguments against doing so and then suggestions how these can be answered. Obviously the pocket-handkerchief plots many city gardeners are cultivating, as a token recognition that a food crisis does exist, cannot hope to raise as much as a single hill of potatoes. No other garden crop is as greedy for space unless it be vining winter squash. The average consumption of potatoes per person in the United States is three bushels annually, so to grow all the potatoes needed by a family of four would mean devoting an area 25 feet by 100 feet to this one crop.

Potatoes

In warm parts of the United States potatoes produce poorly, if at all. The moment soil temperatures reach 80 degrees, suberization or tuber formation stops. Even if the roots have produced tiny tubers as big as a bean, they stop growing and do not develop into edible potatoes. In the South where frosts are infrequent, they can be grown as a winter crop, as they are in Texas and Florida, but the potato plant is so sensitive to freezing that this cannot be done only a few miles farther north.

Even in cooler parts of the country, diseases such as scab and early blight can be extremely harmful. Then too, as a crop, potatoes call for considerable time and labor.

The answer to all these problems, except for that of space, can be met by a device I call lazy man's potato patch. (Mrs. Albert D. Farwell, whose delightful enthusiasm for herbs has led many to start growing them, calls this method straw soufflé.) This begins with digging or tilling the soil and raking it level. Before working up, spread a potato fertilizer (or one recommended for root crops) over the area at the rate recommended by the manufacturer. If you can't find a potato fertilizer, use one recommended for vegetables and add a couple of pounds of muriate of potash or sulfate of potash to the spreader, mixing it in thoroughly. Organic gardeners can use wood ashes instead, but the lime in ashes increases the pH, which is not desirable. If the soil is any more alkaline than 5.6 in pH, it will have to be acidified by adding sulfur. Avoid using lime on potato soil, otherwise the potatoes are almost certain to be scabby.

Once the soil has been raked level, planting can begin. If possible use only potatoes that have been grown especially for seed. Seed potatoes are grown late in summer so they will form during cool fall weather and are harvested before they are fully mature. As a rule they are small enough to plant whole. Because yields of potatoes when grown for seed are low, seed potatoes are relatively expensive. Sometimes regular table stock potatoes are sold as seed, but this fraud can usually be detected by their larger size. The larger the size of the seed piece, the larger the yield in mature potatoes, but only up to pieces no larger than half the size of a seed potato. There is no gain in yield with seed pieces three-quarters as large as the whole or larger.

In America mass production methods make it difficult to use a common practice that produces a better plant. In England, Germany, and Scotland, a visit to the tool shed of a good gardener in early spring will find the floor covered with cut halves of seed potatoes. For two weeks the cut pieces are exposed to moderate light (not direct sunshine) to sprout or "green" them. This produces stocky, green, disease-resistant sprouts. In the process any pieces without eyes or low in vigor can be discarded so that the entire planting will be from healthy seed pieces that will grow and produce well.

Usually, sprouted pieces produce fewer stems but more underground shoots on which the tubers are borne. As a result there are more big tubers from this treatment.

Although dusting the cut pieces with various materials to dry the cut surfaces has been a common practice in the past, allowing them to dry naturally is better. This means that the cut surface should not go down directly on a concrete or other solid surface. Instead spread clean cloth on the floor first so air can get under the cut piece. If gunnysacks are used, they should be washed first in water containing some chlorine bleach and then allowed to dry out before using. Such bags often carry disease unless washed.

Now comes the easy part—planting. With the lazy man's potato patch, the seed is not covered at all but is laid directly on the surface of the soil. It is pressed in just enough to produce firm contact with the soil. Spacing is from six to eight inches apart in the row. Since no cultivation is needed, the rows need be no more than 18 inches apart. Now the entire bed is covered to a depth of at least a foot with clean hay or straw. The purpose of this covering is to protect the seed from drying out and from the sun's heat. After a rain or two the covering will settle and another six inches can be added. From now on, nothing needs to be done until harvest time.

During the summer, if you are a new potato addict, two or three plants can be uncovered in mid-July and a mess of new tubers the size of a golf ball harvested. If you have never eaten these before, you are in for a feast. Cooked whole, with their jackets on, these are not mere potatoes but the vegetable equivalent of caviar or lobster.

What will surprise the gardener growing potatoes in this way for the first time is that harvesting them requires no digging. The tubers form on the surface of the soil and can be picked up by merely stripping off the straw covering.

For storing, wait until the vines turn brown and die. Then remove the straw with a fork and gather the tubers.

Potatoes grown by this method rarely need watering, but better lift some of the mulch from time to time to see that the soil is still moist.

The top layer of straw or hay can be set aside for mulching strawberries in winter, but that in close contact with soil should either be composted or plowed under after the crop has been gathered.

None of the catalogs I have seen list seed potatoes nowadays. This means that you will probably have to visit some farm supply house near you to find them. One seed house, Farmer's Seed & Nursery Co., Faribault, Minnesota 55021 does list potato *eyes*. Although I much prefer more of a seed piece, if handled carefully eyes can be used. Because of the difficulties of finding seed potatoes, I make no recommendations of varieties, since you will probably have to take what is available. Beware of one practice: Don't think you can grow a crop from potatoes bought for food. Nowadays market potatoes are treated with chemical sprout inhibitors. Even when they make feeble sprouts late in winter, this cannot be relied upon as a sign that they will grow. If you are forced to depend on such planting stock, by all means cut the pieces and sprout them as already described. If the sprouts do not double in size in two weeks, throw the cut pieces on the compost pile.

Although the straw method of growing protects tubers from sun, occasionally one or two will get a touch of sunlight and turn green. It is common knowledge that greened potatoes contain solanine, a toxic substance, and should not be eaten. They can be made safe, however (if potatoes are scarce), by peeling them and soaking them in water for an hour or two. Drain and cover with fresh water; boil and drain. Solanine is water soluble; so this treatment gets rid of it. However, since greened potatoes do not taste as good as those without green color, unless badly needed, they should be composted. Do *not* feed to poultry or livestock without treatment.

Sweet Potatoes

In the South, what damyankees call potatoes are usually called Irish or white potatoes. To a considerable extent they are replaced in the diet by sweet potatoes, which some mistakenly call yams.

Sweet potatoes need a long, warm growing season. Any area where night temperatures go below 65 degrees for much of the time is a poor place to grow them. Sweet potatoes are one crop that needs less moisture to grow than probably any other common vegetable. They can be grown in dry parts of the country if well watered up to the time the vines cover the ground, after which they can get along with accumulated soil moisture. However, in areas as dry as New Mexico and western Texas, irrigation will be needed if a profitable crop is to be grown.

On too rich soils, vines are produced at the expense of tubers. On clay soils tubers will be rough and irregular. In moister climates the plants are grown on ridges to avoid wet soils, which are not good for the crop. Plowing should not be too deep, yet good drainage is essential, hence the ridges. On deep soils the vines tend to produce long, slender tubers that are not desirable, but too often soils in the South are only plowed three or four inches, too shallow to give the roots room. Six inches deep is enough if plants are ridged. In dry years, such as occurred in many parts of the United States in 1974, ridging would be a disadvantage.

The sweet potato is a crop that does well on soils low in humus. Commercial fertilizers are best; a single application of about 20 pounds of a vegetable fertilizer when the soil is plowed will be enough for poorer soils. Richer soils need no feeding.

In the North seasons are too short to rely on home-started plants. Most seed houses can supply transplants ready to set out as soon as the weather is warm. These are slips cut off sprouted tubers. The tubers are bedded down in a hotbed with a soil temperature of 80 to 85 degrees when the tubers are first put in, dropping to 75 degrees as they grow. It takes about six weeks to produce slips for planting.

In the South early crops are planted with slips, but the main crop is started by taking vine cuttings from the earlier plantings. The cuttings are rooted in shaded cold frames before setting in the field. All danger from frost must be over before slips are set in the field. Allow 12 to 18 inches between plants.

There are some 200 varieties of sweet potatoes grown by commercial producers, but home gardeners are usually offered little choice, one of either a dry yellow or a moist orange. The dry variety will usually be listed as New Jersey and the orange as Puerto Rico or yam. Northern gardeners will do well to substitute Butternut or Buttercup winter squash for New Jersey sweet potatoes. The flavor is similar, if not superior, and production by squash vines will exceed that of sweet potatoes.

See the chapter Storing Vegetables for Winter Use for information on keeping sweet potatoes over winter.

10

The Gardener's Spice Cabinet—Herbs

Pundits gazing in their crystal balls give us little hope that the world's food crisis will disappear. Instead, predictions for mass starvation, soaring prices, and far more drastic shortages in available food fill the air and face us on the printed page.

Inevitably this means that the American diet, recognized as the most varied and ample in the world, must shrink close to the level of that of other civilized nations. Already our consumption per capita of meat has fallen, yet beef, lamb, and pork keep rising in cost.

One way that Americans can make some progress in improving the quality of cheaper and less palatable foods is by the use of herbs—the gardener's source of flavor.

A good example of a change in diet is the increased use of chicken in place of more expensive beef, lamb, and pork. But how many ways can you serve chicken? By the use of ordinary sauces, combined with mixtures of herbs, I have counted 18 delicious ways to serve this less costly meat.

A step up from chicken (in price, not necessarily in flavor) is pork, cheaper than beef but delicious when its too-rich flavor is subdued by the judicious use of herbs.

Many housewives are still faithful to beef but are switching from steaks and rib roasts to pot roasts and stews; again, cuts that can take on added interest if the flavor is enhanced by the use of herbs. Several years ago I was introduced to a variation on that delectable dish, boiled beef with horseradish sauce, in which fresh dill was used in addition to the horseradish. It was an exciting introduction to combining a common herb with a standard sauce to produce a chef's masterpiece.

(For those who are thinking of a retreat to some farm haven, or even for suburbanites looking for a hobby, I can recommend an investigation of herbal dyes as a project. If coupled with the raising of sheep for meat and wool, it can even be a source of income. Homespun yarn dyed on the farm with vegetable dyes is a highly salable product.)

One advantage to growing herbs is that they seem to thrive on neglect. Most herbs originated along the Mediterranean in poor soils relatively low in fertility and with sharp drainage. These are plants that can be grown in dry soils in sun where few vegetables thrive. Their origin in a relatively mild climate means that in cooler parts of the United States they need some shelter from cold winds, but, in providing a windbreak, they should not be cut off from sunshine.

Herbs need some organic matter in the soil, but this can be lower than for other garden crops. Most herb seeds need exposure to sunlight to germinate, but are injured by drying out. To allow sunshine to reach the seed without excessive drying, use a thin mixture of sand and peat over the row; this covering should be kept moist but not sopping wet. Annual herbs can only be started from seed, but perennial seeds are often weak and take a year or more to produce a strong plant. Buying plants from herb specialists is best.

Because they transplant poorly, it does not pay to start seeds of annual herbs indoors; sowing the seed directly in the open where it is to grow is much more satisfactory. Once established in a relatively dry, sunny spot, practically all herbs grow well.

With most species, fussing with fertilizers, watering heavily, and using other practices that work well with vegetables may do more harm than good.

In catalogs of herb specialists, names are often listed by the botanic genus and species rather than by common names. To help you find them, both common and botanic names are given in the following descriptions.

Annual Herbs Worth Growing

Anise (Pimpinella anisum) Seed of this herb must be fresh as it loses germination rapidly. It transplants poorly. Mature plants should stand about eight inches apart after thinning. Soil should be fairly rich and well drained. Use fresh leaves in salads or as a garnish in place of parsley. Seeds used as flavoring in cookies, candy, applesauce, stew (particularly with chicken and pork) and as a tea with a supposed medicinal value. The flowers are used to flavor muscatel wine.

Sweet Basil (Ocimum basilicum) One of the easiest of all herbs to grow. Seed down in spring germinates in four or five days and quickly forms lush, thick leaves with a distinct clovelike flavor. There are several species of this herb, but the one known as Sweet Basil has as good a flavor as any, and the seed is universally available, It has the same requirements as anise, although it will grow in heavier soils. After extensive or prolonged harvesting, it will respond to a light application of a complete fertilizer. The flavor of varieties with red or purple foliage is inferior to those with green leaves.

Basil is a must in canned tomato juice and tomato paste. It is a necessary ingredient in most Italian regional spaghetti sauces. Sweet basil vinegar is made by steeping the leaves for several weeks, then decanting. It is delightful in salads in place of tarragon vinegar. Because of the strong flavor of Sweet Basil it must be used with a light hand. Pinches of chopped leaves add an interesting touch to soups, stews, chopped meats, boiled potatoes, peas, sausage, and creamed and cottage cheeses.

Benne (Sesamum orientale) This plant produces the sesame seeds of commerce. Culture as for Anise. Principal use for sesame seed is as a flavoring in cookies. One warning: Some individuals are allergic to sesame seed and suffer discomfort if even a single seed is consumed.

Oil of sesame seed is used in salads but can also cause allergic reactions in sensitive individuals.

Calendula (Calendula officinalis) This is the pot marigold so popular with English and Scottish cooks. It should not be confused with French and African marigolds, which belong to an entirely different genus. Culture as for anise with the plants spaced 12 inches apart when thinned out. The large daisylike flowers are bright yellowish orange in color. When fully opened the petals are separated from the flower head and dried. They are used as a substitute for saffron in pastries and puddings. Although slightly bitter, many prefer Calendula to true saffron. Only one or two dried petals in the bottom of a pan of custard will flavor and tint the whole. The Dutch use it in soups and stews. Try adding a scant half teaspoonful in chicken broth. An excellent version of the costly saffron rice can be made with the same amount of powdered Calendula. It also can be used in the gourmet's Bouillabaisse of the French, a noble seafood soup (or is it actually a stew?). Because of its many uses no other herb is more useful to grow in the vegetable garden.

Plant breeders have modified the old-fashioned Calendula by increasing its color range. In buying seeds, which are usually listed in the flower-seed section of catalogs, you may not find the original Pot Marigold. The Pacific Beauty strain will be listed in several varieties. The only variety rich in color is Flame, a deep orange. It still has the old-time Calendula flavor. Incidentally it stands heat better than does the older species.

Chervil (Anthriscus cerefolium) This herb is not widely used, but those who grow it feel quite superior in their affection for it. Its flavor is that of a mild parsley, with a delicately cut leaf similar to that herb. Culture is like that for anise, with plants spaced nine inches apart. The French use it in salad dressing, spinach or sorrel soup, omelets, in béarnaise, ravigote, and fish sauces, butter sauce for chicken, and with wine-and-butter over veal chops. One difference from other herbs: It prefers light shade about noontime. The delicate leaves can't stand the sun at high noon.

Coriander (Coriandrum sativum) Your first sniff of the foliage of this herb will repel you; peasants in France used to say it smelled like bedbugs. When the seeds ripen in fall, however, they are delightfully fragrant. The drier they become, the more pleasing the odor. Except that plants need ten-inch spacing, culture is like that for anise.

The sugar-coated seeds were a favorite comfit in rural England and were carried by mothers to church to quiet restless children. Coriander comfits are still sold in Europe and can be made at home by coating the seeds with egg white and rolling in fine sugar. The ground seed is used in cake, bread, gingerbread, biscuits, cookies, and coffee breads. It adds flavor to baked apples, sausages, poultry stuffing, cream cheese, and (with vinegar) in pickled beets. It is also used in some brands of instant coffee for flavoring a demitasse, although Europeans prefer the whole seed in strong coffee for this purpose.

Dill (Anethum graveolens) Anise culture, with plants spaced ten inches apart. Self-sows readily. The plants are poorly rooted and need protection from wind. The best-known use for the fresh leaves is in dill pickles, but dill is a delicious addition to tomato soup, potato salad, cottage and cream cheese, gravy on fricasseed chicken, chops and steaks, in pastry and apple pie, spiced beets, gravy, and in Swedish bean soup. Use also in cream gravy for boiled beef, and fresh sprigs in green salad. Add seeds sparingly to sauerkraut. Soak the seed head in vinegar to make dill vinegar.

Sweet Marjoram (Majorana hortensis) Often called sausage plant, this is a widely used herb in omelets, soup, sausage, meat pot pies, liver dumplings, custard pudding, beans, and some seafood dishes. In Germany its principal use is in sausages, hence its name Wurstkraut. It is an ingredient in many herb mixtures. (See other marjorams under Perennial Herbs.)

Nasturtium (Tropaeolum majus) Seeds are usually listed in the flower-seed section of catalogs. Grown as a herb for its leaves (used in salads) and for its seeds (pickled as a substitute for costly capers). It will grow in heavier soils than most true herbs but prefers lots of sun. Aphids are a serious pest that should be fought with pyrethrum sprays (in organic gardens) or with

Malathion. The half-ripened seeds can be either pickled in tarragon vinegar or used in mustard pickles.

Parsley (Petroselinum hortense) This is *the* herb for home food gardeners, so universal that we have come to think of it as a vegetable. Although it is a biennial or short-lived perennial, it is practically always grown as an annual. The seed is fiendishly slow in germinating. Old English gardeners used to say it had to go to the devil and back nine times before it would sprout. Germination can be speeded up by soaking it in water as warm as the hand can stand when poured on the seed. In the morning allow lukewarm water out of the tap to flow over it and wash away the brownish water in which it was soaked. Water soaks out a germination inhibitor, which slows up sprouting. When the water runs clear, plant the seed at once.

In the past I urged the planting of Italian or Plain Leaved Parsley instead of the moss curled type, because it had a stronger true parsley flavor. Now, Banquet, a variety developed in Denmark, has all the flavor of the old Italian type, plus the most beautiful finely cut and curled leaves imaginable.

To catalog the uses of parsley seems unnecessary, except to recall an old favorite of Victorian days—cream of parsley soup, a simple cream soup to which a liberal amount of finely chopped parsley is added and heated for a few minutes to extract the flavor.

Safflower (Carthamus tinctorius) Also called American saffron and false saffron. A thistlelike annual used either as an adulterant of true saffron or as a substitute. Culture as for anise. The flowers are used in cooking as a source of yellow coloring. Calendula is more desirable for this purpose except where the pronounced flavor it adds to food is not wanted.

Summer Savory (Satureia hortensis) This is the Bohnenkraut of Germany and Switzerland, which adds a delicate flavor to green and wax beans. It can be used with practically any leafy vegetable cooked for greens. No herb has a longer list of uses. Add a sprig to tomato juice for a flavorful cocktail. Use with eggs—scrambled, deviled, or in omelets. Any fresh or saltwater fish is improved by a touch of Summer Savory. It improves the flavor of mutton, beef, lamb pies, Canadian bacon and ham, roast veal, and meat patties. Poultry-dressing herb mixtures are usually high in this herb. Almost any vegetable is improved with it, as are soups and salads. (For Winter Savory, see Perennial Herbs.)

Perennial Herbs

Angelica (Angelica archangelica) The hollow stems of this plant are used for making candied angelica, the translucent pale green cut-out ornaments on fancy pastries.

The process for making candied angelica is a bit complicated for most cooks, yet the herb should be included in the herb garden, if room is available, to use as a flavoring without being candied. The stems can be cooked with rhubarb to temper its acid flavor, or stewed with apples. Angelica can be used in herbal jellies. The stems are sometimes eaten as celery and are also cut into fine pieces for garnishing various foods. For these purposes, they should be blanched by covering with parchment paper for two or three weeks before harvesting.

Culture is like that for anise except that angelica will thrive in light shade. Mature plants should be spaced about 30 inches apart. If allowed to go to seed, the plant dies, but if faded flower heads are cut off, it is a short-lived perennial.

It can be increased by transplanting the offshoots that form at the base of a two-year-old plant. To grow from seed sow this as soon as it ripens: if this is not practicable, keep the seed over winter in a sealed jar in the refrigerator for planting in spring.

Balm (Melissa officinalis) Practically always called lemon balm because of the delightful lemon-mint fragrance of the leaves. Although many do not care for its flavor in foods, it is widely used in soups, in herb teas, salads, stews, and in flavoring summer beverages. It is also added to tarragon vinegar as an additional flavor. The lemon flavor of its leaves is used to improve Swiss chard, spinach, and New Zealand spinach.

Borage (Borago officinalis) Subsistence farmers who keep bees should plant long rows of this blue-flowered perennial herb. It needs the same culture as anise, with plants spaced about 12 inches apart. The plants do not transplant at all and so it must be started from seed. Once established it self-sows freely, and these volunteer plants are much more vigorous than the first planting. Young leaves used in summer drinks add a pleasant cucumberlike flavor. They can also be used in pickles and salads or cooked as greens.

Caraway (Carum carvi) Actually a biennial rather than a perennial, but self-seeds so freely that it persists for years once it is established. It needs the same conditions as most of the herbs mentioned, although to contradict myself, it persists in growing in great patches on the north side of my summer home in Maine, in soil that has not had a touch of fertilizer in at least 50 years and kept damp by runoff from a rain gutter.

The seed is used in rye bread, cheese, cookies, German sauerkraut, German or Hungarian cabbage soups, cake, baked apples, spiced beets, and in sugar-coated old-fashioned comfits (Sugar-coated seeds are supposed to be good for digestion). The fresh green leaves can be added to soups and salads.

Chives (Allium schoenoprasum) This relative of the garden onion does best in slightly heavier soil than for other herbs but does want sun. It is painfully slow to reach maturity from seed. One row I started could not be cut until the third year. A much easier way to grow it is to buy clumps. These clumps, whether from a produce department in a chain store or from a garden center are actually made up of 50 or more individual plants. These can be broken up into smaller clumps of 10 to 15 plants and set out to form a solid mat.

If the blue flowers are kept cut off, they will keep going for years. However, they do grow coarse after a while; so if a fresh row is started from seed every second or third year, the new plants will be ready to use when the flavor of these older plants drops in quality.

Although the flavor of chives and its use in food are too well known to describe in detail, the fact that it can be frozen is not commonly realized. Green leaves can be cut in late fall and packed in plastic freezer packets. The round plastic tubs used for soft margarine are ideal for this purpose because of their tight-fitting lids.

Fennel (Foeniculum vulgare) The original wild fennel seems to have disappeared from American catalogs except for those of herb specialists. This is no real loss, since Florence or sweet fennel has the same leaves and seeds for flavoring. This is sold as a vegetable. The lower stem forms a bulb that is eaten raw as a salad or braised. Its culture is described under Greens—Salad Crops. As an herb, its seeds are used in puddings, sauerkraut, soups, cakes, and spiced beets. The leaves are used in salads (they add an anise taste), in fish sauces, and all of the uses for which many other herbs are used.

Fennel-flower (Nigella damascena) This is another herb that is usually cataloged in the flower section—the well-known mist flower, also called love-in-a-mist. Its seeds are highly aromatic with a nutmeg flavor and can be substituted for that spice. Seeds are also used on rye bread, the so-called black caraway sprinkled on Russian rye bread. Ordinary garden soils suit fennel-flower. Sow where it is to grow; it doesn't like transplanting.

Marjoram (Species of Majorana and Origanum) Several different marjorams make identification difficult. Sweet marjoram is described under annual herbs, since in most areas north of Washington, D.C., it is likely to kill out in winter if grown as a perennial. Oregano is a name applied to wild marjoram as a rule, but it might be any other plant called marjoram or it could be a species of coleus. To add to the confusion, this coleus is sometimes called purple basil but I also have a common-name record of it as Spanish thyme. To simplify matters plant wild marjoram *(Origanum vulgare)*, along with sweet marjoram *(Majorana hortensis)*, growing the sweet as an annual.

Oregano is an important ingredient along with sweet basil in most true Italian spaghetti sauces. Marjoram is used in soups, poultry seasoning, roast lamb and pork, meat pot pies, beans, stewed tomatoes, and in fish sauces. It is an ingredient in most herb mixtures.

All marjorams are sensitive to winter and need protection from winter sun. Since they grow best in a sunny location, this is a problem. I have found that the plastic rose cones sold for winter protection for roses are ideal for this purpose.

Mint (Species of Mentha) Usually, unless a specialized collection of mints is wanted, as a flavoring for most dishes spearmint *(Mentha spicata var. viridis)* will do as well as any. Orange mint

(Mentha citrata) and apple mint *(Mentha rotundifolia)* both have more delicate flavor but are hard to find.

Mints are rampant growers in almost any soil, so long as it is reasonably rich and moist. They will tolerate light shade. As flavors they are used in so many ways that the simplest way to describe them is to say "If you like mint, try it in any food you think is too bland in flavor." It goes well with everything from roast lamb and pea soup to apple jelly.

Rosemary (Rosmarinus officinalis) Although a perennial, rosemary is not reliably hardy much north of Alabama or the lowlands of South Carolina. It thrives in a sunny window in the North if the temperature can be kept below 70 degrees, and if the soil is kept constantly moist but never saturated. Spraying the foliage once or twice a week helps keep it in good shape. Set the plant out-of-doors on a warm, misty day after the danger of frost is over. It prefers a light, sandy loam soil, but since such soils are inclined to be acid, check the pH. It prefers a reading of 7.0 or above. Bring it indoors in fall before hard frosts occur.

This seems a great deal of fuss for one herb, but rosemary is worth it. No other herb has quite the flavor on meats. Formerly it was hard to measure for use in cooking because the dried leaves (like short, hard pine needles) were all but impossible to reduce to a fine powder. Today less than a minute in a food blender will break up a year's supply to any degree of fineness you prefer. In this form it can be dusted lightly on roast meats and fowl or used in baking powder biscuits or dumplings. Fried potatoes with rosemary and chives are a gourmet's treat. A nonculinary use outside the scope of this book (but that I am tempted to pass on) is to perfume linen with dried lavender. It imparts a heavenly old-fashioned fragrance that conjures up memories of my grandmother's linen closet.

Those in warmer regions who would like to try outdoor culture with protection can try using the styrene plastic cones sold for protecting roses over winter.

Sage (Salvia officinalis) Like most herbs this prefers the sunny location and light loam soils recommended for most herbs, yet will grow well on heavier soils. However, on too rich soils the flavor is not as good. Sage comes easily from seed sown as early as the soil can be worked. If allowed to seed it will produce all the volunteers any garden can use. Old plants will do better if cut to within four or five inches of the soil as soon as new foliage appears in fall. Do not cut off stems or leaves after September 1, however. Late shoots following fall pruning will winter kill.

Its uses are so varied that to list them would require more space than can be spared. One of my favorites is a mixture of cream cheese and powdered sage with a little minced onion and a pinch of salt—a perfect appetizer. Although we are not venison enthusiasts, the gift of a haunch of this strong meat should not be wasted. A touch of sage, perhaps with a touch of thyme and powdered rosemary, goes a long way to make this game more palatable. A single leaf adds flavor to boiled or baked fish. Powdered sage will greatly improve broiled eels and other fat fish, but use with discretion. Boiled fresh vegetables will benefit from a single leaf of fresh sage in the water.

Summer Savory (Satureia hortensis) (See under Annual Herbs.)

Tarragon (Artemisia dracunculus) Where it survives, tarragon is a garden status symbol. It has a unique, almost artistic, flavor that sets it apart from other herbs, although a good flavor chemist could probably duplicate this flavor from a blend of several essential oils. It can only be propagated from plants as it does not set fertile seed. This is one herb that simply must have the light, sandy loam soil if it is to survive. On heavier soils it will winter kill. Even on lighter soils winter protection is desirable, perhaps using a plastic rose cone.

Its uses are so many that listing them would be difficult. Even if you plant it without knowing why, sooner or later on opening a cookbook, you will see it listed in some recipe, from appetizers to meats and salads.

Thyme (Thymus vulgaris) Like tarragon, thyme is used in so many dishes that it is all but indispensable in any well-ordered kitchen. A fresh sprig is an essential ingredient in the French chef's *bouquet garni*. It is the breath and soul of roast lamb, even more valuable than the traditional mint jelly that accompanies it. Grow it and try it in any dish that needs a touch of its special flavor.

A thyme that is not too easy to find, but that is even finer in flavor, is *Thymus herba-barona*, so-called caraway thyme. Its specific name has an interesting history: It was used to sprinkle on the barons of beef roasted for royal banquets. It is available from herb specialists.

Drying Herbs

Don't wait until a day or so before frost strikes to rush out and gather herbs to dry for winter use. By then they will have lost most of the essential oils responsible for flavor. Too, weather will be unfavorable for drying in fall. Instead, harvest them in midsummer about the time the flower is all but fully opened. At this time the leaves, stems, and flowers contain the greatest concentration of essential oils. Don't work in rainy weather; wait for a time when sunshine is predicted for three or four days ahead. On a morning when the sun rises bright and clear, wait until dew has evaporated from the foliage, but harvest before the sun is so high that it is evaporating essential oil from the leaves faster 'than the plant can restore it.

The easiest, and in many ways the best way, to dry herbs is to tie them in bundles of not more than ten stems and hang them in a dry, airy attic. If possible they should be in a completely dark but well-ventilated spot. In the dark many will retain a fresh green color. While retention of green color is not essential to flavor, you will appreciate it when you use the dried leaves in various dishes. There is some slight gain in flavor also, but *dry* and *airy* are the important words to remember.

One step to remember is to have tie-on labels ready to attach to each lot as it is cut. Dried herbs look quite unfamiliar at times. I like the wooden tags with a wire attached that are used to identify nursery stock. As soon as the bundle of stems is tied, tag and name it.

If no dry attic is available, herb leaves stripped from the stems can be dried in the sun on wire screens. Use aluminum screening or the smallest-mesh hardware cloth you can buy. Each batch of leaves will need two screens, mounted on wooden frames for easy handling. The herbs are laid on one screen and the other placed over it before setting both in the sun. The top screen keeps leaves from blowing away and also allows you to turn the screens over to expose the other side of each leaf to sunlight.

Bring in the screens at night or they will take up moisture from night dew. When dry enough to crumble, store leaves to be used whole, such as sage leaves and sprigs of rosemary in glass jars. Most herbs are best stored dry as powders. The modern food blender makes light work of what was once a tedious and dusty chore.

The oven is a poor place to dry herbs, but sometimes in rainy weather it is the only way to save them. Any temperature above 200 degrees will cause a serious loss of essential oils. If the oven does not have a temperature control, work with the oven door open.

If there is space in a freezer, freezing beats drying by any method. If leaves are cut too fine for freezing they can pack down and slow up the freezing process somewhat. Since soft green foliage should freeze quickly, it is best to pack only sprigs or whole leaves rather than cut green material. Parsley and chives are particularly welcome in frozen form. Sweet basil is another herb to freeze. When dried it retains little of the flavor of the fresh leaf, but when frozen, is as good as the day it was picked.

An unusual way to keep herbs is used by Italians to save leaves of sweet basil, which are used almost daily in making spaghetti sauce. They pack them in stoneware crocks, putting down alternate layers of rock salt and leaves. When leaves are taken out for use, the cook just shakes off the salt and uses them as though they were fresh. The flavor is much better than that of any dried sweet basil.

Herbs dried as stems or leaves should be stored in the thinnest possible plastic bags and tied shut. Be sure they are dried to a crisp and crumble easily. If the bundles are left in an attic without bagging they get covered with dust and are attacked by insects.

To store herb seeds don't wait to harvest them until they are thoroughly dry. As soon as the stems of the plant look dry and the seeds have a brown coat, cut the entire seed head and store it on a tray or in a basket lined with cloth. If held in a dry place for two or three weeks, the seed can be shaken out of the stalks and stored in sealed jars in a cool place without actually freezing. A refrigerator can be used for cool storage, but don't seal the jars before you set them in the refrigerator. Instead leave the jars open on the regular food shelves for at least a day. When put in, the air surrounding the seeds is much moister than that in the refrigerator. If the jar is put in sealed, this extra moisture will condense on the seeds.

For those who want to know more about herbs than can be told in one chapter, the following books are recommended (your book dealer may have to advertise for those that are out of print).

Herbs: Their Culture and Their Uses, by Rosetta E. Clarkson (Macmillan, 1940).

Gardening with Herbs, by Helen Morgenthau Fox (Macmillan, 1945).

Herb Gardening in Five Seasons, by Adelma Grenier Simmons (Hawthorn, 1964).

Herbs, the Spice of a Gardener's Life, by Katherine Barnes Williams (Diversity Press).

Herbs for Every Garden, by Gertrude B. Foster (Dutton).

The Art of Cooking with Herbs and Spices, by Milo Miloradovich (Doubleday, 1951).

11

Perennial Food Crops

Providing space for perennial food crops is often a problem. If made a part of the general garden, they are usually in the way when preparing ground for annual crops in spring. If planted separately, they increase the work in caring for them. Access to water and tool storage is another problem.

Cultivated Crops

Because they may take two or three years to come into production, perennial crops are often omitted from first-time gardens with a that-can-come-later attitude. Often, later never comes.

This is unfortunate, since two of the most welcome of all food crops—fresh asparagus and rhubarb in spring—are so delicious that the family is cheated out of much of the pleasure of home food production.

Asparagus

There is no denying that this is at once the most delightful yet the most difficult to establish of all perennial crops. Since it must be left in place without being disturbed for as long as 10 to 15 years, soil preparation must be much more thorough than it

need be for annual vegetables. Today deep plowing or even double-digging to a depth of well over a foot is no longer necessary.
This was common practice when earth was drawn up around
the crowns to blanch the shoots, but today recognition of the
greater nutritional value of green asparagus has all but eliminated blanching.

Preparation of the soil should include working in all the compost or well-decayed organic matter that can be spared. The
addition of a slow-release mixed fertilizer such as Osmocote,
Green-Green, or Mag Amp is highly desirable, since the food
available to asparagus plants the first year they are set out often
determines the vigor of the bed for years ahead.

The most important step in preparing the bed is the elimination insofar as is possible of every bit of perennial weed growth.
Perhaps the worst weed of all is quack grass. Some authorities
speak glibly of plowing this out; something I have never been
able to do. Every broken bit of root is capable of establishing a
new plant. If no other plot is available than one where quack
grass is established, either a chemical control such as Dalapon or
Amizole should be used, or it should be fumigated with Vapam.
(See directions for killing weeds under The Many Reasons for
Mulching—Weed Control.)

Although the idea of gaining a year's time by buying plants
sounds attractive, you are much better off if you raise your own
from seed and transplant them into a permanent bed a year
later. For one thing, since you can buy seed of improved strains
under name, you can be sure of what you are getting. Practically all asparagus roots you buy will be without name. Another
advantage to home-grown plants is that they can be dug and
moved into their new location the same day. Asparagus plants
for sale are usually dug in fall and stored in damp peat or shin-
gle-tow until spring. Storage reduces vitality. If they dry out
only once, they may not survive.

Probably Mary Washington is the most widely sold variety of
asparagus available in seed form. It is highly resistant to rust,
the worst disease affecting this crop. In flavor it is as good as the
best and is delicious eaten fresh, canned, or frozen. Paradise is
supposed to be superior, but I have not seen any difference

between the two. Brock's Imperial is a hybrid variety with some advantage in early bearing. For milder climates California U.C. 66 and California U.C. 72 have slight advantages over regular Mary Washington.

Much fuss is made by commercial growers about whether to set out male or female plants. Asparagus is dioecious, which is to say that the male and female flowers are on different plants. Male plants produce about 25 percent more spears by weight, but female spears are somewhat thicker and command a premium. Since male and female plants cannot be separated until the second year when they bloom, this means they cannot be set into position until the following spring. For a commercial planting where extra production or heavier spears (which command a higher price) is important, this is worth the extra investment, but for the home garden don't pay anyone a premium: Remember this is the age of women's lib and the sexes are equal.

By far the best beds are set with one-year-old home-grown plants. If you grow your own, plan to produce at least double as many plants as you will need. Asparagus seed is an erratic germinator; sometimes it takes from two to six weeks. This can be speeded up by soaking the seed overnight in lukewarm water. In the morning allow warm water to flow over the seed until any sign of color disappears. This washing removes natural inhibitors that prevent rapid germination. As soon as the seed is dry enough to handle, it should be sown at once.

The seed is hardy and should be planted as soon as soil is workable in spring. Any well-prepared seedbed will do. Because of slow germination soil is likely to crust over; covering the row with sand, vermiculite, or leaf mold will prevent this. Keep the bed weeded until the following spring when the plants will be ready to set into permanent position as early as the soil can be worked. While growing in the seedbed they should be spaced out a foot apart in the row. If closer, the roots become meshed and are injured in digging.

As the plants are dug, any weak, small ones should be discarded. Sometimes this means discarding nearly half of those in the seedbed, but future production is determined by the vigor of those planted. Depth of planting is always a subject of argument. In California where canneries demand blanched asparagus for part of their trade, some fields are planted as deep as 14 inches. Elsewhere eight inches is a standard depth. If you are an avid asparagus user, by planting a few crowns with only four inches of soil over the tips, these will produce edible spears nearly a week before those planted at the standard eight-inch depth. Where heavier soils are used for asparagus, a planting depth of six inches should be used. Commercial spacing is 12 inches to 18 inches between plants, but in the home garden where a bed might be kept for as long as 20 years, they will keep increasing in size so that even 18 inches may be too close. Where space permits, 24 inches will insure a longer life to the bed.

Chemical weed controls make cultivation a much easier job than formerly. All tillage operations can injure crowns; so the less the surface is disturbed the better. Deep mulching is not ordinarily used with asparagus.

Removing the tops while still green reduces food supply for next year's crop and is poor practice. The dead stems should be allowed to remain over winter to catch snow. In commercial practice the tops are disked into the soil, going right over the plants as early as possible in spring, but this is impractical in home gardens. Instead remove them to the compost pile and apply a mulch of well-rotted compost as often as it is available. Feed at this time with any complete vegetable garden fertilizer.

A light cutting can be taken from a new bed the year after it is planted, but full production will probably not begin until the third or fourth year. In warm springs, cutting can be done every day for about eight weeks, but if spring is cool and late, a second application of fertilizer at this time improves next year's crop. One fact to keep in mind is that asparagus is like peas; quality goes off rapidly after harvesting. It is better to gather all stalks that are ready to eat and either freeze or can any surplus.

Sevin or methoxychlor will control the asparagus beetle, the only serious pest.

Rhubarb

Where the climate is suitable, this is a valuable crop because it can be used as fruit and is perhaps the easiest of all fruit crops for the home gardener to grow. It can also be forced in the winter, when it can substitute for expensive fruit from the supermarket.

Rhubarb can be grown from seed but does not come true; so seed is seldom used. Instead, divisions of older clumps are used. When dividing your own clumps, be sure each piece of root has one or two strong eyes. Divisions from very old clumps with hollow roots seldom do well.

This is one crop that must have fertile soil. If well-rotted compost is not available, use a slow-release fertilizer if it is available, otherwise use a good mixed vegetable fertilizer. A second application following the harvest season is a must. Spring planting is best. Cover the buds three to four inches, no deeper. Clumps should stand about three feet apart in the row. The soils should be kept moist but not soaking wet. In California it is grown on light, sandy loam soils and goes dormant in summer heat, starting growth again with the coming of winter rains. During drought in cooler climates it can go dormant. This is a crop that is hardly worth growing in the South.

Do not cut rhubarb for at least a year after setting out. On mature plants harvesting should not extend for longer than eight weeks.

The old variety, Victoria, is still being sold. It is a much heavier producer than newer varieties that are all red. The stalks of Victoria are green unless it is growing under very cool conditions, in which case stalks may show a little pink, but the color is much less attractive when cooked than the clear pink and ruby red of varieties such as Mcdonald, Cherry Red, and Ruby.

One warning: Never cook the leaves of rhubarb. They contain large amounts of oxalis acid and can make you ill.

Forced rhubarb in winter is a real treat. Extra roots should be grown for this purpose. Three-year-old clumps are best. Dig them in late fall and store in bushel baskets. Fill around them with soil so they will not dry out, but leave outdoors under shelter until frozen lightly. Any freezing longer than two weeks and below ten degrees will hurt forcing.

Bring them into a cellar with a dirt floor and water enough to keep the soil moist but not wet. Kept at 60 degrees in a dark

room the new shoots will be a rich pink and develop a true rhubarb flavor.

Jerusalem Artichoke

As American as apple pie, the Jerusalem artichoke never saw
Jerusalem and is not an artichoke except that the tuber tastes
something like the base of that vegetable. Years ago I used to
warn gardeners against planting this pernicious weed, but today
with modern weed killers it can be eradicated if it gets out of
control. It is worth planting as a source of food that practically
never fails.

Like most weeds it is tough, survives almost anywhere except
in wet soil, and needs little or no cultivation. The subsistence
farmer will find it a valuable hog feed that needs no harvesting;
hogs will dig them without any urging.

The plant is a relative of the sunflower and grows wild from
Nova Scotia to Georgia. Although hardy in Nova Scotia, this is
along the seashore, not inland. It is not fully hardy along the
Canadian border, where it needs to be mulched in winter. The
edible portion is a tuber about one-fourth the size of a potato
with a crisp, nutty flavor, usually dug before hard freezing weather for winter use. It can be grown in an uncultivated area if no
other place is available, but tubers will be smaller than when
grown under cultivation.

In planting, small tubers are used whole, but larger ones can
be cut into pieces with eyes. Plant about four inches deep in the
South, six inches in the North.

When flower buds form, cut off the upper 12 to 18 inches of
the stalk. This throws all the nutrition meant for flowers back
into the roots so that they grow larger. Never peel Jerusalem
artichokes *before* cooking. The peel is rich in flavor.

Diabetic patients seem to be able to tolerate Jerusalem artichokes as a source of energy because, instead of starch, they
contain inulin. However, I personally would question this, since
the tubers are high in levulose—fruit sugar that is actually
sweeter than cane sugar.

In harvesting dig the tubers as they are needed for the table in
summer. For winter use store in damp sand, above freezing but
below 40 degrees F.

Sea Kale

Although grown very little in the United States, sea kale is a tasty vegetable beloved of British cottage gardeners. It is a member of the mustard family, but unlike most mustards, produces a fleshy root that is forced in winter. It produces a head similar to that of French endive. Culture is like that for rhubarb. Although it is a delicious salad green, I have eaten it (in Canada) cooked in a number of ways. Breaded and fried, it is delicious.

Once established from seed a bed can produce roots for forcing for several years. New plants can be grown from root cuttings. Pieces of root about four to five inches long are planted early in spring, spaced about three feet apart. A light harvest can be taken from a new bed the second year. The shoots must be blanched to be palatable. In milder climates blanching can be done right in the bed by covering with big flower pots and hilling around the pot with soil. Or a drainage tile six inches in diameter can be used instead of a pot but must be covered to exclude light. Hilled up with dry leaves that are wetted with a little soluble fertilizer, heat inside the tile will rise enough to force top growth if this is done after a light frost in fall. This is not always effective but worth trying, because if it doesn't work the roots can be dug and forced inside. If it does, considerable fussy work is avoided.

In the North roots are dug after a light frost and stored, with the bud at the top upright. Held as close to 32 degrees as possible without actually freezing, they will remain dormant until wanted for forcing. In digging the roots you will find many small branching roots that should be cut away. Don't discard them; they are good propagating material. Store these root cuttings in damp sand close to freezing and plant out in spring.

For forcing, plant the trimmed roots in boxes in soil or a mixture of sand and peat moss (half and half by volume) with the large bud exposed. Cover with a pot or tile in the same way as for outdoor forcing, but omit the leaves and hilling. Forcing temperature should be above 55 degrees, but not above 70. Too warm a temperature means a limp shoot. Shoots should be gathered when about four to five inches long.

The only source of seed I can find in the United States is

Thompson & Morgan, Inc., P.O. Box 24, 401 Kennedy Boulevard, Somerdale, New Jersey 08083. Seed planted in spring will produce roots that should be transplanted to a permanent bed the following spring.

Food from Weeds

Every year delicious food that would have provided millions of meals is tossed onto a compost pile or hauled away as rubbish. What is particularly unfortunate is that the plants that could have been eaten did not have to be planted nor did they need time, money, and physical effort to grow them. Most people call them weeds.

One of these is a so-called weed that came to America originally as a food plant, after it had been grown in India for centuries as a crop. Called purslane, it has become one of the gardeners' most hated weeds because of its vigor and ability to survive rough treatment. It has many common names such as pussley, pursley, fat weed, pigweed, and others. Its fat, succulent reddish stems and round fleshy leaves are delicious if harvested before the plant blooms. They need only to be boiled for a few minutes and served with lemon juice and melted butter. Cooked purslane has a rich, gelatinous flavor unlike that of any other vegetable. In the words of the TV commercial, try it, you'll like it.

A weed that is well-nigh universal in its distribution is lamb's-quarters. It belongs to the goosefoot family, which makes it a relative of garden spinach, but to those who know it, superior in flavor to its pampered cousin. I have seen it growing lush and fresh in a patch of spinach where the crop was practically a failure. To see a gardener pull up the lamb's-quarters and discard it was almost ludicrous except that a delicious potherb was being wasted.

Other names for this weed are fat hen, white goosefoot, meal weed, frost blite, and bacon weed.

Lamb's-quarters can be cooked by any method used for spinach. For winter use it can be frozen or canned. Residents of New York City who would like to try it will find it occasionally on sale in shops where Mexican and Italian foods are sold. I also remember seeing bushel baskets of purslane on sale in an Italian market west of the big bus station in midtown Manhattan.

About the only problem with lamb's-quarters is that it attracts black aphids, but even when some plants are infested there will be younger seedlings that are clean.

12

Do Vegetables Cross-Pollinate?

A common belief among gardeners is that if cucumbers and melons are planted in the same garden, there is no way to prevent them from crossing. When this happens, cucumbers are bitter and melons lack flavor. Or was it a melon-squash misalliance?

Today, with seeds costing five to ten times their price a few years back, the same question comes up about saving seeds from your garden to plant next year. Will they have been spoiled by crossing?

Others are thinking about saving seeds if they are on a subsistence farm, trying to become self-sufficient in every way possible.

First a look at the question of whether melons and cucumbers or cucumbers and squash are capable of crossing. The answer is a flat no. Although closely related there are intricate genetic reasons why cross-pollination is all but impossible. The real reason both develop off flavors is much simpler.

When either melons or cucumbers are exposed to low temperatures for several days soon after seedlings emerge, this affects their ability to convert starch into sugar. Since the ripening process is exactly this starch-to-sugar conversion, cucumbers retain the bitter flavor of the immature fruit while melons taste flat. There is no crossing. The same is true in squash-cucumber and squash-melon relations. It just doesn't happen.

Whether or not it is wise to save your own seeds for whatever reasons, this is complicated by the introduction of hybrid vegetables, which scarcely ever come true from seed. They are developed by crossing two unrelated inbred varieties. Even if one or both the parents had a weakness, a cross between the two might have neutralized this weakness in the first generation, but this may crop up in the second.

This is not always true, but chances are not good for growing vegetables of the same high quality as the parents. Only if the cucumbers or melons were open-pollinated and with no other melons or cucumbers in the same garden would saving your own seed be worthwhile.

However, sometimes the second generation does not break up into plants like those in both parents or even remote ancestors of these. You might take a chance and save seeds from hybrid melons and cucumbers, but don't expect too much.

In the case of vegetables we call squash and pumpkin, we are faced with an entirely different picture. Three closely related plants were used to produce the many types and varieties of vegetables in this group. Squashes are pumpkins and pumpkins are squashes; so the names mean little. To make matters worse, if planted within 500 feet of each other they seem to accept foreign pollen as readily as they do from their own kind. As one seedsman put it, squashes and pumpkins have about as much pride in their progeny as a stray tomcat.

Saving seeds from these crops is amusing; the next year's crop will be a mixture of dozens of types. One year I actually grew a Halloween type pumpkin on what should have been a blue Hubbard. Just so you don't expect too much, save them if you don't care what grows.

Tomatoes, peppers, and eggplant are quite safe, since they are self-pollinating and the seeds come true. There might be some variation from seeds of hybrid plants, but the chance that they will produce something much like the parent is reasonably good.

Sweet corn presents a much more critical problem. In most seeds any lack of quality shows up only in the seedlings of the following year, but pollen from one variety of corn can directly affect the ear it pollinates. Since corn pollen is wind-borne, separation by as much as 1,000 feet does not always prevent this from happening. You may plant a variety of superior quality such as Silver Queen only to find the ears you pick are mottled with golden kernels resulting from pollen from a nearby planting of Seneca Chief. Again, if you aren't fussy, there is no reason why you can't save seeds so long as you are willing to accept what grows next year. Hybrids, however, may produce seed that is no longer resistant to Stewart's disease.

Producing seed of some vegetables is beyond the skill of the amateur gardener. For example, beets, Swiss chard, carrots, celery, cabbage, cauliflower, Brussels sprouts, and kale do not produce seed the first year but must be carried over winter, often under careful temperature and humidity control. They are then planted out the following spring to produce flower stalks for seed production. All breed reasonably true if this process is followed, but again the complication from hybrid varieties exists.

Chinese cabbage is a special problem. Seeds are easy to produce by sowing seed early in spring, but all plants from this sowing will be ruined for table use since they will not produce heads but will shoot to seed within 60 days. This means you can grow your own seed, which will probably come reasonably true, but will mean growing a second crop for the table.

Lettuce from early-planted seeds is likely to come true to type if allowed to produce seed stalks, but, again, this is a separate operation from growing lettuce for the table.

Peas and beans are both self-pollinated and crossed by insects: so they can be a mixed bag if more than one variety of either is grown in the same garden. Otherwise they are a good bet for saving.

Perhaps a better idea than saving your own seed is carrying over unused packets for use the following year. This calls for more than tossing them on a pantry shelf and forgetting them until the following spring. Seeds are alive and need to be treated as dormant life, ready to spring into active growth when put in contact with warm, moist soil.

The words *warm* and *moist* are the key to what they need *not* to grow. In other words they want to be dry and cool. In keeping seeds commercially an old rule was that *temperature* and *moisture* combined should not exceed 100. That is, if you could hold temperature down to 50 degrees, and keep the seeds in an atmosphere with less than 50 percent humidity, you were in good shape. Since then, lower humidities and temperatures down to freezing have been used, with increasing seed life. About the best the home gardener can do with his home-saved seed is to allow it to dry naturally in a dry spot after cleaning and then store it in an open glass jar in the refrigerator. Because refrigerator air is drier than that in a room, it will gradually lose moisture for a week. Then the jar should be sealed and kept in the refrigerator until needed for planting.

Most seed packets (except for hybrids) contain more seed than many families want. This is particularly true if a great many different vegetables are wanted to provide variety in the diet. With this in mind, don't expose seed packets to the open air in a garden. Take out as much as you need for planting and keep the rest in a dry, cool place until the planting season is over. Then store the leftover packets as recommended for home-saved seed.

Two crops that are not worth keeping for another season are onion and parsnip. These lose germination so rapidly that they barely reach your hands with enough vitality to produce a good crop. The exposure to which leftover onion and parsnip seeds are subjected after the crop is planted usually means they will not germinate the following spring. If you want to try to save them, place them immediately in the refrigerator when received and put them back as soon as the crop is in the ground.

With seed for a good-sized garden now costing $15 or more, it isn't penny pinching to try to conserve leftovers. True, if neither savings nor survival are important, by far the best practice is to buy fresh, true-to-variety seeds from the seedsman. After all, it is to his best interests to supply you with superior varieties of the greatest possible germination.

II

Home-Grown Fruits

13

Growing Fruits and
Nuts at Home

Most home food production programs do not include fruits and nuts. This is not surprising when the shortage of information (particularly about *varieties*) is examined. Most of the available publications on the subject are written for commercial growers, with the author assuming that the grower knows the basics.

What a pity that *Les Beaux Fruits de France* by Georges Delbard has never been translated into English! Perhaps the most elaborate horticultural work published in the 20th Century, it gives meticulous instructions on the growing of fruits as practiced for a century or more in France.

I am certain that M. Delbard lost thousands of francs on its publication, yet no dedicated amateur (in the true sense of that word) would regret the service he performed by its existence. Although a commercial nurseryman, he was obviously not thinking of financial return as he wrote.

There is no denying that the growing of bush, tree, and vine fruits is somewhat more difficult than producing food by sowing seeds in a vegetable garden. At the same time, if certain basic operations are learned, any early difficulties will be more than paid for by year after year production from plants that will not need annual replanting.

An even more important reason for growing fruits and nuts is their value in the diet. Nutritionists, who in the past insisted that only meat was a safe source of all the essential amino acids needed to form proteins, now are saying that if a wide variety of vegetables and fruits is included in the diet, meats can be eliminated entirely, or limited in their use.* Placing too much emphasis on nutrition, however, might mean overlooking the most important reason of all for growing fruits and nuts—they taste delightful. Most Americans have never tasted a truly great apple, a ripe, mellow pear, or a richly flavored bunch of grapes ripened in the autumn sun.

Not to be overlooked is the actual cash value of home-grown fruits. An interesting but not unusual example is a vine of Himrod grapes, a superb seedless variety developed by the great New York State Experiment Station in Geneva, New York. Not only is Himrod a far better grape than its parent, Thompson Seedless, but it can be grown far north well into Canada. Thompson Seedless grows well only in California.

On my recommendation a friend planted a vine of this variety that cost him $2.75. Two years after he planted it, it bore over 36 pounds of delectable amber-green grapes. Surprisingly his family of five consumed all 36 pounds over a period of three weeks. At the time Thompson Seedless grapes were selling for 49 cents a pound in supermarkets. And that vine continued to bear at a rate of 10 to 15 pounds a year.

Although first harvests of some fruit crops may be delayed for one to four years, dollar returns from fruit crops are much

---

* The findings of researchers studying vitamin B_{12} that contradict the statement by others that vegetables can supply complete proteins should be mentioned here. They find that in human nutrition only meat products can supply that essential ingredient. What has thrown off previous experiments is that the liver can store B_{12} for more than a year, and very slight amounts of that vitamin are produced in saliva when food is chewed for longer than normal.

Although these two reserves can keep a human being from suffering B_{12} deficiency, eventually the supply runs out and can cause latent symptoms that may not become critical for several years.

For this reason the need for home-grown sources of meat is discussed in the section on modern homesteading.

higher than from vegetables. The subsistence farmer or modern homesteader should give particular attention to home-grown fruits and nuts, since he (and particularly she) is located at a distance from big city markets. In small towns the housewife usually can find only apples and oranges, good as far as they go, but which can get monotonous as a steady diet.

One advantage the home orchardist has over commercial growers is that trees can be given close personal attention, which would be too costly for big growers to provide. For example, a pleasant task in early summer is that of thinning the fruits on apple trees that have set too thickly. Commercially this is done with chemical sprays, but is much less perfect than when done by hand, with each apple given all the space it needs to develop into a perfect specimen.

One of the delights of growing your own fruit is that you are not limited to commercial varieties. Although I would like to warn those contemplating planting an orchard against going all out for old varieties, there is much to be said for doing so if you have a nostalgic yearning for such antiques as Spitzbergen (which was Thomas Jefferson's favorite apple), Pound Sweet with its huge fruits, Golden Russet, which was dropped by commercial growers because of its erratic bearing, and Summer Rambo, perhaps the oldest apple variety in existence.

The danger in planting these older gems too heavily is that they are often alternate bearers; that is, producing a crop only every other year. This can be tolerated if you are growing half a dozen or more trees so that at least two of them will give you fruit each year. If only two or three trees are planted, better stick to commercial varieties such as McIntosh and its many descendants or Jonathan and Golden Delicious. Incidentally, Jonathan *is* an old variety, introduced in 1840. McIntosh is also an old variety, first discovered in 1796.

Another reason for growing your own apples is the differences in taste. My wife thinks that a McIntosh (even an apple harvested green and stored under CO_2) is about the only acceptable commercial apple worth eating. I formerly preferred the true Jonathan with a tart-crisp flavor that jolted my taste buds. What is sold as Jonathan today is obviously one of its sports, selected for some quality that is profitable for the orchardist but that degrades a wonderful apple.

One important fact must be emphasized when talking about apple flavor. Not all old apples, even some that have survived for a century or more, are high flavored. In fact many fell by the wayside because they had poor flavor. I know individuals who swear by Baldwin and Ben Davis. In 1912 Liberty Hyde Bailey condemned these two varieties in the following words: "the former, of secondary quality and the latter, of worse."

My advice is that before you invest time, effort, and money in any fruit you plan to buy—whether apples, pears, grapes, strawberries, plums, peaches, or apricots—sample them first. Although I shall make some specific recommendations, remember that these are as personal as a toothbrush. If you are unable to make actual taste tests and must take my recommendations you will still eat better fruit than 90 percent of the misused, bruised stuff on the market.

Although what has been said has been largely about apples, since this is by far the favorite fruit of most Americans, the real opportunity for adding interest and variety to the diet lies in growing as many species as your climate will allow. For example, if you can give it a damp and cool but frostless storage for the winter, a fig tree in a tub is worth the extra attention it demands, even if you live north of the Ohio River. In a full-sized greenhouse I once grew one that had a spread of 25 feet, a real conversation piece.

If pears have not appealed to you, the first taste of a properly ripened Anjou or Dumont pear will be a gourmet event. Compared with the cold storage green fruit offered in the market, your own pears will be pure ambrosia.

Peaches, plums, apricots, and cherries are similarly improved when tasted an hour or two after harvesting. As for strawberries, no one dependent on commercial sources for this highly praised fruit has ever tasted them in the perfect condition that led Dr. Butler to laud them as God's perfect berry.

Nuts belong in any larger collection of food plants for two reasons. First and most important in my book is flavor. There is no substitute for the special tang and texture of nutmeats in the diet. Second, they are concentrated nutrition, one of the richest sources of energy, a source that can be kept for months without spoilage. True, they can be overdone; it is hard to stop eating them. Resist the impulse to eat the entire dish of walnuts or pecans; save them for use through the entire winter.

14

The Strawberry

Dr. William Butler, an English physician in the 16th Century, lauded the strawberry in words that have been parroted ever since. "Doubtless God could have made a better berry, but doubtless God never did." His comment was quoted in *The Compleat Angler* by Izaak Walton.

Although I would differ with the good doctor (apparently he never tasted the glorious flavor of a fully ripened modern red raspberry) it would be blasphemy to deny that the strawberry might be the *second-best*-tasting berry in the world. When both are in season at the same time, I find myself emulating the donkey with a bale of hay on each side of its head, unable to decide which is the most tempting.

Whatever their respective rank flavorwise, the strawberry is by far the most important of garden fruits. Perhaps this is because it most closely resembles a vegetable in its cultural needs. Not surprisingly, in some sections truck gardeners switch from vegetable crops to strawberries almost at will, and back again when the shift is to their advantage.

Strawberries are short-lived perennials and in the hill system described below can be kept in production for as long as five years. Usual practice, however, is to have three rows growing.

The first is a newly planted row set out in spring to produce the main crop next year. If it is a June fruiting variety, all blossoms are kept picked off that season. If, however, it is an everbearer, some fruits are allowed to form after mid-July.

The second row is for heavy production that year (its 2nd year). After it has fruited (if it is a June bearer) it is renovated as described later, to produce a second crop the following year.

The third row is the one planted two seasons before and in most cases is producing a crop of small berries after which it is plowed under.

Strawberries are often grown in vegetable gardens even though they spread out and occupy a space about three feet wide, allowing no space for cultivating between the plants.

Good air drainage is important when picking a spot for strawberries, otherwise late frosts and winter thaws can cause trouble. This is one crop that cannot stand flooding of the root system for more than a day before it develops damage to the roots. Don't try to grow strawberries on clay soils unless you are willing to accept small yields and weak plants. If drainage is poor, raised beds are a possible remedy on a small scale. Or raised ridges (growing the plants on the hill system) are often used. In heavier soils it is important to plant only varieties that are known to be resistant to red stele disease.

Because the root system of strawberries is quite shallow and does not penetrate to any depth, any soil used for this crop must drain well, yet hold moisture, which always means high organic content. This is a good place to use any well-rotted compost you have available.

Strawberries are peculiarly subject to injury by white grubs, the larvae of various beetles. To use soil infested with white grubs for strawberries is asking for trouble. Now that DDT can no longer be used for grub proofing, about the only chemical we have left is old-fashioned arsenate of lead. Treatment should be made the season before planting so the arsenate of lead can be "fixed" on soil particles to prevent root injury.

Quack, twitch, or couch grass is a serious pest in strawberry beds and if at all possible should be killed out by a combination of spraying with either Amizole or Dowpon and cultivation. This should be done the year before planting, with a final cultivation just before the plants are set. The year before planting would be a good time to plant a green manure crop to be plowed under late in fall. This could be sown in September in the North, using cereal rye.

Plowing under about twenty pounds of superphosphate and ten pounds of muriate of potash to 1,000 square feet in poor soils, half that amount in richer soils, will help plants get established. Strawberries will tolerate soils as low as 5.0 pH or as high as 7.0—6.3 to 6.7 is considered ideal.

Variety is Important

What to plant depends on where you live. No small fruit has been the subject of as intense concentration on breeding for qualities wanted in the perfect berry. Although my nomination for the best-flavored berry I have ever tasted would be Royal Sovereign or George IV from England, I would not plant either variety where I garden. Lack of hardiness alone would eliminate it.

Perhaps the outstanding variety north of the Ohio River and into Maine would be Surecrop. Experts also rate it as the best-adapted variety for the South. Although it rates only a step below the outstanding varieties for flavor, in every other respect, it is without an equal. No other berry will do as well on dry or poor soils. It is the only variety that combines these qualities with multiple resistance to diseases, including red stele, verticillium wilt, and various leaf troubles. It is also one of the heaviest producers among modern strawberries, with one commercial grower reporting 13,000 quarts to the acre. It is an excellent berry for freezing.

If grown in the far north, it will need heavier mulching than varieties such as Premier, Catskill, Fletcher, Midway, and Robinson.

If high flavor is your objective, along with hardiness, your choice would be limited to Fletcher, Sparkle, and Midway. But if you wanted resistance to both red stele disease and cold in a berry with high flavor, you would have to confine your choice to Sparkle. But if you had to avoid verticillium wilt (which is almost certain to be present in most soils used for general vegetable gardening) you might have to give up superflavor and settle for Surecrop.

An old variety that persists in bobbing up among new varieties, perhaps because of its high resistance to both leaf diseases and verticillium, is Premier. Introduced in 1918, it was for many years America's leading variety. It ripens early, with plenty of light red berries that are as good or better in flavor than those you will find in most markets. It is a sure-fire variety so widely offered that millions of home gardeners know it and still like it. However, growers who know quality berries are replacing it with Empire, which improves on it in every way.

One quality to consider is, of course, flavor. But what flavor do you prefer? To some a strawberry must be tart, but the majority of home gardeners want a berry that is sweet when ripe. Some varieties turn a dark, dull red before they develop sweetness, which is against them on the market because housewives shop with their eyes—and bright, shiny red berries get preference.

Among the top-rated varieties for a sweet-flavored berry is Fairfax, which is not too popular as a market berry because it must develop a deep red color before it is at its best. This is *the* strawberry for home gardeners who do not object to this color. Production is good but not sensational. It is reliably hardy except in the far north. A similar variety is Suwanee, which some consider the best-flavored of all strawberries. It is light red when ripe. The berries are somewhat softer than Fairfax and bruise if not handled carefully. It is the one high-flavored strawberry that does well in the South.

An excellent all-around variety is Sparkle. While the berries do actually sparkle on the plant they do darken later. Sparkle is rated among the top varieties for flavor. It is the leading commercial variety in most of the northeastern United States. It is one of the hardiest of all varieties, doing well into Maine. It is resistant to red stele disease but only fair in resistance to verticillium and leaf troubles.

Southern growers do plant all of the varieties already described, but of these, Surecrop is the only one of any importance. None of the strawberries usually recommended for the South rank with the best-flavored varieties, although some were considered in that class before they were pushed out by Sparkle, Suwanee, and Fairfax. The leading variety south of the Ohio River is Albritton, which would rank just under today's top favorites. Except where a strawberry is wanted for freezing, it is perhaps the best variety for home gardens in the South. The second-best variety for that region is perhaps Pocahontas, which is even better than Albritton as a freezing berry. This does well everywhere in the South as far west as Texas. Another freezing variety for the South is Tennessee Beauty, widely grown as a shipping berry. Except that it is slightly tart it has excellent flavor. Suwanee is the only full-flavored variety that does well south of the Ohio River.

Hill, Matted Row, or Spaced Row?

Most commercial crops of strawberries are grown in what are called matted rows. In this method of culture, a single row is used, with plants spaced about 18 inches apart in the row and in home gardens, about four feet between rows. Planting can be done as early as the soil can be worked. Properly stored plants delivered in spring are hardy and will even tolerate light snow drifting over them. However, little is gained in planting before soil temperatures go above 40 to 45 degrees, since no growth takes place.

Nowadays strawberry specialists keep plants in cold storage so they can be planted as late as July 15. There is an advantage to late planting if the soil needs preparation beforehand. If space permits, plant 25 or more plants for each family member.

The plants must be set at the proper depth. Just above the point at which the roots come together is a sheath that surrounds the growing tip of the plant. This sheath should be right at ground level so that the roots are buried completely, but the growing tip is out of the ground. Dirt over the growing tip can kill it. Roots left exposed will never produce a good plant.

In the matted-row system the plants are allowed to make all the runners they can until they form a solid carpet of plants—small, medium, and large.

The outside plants in the row are cut out, leaving about 18

inches between rows as a walk. Before runners begin to form, all flowers must be removed to prevent plants from setting berries the first year. If. allowed to fruit, they will be weakened so that the crop the following spring will be poor. There is always a temptation to leave a few flowers for a taste the first year plants are set, but. the impulse must be resisted.

Earlier, the plowing under of phosphorus and potash was recommended, but no mention was made of nitrogen. The time this. element is needed is in August and September, at the time plants are forming flower buds for next year's crop.

Mulching the plants is necessary, even in the South. Strawberries are so shallow rooted that they heave out of the ground if the soil alternately freezes and thaws. This particular danger is actually greater in the South than in the North where the ground is likely to freeze and stay frozen all winter long.

In the North a mulch should be applied before the temperature drops as low as 20 degrees above zero. Below that temperature crowns are killed on even the hardiest varieties.

Straw is by far the best mulch, but if you don't have it, dry, fluffy leaves will do. Personally I use spruce needle duff collected from under spruces, not because it is perfect, but with no deciduous trees on our island, it is all I have. Even excelsior will do if used thick enough. Avoid leaves that pack down such as those from cottonwoods. The mulch goes right over the plants. If you are in doubt about smothering the plants, try laying a few evergreen boughs over them first.

In areas where zero weather occurs at times, you will need about four inches of mulch. In the South two inches should provide an umbrella that will keep soil temperatures from fluctuating. The idea in mulching is *not* to prevent freezing but to keep the soil frozen so the plants won't be pushed out of the ground by frost action.

In the North soil should be crusted enough to bear your weight before mulching. Otherwise field mice are likely to move in for the winter and dine on strawberry foliage.

The description of matted-row culture is not meant to recommend this way of growing strawberries unless you are too busy to use one of two better methods. ·

Matted-row culture is used commercially because the other

two methods require so much hand labor that the grower cannot afford to employ them. In the home garden, however, the easiest and in many ways the best method is the spaced-row system. It is based on setting the plants in rows as with matted rows and allowing runner formation to begin. The difference is that no more runners are allowed to form after June 1 to 15. Any runners that form after that time are cut away so that those formed earlier will have more space, more light, more moisture, and fertility from the soil.

Experiments at a number of stations have shown that a runner rooted in June will produce 15 *times* as many berries and larger, more perfect, ones than will a runner rooted in September.

A third method of growing strawberries is by the hill system in which plants are not allowed to produce any runners. All are cut away as soon as they appear. That this method produces the largest berries and of top quality cannot be denied, but unless you are trying for a prize in a show the difference is not enough to justify the extra labor. In addition to the added labor is the loss of plants for new rows from runners that can be rooted in either the matted- or spaced-row methods.

There is the advantage of a perennial planting when growing by the hill system. You don't replant hill-grown strawberries every year; they have survived as long as five years or more. As plants grow older and have more leaves, they produce more fruit. A plant with two or three leaves in fall will probably throw out one flower cluster the following spring that will ripen three to five berries. One with 50 leaves can produce as much as a quart of larger berries. Even so, the total production under hill culture will usually be less than a spaced row occupying the same area.

To grow strawberries by the hill system, plant one foot apart in rows 18 inches apart. Cut off all runners as they develop. Again, be religious about cutting off all flowers as they form.

One advantage to the hill system is worth considering. Since runners do not need to root but are cut away, the original plants can be grown under black plastic mulch. This eliminates cultivation, weeding, and reduces the amount of watering needed. Black plastic mulch increases soil temperature in early spring, resulting in earlier crops. However, it is not practical in the South, where the extra heat will be too much for the plants.

General Treatment for All Cultures

No matter how you grow, there are certain basic rules that apply to all three methods. First, because of their shallow root systems, strawberries must be kept moist but not sopping wet This is one crop that is hard to grow on sandy loam soils with out some form of irrigation. Even so, when well watered, sandy loams produce quality berries if fertilized.

Strawberries are a full-sun crop. Never plant where they must compete with tree roots for food and moisture, even if on the sunny side of the tree.

Insect control is more important with strawberries than with most crops. Spider mites and aphids are the worst pests. Fortunately both are easily controlled with Malathion, an insecticide less toxic to humans than natural materials preferred by organic gardeners. Aphid control is vital to keeping plants free of virus disease.

The importance of buying from reliable sources is nowhere greater than in the case of strawberries. Today it is possible to buy virus-free plants of all desirable varieties. The importance of this is difficult to overemphasize. The work of two great horticulturists, Dr. George Slate and Dr. George Darrow (both now retired), in developing methods for indexing and eliminating viruses in strawberries has been one of the great forward advances in fruit culture. Both have been responsible for some of our finest new varieties of small fruits.

Don't let your failure to demand virus-free plants spoil their contribution to better strawberries.

Renewing Old Beds

In commercial production, matted and spaced rows are kept for two years. The best time to renew a row for another year's production is immediately after the crop is harvested. The first step is to mow off the old leaves, either by hand with a sickle, or with a power mower set as high as the blade can be raised. This can only be done with a rotary mower or one with a sickle bar, since a reel type cannot be raised high enough to miss the crowns. Plants in poor shape can be cut out before mowing.

If the soil is heavy enough to retain moisture well, water the day before mowing. After mowing allow the leaves to dry for a day or two, then set them on fire. The day should be breezy so the fire doesn't smolder around the leaves but runs quickly along the row. Burning, if it does not injure the crown, helps control many leaf diseases and insects. If burning in the row is impracticable, rake off the leaves and burn them.

Here is where one of the slow-release fertilizers used on lawns can be useful on a garden crop. One with a formula of 20-10-5 containing either IBDU or Ureaform nitrogen used at about the rate recommended for lawns will supply nitrogen at the time when strawberries need it most. The new Green-Green formula would be ideal. Some so-called slow-release fertilizers also contain other forms of nitrogen that will injure plants unless watered immediately. Be ready with the hose and wash the fertilizer off the plants and into the soil.

If a lawn fertilizer is not available, use any high-nitrogen plant food. Remember the first figure in the formula shows the percentage of nitrogen.

If the row has spread too much, it can be cut down by working under the sides until it is about 15 inches wide. If a matted row is too thick, in thinning always leave the oldest runners (the ones nearest the plants) and remove the smallest ones at the tip of the string.

A good plan for the home gardener is to keep three rows growing. One should be the newly planted row for fruiting the following year and one additional year. The second is the fruiting row of the current year, to be renovated following harvest. The third is the row that was renovated the year before, to be plowed under as soon as harvested. If no other space is available, this row can be reset.

To provide plants for setting a new row where the oldest one is plowed under, set clay pots three inches in diameter under healthy runners as early as they throw out a small plant. These are filled with good soil and the small plant pinned down to the soil. For this purpose I like wooden clothespins, which don't get hot and stunt the runner. Don't use wire loops or stones to pin the plant; both can get so hot that the runner will be damaged.

As soon as these spring-rooted plants have filled the pot with fine white roots they can be used to set a new row. Preferably this should be in new soil, but if no other space is available use the three-year-old row that was plowed under.

Good Garden Varieties
Everbearing Varieties
In the past, everbearing varieties were a poor crop. In summer the berries were soft and in cool fall months they lacked flavor and were sour. In the past decade the picture has changed because of the development of high-flavored, vigorous varieties. The first of these was the variety Red Rich, which I viewed with skepticism at first. Victor Judson, who was responsible for its introduction, insisted that I must try it, which I agreed to do. For some reason he insisted on sending me 1,000 plants, when I had space for only 100. My friends benefited as a result, and we have all been Red Rich fans ever since.

Unlike older varieties Red Rich did not lose flavor when autumn nights turned cool. Its berries have a full, rich strawberry flavor from early summer until frost. Its one fault is that it does not like hot weather and the berries from the June-July crop tend to be small. It was bred in Minnesota, where it is an outstanding variety. Later introductions are even better. It makes very few runners, which means it is well adapted to hill culture.

A seedling of Red Rich, Ozark Beauty makes more runners, but the runners do not fruit well. It has flavor equal to its parent but is an improvement in that berries are more resistant to heat. The flavor is equal to Red Rich.

Ogallala is a high-flavored everbearing variety that is extremely hardy and resistant to leaf spot. It originated at North Platte, Nebraska.

Geneva, bred by George Slate at the New York Agricultural Experiment Station bears large, high-flavored berries, a deep, rich red in color.

Any of the varieties mentioned are worth planting in home gardens, preferably on the hill system. Everbearers are not too successful south of the Ohio River except at higher altitudes in the Appalachians in the Carolinas.

Strawberries in the Northwest

Here, growers are practically limited to a single variety, Northwest, except that where plants are available, the older variety Marshall does well in this area. Northwest is so specific to this area that it has become the most widely grown strawberry (by acreage, not tonnage) in the United States. It is used principally for freezing although not large enough to suit commercial processors. Plants are tolerant of virus disease but are not resistant to red stele.

California Varieties

The variety Shasta is the dominant strawberry on the coast of California, where it fruits all summer long. Production is enormous; probably more tons of strawberries of this variety are sold than of any other. It is the perfect market berry, appealing to the housewife by its attractive berries—huge, brightly colored, and firm. Wonderful on the market, but on the table a disappointment for anyone familiar with true strawberry flavor. One friend of mine in California called it "a big blob of nothing."

The variety Lassen is similar but has a much shorter rest period and so can be grown farther south along the coast. It is being replaced by Fresno, Torrey, and Tioga. All are better flavored and need an even shorter rest period than Lassen, with firmer berries better suited to freezing.

Canadian Varieties

For years Premier and Dunlap were the dominant varieties in Canada. In the Golden Triangle north of Lake Erie practically all of the varieties adapted to Northeastern United States can be grown. Another type that should be of interest to home gardeners is British Sovereign, a variety of superb flavor particularly adapted to British Columbia. Why this variety has not taken over (at least in home gardens) in Northwestern United

States is difficult to understand. Although not red stele resistant and subject to mildew its quality should mean wider distribution.

Redcoat, which was tested in the United States but proved too soft, is another favorite in Canada because of its extremely high yield and its earliness. It has replaced Dunlap over much of eastern Canada as a commercial variety. There, it does not become soft at maturity but is a firm berry suitable for shipping. It is suitable for home garden use.

For the Prairie Provinces only hardy varieties such as Glenheart, Soarta, Jubilee, and Parkland (all everbearing) are grown. Two of the best-flavored varieties for this area are Guardsman and Grenadier. Of these, early berries are of good size, but later they run down in size.

Diseases
Virus
Several virus diseases attack strawberries, and since there are no cures for plants once infected, the only remedy is prevention. This begins with buying plants that are identified as virus-free. Never buy plants that are not identified as uncontaminated by viruses.

Red Stele
This is another disease where the remedy begins with the stock you buy. In this case, however, the answer is to buy varieties that are resistant to the disease. When you plant a variety that is not specifically identified as stele resistant, you may wake up about the time the first berries are maturing to find leaves wilting and rolling. As the disease progresses they turn a dull leaden green in contrast to the normal fresh green of healthy plants. The plants become stunted and berries dry up. Digging up infected plants you will find that the core of infested roots has turned a brown color and the tips are dead.

The disease is worse on low, poorly drained soils.

Gray Mold
In wet seasons plants in matted rows in particular are attacked by gray mold that forms a fuzzy, fluffy light gray coating on the fruits, ruining them for use as food. Spaced rows are less likely

to attack, while hill rows are seldom affected. In addition to opening up the plants to free air movement, you can spray with Captan. The first spray should go on when the first blossoms open and a second ten days later. If muggy, wet weather continues while berries are ripening, a third application might be needed.

In sunny, bright springs, spraying will not be needed. However, if leaf spot diseases appear on foliage, the same two or three sprays are needed. I have found that if either Chlordane or Methoxychlor are included in the Captan spray, most harmful insects (other than white grubs in the soil) are controlled well enough to insure a crop.

15

Grapes for Table and Wine

The grape is one of the oldest of all cultivated fruits and among the most valued. With the proper selections of types and varieties, it can be grown anywhere in the United States, except in the driest regions. Once limited by cold winters, there are even grapes that will survive on the northern edge of the Great Plains if irrigated. In discussing grapes for growing in the home food garden, emphasis will be on varieties that are both good table grapes and will also make good wine if properly handled.

Good Growing Varieties

Where the production of wine is considered more important than table use, it is suggested that you send four dollars to the New York State Fruit Testing Association, Geneva, New York 14456, a nonprofit organization established to test all types of fruits. The association offers over sixty tested varieties of the better hybrids between the European wine grape and American table grapes. Their catalog rates wine grapes by color, season, hardiness, and quality of the wine each produces.

Some of these hybrids, however, are both excellent table

grapes and good for wine as well, with enough hardiness to survive in all but the coldest parts of the country.

For colder parts of the Northeast, the hardiest of the varieties described below is Van Buren, which has fruited after 25 degrees below zero. The vine itself is hardy to 30 degrees below. Other hardy grapes are Concord, Ontario, Delaware, and Worden. Temperatures listed are for fruiting, not vine.

The following varieties are listed more or less in the order of their ripening in the Finger Lakes region of New York State.

Interlaken Seedless. An amber or light gold-colored grape far superior to the Thompson Seedless, an older, more tender variety that can be grown only in California. Ripens about August 15. Probably will not fruit at temperatures below -10. Delightful fresh flavor.

Himrod Seedless. A sister seedling of Interlaken Seedless and even a shade finer in flavor but a week later in ripening. It is hardier than Interlaken. A terrific grape.

Ontario. Ripens with Himrod. Although not seedless, it is a superior white table grape with a distinctive flavor.

Van Buren. Perhaps the hardiest quality grape that produced a crop after 25 below zero. Ripens about September 1. A better grape than Concord but of the same slip-skin type. Preferred for jams and jellies. Needs somewhat less sugar than Concord.

Schuyler. A relatively new variety from the New York State Fruit Testing Association. The fruit is like French grapes with a clean vinous flavor. Not a slip-skin variety. Hardy to ten below zero. A heavy producer and needs hard pruning to keep it from overbearing. Ripens the last of August. Fruit has a beautiful blue bloom.

Seneca. Another European-type white grape but is hardy to about 15 below zero. An outstanding dessert grape. Makes a fair white wine.

Aurora. Although an excellent dessert grape, it is one of the best of the French-American hybrids for white wine and the hardiest. Ripens about September 1. A heavy producer.

Captivator. An old 19th Century variety but one of the best of all red table grapes. A French-American hybrid but fully hardy and vigorous. Ripens September 1.

Brighton. Because it is self-sterile and not planted in commercial vineyards, Brighton has been lost sight of in many catalogs. It is one of the best highly flavored red grapes ripening about September 5 to 10. Should have another grape as a pollinator.

Fredonia. A seedling of Concord with bunches two to three times the size of its parent and better flavored sounds spectacular, and to the commercial grower, it is. In the home garden, however, it must compete with Buffalo, described below and perhaps the finest of all grapes of the Concord type.

Buffalo. In addition to its high quality, Buffalo is an excellent variety for homemade wines, lacking some of the "foxy" flavor of other Concord seedlings. What makes it an ideal variety for home gardens, however, is that it is so highly disease resistant it can be grown without spraying. September 10 maturity.

Worden. For those who prefer Concord above all other grapes, this old-time variety is not only hardier but ripens September 10, two weeks earlier. It requires a minimum of spraying to keep it pest free. The clusters are larger and juicier than Concord. Some grape nursery specialists still list this variety. I prefer Buffalo, but the greater hardiness of Worden makes it worth planting.

Alden. If the thought of individual grape berries as big as Damson plums is intriguing, Alden is your grape. For those who are not familiar with Damson plums, I should explain that they are only about an inch long, small for plums but huge for grapes. The oval, purple-blue berries are identical with European wine grapes in texture but to American tastes the flavor is better, since it does have some of the sprightly flavor of American varieties. Hardy to 15 degrees below zero. Vines are productive, up to 20 pounds from a single vine. Ripens September 20. One of the best of all wine grapes among American hybrids. Needs pruning to keep it from overbearing.

Caco. A high-quality red grape that has suffered because it ripens in the same season as Delaware. In addition it is sweet two weeks before it actually ripens; so it is seldom eaten when it is at its best. A much heavier producer than Delaware and for most food gardeners, an easier variety to grow.

Suffolk Red Seedless. This gives the home food gardener a truly seedless red grape of Interlaken Seedless quality. Although rated as ripening Sept. 10, I am told the flavor will improve up to Sept. 20. I tasted it at the earlier date and if the flavor improves after that, this is truly a great grape. Hardy to about five degrees below zero.

Lakemont Seedless. Another green seedless variety turning golden when fully ripe. It is edible by Sept. 10, but another ten days on the vine will improve flavor. Fruit will keep well in cold storage. The flavor is honey sweet when fully mature.

Delaware. This high-quality red grape has for years been *the* wine grape among American vintners. It is also a superb table grape. It is hardy and not fussy as to soil so long as it is rich. It is a weak grower and for that reason needs extra care. Do not prune too closely. In season about Sept. 20.

Niagara. A heavy producer of very good, sweet, and juicy "white" grapes, actually a delicate pale green. Next to Concord perhaps America's best-known grape. In season with Delaware. Vigorous vine, suitable for growing on a trellis.

Concord. By far the best known of all American grapes, but far from the best. There is no question that it is refreshing and tasty, but the tough skin means that most of the flavor has to be spit out. Makes excellent jelly and grape juice, but as a wine grape it is rated last on the list. Should not be planted if you can find such better blue varieties as Buffalo, Van Buren, or Worden. Snobbish enologists sneer at the "foxy" flavor of Concord, but Americans are accustomed to it and do not enjoy the lack of it in French varieties. Concord is in season about September 25. It is the perfect vine for covering a trellis, thriving even without pruning.

Sheridan. Not only is this one of the finest of all American varieties but one that can be stored until Christmas, prolonging its sweet, delicate flavor for nearly two months. It is the best of the late blue grapes. I have never seen it grow on a trellis, but from its vigorous growth I would guess that it would come close to Concord or Niagara for this purpose. In season about October 1. Needs close pruning or it will wear itself out producing fruit.

Catawba. Here is another grape to grace your Christmas dinner table but red in color instead of blue. It has maintained a place as one of America's good grapes for well over a century. While there are grapes that have a finer, more refined flavor than Catawba, it is well worth planting for its reliability as a producer of a grape that has even inspired poetry. In season about October 1.

Steuben. Here is a grape that is a catalog writer's dream. Developed at the New York State Experiment Station, it has a flavor that is almost a perfume. The oversized clusters are long and slender and so fully packed that they resemble a model of the perfect grape. It will produce a full crop even after 20 degrees below zero temperatures. It ripens with Concord and will keep until Christmas. Even in unfavorable climates it does not seem to need spraying. My one regret is that we leave our summer garden before it is ripe; so I must enjoy it from a friend's vine. For him it ripens *before* Concord.

Golden Muscat. I happen to dislike the musk undertone in grapes and so must depend on a friend's analysis of the flavor of this dramatic grape. Its clusters of golden oval berries weigh as much as six pounds each. They are highly flavored with a distinctive taste similar to that of muscatel wine. A strong grower. In season about October 10. Can be kept for about a month. For those who like the muscat flavor it is an excellent wine grape. Hardy down to about five degrees below zero.

Urbana. This is a grape that came out originally in 1912, then disappeared from commerce, but was revived because those who planted it originally praised it highly. Under refrigeration it has been kept until nearly February, enough to recommend it even if it were not good. Instead it is one of the finest of all late red grapes. About the only listing I can find is in the catalog of the New York State Fruit Testing Association, Geneva, New York 14456.

Culture for Northern Bunch Grapes

One operation in the culture of grapes stops many from growing them—pruning. At least that is what most amateurs call the operation. Actually pruning is only one step in a much more involved operation—training. For centuries the grape has been subjected to discipline far more rigid and restrictive than any other crop. Vines can survive and fruit without training or pruning, as anyone can see who has gathered grapes in the wild. I have a vine of Seibel 1000, a French wine grape that has not been pruned in 20 years, which I abandoned because the starlings ate all the berries before they were fully ripe. It still bears an abundant crop of small clusters.

For anyone too busy to go through the rituals of training, a satisfactory way to grow grapes is on a latticework wooden trellis high enough to walk under and wide enough to allow the gardener to relax under its shade. If made 16 to 20 feet long, it can support about four vines on each side, which can be allowed to scramble over the trellis at will. At first the canes will have to be tied up, but by the time they reach the top they will form a roof that can even shed light showers. For this purpose I would prefer varieties that are both strong growing and that need little or no spraying. Old-fashioned Worden would be one. Buffalo is another. Steuben is a third. All three of these are blue grapes of the Concord type. For a white variety Interlaken would be a good choice if temperatures do not drop too low. Niagara is hardier but not seedless.

I know of one trellis planting of this type that has been producing more grapes than the owner can eat or give away that has not missed a crop in 40 years. About the only care it gets, every three or four years, is to have the older woody canes cut away to the main stems.

Much finer fruit can, of course, be produced when grown on a conventional three-wire grape trellis. Today a relatively new system of pruning and training, developed by Dr. Nelson Shaulis of the Geneva, New York, experiment station, has improved both the size and production of clusters. It utilizes an old trick in improving the size and floriferousness of climbing roses. When a rose cane is trained downward at the tip instead of horizontally, the effect is a substantial increase in the number of flower buds. The Shaulis system trains two canes to the top wire of a trellis and then bends their tips down and ties them to the lower wires.

Spring planting as soon as the soil is workable, is best. If planted in autumn after leaf-fall, mulch well.

Grapes require much more careful soil preparation than do vegetable crops, not because they are heavy feeders, but because they might remain in the same spot, without a chance for soil improvement, for half a century or more. The one important need is for good drainage. No species of grape can tolerate wet feet. At the same time enough humus in the form of well-decayed compost, old, rotted manure, leaf mold or similar organic matter, is highly desirable.

In traditional vineyard practice whole or coarsely crushed bones were buried under grapevines. Originally this material contained some nitrogen and other food elements, which were probably exhausted during the first year or two of growth. I was present in a French vineyard when grapevines that had been killed by root lice (phylloxera) were being dug up. Although they had been planted half a century before, the bone was still intact. Most of the phosphorus they contained had not been of any use to the vines.

The need for phosphorus can be supplied by the use of superphosphate plowed under before planting. Few home food gardens would have a grape trellis longer than 25 feet. Scatter ten pounds of superphosphate along that 25-foot row and dig or till it under. In any soil containing enough organic matter this should take care of the nutrient needs of grapes for several years. If at any time in the future vegetative growth seems weak, light feeding with ammonium nitrate or ammonium sulfate, say five pounds along that 25-foot trellis, should be enough.

Overfertilizing grapes means they will make long vegetative canes with few fruiting buds. Too, fruit will lack flavor. Only in sandy loams is regular feeding needed.

Although the vines will not need support until the second year, it is best to set up the trellis before planting, since the work required will mean that the soil will be tramped down. Even though it can be worked up again, there is much less chance of injury to spreading roots the first year.

For practically all American grapes eight feet between vines is standard practice. One-year-old vines are best. Paying extra money for so-called bearing age or quick-crop plants is not only a waste of money but may result in setting out poorer plants than one-year-old vines that cost less. Since both must be cut back to form bearing canes, there is seldom any gain in earlier fruiting.

If the vines are dry when received, soak them overnight, completely immersed in water over the canes. I like to have a soupy slurry of clay soil when planting, into which I dip the roots to conserve moisture.

When planting, remember you may be setting vines for a lifetime and do the job right. The hole should be wide enough and deep enough so the roots can be spread out in natural position. The roots should be trimmed back as little as possible, unless they are broken, in which case cut them back to clean wood. The top should be cut back to a single trunk as straight as possible. Leave four buds, but nip out two of the weakest after growth starts.

In setting the plant, plant it so the soil marks on the roots and stem are about an inch below ground level. That is, it should stand about an inch deeper than it grew in the nursery.

I am a strong advocate of setting a stout stake, say one inch by one inch, beside the vine when planted. All too often this is left to be inserted the second year, injuring the roots. As soon as set, tie it to the lowest wire. Since the cut-back plant has no canes, it cannot be tied to the stake until the following year.

The first year of growth calls for clean cultivation. Your chance of success in controlling weeds in future years depends on how well you get rid of perennial weeds and how completely you prevent annuals from seeding.

From the second year on the only practical way to grow grapes is under a mulch. If available, sawdust is ideal. It must, however, be supplied with extra nitrogen to prevent soil bacteria from robbing the soil for nitrogen as they rot down the wood fibers. Our 25-foot trellis would need about a pound or two of urea or three pounds of ammonium sulfate added to the sawdust needed to cover the row with six inches of sawdust, spread out three feet on either side of the wires.

Since a mulch will not be needed until the second year, the first year can be used to compost other mulching materials for use, if sawdust is not readily available. Leaves, straw, old sod, or other organic matter piled as recommended for composting, should be weed-free and well rotted within a year. These will need no additional source of nitrogen when used under the vines.

Watering the first year is important. Grapevines are able to grow deep for water, but when newly planted the limited root system often cannot draw up enough moisture for best growth.

Training and pruning are all but impossible to explain. Although the rudiments of the umbrella system of Dr. Shaulis are given below, the grape grower must interpret them vine by vine. Varieties differ in their response to pruning. A vine that shows by its vigor that it can support more clusters can be given more buds for the following season's crop. A weak grower such as Delaware should be left fewer buds.

Even the experts differ. At one meeting I heard a specialist say, "Use the largest, dark brown, well-matured canes. Wood larger than a pencil is more productive than wood smaller than a pencil when there is a choice. Unfortunately too many growers are inclined to pass up too much fruitful wood in order to save fruit wood one-quarter inch (pencil size) in diameter."

The other speaker, equally competent and nationally recognized as an expert, told big vineyard operators to strive for a trellis filled with lean vines about one-quarter inch in diameter. If you keep that size in mind, you won't be too far off.

On mature vines leave between 35 and 45 buds on the two canes selected for the umbrella. If the variety seems particularly vigorous and you can use more grapes, it can be allowed to develop an extra cane. In choosing the canes to be retained, these will fruit better if they are not much bigger than a lead pencil in diameter, well matured and with dark brown bark.

Some discretion is needed in applying that one-quarter-inch standard, since sometimes a really vigorous variety will have no suitable canes that small.

If the larger canes bear fruit, continue using them. Always keep in mind that grapes bear on two-year-old wood. Don't retain old canes if not useful or expect fruit on the current year's wood.

Write your state experiment station for spray schedules for grapes. They will tell you if any serious pests are likely to prevent success. If varieties are selected carefully, it is often possible to grow grapes for years without the need of spraying.

Speaking of sprays, it is interesting to note that the first time chemicals were used against plant diseases was in France on grapevines.

For training the vines see the chapter on pruning.

Harvesting and Storing

In harvesting grapes do not pull the bunches from the vine. Instead, cut the stem, leaving a stub about an inch long attached to the cluster. If not wanted for immediate use most varieties will keep for a week or more in the crisper pan of a refrigerator. For longer storage use varieties known to keep well such as Sheridan, Catawba, Alden, and Steuben, which last for several weeks in moist storage between 33 and 40 degrees.

I have had success prolonging the length of storage by placing clusters in individual small cartons and pouring vermiculite over them. This should be the coarser house fill grade, not the fine horticultural size. Vermiculite will absorb surface moisture without sucking the juice out of the berries.

Grapes for the South

Although some northern grapes, including the French-American hybrids, do fairly well in the South, they are seldom long-lived and production is low. Here they are called "bunch" grapes to distinguish them from Muscadine varieties. Best chances for success are at higher elevations in the south end of the Appalachians and Blue Ridge. They should be planted from early December until late March.

In lower altitudes only the Muscadine varieties can be relied upon. The Scuppernong, often thought of as a separate species, is only a variety of *Vitis rotundifolia,* the Muscadine grape. The flavor of these grapes is disappointing to those accustomed to Northern species, but loved by most Southerners. Damyankees condemn it as nothing but sweet juice with a musky taste. Once you accept it as a different fruit, you learn to love it.

There are both self-fertile and self-sterile varieties. The latter need one fertile pollinator for every six self-sterile vines. The following, all desirable varieties of good flavor, are self-sterile and need pollinators: Nevermiss Scuppernong, Creek, Higgins Bronze, and Hunt. Among self-fertile varieties that can be used as pollen parents are Cowart, Albemarle, Magnolia, Roanoke, Magoon, and Southland.

Southern growers of Muscadines are spared the pains of pruning. This type of grape is trained on arbors and keeps growing endlessly. I have seen one Scuppernong vine that was growing on a trellis that had been extended three times until it reached a length of 80 feet, at which point the owner cried "Enough" and kept pruning off the ends of the canes.

Muscadine wine is not bad. The flavor is mostly sweet and musky. I have even been introduced to Scuppernong brandy, a fitting companion for Kentucky Mountain Dew!

The vines are seldom cultivated, though I have seen a furrow plowed along each side of a trellis, intended to check too vigorous growth.

16

The Brambles or Cane Fruits

If it were not for the fact that among cane fruits we find the most delicious of all berries that can be grown in home gardens, few people would trouble to grow them. Their thorns alone would discourage most home food gardeners. Unless the bushes are pruned and trained carefully, gathering the berries can be an adventure in frustration.

All the difficulties of bringing a crop to maturity are forgotten, however, with the first taste of a fully ripened red raspberry or the robust flavor of a blackberry, so unlike the dry, bitter taste of what can be bought on the market that it seems like an entirely different fruit.

One advantage enjoyed by brambles is that they can produce over a longer period than almost any other group of berries. Beginning with the earliest fruits in June (along the southern limits of their range) regular raspberries continue to bear well into August, at which time the fall-bearing varieties begin ripening and carry on until frost.

The ease with which new plants can be propagated from a few purchased at a nursery is another advantage that appeals to those for whom the cost of a dollar a plant for a single raspberry means they must start small and increase their own. From suckers alone I was able to increase a dozen plants of Heritage fall-bearing raspberries to an additional 50 by the spring following planting. If I had had more time, by the use of leaf-bud cuttings I could easily have produced at least 200 more.

A real advantage that raspberries share with strawberries is that they bear a full crop the year after they are planted. Once in bearing they can be counted on for five or six years of full production. In the meantime a new row can easily be started from the old.

When all is said and done, flavor is by far the most convincing argument for growing all the brambles in home gardens. This is particularly true in the case of raspberries, whether they bear red, gold, purple, or black fruit. These are berries so succulent and delicate when fully ripe that in commerce they are picked before they are mature. Too, because they cannot stand handling, only dry, firm varieties are grown commercially, which are a far cry in flavor from the tender home varieties that drip juice if barely squeezed in picking.

If anyone needs to be convinced that there is a vast difference between home-grown and the commercial product, let him plant a few bushes of Fall Gold, a new everbearing raspberry introduced by the University of New Hampshire. Its extra-large berries are rich gold in color and are produced from July until frost without a break between the summer crop and fall. In flavor nothing I have ever tasted can equal them. Pure ambrosia. It is treated as a red raspberry culturally.

The ease with which Heritage can be increased has already been mentioned. It is also by far the most outstanding new raspberry, with fruit of superior flavor, on healthy upright canes. The summer crop ripens in early July and continues for two weeks, with the fall crop beginning about September 1 and continuing until frost. If a heavy fall crop is wanted on one row, it can be cut to the ground before growth begins in spring, in which case there will be no summer crop. This is something to think about after you have increased the number of plants from those planted initially.

One of the best of the newer summer-fruiting red raspberries is Taylor, with delicious bright red berries over an inch long. It begins bearing right after the Fourth of July and continues for three weeks. It is first choice for a variety for a summer crop. If Heritage is cut down to increase yield in fall, Taylor would make a good companion variety for it.

Another fall bearer that produces a fair summer crop is Fall Red, a companion variety of Fall Gold. Although its berries are of high quality, its chief distinction is hardiness, having produced full crops after temperatures of 25 degrees below zero.

Although purple raspberries are not widely grown, to my taste they are superior to black cap raspberries and worth planting for their distinctive flavor. They are particularly delicious in jams and as pie filling. The newest variety is Clyde from the New York State Experiment Station. The berries are large, somewhat darker than a medium purple in color, highly flavored, and tart. They ripen in mid-July.

Of the varieties already mentioned, all will do well north of a line from southern Iowa east to southern Connecticut. South of that line raspberries are generally unsatisfactory, except at higher altitudes.

Along the East Coast, where temperatures fluctuate widely in winter (usually referred to as the Middle Atlantic area) varieties hardy in the north may not do well. The Maryland Experiment Station has been breeding for this area and has introduced Reveille, a red raspberry that has proved too soft for commercial use but is unusually high in quality and perfect for home garden use. It is very early. Two other Maryland introductions—Citadel and Scepter—are of good quality. Citadel is a summer variety, late midseason and highly disease-resistant. Scepter bears a spring crop in July, with a fall crop in early September.

Raspberry and Blackberry Culture

Except for Clyde (purple) and Fall Gold (yellow), which require the same treatment as do red raspberries, they differ from black caps and purple varieties largely in the method of propagation and in the pruning required. Red raspberries are propagated from suckers that develop from the roots, at times much too abundantly. In either spring or fall suckers can be cut off from the mother plant and lifted with as much of the root system intact as possible. If planted immediately they are almost certain to take off and grow. Red raspberry plants ordered from a nursery should be soaked overnight before planting to be sure the roots and bark are moist. If soil with considerable clay is available, make a slurry or thin paste of this and dip the roots in it before planting.

Set the plants about an inch lower than the soil level shown on the roots. The distance apart for planting depends on the system used for growing. One, and the easiest to use until the plants begin to matt together, is the hedge row. Set the plants about two feet apart. If more than one row is planted, space them six to eight feet apart. The soil should be prepared deeply and fertilized beforehand with a slow-release fertilizer at the rate recommended by the manufacturer.

If possible avoid soil infested with Canada thistle and quack grass. These pests are difficult to hoe out when they grow in a row of brambles. Cut back newly set brambles of all types to within 8 inches to 12 inches of the ground. The first season, regular cultivation, as shallow as possible to avoid injuring roots and suckers, is important. If compost or other organic matter was plowed under before plants were set out, no further fertilizer will be needed the first year.

After the first summer's growth, the following spring, remove all but four or five of the most vigorous canes. Those left should be cut back to remove any winter-injured wood at the tips. Just how much depends on the vigor of the variety. Too much removed will not improve the size of the fruit, and it will reduce the size of the crop. Some canes should be left four feet tall; vigorous varieties can be left at six feet.

Most home gardeners will find it easier to grow all raspberries and erect blackberries on the hill system rather than on the hedge row. This means that each plant stands apart in the row so that it can be cultivated on all sides rather than just along the row. Red raspberry plants are set six feet apart, with six feet between the rows. My own experience has been that even varieties with stiff upright canes are better off if supported along the row with two wires on each side attached to stakes at the end of the row. If you have ever tried to prune cane fruits on a windy day in spring, the value of restraining the waving canes will be obvious.

Some growers depend on individual stakes for each plant, which works well, but it takes more work tying up long canes to these stakes.

An important problem to consider when buying planting stock of brambles is virus disease. At the great Beltsville Station of the U.S. Department of Agriculture, scientists have learned that all raspberries might be infected with virus diseases that produce no visible symptoms but can cut production as much as 50 percent, reduce plant vigor, and can be transmitted to other healthy plants. To be safe plant only stock that is clearly identified as virus-free.

This does not remove all danger from infection, however. Aphids can carry the disease as can leaf hoppers. Even when virus-free stocks have been planted, if any raspberries are growing within 1,200 feet of your planting, there is a chance that an infected leaf hopper or aphid might reach your healthy plants.

In spite of this problem raspberries are worth the risk, since even infected plants will usually produce some fruit.

Blackberries can be planted about three feet apart in the row. Thin out the first spring as recommended for red raspberries, but wait to head back the canes that are left until they have made strong growth. If these are cut back about six inches in late June or early July, this will force lateral fruiting branches and increase the crop.

The fruiting canes of brambles are annual, that is they only bear a crop once. If left they may survive and send out laterals that will fruit weakly, but if they are cut to the ground once they have borne fruit, they will be replaced by strong young shoots that will bear much more fruit. In the hedge-row system remove all the weak and short canes that were not cut away after fruiting, leaving only strong, vigorous canes spaced about six inches apart. In the hill system leave six to eight strong canes to each plant.

An exception must be made in handling everbearing red raspberries. The same cane that bears the summer crop will also fruit again in fall. Hence the canes should not be removed after the summer crop has been gathered, but only after the fall crop is stopped by freezing weather.

Bramble canes are tough and the right tools will make work much easier. For small cuts, hand pruning shears are satisfactory and if stiff leather gloves are worn, can even be used to cut out entire canes. However, if any number of cane fruits are grown, a long-handled lopping shear is a back saver.

A special tool is a bramble hook, which is a knife mounted across the end of a long shaft and worked by holding the knife against a cane and pulling toward you. A search of American catalogs has failed to turn up a source, but a blacksmith can usually make one to order.

One important point is to be sure that when you use a bramble hook, it must be sharp and free from rust. Otherwise you can pull out an entire plant by the roots.

Black and purple raspberries are allowed to grow until early summer or late June in most areas. The blacks will be about two feet tall, at which time the tips of the canes, not more than three inches long, should be nipped off. Purple canes are more vigorous and should be topped at 30 to 36 inches. Any canes less than half an inch in diameter should be cut away at this time. All other vigorous canes should be left, since brambles of this type are able to produce fruit on about all the canes they send up.

By this time of the year both will have produced strong lateral branches. Laterals on black caps should be nipped back to about eight inches; the purples can be left as long as a foot.

Other Berries

In Southeastern and Southwestern United States, boysenberries, dewberries, youngberries, and loganberries replace blackberries of the North, which many gourmet gardeners consider an improvement, while others find their flavor less brisk and tangy than erect blackberries. These are actually crosses between native blackberries, dewberries, and raspberries, which are not hardy North. Like the Northern dewberry, they are scrambling vines rather than cane bushes.

Although I consider the dewberry not worthwhile where erect blackberries can be grown, this cannot be said of dewberry hybrids such as the boysenberry. The one problem is that they make such rampant growth as to make growing them on stakes difficult. They are sometimes grown on two or three wire trellises like grapes, with the long trailing branches tied to the wires. An easier way I discovered when growing them in the Midwest (a difficult thing at best), was to train them on top of a flat trellis resembling a table. This was in sections covered with chicken wire, three feet wide and eight feet long. Set on wooden horses so they could be lowered for winter protection, these panels were spaced between plants so the vines could be brought up over them for the summer. This spaces the plants eight feet apart.

In winter the horses were removed, the panels lowered to the ground, and the vines protected with a layer of straw or hay. In mild climates where winter protection is not needed, the wire panels could be fixed permanently.

Grown in this way the fruit is kept off the ground and ripens better. Little pruning is needed except to thin out the vines when they become too thick. Then all but the strongest four or five canes can be left, cutting away all the rest. Heading back the long canes before growth starts in spring may be needed if they pile up over the next plant in the row.

Nothing has been said about dewberry varieties other than the western hybrids, because nurseries don't seem to handle them. Vines can be collected from the wild if the special flavor of the dewberry is wanted. If possible mark superior vines during the summer fruiting season, to be dug the following spring just as growth begins.

Up to a few years ago I found that this method made it easy to pick out superior erect blackberry plants from the wild, often better than the old Eldorado cultivated variety. Alfred was a good variety with superior flavor but has all but disappeared because of its susceptibility to orange rust. The variety Darrow, named for the great small fruit breeder of the U.S.D.A., has proved so superior that I can find no other varieties listed today. It has a concentrated blackberry flavor that makes it outstanding.

If only the new Thornfree blackberry introduced by the U.S.D.A. were hardier! Anyone who has struggled through a thicket of thorny wild blackberries (as I do every summer) will appreciate the delightful experience of picking berries from thorn-free vines. Unfortunately, Thornfree is not reliably hardy much north of a line drawn from Chicago to New York City. Its flavor is a shade less perfect than Darrow, yet better than most wild berries.

Insect and Disease Controls

In the case of brambles little or no hybrid breeding has been carried on for resistance to insects and diseases. All are subject to infection by anthracnose, but the most seriously affected are the black caps. On highly susceptible varieties anthracnose can kill canes right down to the ground. In less susceptible black caps the canes may suffer winter injury. During hot weather the berries may shrivel.

Blackberries and dewberries are also susceptible. Only the shoots that produce berries are affected. They shrivel and the crop is ruined. During dry spells the leaves also may dry up on badly infested plants while healthy canes do not shrivel.

Red raspberries are attacked on the bark, which turns gray. Pit lesions on the bark form round or oval dead spots. I have seen no direct report on Benomyl as a control, but because of the fungi it does kill, it should be tried. Sulfur is sometimes recommended, but burns all brambles. Ferbam and Captan are safer. These should be applied about the time leaf buds are opening in spring. Plants grown in hills are less susceptible than those grown in hedge rows because the sun has a better chance to reach the fungi.

Since the disease winters over on dead canes and foliage, sanitation is the best control. Cut down canes that have fruited as close to the ground as possible. Burn the canes and rake up foliage and burn it. Spraying the soil with Captan or Fermate after the harvest is an excellent control measure. Since black raspberries are most seriously attacked, only varieties with some resistance should be planted. Jewel from the New York State Fruit Testing Association has been the most resistant variety, not only to anthracnose but all other serious diseases of cane fruits. Huron is another resistant variety. The varieties Dundee and Bristol are widely grown because of their vigor and resistance to disease. The best-flavored black cap I have tasted is Allen, which has been disease-free wherever grown. This would be my first choice where only one variety is grown.

Crown gall and cane gall are about the only other serious diseases on raspberries. Although these bacterial diseases also attack blackberries and dewberries, they do not seem to affect either fruit production or the vigor of the plant.

Crown gall forms lesions on roots; cane gall affects stems. The bacterium that causes these galls enters through breaks in the bark. Pruning wounds are one source of entry. Since there is no chemical cure, sanitation is the best control. Most reliable nurseries discard any plants showing signs of infection, but a second inspection when planting is desirable. Soil insects, especially white grubs, feed on roots, opening up lesions where crown gall bacteria can enter. Treating the soil for grubs with Chlordane or arsenate of lead is desirable if planting in old sod.

Orange Rust

Blackberries and dewberries are often attacked by a spectacular orange-colored rust. Early in spring, usually about the first of May, small yellow spots develop both on the upper and lower surfaces of new leaves. These develop into lighter-colored patches that soon erupt into striking bright orange areas. Once a plant is infected it is never cured and should be killed at once. Cut off all canes and leaves and burn them. I find that the easiest way to kill the roots is to carry an oil can filled with a strong solution of brush killer and to squirt this on the tips of the cut-off canes. The variety Darrow seems to be resistant to orange rust.

Insects

Rose scale infests red raspberries. It is a reddish insect that covers itself with a waxy coating, under which it lays eggs in fall. They are protected under the wax until spring, when the eggs hatch into minute crawlers that penetrate bark with their sharp beaks and start sucking. They cover themselves with a waxy coating in a day or less. They are easily killed with Malathion at this stage, but this is a matter of finding them within an hour or two after hatching. A much easier way is to spray the dormant canes with a dormant oil emulsion just before they leaf out.

Dormant oils should be applied when air temperatures can be expected to remain above 45 degrees for at least eight hours after spraying. If chilled the oil emulsion may break and the oil separate out, injuring bark and dormant buds. Above 45 degrees the oil will continue to evaporate and is gone within eight hours.

In some parts of the country the red-necked cane borer is a serious pest. In winter examine canes for swollen areas, which may be from one-half inch to one-and-a-half inches in diameter. Slit these open and they will contain an ivory-colored slender grub about one-half inch long. During the month of May these develop into bluish-black beetles about one-quarter inch long. The name *red-necked* comes from the forepart, which is a rusty red.

In June the beetles deposit eggs under the bark, which hatch into the grubs that cause swollen areas on the bark.

The simplest control is to cut out all infected canes and burn them as soon as the swellings occur.

17

Gooseberries and Currants

Although these two valuable small fruits are often lumped with the brambles under the label "bush fruits," they need to be considered separately because of serious limitations to their culture, both legal and climatic.

Because gooseberries and currants are closely related and require the same culture, the French lump them under the name groselles. About the most important way groselles differ from brambles—blackberries and raspberries—is that the canes or brambles bear only for one year and are then removed, while the fruiting branches of groselles can be left for three years or more and will still bear.

Both gooseberries and currants are fruits for the connoisseur. They practically never show up on supermarket counters, except for an occasional box of currants at a fancy price. As for gooseberries our family has been able to buy them only twice in the past several years, and those that were available were unripe hard green bullets, so acid that they needed twice as much sugar to make them palatable as would have been needed for berries ripened on the bush.

Few Americans have ever tasted the true flavor of a ripe

gooseberry unless they grew it at home. This is a fruit that thrives only in a limited area of the United States and really comes into its own north of the Great Lakes in Canada. If grown farther south than central Illinois, Indiana, and Ohio, it will barely survive in full sun. It is one fruit crop (along with its companion currants) that thrives in light filtered shade. Farther north, it will thrive in full sun if nights are cool.

In England, where the gooseberry is considered a choice fruit, it is served in many ways unknown to American cooks. It appears on the table as a sauce with meats (particularly pork and game), as tarts, puddings, jams, gooseberry fool, and gooseberry catsup. I have even had it served to me as breakfast fruit with sugar and cream. When fully ripened, the big English type of gooseberry was delightful.

What makes America's neglect of this fruit inexcusable is that our gooseberries are superior in flavor to all but the top few English varieties. The British gooseberry is larger and often more colorful than ours but lacks the sprightly flavors of ours. Too, English varieties are usually badly infested with mildew.

In America the gooseberry does have one major handicap that severely limits its distribution—it is an alternate host to white pine blister rust. If you live less than 1,000 feet from a group of five-needled white pines, in many states you will be forbidden to plant either gooseberries or currants. In others a substantial number of white pines within 200 miles of your garden will mean a similar ban.

This disease, a fungus that forms blisters on infected trees, propagates from tiny spores that form inside these blisters. When the blister explodes, it releases millions of these spores that are so light they can be borne for 200 miles on the wind.

When they light on other white pines, they are incapable of causing harm. If, however, they happen to light on a currant or gooseberry bush they form pinhead-size blisters in clusters on a background of yellowing leaf tissue. These release spores that are wet and sticky and cannot be carried much farther than 300 yards. If there are no pines within 1,000 feet, currants and gooseberries are not dangerous to pines, although they themselves can be infected by the spores from pines.

States in which white pines are important timber and ornamental trees have strict laws governing the planting of
groselles. The laws vary from state to state, but to order gooseberries or currants by mail without first consulting the law can
lead to trouble and loss of money, since most states will destroy
plants they consider dangerous to white pines. The following
states are those where you may need a permit to bring them in:

California	Massachusetts	Oregon
Connecticut	Michigan	Pennsylvania
Delaware	Minnesota	Rhode Island
Georgia	Montana	Tennessee
Idaho	New Hampshire	Vermont
Illinois	New Jersey	Virginia
Kentucky	New York	Washington
Maine	North Carolina	West Virginia
Maryland	Ohio	Wisconsin

In spite of the complications in growing groselles, once they
are established and growing, no small fruits are more satisfying. To recommend varieties of gooseberries is difficult, since
the only three offered in American catalogs are Poorman, Fredonia, and Pixwell. Pixwell is closest to the wild gooseberry,
smaller in size but excellent in flavor. Its name comes from its
habit of fruiting. The berries are produced along the underside
of the fruiting branch and can be stripped readily. But wear
gloves; the branch is not thornless.

Poorman is the largest-fruited and perhaps best-flavored of
all American varieties.

Fredonia originated in America but is of the English type with
very large, dark red berries of delightful flavor. If space permits, grow all three.

Domestic varieties of red currants are less susceptible to
white pine blister rust than are gooseberries and not all states
ban them, but consult authorities before planting them.

Among currants, varieties are almost as limited as in gooseberries. I happen to be lucky in that I acquired a grand old
variety, Cherry, when buying our summer home in Maine. It is

rarely offered today, largely because it is less hardy than most. It survives on our island largely because we are less than 50 miles from the Gulf Stream and seldom experience zero weather. As a variety for similar climates, it is superb.

Red Lake, Minnesota 71, and Perfection are offered by some dealers, along with White Imperial, about the only white variety in American commerce.

To even mention black currants is likely to bring down on my head the wrath of disease-control authorities, since these are without doubt the most dangerous of all carriers of blister rust. Most American nurserymen have given up growing them. Nonetheless, for those who have acquired a taste for this odd-flavored fruit, they long for it with nostalgia. The flavor is unusual, musty, yet rich. Some claim the berries have a "buggy" odor, but those who love it will go miles for a small basket to make black currant syrup and jam. About the only way to acquire it nowadays is by finding someone who has a bush and making your own cuttings.

Plant Culture

The culture of groselles is simple. In warmer areas plants should be set where they have light-filtered shade most of the day but direct sun for an hour or two in the morning and again in the evening. Set the plant so the stems are covered to about an inch deeper than they grew in the nursery. Groselles need a moist soil at all times. They prefer a clay loam soil, yet will grow in anything but sandy loam.

Groselles produce their best fruits on two- and three-year-old wood. You can tell the age of branches by color. They grow progressively darker with age. Any wood over three years old should be cut away after the harvest is over. An easy way to pick currants is to cut out the berry-laden three-year-old branches and sit down to strip them. Do not, however, do this with two-year-old branches. They will bear your best berries the following year.

Groselles are heavy feeders. Use compost, if you have it, in preparing the soil. Remember that a planting can last 30 or 40 years, and you won't be able to work up the soil again for that length of time. A feeding with a good mixed fertilizer after the harvest is over will feed the bush while it is setting buds for next year's crop.

Propagation by Rooting Cuttings

Softwood cuttings are easy to make, but rooting is less than 25 percent. Even so, it pays to cut off tips about five to six inches long in mid-August and root them in a shaded cold frame. With nursery stock high in price and going higher, this is one way to increase the size of your plantings without cost.

Groselles go dormant earlier than do most woody plants. In making woody cuttings, wait until after a light frost and cut away any extra first-year shoots you can spare. The plant does not need more than five or six such shoots to renew itself. Cut the shoot into six-inch-long pieces and tie them in bundles. Bury them in slightly damp peat moss or sawdust in as cool a spot as possible but not so cold that it freezes. Bury the bundles with the lower end up. In time a callus will form on the upper end. In spring line out these callused roots with that end down, leaving two or three buds above ground. In time you will have small, sturdy bushes for either extending your planting or replacing poor plants.

Fall planting is best for groselles because they start growing earlier than most woody plants. Nurseries carry plants in cold storage for spring planting, but this must be done as soon as the soil is workable. Out on the Great Plains where fall and winter are apt to be dry, spring planting is preferred.

Best spacing is four feet apart in rows six feet apart. If all the weak canes are cut out in May, this will usually get rid of the borer, perhaps the most serious insect pest. Malathion, Methoxychlor and Sevin will control most insect pests other than the borer.

18

Blueberries as a Home Fruit Crop

No one can deny the appeal of modern cultivated blueberries. Distinct in flavor and texture, they add variety and interest to the fruits that many can gather from back-yard gardens. Unfortunately, among home fruit crops, there have probably been more failures with blueberries than with any other bush fruits.

This is not a sign that they are difficult to grow, but it does mean that they have definite requirements that must be met. Unless they are met, blueberries sulk and refuse to produce the huge crops of luscious fruit so temptingly pictured in books and articles.

When conditions are right, no crop (unless it be wild blackberries) is easier to grow. On our summer island off the coast of Maine, we must leave unpicked most of the fruit from 20 acres of low-bush blueberries that have never been sprayed, fertilized, or cut back. The other side of the coin is my experience in trying to grow high-bush-cultivated varieties in the Midwest. After years of struggling to keep soil acid enough to keep them happy, I gave up. The handful of berries they yielded wasn't worth the effort.

183

My recommendation is that unless you live in natural blue-berry country, don't try to grow them unless you are willing to spend at least five times as much time, effort, and money on them as would be needed to grow grapes, strawberries, black-berries, raspberries, or almost any other fruit crop. Be prepared to fight off robins and starlings; for some reason blueberries are particularly attractive to birds in areas where this crop is not commonly grown, perhaps because in blueberry country they can find all they can eat in the wild. This calls for caging or netting the bushes if you are to harvest the scanty crops they might produce.

For those who live where they thrive, blueberries can be a delight. Perhaps they were granted this crop to compensate them for the trouble they have trying to grow other crops that need a sweeter soil. That blueberries need acidity is a funda-mental fact. They demand a pH of 4.8 or less, a reading so low few other food plants will thrive. Although lowering the acid-ity by adding sulfur can be done, this is not permanent. Earth-worms will bring in lime (they line their burrows with a paste made with lime). Water drainage can upset the gardener's efforts to keep soil acid. So will watering from city water mains in limestone regions or where some methods of softening water are used. If your soil does not test higher in pH than 5.5, it can be made suitable for blueberries by using peat moss along with dusting sulfur to reduce pH readings to below 4.8. In limestone areas my advice is brief: Forget blueberries.

The regions where blueberries grow naturally and where they are cultivated as a commercial crop occupy only about one-sixth of the country, fortunately with much of this area in the populous Northeast. Seven native species account for most of the berries harvested from the wild, but of these only three are important. The low-bush blueberry, of which there are no cul-tivated varieties, dominates an area from Minnesota to Maine south to the Pennsylvania-West Virginia line. Although it is by far the most important source of canned and frozen berries for the market, it will not be discussed further. If it does well in your area, all that needs to be done is to cultivate what plants exist, keep weeds and other growth from crowding, and feed every year or two with a high nitrogen fertilizer as soon as the berries are picked.

Blueberry Varieties

The principal cultivated blueberry is the high-bush variety, which grows well from the center of the Maine coast in a narrow strip along the Atlantic down to North Carolina. South of this area it has been challenged within the past two decades by outstanding hybrids between the high-bush and the rabbit-eye blueberries developed at the Georgia Coastal Plain Experiment Station. The original rabbit-eye species is still grown but lacks the quality of the newer hybrids.

In the Pacific Northwest and as far south as San Francisco the evergreen or box blueberry is native. Its fruits are edible but of lower quality than modern high-bush and rabbit-eye hybrids. Gardens from the Oregon-California line south would do well to use the rabbit-eye hybrids, while in the Northwest, modern high-bush varieties are already well established.

The High-Bush Varieties

When considering varieties, attention must be paid to the need for pollination. Blueberries are not self-fertile; at least two varieties must be planted. Among high-bush varieties recommended for as far south as North Carolina, the following are outstanding and are listed in the order of their ripening:

Earliblue. This is usually the first variety to ripen, and for an early variety, unusually good in flavor, mild and sweet. It is superior to Weymouth, which has been the leading early berry in the past.

Collins. This is an improvement on Ivanhoe, previously considered the best second-early variety. The fruit is highly flavored with a sweet but mild sub-acid taste, which most people prefer.

Blueray. Richly flavored second-early variety that is unusually vigorous in growth and hardy wherever peaches survive.

Bluecrop. Of the same breeding as Blueray, it follows that variety in order of ripening, and if anything is hardier. A high-quality variety.

Berkeley. This variety has the most beautiful berries of any blueberry. The flavor is mild and sweet (some think it is too bland). It is a shade less hardy than the varieties already mentioned.

Herbert. The best berry to prolong the picking season as it ripens 25 days after Earliblue. It is by far the best-flavored of the late varieties and a heavy producer. It has better flavor than Coville unless the latter is allowed to ripen fully.

Coville. For those who want to hang on to fresh blueberries as late in the season as possible, this is the variety to include in any planting. It is a full month later than Earliblue. Unless allowed to ripen fully on the bush, it is quite tart, which is not a disadvantage when used in muffins or pies, but not too desirable when eaten fresh.

Rabbit-Eye Hybrids

Woodward. One of the newer varieties and one that sets fruits early. One of the best for flavor.

Tifblue. The most popular and widely planted of the rabbit-eye hybrids. The flavor is outstanding. Does well throughout the area where these hybrids are grown.

Southland. Not only a quality berry in flavor, but ripens its fruits over a long season.

Homebell. Should be one of the varieties in every planting because of its value as a pollinator. The berries are of high quality but are too soft to ship well. It has stayed in the nursery trade in spite of its rejection by commercial growers because it is perhaps the best all-around variety for home fruit gardens. The bush has more of a spreading habit of growth than other rabbit-eye hybrids and is often used in shrubbery borders.

Blueberry Culture

Both the rabbit-eye and high-bush blueberries thrive under the same culture. High-bush varieties are slightly more sensitive to pH, but even the rabbit-eye hybrids do best if the soil is below a pH of 5.0. A peculiarity of both types is that they prefer ammonium sulfate as a source of nitrogen over all other chemicals. In tests this fertilizer has produced yields as high as four to five times that of nitrate of soda. Blueberries will thrive in soil as high in organic matter as half peat moss.

Organic gardeners are pretty well limited to cottonseed meal, which is a complete fertilizer for this crop. Mature plants need about half a pound of cottonseed meal, half applied in April or early May, half in late June. If the plants are mulched with pine needles, leaf mold, or well-rotted compost, they should need no other feeding. First-year plantings need about half the amounts used on mature plants.

When using ammonium sulfate as a fertilizer, a mulch such as recommended for use in organic culture can supply much of the food needed, but on sandy soils a light application of acid-soil fertilizer such as is recommended for use on azaleas and rhododendrons may be needed for heavy fruit production. Half a pound of ammonium sulfate on old plants, a quarter of a pound on newly planted bushes. Again, on sandy soils, more acid-soil fertilizer will be needed.

The condition of blueberry roots when planting is highly important. They do not produce root hairs but rely on certain fungi called mycorrhiza, which serve in absorbing food elements from the soil and passing it on to the plant. If the root dries out too much in shipment, mycorrhiza can be killed. It is a good idea to soak the roots for an hour or so before planting and to protect them from drying until in the ground.

The earlier they can be planted, once the soil is workable, the better. Even if late snows drift over the newly set bushes, this will do no harm.

Soil moisture is highly important. High-bush blueberries are actually swamp plants, but this does not mean they can survive with their roots under water. In swamps they will be found growing on hummocks or raised mounds that are kept constantly moistened by water rising up into them from below. If submerged, blueberry roots lose their mycorrhiza and die.

This means that the soil in which they are planted needs to be filled with peat moss or some compost with an acid reaction, such as rotted pine needles. Try to keep the soil moist but never soggy. This calls for near-perfect drainage.

In planting, the roots must not be set too deeply. The upper roots should not be more than an inch below the surface. Water in with a solution of an acid soil fertilizer dissolved in water, about a handful to a ten-quart pail. Be sure the acid fertilizer does *not* contain aluminum sulfate; this can damage both roots and mycorrhiza.

Trying to grow blueberries without a mulch is asking for trouble—and extra work. The most practical and the easiest mulch to find nowadays is sawdust. But if used without treatment, as sawdust breaks down the bacteria at work will rob the soil to satisfy their appetite for nitrogen. Use about a pound of ammonium sulfate to a bushel of sawdust to provide them with the nitrogen they need. A four- to six-inch layer of sawdust will keep down weeds, hold soil moisture, and provide ideal conditions for growth. Don't worry about the difference between sawdust from pine or other softwoods and that from oaks or other broad-leaved trees. Either will do.

When setting the plant, cut off the upper half of all the branches. This removes the fruit buds, which should not be allowed to bear the first year. No further pruning should be needed until the third year when weak, bushy growth at the base of the stems should be cut away. In following years pruning should consist of removing old stems or parts of stems that have lost their vigor. Also remove the thin, bushy growths that accumulate on older bushes.

The lighter you prune, the smaller berries will be and they will mature later, but the yields will be higher. If size is not important, as when berries are wanted for pies and muffins, light pruning can be practiced. When big berries are wanted early, prune heavily. Pruning can begin as soon as the leaves fall after frost and can be continued up to the time flower buds show on the bushes in spring.

Insect and Disease Controls

Insect pests are few, but the cranberry fruitworm and the blueberry maggot are most likely to be serious. Because of rapid changes in clearances for plant-protection chemicals no recommendations can be given but your county agent or state agricultural station can advise you.

Stunt is a virus disease for which no cure is known. It dwarfs the plants. The leaves cup and become mottled. If the plant produces berries, they are small and worthless. As soon as an infected bush is detected, it should be dug up and burned.

Mummy berry is a fungus disease in which the berries do not ripen but turn gray and shrivel. If infection is widespread, the mulch should be removed, the soil sprayed with Captan, and the old mulch replaced with new. This should be done before the plants blossom. Infection comes from old mummified berries that have dropped to the soil.

Other Blueberries

Dryland Blueberry. This is sometimes called low huckleberry and has not been cultivated to any extent. It does hybridize with the high bush, but no work has been done to improve this species as a garden plant. Those gardening in mountainous areas from Georgia to the Pennsylvania line might find breeding better varieties from native berries an interesting hobby. Since both parents have good flavor, a really desirable fruit might result.

Evergreen Blueberry. Commonly called huckleberry in the Pacific Northwest, the berries are inferior in flavor to both high-bush and rabbit-eye hybrid blueberries, which will survive in the same area. As a cash crop for subsistence farmers, the evergreen blueberry has advantages. Its foliage is in big demand by florists, for which purpose it is harvested extensively. The fruit is edible but has a strong musty flavor that many find unpleasant.

Mountain Blueberry. The berry of this wild species is the best-flavored of any of the wild blueberries of the Pacific Northwest but is not very productive and is not grown under cultivation. Its pear-shaped fruits are juicy, highly flavored, and somewhat tart but refreshing. It has the advantage of tolerating drought and dry soils better than any other species, and should be interesting to use as breeding material.

19

The Stone Fruits:
Peaches, Plums, and Cherries

Anyone who has gone farm hunting north of the Ohio River will recall that every old-time farm, whether still under cultivation or abandoned to the weeds, had a few ancient apple trees near the barn, with perhaps a single pear to keep them company.

Seldom will you find peaches, plums, apricots, cherries, or nectarines. Because they were short-lived, farmers neglected them; so they rarely survived. These fruits, some of the most delicious morsels the home garden and subsistence farmers can grow, deserve better treatment. No one who is familiar only with the commercial peach as sold in mass-merchandising outlets has ever tasted the heavenly flavor of that fruit as picked fully ripened in the sun and eaten within a few hours.

One reason for the lack of peaches on old farms is the short life of the tree. Once it comes into bearing, unless grown under good conditions, it seldom lasts more than seven to ten years.

Neglect of hardy apricots has robbed home orchardists of one of Europe's favorite fruits.

Now that hardy Manchurian apricots are available that will survive at 20 to 25 degrees below zero, more home orchardists and farm families can enjoy the fruit that some claim was the "apple" that tempted Adam. Here is a fruit that, when dried, is almost too powerful in its intense, rich flavor. Eaten fresh, it is a true luxury fruit that sells for as high as 85 cents a pound in city markets. Ripening during the last half of July, apricots come at a time when no other tree fruit competes directly with them.

America's neglect of plums is difficult to understand. This is one fruit that actually improves in flavor when canned. Whether canned plums are like wine and improve with age would be difficult to prove. We found, however, that a jar of Green Gage seemed even richer than when first canned when we discovered it hidden back of later harvests five years after it was processed.

Anyone living where sweet cherries can be grown is missing an opportunity by not planting these delectable fruits. I have seen more than one person, unfamiliar with the special flavor of a tree-ripened sweet cherry, sit down and consume half a pound at a sitting, almost unconscious of biting into cherry after cherry. As for sour cherries the only reason apple pie is America's favorite dessert is because there aren't enough sour cherry trees to meet the demand. Any real cook would welcome canned or frozen cherries in place of stored apples as filling for pies.

Peaches

If space is limited and only a tree or two of stone fruits can be planted, the peach will probably be given top preference, except where temperatures of ten degrees below zero occur. Two varieties that will tolerate 20 to 30 degrees below zero are available for colder regions. Dwarf peaches are available, but these are budded on sand cherry rootstocks and are so short-lived as to be not worth planting. The New York State Fruit Testing Association previously mentioned is budding them on the Nanking cherry, which is longer-lived but difficult to produce.

Since the Nanking cherry is a large shrub rather than a tree, there is a constriction at the union. This might seem to be a drawback, but actually holds back plant foods in the top longer, which means larger fruits. The one precaution is to not let the tree overbear; June thinning is desirable.

Peaches have a slip bark, which means that the bark on both stems and roots bruises easily and separates from the wood. For this reason they should be planted only in spring, so that injuries (sometimes not visible) will have a chance to heal before the tree is subjected to winter cold.

Most stone fruits are attacked by borers. These do not, however, pose the threat they once did. I can remember my father carefully examining peach trees at regular intervals for the purpose of discovering borers at work. Their tunnels could be detected by the debris they threw out. When found, they were killed by probing in the tunnel with a wire. Today, spraying four times at two-week intervals, beginning on June 1 to 15, will catch both the peach tree borer and the lesser peach tree borer.

Since both may be present, the trunk should be sprayed carefully at ground level and spraying continued up the trunk until the scaffold branches begin. The chemical to use is Malathion, one of the safest sprays available to home gardeners. If, however, you are using a mixed fruit tree spray sold for general fruit tree spraying, check the formula; if it contains Malathion it will control borers along with other pests if the bark is wetted when spraying.

These general sprays containing Malathion can also be used on other stone fruits.

Practically all peaches as shipped by nurserymen are only a year old. Two-year-old trees are usually too big to transplant well, with big roots and tops that need severe cutting back when planted. So-called bearing age trees are a poor bet. When planting, all branches are cut back to stubs with two or three buds each. Unless you are planting dwarf trees on *Prunus tomentosa* rootstocks, space peaches 15 to 20 feet apart. Dwarf peaches make small specimens, more like bushes than trees. Twelve feet between them is enough.

When peach trees have been growing for about five to six years, they should be cut back severely to keep them from growing too tall and to renew the vigor of the old wood. They can be cut back by removing all wood produced in the two previous years.

If the spring bloom has been killed or branches killed in winter, this same treatment may be needed on younger trees to maintain vigor. It is better to lose a season's fruit than the entire tree. Following a severe winter, a tree can leaf out weakly and grow all summer, but die the following winter.

Varieties

Reliance. This variety is mentioned first because of its high resistance to cold. It has fruited after three days of temperatures down to 25 degrees below zero. The flavor is only fair, but when compared with the bullet-hard peaches sold in markets, it is ambrosia. It is a perfect freestone, bright yellow with a red cheek. Ripens in mid-August around Lake Ontario.

Madison. Hardy and will fruit if temperatures do not go lower than 15 degrees below zero. The quality is better than Reliance, and while my own tree of this variety has survived 18 degrees below, it did not bloom. It ripens in early September. Freestone. Yellow-fleshed.

Prairie Dawn. Another cold-resistant variety, somewhat hardier than Madison. Slightly less flavorsome, but still a good quality peach. Yellow flesh. It is a clingstone variety, which some would consider a disadvantage. For those who love canned clingstone peaches and who live in cooler climates, it might be food for the gods.

Sunhaven. Another "snow bunny" that has borne peaches after 16 degrees below but did not do so at 19 degrees below. This is about the earliest of the hardy peaches, ripening 40 days before Elberta. A quality peach but a semi-clingstone, sweet and fine-grained. Yellow-fleshed. Fruits are about 80 percent red, suggesting its Redhaven parent.

Redhaven. One of the most important varieties from the famous peach-breeding program of the South Haven Experiment Station in Michigan. A yellow freestone of high quality, almost entirely red in color, it is a favorite market variety. It can only be appreciated, however, when grown at home and allowed to ripen fully on the tree. It can be left unpicked longer than any peach, clinging to the branch even when fully ripe. Reasonably hardy. Ripens a full month before Elberta (early August).

Champion. Perhaps the last of the old white-fleshed peaches and should be in every orchard where more than two or three peaches are grown. There is a distinct aroma and flavor to white peaches that makes them something special. Freestone. Ripens about August 15. Too tender as a commercial shipper; handle Champion delicately.

Richhaven. Another excellent peach from Michigan, a yellow freestone that resists browning. Flavor is superb when fully ripe. Tree is hardy to 19 degrees below zero; flower buds survive down to 10 degrees below. Ripens in late August, nearly three weeks before Elberta.

Elberta. Only mentioned here because it is usually the only variety offered in garden centers. Might be desirable if peaches for canning are wanted. Freestone. Quality only good.

Belle of Georgia. Some rate this as the best-flavored white peach. The flesh is somewhat firmer than Champion so that it cans somewhat better, but for fresh use, my vote is for Champion. In spite of its name, is hardy in New England.

Harbinger. One of the earliest of all peaches, ripening late July in some areas. It is tree-hardy down to 20 degrees below zero; flower-bud hardy down to 15 degrees below. A yellow-fleshed, yellow-skinned peach with about a ten percent red cheek. A clingstone.

Harvesting Peaches

Even home orchardists are apt to harvest peaches much too soon. Any trace of green on the skin, except perhaps in one of the white-fleshed peaches should signal that it is too green to pick. A thumb pressed into the skin indicates full maturity. Of the varieties mentioned, Reliance and Champion need special care in harvesting because they are soft-fleshed and bruise easily.

Plums and Prunes

Although all prunes are plums, not all plums are prunes. Hence the need to treat them separately. In favorable areas for sun-drying, as in California and the arid Southwest, prunes can be preserved for winter use by dehydration. Elsewhere, special treatment will be needed. Ask your county farm adviser (usually located at your county farm bureau) for directions, or write to the Agricultural Extension Service at your state college. They can supply information on making driers, treatment, etc.

America is particularly fortunate in the variety of plums and prunes that can be grown here. Three types, the European, the Japanese, and the American or native varieties, are available in all but the coldest parts of the United States. For northern Maine, upper Michigan, and Minnesota, only the hardiest varieties, mostly of American origin, will survive and bear fruit.

The plum and prune are cultivated much like peaches and need the same protection against borers.

Hardiest Varieties for Cold Climates

Sapa Plum. This is actually a hybrid between a true plum and a western bush cherry. It is self-sterile and needs a Western bush cherry for pollination. Fruit is small with a pit that is even smaller in proportion. The flavor is delicious. The color is a rich Burgundy red. Somewhat tart for eating fresh but makes appetizing pies and sauces. Usually bears the year after planting in late July. Clingstone; hard to pit.

Sapalta. A cherry-plum like Sapa but sweeter and more of a freestone. Larger. Best pollinator is the following variety. In season in midsummer.

Compass. Fruit slightly smaller than Sapalta but needed as a pollinator for that variety. Excellent deep red fruits make delicious preserves and pie filling.

Purple Heart. Bred in New Hampshire, this bears somewhat larger fruits than the above. Extremely hardy with rich red fruits that are sweeter and juicier than most other plums in this class. The small pit makes it excellent for canning.

Underwood. Large reddish-bronze fruits in mid-August that are delightfully sweet and juicy. Perhaps the best-flavored plums for Northern regions. Is not self-fertile; plant with the following as a pollinator.

Toka. Red-skin and yellow-flesh fruits ripen in late August. The sweet flesh has a slightly spicy tang that makes it different.

Superior. Similar to Underwood. It is a cross between a hardy native plum and the Burbank plum from California, but it is fully hardy in the North. Superior to the rather insipid Burbank flavor. An August bearer.

Mount Royal. Hardy well into Canada, this resembles the high-quality European plums in flavor. Bright blue color and excellent flavor. It sets fruit without a pollinator.

Pipestone. One of the largest-fruited plums that can be grown in the North and of high quality. Ripens in early August. Makes a bigger tree than most plums.

Stanley Prune. The hardiest of the true prunes and the only one recommended for growing in the North. It is excellent for eating fresh as well as for canning and drying. Freestone. Bears in late August. Needs no pollinator.

Japanese Plums

Many of these are almost hardy enough to belong in the above class, but do best slightly south of the area where "toughie" varieties are needed. They ripen somewhat earlier, usually in early August. Plant two varieties; Japanese plums are self-sterile.

Early Golden. The earliest yellow Japanese plum generally available. Quality is fair. A better plum when named and distributed is New York 1502. It matures slightly ahead of Early Golden and is of better quality. It remains in good condition on the tree for two weeks after ripening.

Shiro. The best of the yellow Japanese varieties. I like it because the tree is lower-growing than other plums. Sweet and good.

Santa Rosa. Considered to be the best plum originated by Burbank, fruits are deep red in skin and flesh, and of good quality. It is not quite as hardy as other Japanese varieties. During the test winter of 1933-34 in southern Vermont, trees suffered severe kill-back of branches but recovered after pruning the following spring.

European Plums

In Europe plums are considered a gourmet's fruit and many superb varieties are available. No one can claim to have eaten plum jam at its best until he has tried one made from the variety

Mirabelle. Some gourmets who prefer a more tart jam or jelly, swear by that made from the true Damson, quite unlike the honey sweetness of Mirabelle. The contrast between these two choice fruits is an indication of the variety of flavors available, differences that make the plum one of the most delightful of all fruits. Although called European, many varieties originated in the U.S.A.

Stanley & Fellembery. Since a home gardener would find no difference between these two varieties, they are described together. Both are true prunes and over much of the United States have replaced the older Italian Prune. Both bear richly flavored bluish purple large fruit, delicious for eating fresh, canning, or drying. For my money there is no finer fruit pie than one with either of these prunes (used fresh, of course) as a filling. The juice is pure ambrosia. Both varieties are self-fertile. Ripen in early September.

French Damson. The largest of the true Damsons with fruits about one and a half inches in diameter (large for this type) with the typical brisk, tart flavor that makes this plum so desirable for jams and jellies. Fruits in late August. Other Damsons equally desirable for preserves, but usually measure about one inch in diameter.

Golden Transparent Gage. A delectable plum with the true rich Gage flavor, golden yellow with tiny red spots, ripening in early September. The tree is semi-dwarf in habit. Be sure to allow it to ripen fully and it will be a delightful plum.

Green Gage. Ripening about a week before the above variety. European plum connoisseurs consider this the finest of all. Fruit is only medium in size, yellowish-green in color with light red mottling. Not prepossessing in color, but one bite will convince you that it is a quality variety.

Laxton Gage. It is the best-quality early variety of the Gage family. In the Michigan fruit belt I have seen it fully ripe the first of August. Not too heavy a bearer but most welcome in its season. The tree tends to grow tall.

Red Gage. Also called Reine Red since it is identical to the famous old plum Reine Claude in every way except that it is a late red variety ripening in mid-September. Typical Gage flavor. Reine Claude is another name for Green Gage in France.

Bradshaw. One of the most beautiful of all European plums, with rich, deep purple fruits in late August. It is best as a dessert fruit eaten fresh. Canned, it loses flavor.

Cherries

Sour Cherries

The old test for a prospective wife ("Can She Bake a Cherry Pie, Billy Boy?") sums up the affection many Americans have for the sour cherry. In pies, cobblers, tarts, and crèmes, probably cherries are rated only slightly below apples as ingredients in desserts. A limiting factor in their availability is temperature. Unlike apples, they are fussy about long, hot summers. Where winter temperatures are high for short periods, the flower buds become active and are killed when the thermometer drops. If they are planted in the South, they only thrive at higher altitudes.

Their blossoms are even more subject to injury by low temperatures in spring than are peaches, because they tend to start growing during warm spells in late March and are killed by freezing that might occur later. Rapid changes in winter can cause serious bark injury.

In spite of these drawbacks a sour cherry tree or two belongs in every home orchard where cherries survive. The trees are hardier than the blossoms. If they can bear about two years out of three, they will pay their way in some of the most delightful fruit that can be produced in the home orchard.

Sour cherries are in season the last of June and the first of July. All cherries draw birds like flies to honey; so be prepared to fight for your crop. The Ross GroNet, mentioned in the chapter Tools and Other Equipment, is available in lengths up to 75 feet. It can be thrown over a cherry tree to keep out birds. Even robins, which seem to defy anyone to protect a cherry tree, will not venture *under* a net to feed.

Another way to keep away robins, if nothing else helps, is to shoot a bird or two and hang it by one leg to a branch. Although shooting song birds is illegal, it is permitted if they are destructive to crops.

Montmorency. Chances are that you will find no other sour cherry listed in most catalogs. Early Richmond and English Morello are so much like Montmorency that there is little to choose between them. As a result, either by agreement or chance, the two latter varieties seem to have disappeared but are still good if you find them listed. All are self-fertile and need no pollinators. English Morellos have one advantage; they are semi-dwarf where space is limited.

North Star. An important variety where space is limited, as well as for colder climates, this dwarf sour cherry originated in Minnesota. It is a true dwarf; the original tree never grew taller than six feet. It will fruit farther north than any other variety. It is self-fertile and produces cherries larger than Montmorency or than one of its parents, English Morello. It is in season from mid to late July. A perfect pie cherry.

Another futile search was for any listing of the Duke varieties, which were favorites in Grandfather's day. True, they were difficult to bring into fruit because the early-flowering Dukes needed sweet cherries to pollinate them, and the later varieties would only set fruit if pollinated by sour cherries, but once you found the right combination they were truly delectable in flavor when eaten fresh. They lacked the almost-too-tangy flavor of the sour varieties and the milder sugary taste of the sweets. They are still to be found in specialists' catalogs, but be sure you ask for the name of the proper pollinator.

Sweet Cherries

Not only are sweet cherries less hardy than sour varieties, their culture is further limited by the fact that all sweet cherries are self-sterile and need another variety to pollinate them, but not any other variety will do. For example, the leading commercial variety, Bing, is self-sterile and in addition, will not set fruit with pollen from Lambert, Napoleon, or Emperor Francis. Similar behavior in other sweet cherry varieties means that at least two trees that are known to be good pollinators must be planted, since there are two different types of sweet cherries. These are the "Hearts," which have soft flesh, and the Bigarreaus, which are firmer. Merton Bigarreau will pollinate most of the sweet cherries in commerce, but not Windsor, Van, and Venus. Two varieties widely planted as pollinators are Sam and Van, both originating in British Columbia.

The need for planting at least two varieties, plus more if you want variety and a longer harvest period, plus the lack of winter hardiness make sweet cherries not too good a crop for the home fruit gardener. At the same time the fruit is so delectable that many who have the space are willing to do the necessary sorting out of varieties.

Bing. The workhorse of the sweet cherry industry. Cherries are large mahogany red, firm in flesh, thick, crisp, and juicy. Its balanced flavor—high in sugar but also high in acid—gives Bing a distinctive, tangy flavor. Ripens in midsummer, but for home orchards ripens all at once; so the picking season is short. Not hardy much below zero.

Lambert. Trees are hardier than Bing, fruit is slightly softer, juicier, and milder in flavor. A more reliable grower for the non-expert. Fruit ripens a week later than Bing but remains in good condition longer.

Black Tartarian. Probably the most widely grown cherry in the world and the standard variety for early crops. It is not too hardy if fall freezes catch it with foliage still succulent. Because of its high flavor, it remains a favorite in spite of its faults.

Early Rivers. Apparently a seedling of Black Tartarian but firmer and earlier. Preferred for the earliest sweet cherries.

Sam. Mentioned as a good pollinator, Sam is also a desirable, firm, large black cherry of excellent flavor. It flowers profusely and sets more fruit than it can mature. In spite of a heavy June drop, it is highly productive. (It is such a vigorous grower that every spring when I return to Maine, I expect it to be winter-killed, but apparently it matures wood early enough to escape.) Ripens early.

Van. Much like Lambert but less susceptible to cracking and a more reliable bearer. Fruit is black. It is much later in season than Sam. The fruit is of high quality, black with an attractive sheen. One of the hardiest sweet cherries.

Nectarines
Nectarines are actually peaches without fuzz and their culture is

the same as other peaches. The smooth skin makes them more subject to insects that feed by puncturing, which in turn means they are more subject to brown rot. If, however, a mixed fruit spray, such as those sold by every good garden center, is used according to directions, brown rot should not be a problem. Since all nectarines are self-fruitful, a single tree should be enough for a family. The flavor is slightly different from that of a peach and adds variety to any home orchard where space permits.

Nectacrest. This variety has white flesh with perhaps the best flavor of any nectarine. Ripens in early September just before Elberta peaches. Hardy to about ten degrees below zero.

Cherokee. Although the flesh is slightly coarse grained, this variety has a sweet, rich flavor that makes it particularly welcome in its season. It ripens about August 1. Tree is hardy to about zero. Semi-cling.

Lexington. Desirable because of its hardiness to 15 degrees below zero. Flavor is sweet, rich, and tangy. Semi-cling. Ripens with or slightly ahead of Nectacrest.

Surecrop. Perhaps the most reliable of all nectarines. Fruits are large, white with a red overlay. Flesh is tender, freestone with a delightful, sprightly flavor. Its pink bloom is an attraction in spring. Self-fertile.

Apricots

Once strictly a fruit for areas where temperatures did not drop much below zero, apricots can now be grown in areas where readings of 20 to 25 degrees below might occur. Two varieties from the University of Minnesota were produced by crossing high-quality American apricots with a Manchurian species of miserable flavor.

Although all stone fruits need a location that protects them from too-early blooming, this is particularly important with apricots because they are the first of all to bloom. If at all possible, plant them on a north slope.

Moongold. A University of Minnesota variety that has borne fruit after 20 below. The light gold-colored fruits are smaller than American varieties but have a true apricot flavor. They are freestone. Self-sterile. Plant the following variety as a pollinator. Ripens in July.

Sungold. Fruits are deeper and richer in color than the above variety and ripen about a week later. The flesh is closer to a true apricot color than Moongold, juicier and mild.

Alfred. Fruit is larger in size than either of the above, fine grained, juicy, sweet, and rich. It does not need a pollinator. Ripens in early July. One of the hardiest American varieties but not as hardy as Farmingdale.

Farmingdale. Originally I ordered Alfred, which was out of stock, but received Farmingdale as a substitute. It has proved hardier (down to 15 degrees below). It ripens in late July or early August. The fruit is larger than that of Alfred, sweet and rich. The one fault is that it must be watched carefully as the fruit is soft and has a tendency to crack if heavy rains occur at harvesttime. Nonetheless I prefer it to Alfred.

Moorpark. For those who live where temperatures as low as zero are rare, this is by far the choicest apricot to grow. Fruits are extra large, freestone, sweet, and tender.

20

Tree Fruits:
Apples and Pears

When I recommend growing tree fruits in home gardens, a common remark is, "Why bother? I'll be dead before they produce any apples."

This remark by a man or woman of 40 reminds me of a delightful trip I had around Long Island with one of America's great nurserymen. Henry Hicks was then pushing 90, but still operating a nursery. Everywhere we went, we saw some of the finest gardens on the North American continent, with exotic woody plants. Whenever Henry saw a tree or shrub that was rare, unusual, or outstanding for its kind, he would try to gather seeds or berries for propagating superior plants for his customers.

Many of the species he intended to propagate would take 20 to 50 years to reach maturity, yet he felt compelled to preserve outstanding specimens for future generations.

Fortunately the home fruit grower of today does not have to wait a decade or half a century for the fruit trees he plants to come into production. Instead of standard trees of the past, he can now use the same varieties of apples they produced, but grown on trees propagated on a dwarfing rootstock that will begin bearing in two or three years. Recently I set out apples grown on M-M 106 rootstocks that bloomed the following year but did not set fruit. The second year they bore enough apples for a generous sampling.

A common mistake is to think that dwarf trees bear smaller fruit. Actually it is usually larger, since thinning for fruit size is much easier with dwarf trees. By spacing the apples on the branch, nipping out those that would otherwise be small even after ripening, specimen fruits can be produced that would be difficult or impossible with a standard tree. The effect of root-stocks is also to increase fruit size. Pears on quince roots are noticeably larger.

The advantages of dwarf trees are so important that today many commercial orchard operators are using them. For example, they occupy less space so that more trees can be crowded onto an acre. The production per tree may be lower, but by the acre is substantially greater. Equally important, because the dwarf trees come into bearing sooner, as many as four full crops can be harvested before standard trees would begin to produce.

The saving in labor when pruning, spraying, and harvesting is enormous. A friend who operates a 160-acre orchard told me that even the savings in insurance on his help was a factor in his decision to switch to dwarf trees.

The most spectacular use of dwarf trees is in Holland, where a special dwarfing rootstock allows the grower to plant over 600 trees to the acre, instead of 55 standards. Such intensive culture is, of course, beyond the skills of most amateurs but does illustrate that dwarf trees do grow good fruit.

Many of these innovations in fruit growing took place in the years following World War II. Although dwarf trees have been known for generations, the widespread use of a series of root-stocks developed at the Malling Station in England sparked a new interest in their possibilities. The station propagated hundreds of apple rootstocks that had been used in the past, along with new varieties, and compared their good and bad qualities. Of these the most striking was one named Malling 9, which produced a tree no higher than a man. A tree grafted onto Malling 9 will begin fruiting a year or two after planting. It is still used but has one serious fault. It makes such a weak union with the variety grafted onto it that unless kept tied to a stout, tough stake it is likely to snap off in a stiff wind.

I once had an orchard of ten trees on Malling 9, which I dug up and gave to a friend. His experience is interesting as a lesson in dwarf tree culture. Thinking to brace the trunks, he planted them with the graft union six inches below the surface. This supported them well, but since the scion or top part of the tree was in contact with the soil it took root and grew to near normal height for that variety. Of culture, more later.

A fascinating new Malling stock is M 27, which is even smaller than M 9. It will probably be available about 1978 or 1979. Commercial growers are looking forward to growing apples on bushes when this is available.

A rootstock used widely in Europe that is becoming popular in the United States is M 26, which produces a tree two or three feet taller than M 9, but still easy to cultivate without a ladder. It is hardier than any of the other Malling stocks and survives well into Canada. Staking is wise, although it is better-anchored than M 9.

The variety M 7 produces a tree about half the height of a standard tree, but it needs to be cared for on a ladder. I would not recommend it for the home garden and only mention it because it is sometimes sold for that purpose.

Even newer in the nursery trade are the so-called Malling-Merton rootstocks, which were developed as improvements on the original Malling varieties by workers at the Merton Station in England.

My personal preference among all dwarf stocks is Malling-Merton 106. Although it is slightly larger than M 7, it can be kept down in height by the use of spreaders (sticks that force the branches to grow horizontally). It is much better anchored than any of the rootstocks already mentioned. Most important, stocks available are virus-free. It does not sucker, a fault with others of these special understocks. Best of all, it is resistant to the woolly apple aphid, which is a harmful pest the world over.

In my judgment M 26 would be a second choice when MM 106 is not available. Where space is limited, M 9 can be used, but only if a two-inch by two-inch stake four feet long, driven two feet into the ground at the time of planting, is used to support it. This should either be of cypress or some other durable wood, or treated with Penta at least a month before use and allowed to air dry. This stake must be left in place for the life of the tree. Few people realize what leverage there is from the top on the graft union in a high wind.

Unless you want your dwarf tree to grow into a full-sized space hog, you must plant it with the graft union (a knuckle where the straight root joins the trunk at a slight angle) at least an inch above the ground. Otherwise the top will form its own roots and grow to full size.

It may seem as though I am putting too much emphasis on the use of dwarf trees, but I know that full-sized apples or pears are seldom given good care once they reach maturity. Another rea son for dwarfs is that three or four trees can be planted in the same space as a single standard. Any home food garden should contain at least three varieties of apple—an early season, a mid-season, and a late season. This may not be possible if space is limited, but is a goal to try for.

Although I am not too keen about the so-called five-in-one trees, which are budded to five different varieties on the same trunk, they are one answer to the problem of producing an assortment of apples rather than just one. Perhaps my objection to this type of tree is that one of the varieties is certain to be Red Delicious, a variety that has killed an appreciation of true apple flavor in America.

Spacing of dwarf trees varies with the rootstock used. M 9 can be planted as close as six feet apart in rows 12 feet apart. M 26 is usually planted ten by eighteen feet. MM 106 does best 14 feet by 22 feet.

Siting the Orchard

All things being equal, a slight slope to the north is best. Such a site is cooler in spring so that blossoming is held back enough to escape some late spring frosts, which can kill newly opened flowers. The slope also drains off colder air, which can make a difference of a few degrees in temperature during such frosts, often enough to save that year's crop.

If space is limited and the area devoted to orchard is on good garden soil, the area between rows can be used for growing catch crops of vegetables. If they are kept within bounds by tilling close to the plants, gooseberries and currants will also do well, even after the trees have reached maturity, since they will bear in light shade. The tilling necessary to keep them within bounds cuts production somewhat.

There are three ways to solve the problem of weed control. Many orchards are grown under sod, with the grass mown regularly. Some growers feel that when grown under sod the trees are not likely to grow too big. There is danger of nicking the tree trunks with a mower unless care is used. Bruises can develop into rot.

Clean cultivation is also practiced but means going over the soil regularly with some tilling device.

My preference is for a heavy mulch surrounding the trunk for a distance of three feet or more on all sides of the trunk. The area outside the mulch can either be tilled or kept mowed. I find mowing easier to maintain than tilled soil. One danger with a mulch is that unless the trunks are protected against mice these pests will move in and set up housekeeping. I wrap the trunks with aluminum foil to a height of three feet, which protects against both mice and rabbits, unless snows are deep, in which case the foil must go high enough so a rabbit cannot reach bare bark.

In rich soils fertilizing might mean too much lush vegetative growth, but few soils are in that class. An average feeding for 100 square feet of area under the trees would be about 10 to 12 pounds of a fertilizer containing 10 pounds of nitrogen per 100 pounds, such as 10-6-4. This should be applied in early spring; late applications may prevent fruit from coloring.

If this does not keep the foliage a good dark green color during the summer, double the application the following year. The best placement of this fertilizer is under the drip of the branches, not around the trunk.

All fruit trees are sensitive to wet feet; never plant them in ground where water stands for long periods. Good drainage is more important than the type of soil, although light, sandy loams are usually too dry for best results.

Apples

Varieties to Plant

This is probably the most difficult decision to make. Much fuss has been made about old-time varieties as superior to modern apples sold in stores. I must admit that among old-time apples many stand out for their distinctive and unique flavor. I am thinking of a summer apple that is all but impossible to find nowadays, which often matures in late July. Called Irish Peach, it is close to the ideal apple flavor with just the right blend of tartness and sweetness.

Yet among old varieties there are just as many vapid, uninteresting apples as can be found in today's catalogs. I am remembering Chenango Strawberry, a variety that may have been the parent of Red Delicious. For about two weeks in fall, it is delightful with a mild, yet slightly tart flavor, but once its brief season is over, it is punky and a disappointment, both in flavor and texture. If there is room to spare in the home orchard, I would personally like to have a tree of Chenango Strawberry, but I have already planted 15 other apples and plan to set out a dozen more that I would rate as more desirable.

There is an unsolved problem in the nursery trade—how to let prospective home orchardists actually taste the apples they hope to plant. Catalog descriptions are of little value. I once suggested to the late Paul Stark, Sr., that what should be done for prospects is to sell a box of a dozen or more varieties to allow them to sample those they had in mind. Such a box even at a fairly high price would be a good investment. After all, planting an apple, pear, plum, peach, or apricot and growing it for three or four years before it fruits, only to find you don't like it, is an experience worth avoiding.

One fact to keep in mind about old varieties, if you are tempted to invest in them, is that about half of those that have survived were originally selected because they were sweet. They were intended to be cooked for sauce or baked in pies and tarts, using as little as possible of "boughten" sugar. Unless you are a lover of sweet apples, select with care.

This somewhat lengthy description of the pitfalls in buying old-time varieties will explain why the following list avoids any attempt to recommend such varieties. Listing is in order of ripening, with earliest varieties first.

Summer Apples

NJ 36. I must explain that I have not tasted this apple, but it is from one of the leading apple-breeding stations in the United States. It's located in New Jersey. It is said to be better-flavored than July Red, an apple I have in my orchard and that is quite good for so early a variety.

Lodi. This variety replaces an old favorite, Yellow Transparent, which it resembles, but is healthier, more vigorous, and bears more regularly. An excellent early cooking apple that is good to eat right off the tree if fully ripe. An apple tree of this type probably should be in any collection of more than five varieties, but the season is short, as are most early summer apples.

Quinte. One of the earliest red apples to ripen. The flesh is rather soft but of very good quality. The tree is a regular bearer. A better apple than July Red.

Jerseymac. For those who like the McIntosh flavor here is an apple with even more of the McIntosh sprightly flavor and ripens a full month before that variety. It is a soft apple and bruises easily, not a drawback in an apple for home use. It reminds me of the old Fameuse or Snow apple touted so highly by old variety fans. I find Jerseymac a better apple.

Ozark Gold. I happen to like Golden Delicious even though it is a sweet apple and I prefer them tart. Ozark Gold ripens three weeks before its Golden Delicious parent but is a shade below it in quality. Still it is probably the best yellow among early fall apples.

Jonamac. A cross between two of our best commercial apples—Jonathan and McIntosh. It is superior to McIntosh in flavor, ripens ten days earlier and is a more uniform red in color. I don't pay too much attention to color except that if an apple excels in this quality, it doesn't hurt to have one with eye appeal. Jonamac is one of the better early fall varieties.

Macoun. Many orchardists consider this the highest-quality dessert apple that can be grown in Northeastern United States. It is a McIntosh type, about the same season, but a better apple. It needs hand thinning or fruit may be small.

Empire. Mentioning McIntosh as often as is necessary to describe present-day apples is a bit monotonous but cannot be helped, since 75 percent of all the good dessert apples today are crosses with that variety. Not only does Empire have high quality (nearly as good as Macoun) but it keeps longer in storage than other McIntosh varieties.

Holly. For those who like the Red Delicious flavor, here is an apple with better texture and more juice. Although it is similar to Red Delicious in flavor, it is slightly more tart. It does not become as mealy in storage as its parent. The color is its biggest asset—the bright red of the holly berry.

Jonagold. Here is an apple that is hard to fault. Some call it the best-flavored new apple of the 20th Century. The flavor is outstanding—just the right blend of acidity and sweetness. It is a big apple. It is of no value as a pollinator but needs outside pollen to set fruit. What this means is it should not be planted if your home orchard consists of only two trees. In such an arrangement only Jonagold would set fruit. In a group of three or four trees, it should be a first choice. Not only is it excellent as a dessert apple, but it also is rated high for use in cooking. In 35-degree storage it will keep until spring. color is bright scarlet stripes over a yellow ground.

Jonathan. Not a new apple by any means, but for those who like an apple that wakes up the taste buds, there is nothing better than a Jonathan. Its fruits are small and dark but still sparkling red. Flesh is crisp and juicy. Unfortunately in recent years the variety Melrose is being substituted for it, even on the market and marked as Jonathan. Melrose is a better keeper, but not one-two-three with Jonathan in flavor.

Golden Delicious. Being phased out in home gardens by Jonagold and Spigold.

Spigold. Much of what has been said of Jonagold could be repeated about Spigold. Both do not produce fertile pollen; so they cannot be planted alone or as the only two varieties in a home orchard. The fruits are among the largest of all apples on the market. It is about 75 percent red striped over a clear yellow base. It is a cross between two top varieties—Golden Delicious and Northern Spy.

Old Apples

I may be playing the coward by being unwilling to make recommendations of old-time varieties, but discretion is the better part of valor. My own experience has been disappointing in running down a variety highly touted by some gardening friend, only to find it tasting like a woolen mitten. An old friend, the late Lewis J. West, was a true old-variety enthusiast with a home orchard of over 100 trees. Out of 25 varieties several of us sampled one autumn day, I would give top marks to only three, with six or seven more that would rate better than McIntosh or Jonathan.

For those who still want to try the oldies, let me list three possible sources:

Southmeadow Fruit Gardens, 2363 Tilbury Place, Birmingham, Michigan 48009. The owner sells no trees but provides scions to a commercial grower of some 300 choice varieties of apples, including some modern commercial varieties that he feels rates with the old. Also lists hundreds of older peaches, grapes, pears, etc. I am reassured by the fact that he rates Jonathan among these. Catalog is one dollar and worth it as delightful reading, including history of old varieties.

J.E. Miller Nurseries, Canandaigua, New York 14424. An important grape nursery that also lists 14 of the best-known older varieties, including the 16th Century French variety, Summer Rambo. Catalog is free.

New York State Fruit Testing Association, Geneva, New York 14456. This is a cooperative organization dedicated to the dissemination of new fruits, but it has had so many demands for old varieties that it propagates 15 varieties on semi-dwarf rootstocks. You can become a member for an annual fee of four dollars, refunded if you order from the catalog. The Association is conservative in its descriptions; only one of the 15 varieties listed is rated "best quality."

One of the most important collections of old apples is owned by the Worcester County Horticultural Society, 30 Elm Street, Worcester, Massachusetts 01608. More than 60 varieties are listed by the society. They do not sell trees, but they do offer scions for grafting, which is one way to improve an old orchard that exists on a farm you buy.

Scions cost very little as compared with present-day prices for one- and two-year-old trees. Directions for grafting will be found at the end of this chapter.

Disease and Insect Control for Apples

This is a problem for which no general directions are possible, since the most important pest, the codling moth, might produce two broods a season or only one, depending on where you live. It can vary as much as a month and a half in hatching in spring; so only your state experiment station is able to tell you the right time to spray. If apples are an important crop in your area, they will maintain a codling moth watch, advising apple growers when to apply sprays to kill them. Get on this list; it will help you produce clean fruit. For control of fire blight, see information under Pears.

Over much of Northeastern United States, inexperienced apple growers are alarmed when they see their trees shedding immature fruits. Under some weather conditions and on certain varieties, this drop is so heavy that it seems no apples will be left to mature.

This shedding is perfectly natural and is known as June drop. Unless the immature apples are spaced farther apart than two inches, it is helpful rather than harmful. Some varieties tend to set so heavily that even after the June drop they will be too closely spaced. Unless further thinned by hand, fruit size will be seriously reduced.

If the June drop continues year after year, possibly drainage is too sharp and the soil dries out too much. This is a difficult condition to correct, since it means trying to incorporate heavy amounts of organic matter into the root area. Heavy mulching is sometimes enough to check loss of soil moisture. For a tree or two in a home garden, irrigation with a hose can be tried.

Espalier Trained Apples

The idea of an orchard of carefully trained and disciplined trees growing on a stone wall is tempting to many amateur gardeners, but unless you want to make a career out of their care, don't try it. Actually this is a poor way to grow fruit over most of the United States. In northern France and Germany, where the summer sun is not as hot as it is here, growing trees against a stone wall (which absorbs heat and helps keep the trees warmer at night so fruit will ripen) can cause injury to bark, leaves and fruit buds if used here.

Take it from someone who has managed by hook and crook to make these trained trees bear fruit; no matter how striking and artistic they may be, the time, energy, and money spent on them is not worth it.

An example of the difficulties encountered is that of timing the essential cutting of the branch leader. It took me several years to learn that this had to be done between July 1 and July 15 in my area, no sooner and no later. This varies with the location of the tree, earlier in the South and gradually later day by day as you move north, but by some twist of apple physiology, going up earlier in the Golden Triangle, the heart of Canada's fruit belt in southern Ontario. Other difficult cultural practices make espalier trees a type of culture best left to advanced amateurs.

Pears

Many gourmets consider pears the choicest fruit of all, a dessert that they can serve without apologies to the most critical of their friends. The fanciest pastry any Cordon Bleu chef can concoct must take second place to a fully ripened and chilled Beurre D'Anjou or Doyen du Comice pear served with cream cheese or a superb Brie at the end of a perfect meal.

Pears are much fussier about where they grow than are apples. They are less resistant to extremes of heat and cold.

Because of this, they do best in the milder climate of California and the Pacific Northwest. Although, by taking infinite care, pears can be kept alive on the Great Plains, they are hardly worth the effort. In the South about the only variety that does moderately well is Keiffer, a poor choice at best. Formerly the variety Conte was popular but has all but disappeared and as far as I can learn is offered by no nurseryman. Blight, always a threat to pears, is at its worse in the South.

One feature of pear culture that interests the home fruit grower is that the trees require far less care than do apples or other tree crops. Left unpruned they will still continue to bear. However, because many pear varieties tend to grow upright, training as recommended in the chapter on pruning tree fruits is important if you want to keep the trees low enough for picking without a ladder. As with dwarf apples, it is important to plant the graft union above the soil.

Pears are dwarfed by budding or grafting on quince rootstocks. Since many varieties do not unite well with quince, pears are double-worked. That is, the rootstock is first budded to a variety that knits well with it, usually Old Home. When this has grown for a year, it is in turn budded to the desired variety that forms the top and fruiting part of the tree. This leaves a short trunk of Old Home between root and top. Double-worked pears are offered by the New York State Fruit Testing Association.

Pear blight is a serious problem in growing pears. It is also called fire blight. It is a bacterial disease that causes the tips of branches and twigs to wilt suddenly, then turn dark brown, then black. They look as though scorched by fire, hence the name fire blight. Bark on the affected twigs turns black or brown, sometimes oozing a whitish gum. The gum is particularly dangerous because it contains spores that dry up and fly to other susceptible trees.

Some varieties are resistant or even immune to fire blight. Unless you are willing to spray for control, only resistant varieties should be planted. To control, spray with a streptomycin antibiotic spray called Actidione, an UpJohn product.

Fresh infestations may occur during the summer. If these appear, cut off the affected branch a foot below the lowest withered leaf. Dip the shears in a strong disinfectant (household Clorox or Purex bleaches are good) before making another cut.

Sometimes an orchard will go for years without any sign of this trouble and may escape permanently, but it is well to keep an eye out for this, the most serious problem with pears. In the following list of varieties, those partially resistant to fire blight are marked FBR. This is not a guarantee, however, that trees will not become infected under some conditions.

Varieties Available

Bartlett. Planted so universally that to omit mention of it would incur the wrath of many lovers of highly flavored pears. In the East it ripens in late August to September, in California and the Pacific Northwest from the last of June to September. It is not fire blight resistant but I once had a tree that became infected every year for ten years. By cutting out the blighted twigs and spraying with Bordeaux mixture (this was before the days of streptomycin) I was able to renew the top enough to harvest all the Bartlett pears we could eat.

Beurre Hardy. FBR. Greenish-yellow rather than the clear yellow of Bartlett when ripe. Somewhat less susceptible to blight. Some rate this with or above Bartlett in flavor.

Kieffer. FBR. If it were not so resistant to blight, no one would grow this inferior variety. All but worthless for eating fresh, but when canned it is often difficult to distinguish from Bartlett. This is a variety worth planting only if you intend to neglect your trees, or want pears only for canning.

Beurre d'Anjou. FBR. Although only moderately resistant to blight, Anjou (as it is usually cataloged in America) seems to recover well if this disease does invade and bears well. It bears large green fruits, which will keep in ordinary cellar temperature until January. It is hardy in southern Vermont. For its season, it is the only competitor of du Comice (usually sold as Doyenne du Comice, sold in fancy packs at Christmastime) in the East since that variety does not do well away from the Pacific Coast.

Max-red Bartlett. A variety I have not grown and have only tasted once, but so highly praised by many that it deserves mention. The flavor is definitely sweeter than the true Bartlett and the color is an all-over cherry red, unusual in a pear. Hardy to 20 degrees below zero. Self-sterile and needs a pollinator. A week later in season than its parent.

Clapp's Favorite. I have had conflicting reports on the blight resistance of this old variety. Probably it has considerable resistance. It ripens early, in mid-August, and in its season is perhaps the best variety available. It is one of the best pollinators for sterile varieties. The following variety, however, may be better.

Moonglow. FBR. Ripening two weeks ahead of Bartlett, this competes with Clapp's Favorite. It has an unusual flavor, both sweet and yet sprightly. It was developed by the U.S.D.A. for blight resistance. It is self-sterile and needs another pear to pollinate it.

Seckel. FBR. Perhaps the most delectable pear of all. Its bronze colored fruits are nuggets of pure flavor, but so small that they are frustrating to eat. It is perfect for pickling. At our house, fall is not complete until we have put up at least a peck of Seckels in sweet spiced vinegar. If you have room for only one pear tree, this is it. Ripens about Sept. 1.

Parker. This was developed as a pear that would be fully hardy in southern Minnesota. Not as good as Bartlett but does resemble it somewhat in flavor. In that area it ripens in early September. I have had no reports of its performance elsewhere, but it should be the variety of choice for cold climates.

Patton. Another University of Minnesota variety, similar to the above, but somewhat better in quality and about as hardy in the same area. A few days later in season.

Collette. A new patented variety. No information on its resistance to blight. It is remarkable because of its so-called ever-bearing habit. This should really be called "long-season" instead. Its fruits begin ripening about the end of August and continue maturing until frost kills the leaves. This would be a poor habit for a commercial variety, but desirable for a home orchard pear. If frost holds off in areas north of the Ohio River, this may mean pears until November. When canned it is superior to Bartlett, with a distinctive flavor. Eaten fresh, the flavor is perhaps better than any variety other than Seckel.

Beurre Bosc. Perhaps I should not comment on this pear, which I find undistinguished, but that many gourmets consider superb. It has about the toughest skin of any pear that keeps well. Unless fully mellow it is gritty and not too tasty. Because it will last in storage until March, it does have a place if your fruit garden will allow several pear varieties to be planted.

Conference. This is a tantalizing will-o'-the-wisp variety that I have always missed when visiting pear collections in which it was included. The late Dr. Harold B. Tukey, one of the great authorities on fruits, recommended it to me years ago as perhaps the best variety introduced in the 19th Century. Without a chance to taste it, I can only pass on this opinion from a man who knew his pears.

Duchesse D' Angouleme. FBR. Usually listed as Duchess in American catalogs, this is one of the great pears of France. On the Covent Garden in London, it is sold in great quantities in October and November. In flavor it resembles Doyenne du Comice, but it is a more reliable grower. Although it will not keep as long as Anjou, it is considered slightly better in flavor.

Aurora. This is a pear that I would prefer to Bartlett. It ripens a few days earlier, yet if picked at the right stage it will keep in a cool cellar until nearly Christmas. It is no more blight resistant than Bartlett, but many claim it is superior in flavor. The flesh is smooth, juicy, melting, and the flavor is sweet and aromatic.

Dumont. A delicious old French pear but has not been grown widely enough in America to test its blight resistance. It has a habit of alternate bearing on mature trees, but I am guessing if grown on quince rootstocks, perhaps with an Old Home interstem, this would be overcome. It is worth the trouble of coddling since it is rated among the top ten winter pears by connoisseurs. In America it ripens in the last two weeks of October and can be stored until the first of the year.

Sirrine. FBR. A high-quality dessert pear with a very sweet flavor and smooth, juicy flesh that is in season with Bartlett, resembles it, but is more resistant to fire blight. Commercial orchardists feel it may replace that variety.

Highland. Since this is about as susceptible as Bartlett to blight, its greatest value is that it ripens a month later. It can be picked a month before it ripens and stored as cool as possible, under which treatment it can be kept until January. It is a cross between Bartlett and Comice and is, if anything, better in flavor than Bartlett.

Harvesting Pears

This is one fruit that should not be allowed to ripen on the tree. If this is done, pears go off in quality so quickly that the season is too short. Instead they should be picked in a way developed by old-time French pear growers. They watch the fruit until there is a slight tinge of lighter green on the skin. Then they place a hand on the pear and raise it slowly from a vertical to a horizontal position.

Experience is needed to feel whether it is ready to be removed from the tree. There is an almost imperceptible feeling of separation of the stem that tells you that a pear has stored enough food so that it will go on and ripen after picking. If picked too green, it will not mature in storage.

Summer pears can usually be ripened on a kitchen counter, but those intended for later use should be wrapped carefully in tissue paper and held in a cool cellar until the first light color change has progressed and light pressure shows the fruit is ripe. In my experience a temperature of 40 degrees is better for storage than one of 33 degrees. For some reason I don't fully understand, fewer pears rot in the higher reading. Fully ripe pears should not remain in a refrigerator for much longer than overnight.

Budding and Grafting Pears and Apples

Although budding and grafting do require careful attention to details, they are not beyond the skill of amateur orchardists. Grafting consists of placing two separate parts of a tree, the rootstock and the scion or top part, in such a position that they can unite and form a complete new tree. The rootstocks used for dwarf apples have already been described. Also the method for grafting pears onto quince rootstocks with an intermediate stem has been mentioned.

For these operations to succeed, certain fundamentals must be observed. First, in order to insure clean cuts, all tools used must be razor sharp. Second, the cambium (a thin greenish-white living layer just under the outer bark) of both the scion and rootstock must be in contact. This is true whether the graft is made up in the tree where mature branches have been removed, or close to the ground.

About the only type of grafting attempted by amateurs is the cleft graft. As shown in figure 1, a branch is cut off squarely,

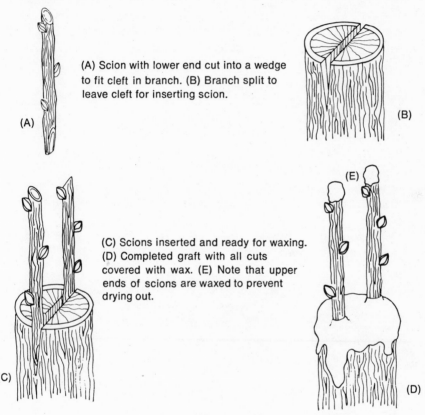

(A) Scion with lower end cut into a wedge to fit cleft in branch. (B) Branch split to leave cleft for inserting scion.

(C) Scions inserted and ready for waxing. (D) Completed graft with all cuts covered with wax. (E) Note that upper ends of scions are waxed to prevent drying out.

Fig. 1

exposing the cambium (B). Best success in getting the two parts to unite is with branches less than six inches in diameter. The stub left on the tree is then split down a short distance. There is a special tool made for this purpose, but for only a few trees a heavy old butcher knife or thin cleaver can be used. The important thing is to be sure that the cut is clean with no fuzzy edges.

Next, the scion is cut on the lower end in a wedge shape (A) and carefully inserted in the split (C). This is the tricky part of the operation; the cambium layers of both scion and rootstock must touch so they can grow into each other.

All cut surfaces of the graft, including the sides of the branch along the split, must be covered with grafting wax (D). Most garden centers and orchard supply houses carry grafting wax. If it can't be found (and at times this is difficult), you can make your own by melting together four parts of rosin, two parts of beeswax and one part of beef tallow. For the small amount needed in grafting a tree or two, music stores sell violin bow rosin. When thoroughly melted, pour the mixture into a pail of ice water and before it is cold, pull it like taffy. When ready for use, it will look about the color of Kraft paper.

Although there are many complicated types of grafts, the only one that is practical for top-working old trees is the cleft graft. As already mentioned, the cambium layer of the scion must be in firm, direct contact with the cambium of the cleft in the branch. In smaller branches up to one-and-a-half inches in diameter, use only a single scion; in larger branches two can be inserted.

In my experience branches larger than three inches in diameter make poor grafts. No matter how well the scions grow, there is always an unfilled space inside the graft. The only plant tissue holding the cleft together is the bark union at the cambium. This is amazingly strong but still weaker than a normal crotch on a branch. On larger branches the cambium and bark that forms over it are not enough.

Scions for grafting can be purchased for old apples (and some used commercially) from the Worcester Horticultural Society. They must be ordered early, as grafts should be made before growth starts in spring, just when the buds on the tree to be grafted begin to show signs of swelling.

If two scions are used, one should be cut away when the other is strongly fixed and growing well.

As soon as scions are inserted, they should be covered with grafting wax, leaving no opening for air to reach inside the cleft. One area often neglected is the upper tip of the scion, which should also be waxed.

Budding (figure 2) is a much more delicate operation than

grafting but more likely to succeed in the hands of an amateur. It is an operation at which the wife of a family is more likely to excel than are male members. One advantage to budding is that it is done in pleasant summer weather rather than on chilly spring days before the sap is running.

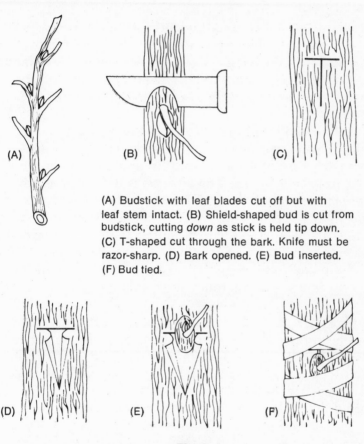

(A) Budstick with leaf blades cut off but with leaf stem intact. (B) Shield-shaped bud is cut from budstick, cutting *down* as stick is held tip down. (C) T-shaped cut through the bark. Knife must be razor-sharp. (D) Bark opened. (E) Bud inserted. (F) Bud tied.

Fig. 2

It calls for inserting a mature bud of the current season's growth under the bark of the rootstock. A bud stick is cut from a tree of the desired variety in July or August, or even in September in areas close to the Ohio River (A, B). It should be of the current season's growth with well-developed but fully dormant buds formed at the base of the leaf stem where it joins the main stem. The leaf stem should be left attached to the stick, but the leaf blade should be cut away. This leaves the stem as a handle so the bud can be inserted without touching the moist bark. As soon as cut from the tree a bud stick should be wrapped in a damp cloth to keep from drying out and taken out only to cut a bud immediately before inserting.

A trick used by professional budders is to hold the bud stick by the lower end, with the tip pointed down. Buds are removed by cutting upward, removing a shield-shaped piece of bark and a barely visible sliver of the wood. The art lies in cutting this so that a thin, wide surface of the cambium layer surrounds this bit of wood.

Before the bud is cut, however, a T-shaped slot is cut in the bark (C). If you are using a regular budding knife, it will have a bone or ivory tip on the handle, but for only a few buds there is no need to have this tool. The bone tip is used to carefully lift and spread the T-shaped slot (D) so the bud can be inserted (E). It is carefully pulled downward with the leaf stem as a handle until you can feel that it is in firm contact with the bare wood.

This step is critical. Be sure the bud is in place, then with a razor-sharp knife, cut along the cross-cut of the T so the upper part of the bud shield will touch the cambium of the rootstock bark.

Step F shows the bud in place and tied, but the inserted bud has not been fully covered. Professional budders can get away with this, but I prefer to leave only the bud and leaf stem exposed. The traditional binding material was raffia, with rubber budding strips now the standard. My preference is for strips of knitted cloth (old T shirts are ideal) rubbed with soft grafting wax.

The binding is left in place for three weeks. If the bud has not taken by that time, it probably never will.

All this may sound like a lot of fuss to the city gardener, but for anyone whose abandoned meadows are filled with volunteer apples, budding is an excellent way to develop an orchard at practically no cost. The fact that these volunteer trees were aggressive enough to survive is evidence that they should be good rootstock material.

If the bud does catch, it will not make growth that year, but the following year it will leaf out. When this happens, cut off the main stem of the rootstock tree about an inch above the bud site. Train the stem upright and it will become the trunk of a full-sized apple tree.

Budding can also be used to convert a worthless tree to one of a desirable variety by budding individual branches. This is a good way to make your own five-in-one tree of varieties you like rather than those selected by the nurseryman.

21

Pruning:
Discipline for Plants

Anyone who sets out to explain pruning faces a difficult task. This is one of the most puzzling of all cultural practices. In many cases, it is a self-taught art or a version of the old master craftsman and apprentice relationship. If at all possible, try to watch someone prune a tree or grapevine. Even this will be meaningless if he does not explain what he is doing.

Perhaps the most important principle to understand is this: If you don't know why you are pruning, don't. To whack away at a living organism that can't tell you when it hurts is almost certain to do more harm than good.

But why prune at all? In the wild, apple trees that are not pruned, yet bear fruit, often set more apples than on a tree in a well-cared-for orchard. What should be noticed is that these wild apples are small, poorly ripened, and worm-infested. Examine a wild tree laden with fruit and you will see that the apples are born in clusters, with two or three apples touching. Separate them and almost always there will be a worm hole from the side where a codling moth larva has eaten its way in rather than entering through the blossom end. This is only one of the effects of allowing fruit trees to grow without the discipline of pruning.

Pruning Apples and Pears

When a tree is grown under cultivation, the aim of the orchard owner is not to produce the most apples a tree can bear, but the most high-quality fruit it can ripen.

An important fact to keep in mind before you pick up a pruning shear is that what you do not cut away is just as important as what you remove. All too often, beginners think the removal of unwanted wood is the sole purpose of pruning. Before you make a single cut, examine the newly planted tree from a nursery. It should look something like figure 3A, unless you are planting a one-year-old whip. If the latter, let it grow for a year, by which time it will resemble that figure.

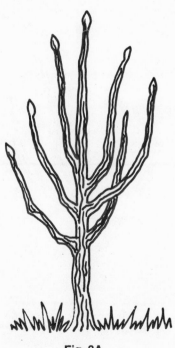

Fig. 3A

A two-year-old tree will probably have too many branches unless it is poorly grown. If all of these are allowed to grow the tree will be a mass of thin, weak branches. It will also have one stem that is taller than the rest. This is the leader, or trunk.

It differs from other branches in one important way. Certain growth-regulating substances called growth hormones are manufactured in the tip of the leader and are then moved down into the root, from which point they are redistributed to control the amount of growth made by the branches. If allowed to continue growing without a check, it will outgrow the lower branches. This reaction is called apical dominance. If the lower branches are to develop so that fruiting rather than vegetative growth of the tree is encouraged, apical dominance must be repressed. This can be done temporarily so the lower branches can become stronger by cutting off the leader, as shown in figure 3B.

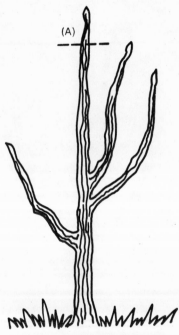

Fig. 3B

At the same time the tip is cut off, three or four of the strongest, best-placed branches are selected for fruit production. Arrangement of these branches around the trunk is important if they are to be strong enough to support heavy crops of fruit. If two branches join the trunk directly opposite each other, they will exert enough leverage under a bumper crop to split off where they are attached. Instead the tree should be pruned so that no two branches are paired to form a crotch.

Only three or four strong branches should be left in addition to the leader. The lowest should, if possible, start between one and two feet above ground, but if there is no strong branch so low, it is better to choose one somewhat farther up than to use a weaker one that is thin and spindly.

Above the lowest branch select another strong grower above it that is not pointed in the same direction. See figure 4 (A, B) for the spacing of three or four branches around the trunk. These

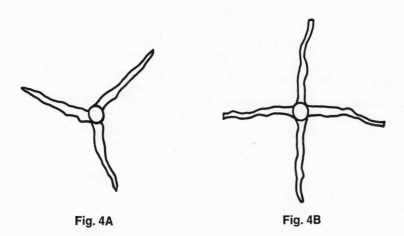

Fig. 4A   **Fig. 4B**

arrangements distribute the strain of fruit bearing (also of ice loads in areas where icing occurs). The branches should form strong connections with the main trunk at an angle of between 45 and 90 degrees. Most two-year-old nursery-grown trees will not have such wide-angled branches naturally. In this case the wide-angled connection with the trunk can be formed by spreaders or braces made from a wooden lath. A finishing nail is driven into each end of the lath and the head cut off to form a small spike, with one end stuck into the trunk and the other into a branch (figure 5). However, this operation is often left until after the first year's growth to improve the strength of branches.

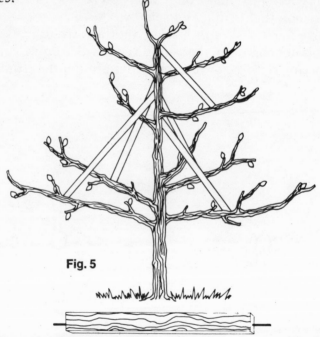

Fig. 5

Do not try to do this bracing in the winter when wood is frozen and brittle. In spring when sap is rising, branches are much more resilient.

Up to this time the object of pruning and training has been to form a tree that is roughly cone-shaped (figure 6). From this point on, about all the pruning that will be required in a home orchard is snipping out weak, spindly growth and removing water sprouts.

As a rule water sprouts arise from stubs where branches have been cut off. Note that in figure 6, stubs are shown at (B). In actual practice these should not be left as stubs but should be cut off as close to the trunk as possible, even if a ring of bark at the base is sliced off. This ring contains dormant buds. When the branch is cut away, if they are left intact, growth substances will stimulate them into growth and long, straight shoots will grow.

Although water sprouts will bear fruit if allowed to remain, this will be at the expense of better-bearing wood. Too, two or three years must elapse before they do fruit.

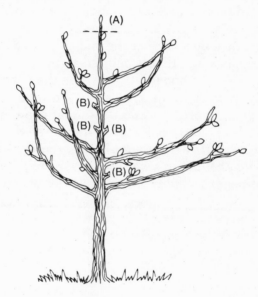

Fig. 6

If you are near a good orchard supply house, ask if they carry a sprout inhibitor. This is a chemical (usually in an aerosol can) that can be sprayed onto cut ends of stubs and will stop water sprouts from forming. If not, and if a ring of bark was left, in a small home orchard remove any buds that start to grow with a pen knife. Whenever bark is injured or cut away, the shape of the debarked area is important. If the area is wider than it is up-and-down, sap cannot flow around it. Any debarked areas should be trimmed down to bare wood so that they look like a canoe going upstream toward the tip of the leader. This allows sap to flow around both sides of the cut and stimulates formation of new bark to cover the wound.

Watch the tip of the leader. Let it grow for a year, then cut it off, leaving a strong bud to form a new one. Be careful that *two* buds do not compete for this place. If two equal leaders are allowed to grow, the tree can be split in two under a load of ice or in a high wind.

Remember that branches do not grow around corners. When you want a branch to grow in a certain direction, pick a bud that is pointed in that direction, cutting just above it. For example, when a tree spreads too widely with age, some branches should be shortened. Be sure that the bud at the end of the stub left on the tree has a bud that is pointed away from the trunk and on the *lower* side. If a bud is left that is on the upper side, it will probably grow straight up, at an awkward angle. Upright branches do not fruit as freely as do those that grow horizontally.

In reading older books on pruning, the directions given are intended to form a tree with a hollow center, called vase-shaped. The theory behind this was that a vase-shaped tree allowed sunlight to penetrate to fruit on inside branches so it could ripen well. In practice this does not work out because by the time apples and pears are ripening, the sun is too low in the southern sky to reach the hollow center. Vase-shaped trees are more liable to splitting and other ills, so the practice is not as common as it once was.

Pruning Peaches

Peaches are an exception to the practice of pruning for a vase-shaped tree. This is due partially to the fact that widespread branches are easier to produce on this form of tree. Space branches as you would for apples or pears, but allow the central leader to grow only for the first year. In figure 7 the stump is shown on a mature tree, but in practice this should be removed completely

Fig. 7

Peach trees are short-lived and need more regular pruning and snipping to keep them fruitful. Snip out all twigs and weak branches that have only single buds on them. Fruit-bearing twigs carry triple buds; the two outside buds will produce fruit, the center bud will produce leafy growth. The branches keep spreading outward and two or three years after the tree starts bearing should be cut back one-third to one-half their length. Otherwise a heavy crop will exert so much leverage that they will split off.

Pruning in home orchards should only be done when temperatures are 25 degrees or above. At these temperatures the wood is not frozen. True, commercial orchard operators prune all winter long, but their workers are more experienced and the operation needs much more time than does a home farm orchard.

Pruning Grapes
To simplify a highly complex subject—training and pruning

grapes—I am limiting directions to a single method, the two-cane high umbrella system developed at Cornell University. Not only will this system produce as much or more fruit than any other, but it is relatively simple to use when compared with those used in commercial vineyards.

Although a three-wire trellis is not essential for training grapes on this system, it is more convenient and allows for more secure tying of the fruiting canes. Wooden poles or steel fence posts eight feet long are erected at each end, buried two feet for support. If wooden posts are used, treat the lower end with a good wood preservative such as copper napthenate (Cuprinol) or pentachlorophenol. Do *not* use creosote; this has no place around plants.

A way to stretch the top wire is to use the weight of a heavy stone at each end (figure 8). The stones are fastened to the top wire and the wire run over the tops of the posts. By digging away under the stones, they put tension on the wire. This is then stapled into the wood and the stones buried. If a wire puller is not available for the two lower wires, use turnbuckles on both and draw them fairly tight. Remember, however, that in win-

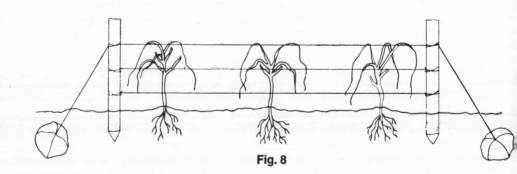

Fig. 8

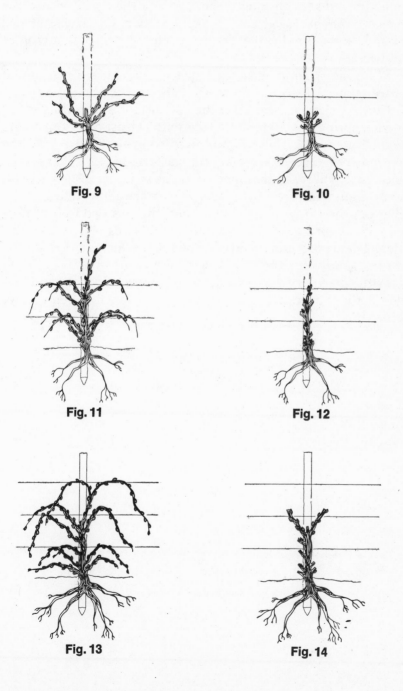

Fig. 9

Fig. 10

Fig. 11

Fig. 12

Fig. 13

Fig. 14

ter in cold climates the wire will get much tighter. With this in mind, install a turnbuckle at the center of the upper wire so the tension can be eased off in cold weather. Otherwise it will stretch and cannot be made taut under the load of a crop of grapes.

Best spacing for home garden grapes is eight feet apart, but if space is limited, six- to seven-foot spacing can be used.

Figure 9 shows a vine after the first season's growth. The following spring it is cut back to stubs with at least one stout bud to each (figure 10). These are allowed to grow (figure 11). The second spring, canes are again cut back (figure 12). That season the canes will reach the upper wire, as in figure 13. This is cut back (figure 14), from which two canes are allowed to grow to the top, then trained downward and the tips tied to the lower wire. Each spring, in addition to the fruiting canes for that year, strong buds are left on two stubs from which are grown the renewal canes for the following year's crop.

With some very vigorous growers such as Concord and Fredonia, three canes may have to be left to allow for their greater growth.

22

Little-Grown Fruiting Trees and Shrubs

Although many of the trees and shrubs described in this chapter are not widely used for their fruit, many of them may be growing at the present time in your own back yard. A good example is the so-called high bush cranberry, not related to the true cranberry but an ornamental shrub known to botanists as *Viburnum opulus.* The similar European cranberry bush, *Viburnum trilobum* is considered by some botanists to be identical.

Although it is widely used as an ornamental shrub, the bright red berries are almost never used as food. While they do not have the identical flavor of the true cranberry, they are so similar that those who do not know that high bush cranberry fruit is edible are often fooled into thinking a sauce served to them actually came from the former plant. Only a faint musky tang gives the substitution away to those who know both.

But why grow a substitute? The best reason is that the true cranberry has a very limited range. It grows in swampy soils from Massachusetts to Nova Scotia and across northern Michigan and Wisconsin, but anyone in the Midwest or living in similar climates can't grow it.

The same is true of many of these out-of-the-ordinary fruits.

Here are a number of these that will add variety to the diet and that can be grown in the home fruit garden.

Cherries

Bush cherries. The genus Prunus, which includes cherries, plums and peaches, gives us several cherrylike fruits that are delightful when made into jams, jellies, and fruit butters. The Western sand cherry, *Prunus bessevi* is one of the few fruits that is hardy at the northern end of the Great Plains. It likes dry conditions. If grown in the humid East, it often develops brown rot. It usually bears the second year after planting. Bushes sold by some nurserymen were collected from the wild and are likely to bear only sour, harsh-tasting fruits. Be sure to ask for named varieties of this shrub, of which there are a number.

The beach plum of the Cape Cod area is more cherry-like than plum-like. I would not recommend planting it for eating fresh, but it does make a tasty jelly. It is tolerant of salt spray and sandy soils. A fruit for special locations.

Korean Cherry. This is the single form of an ornamental shrub called flowering almond. Botanically it is *Prunus japonica*. The fruits are bright red and make excellent jams and jellies. It grows about six feet tall. Birds will strip the bushes unless netting is used. Except that it is more dwarf, it looks much like the Nanking cherry. Two bushes are needed for good pollination.

Nanking Cherry. Its bright red fruits are smaller than a sour cherry but delightfully acid in flavor, juicy, and much like true cherries. It forms a small tree or shrub, eight to ten feet tall. Will fruit after 15 to 20 degrees below zero. Botanically it is *Prunus tomentosa* from northern China. Its white flowers open in early spring before most other fruit trees. This is probably the best substitute for the true cherry where that tree is not fully hardy.

Berries

Elderberry. Even those who recall with nostalgia the tantalizing flavor of the wild elderberry have no idea of how superior the new cultivated varieties can be. Not only are the individual berries larger and juicier, but they are borne in huge clusters that measure several inches across. Four improved varieties are Johns, Adams, Nova, and York. The heaviest bearers are Nova and York. Cultivated elderberries are hardy as far north as Nova Scotia, in which country Nova originated. Elderberries make good landscape plants or can be planted out in fence rows and on wasteland where they will thrive. Two or more bushes are required for good pollination.

Elderberries are usually made into jelly or jam and wine. A use that I feel is best of all is as filling in an elderberry pie, one of the truly epicurean dishes in the American cuisine. If fully ripe, a touch of lemon is needed to round out the delicate flavor.

Mulberry. Although somewhat insipid in taste, many like the flavor. Its principal use is to lure birds away from cherries. They prefer mulberries if they are ripe at the same time. The New York Fruit Testing Association offers Wellington mulberry, which is superior in flavor and texture.

Barberry. In England, Barberry jelly is considered a delicacy; in the United States it is all but unknown. The best source is the English barberry, *Berberis vulgaris*, but this has been all but exterminated in the United States because of its association with wheat rust. Here and there, wild plants can occasionally be found. The Japanese barberry also produces fruits that can be made into jelly.

Rosa rugosa. This rose grows wild along the New England coast where its fruits, which are larger than many crabapples, are used to make a delicious jam or jelly. The all-too-numerous seeds must be discarded before cooking. The jelly has a flavor and odor that are a subtle blend of tea and honey, delightful on toast. A hedge of rugosa roses should yield a bushel or more of hips, far more than any family would consume as jam and jelly.

Juneberries. This name is applied without distinction to various members of the genus *Amelanchier*. Although a great fuss is made over the tastiness of their berries, they are rather insipid and seedy. They do make an interesting jelly when gathered from the wild, but they are not worth growing for this purpose in a fruit garden. As ornamentals they are useful because of their airy white bloom in May, which is responsible for the name shadblow applied to this genus. One advantage is that they do produce berries in late June or early July before blueberries are ripe. The ripe berries do resemble that fruit. Another reason a home fruit grower might plant one of the Juneberries is that they will survive and fruit much farther north than other berried shrubs.

Buffalo Berry. Two species of *Shepardia* are called by this common name. One, *Shepardia argentia,* is also known as silverleaf and wild oleaster. It is a large shrub and sometimes trimmed up as a tree, from 10 to 18 feet tall. The leaves are silvery on both sides. The fruit is a berry, yellow to red in color and much too sour to eat fresh. It does, however, make a marvelous tart jelly. This shrub and the following will survive even in the sub-Arctic.

Another buffalo berry is *Shepardia canadensis,* which grows much lower, never over eight feet tall. Its fruit is insipid and can only be made into a jelly with the addition of lemon juice, although Indians ate it for its moisture content when thirsty.

Other Fruits

Flowering Quince. Anyone who has tried to eat the green fruits of the flowering quince will attest that it is inedible. At the same time, they do make a marvelous quince jelly and conserve used in place of the true quince in any recipe.

Hawthorn. Because this genus is filled with mongrels (it is as promiscuous as a tomcat) it hardly pays to plant it unless you can locate a nursery that sells the true Pekin Hawthorn, *Crataegus pinnatifida.* This is grown in China as a fruit. The individual "apples" are nearly two inches across in some trees and are eaten in the same way as apples. They make a marvelous jam or jelly, as do selected wild trees that bear larger fruits.

Oregon Holly Grape. A close relative of the barberry, its fruits can be used for jellies and made into juice for a drink with a fresh, tart flavor. In the East it does not fruit as freely as it does in the Pacific Northwest. The blue berries are often eaten fresh by hunters.

23

Nuts as a Food Crop

In the past nuts have been a subject of amusement when mentioned as food, perhaps because of their association with the nuts-and-berries school of back-to-nature faddists.

In recent years some doctors have frowned on the too frequent use of nuts in the diet because of their lack of bulk and roughage as well as their high caloric value. This is a legitimate criticism if they are used in quantity every day to the exclusion of less concentrated foods containing less fat. As a source of protein and vitamins, they have provided the equivalent of meat to many native diets.

Their place on the menu should be that of a dessert rather than a day-to-day food, except perhaps when the use of meat is limited for financial, religious, or dietary reasons. This alone would not justify their planting where space is limited, except that they also serve as shade and landscape specimens. The cracking of nuts at family gatherings on winter evenings is one of the simple pleasures that fit so comfortably into rural living.

Climatic Adaptation and Nut Tree Culture
Nut trees vary in their hardiness from coconuts, which are truly

239

tropical, to the butternut, which survives well into Maine and New Brunswick.

Any soil that will produce good apples will do for nut trees. Many are tap-rooted so that trees dug from the wild are hard to transplant. Root-pruned nursery-grown specimens are much more likely to survive.

Trees to Plant

Coconut. A true palm, it is the best-known and most widely planted of all the palms in southern Florida. The curving trunks are often as tall as 80 feet, which is much too tall to fit in with modern low homes, yet it is not unusual to see a specimen of this height towering over a one-story ranch house.

Nurserymen usually stock a variety called Dwarf Malayan, which is immune to a disease called lethal yellowing that has destroyed most of the native coconuts on Key West. The trees are easy to grow from seed, which should be planted half-buried in a horizontal position in a shady spot and kept moist. However, do not expect fruit from a seedling for much less than ten years.

Cashew

See the warning about toxic effects from this nut under Sub-tropical Fruits. Although the processed nut is perfectly edible, the plant itself belongs to the same genus as poison ivy and secretes a similar toxin.

Almond

A relative of the peach and nearly as hardy in its wood, the almond flowers so early that, except in California, the blooms are killed and nuts are seldom produced. One exception is Hall's Hardy, a variety that will often produce nuts as far north as Central Illinois in sheltered spots. Its nuts are much coarser and have a thicker shell than do the varieties grown in California. In the latter state, at least two varieties should be planted for cross-pollination as most almond varieties are self-sterile. Culture of the almond is much like that of the peach.

English Walnut

In the United States the culture of this nut is confined to California and milder areas of Oregon and Washington. This is actually a native of Persia and as such is not reliably hardy elsewhere in the United States. Plant two trees for pollination.

Carpathian Walnut

Although this is identical to the regular English or Persian walnut, it was collected from an area in the Carpathian mountains where winter temperatures drop as low as 40 degrees below zero. It has borne nuts well into Canada and central Maine. The nuts are slightly smaller than the English walnut but thin-shelled and just as tasty. The trees at the northern limit of its range seldom grow taller than 30 feet but may grow to 40 feet farther south. Unlike the black walnut the trees grow dense with a well-filled head that throws good shade.

Like all walnuts the trees give off a substance that is toxic to tomatoes and other sensitive plants; so they should not be planted near the vegetable garden. At least two trees are needed for pollination.

Chinese Chestnut

This exotic species replaces the now extinct American chestnut. It is immune to a blight that killed the latter species. The nuts are larger and many claim the flavor is as good. The trees grow to about 35 feet and are good as shade trees. In addition to serving in place of both the American and Spanish chestnut in the diet, the nuts are valuable as hog food. Although a single tree will bear some nuts, two or more trees should be planted for heavier production and should produce a surplus of hog feed. Do not, however, feed chestnuts to hogs without removing the nuts from the burrs that surround them before they are ripe. This chestnut is flower-bud hardy to about ten below zero, but the tree itself will survive 15 to 20 degrees below.

Black Walnut

If you have space to spare, plant this nut in groves, spacing the trees about 25 feet apart. Mature walnuts are valuable for timber and increase each year in value. A friend of mine sold four logs over a foot in diameter for $4,000. True, not all walnut logs are that valuable, but you will never lose money on those you plant. For this purpose, seedlings are good. Although they vary in quality, at least one or two trees in a large planting will produce superior nuts for eating.

Where only one tree can be planted (black walnuts do not need a pollinator), select named, grafted varieties such as Thomas, Snyder, Patterson, or Michigan.

Butternut

The hardiest of nut trees and one of the tastiest. The flavor is known largely to farm families because the nuts seldom reach commerce. The shells are hard to crack, but the following varieties can usually be opened so the two halves can be extracted whole: Thill, Craxeasy, Ayers, Van Syckle, and Johnson.

Butternuts are among the earliest bearers of all nuts, fruiting in two to three years after planting.

Japanese Walnut

Much inferior to other walnuts. The nuts resemble those of the butternut but are poorer in flavor. It makes a handsome landscape specimen that has a tropical appearance with very large compound leaves. Not worth planting as the only nut tree on a farm or home property. Sometimes called Heartnut.

Hickory

The hickory most often sold by nurserymen is the shell-bark hickory. However, the shagbark produces more flavorsome nuts. All hickories are hard to transplant and slow growing. Where space permits, sow the nuts for timber; any farm with a stand of hickory has a valuable asset in the toughest wood of any tree. Hickories are not too hardy outside their normal range—the Middle West.

Pecan

Although you will see "hardy" pecans advertised, this name is only relative. Even the hardiest will not produce nuts too far north of Central Illinois. This is the most desirable of all nut trees for southern states such as Mississippi, Alabama, and the Florida panhandle. Makes an excellent shade tree even for small properties, with the delicious nuts as a bonus.

Filberts

The filberts, also known as hazelnuts, are big shrubs rather than trees, growing to about 15 feet at maturity. The American filbert will pollinate the European and vice versa. In flavor there is little difference between them. Nurserymen do not offer named varieties, although these are available in Europe. Plant one of each type to insure pollination.

Filberts are about as hardy as peaches. In English cookbooks, cobnuts are mentioned in some recipes. These are round varieties of filberts, but there is no reason whatever why the longer filberts cannot be used as well. Either variety can be used in the famed hazelnut torte so popular in Vienna.

24

Subtropical Fruits

The area in which tropical fruits can be grown in the United States is limited to the frostless areas around Key West and a small area near the Mexican border in south Texas. To those who don't mind gambling with an occasional freeze, they can be grown along the Florida coasts from Palm Beach and Bradenton south. When I worked as an agronomist in the Southeast, a request that was made perhaps as often as any other was for information on protecting these tropical exotics from damage by frost.

I recall vividly an enormous specimen of the true rubber tree, *Hevea brasiliensis*, which was growing on an old estate in Winter Park, Florida. After most of the top had been killed by a 30-degree freeze, the owner cut it down and dug up the stump. On my recommendation a friend of mine took the stump and transplanted it to the patio of his home in nearby Orlando. It sprouted and grew into a magnificent specimen, but the care it needed to survive will explain why I do not recommend trying to grow true tropicals in subtropical country.

Every time the temperature went below 40 degrees, my friend hauled out a huge tarpaulin and hung it over the patio. With a charcoal salamander fired up early in the evening and replenished at midnight, we saved the foliage of this plant half a dozen times.

If you are willing to go through a similar operation every other year or so (even oftener at the north end of the Palm Beach-Bradenton limits) you can grow many of the trees, shrubs, and herbaceous plants described later. One fact must be understood, however, about growing plants in Florida and in the sterile sandy soils of Florida and south Texas. These are areas where humus and other organic matter seem to flow out of soils. Because of more persistent, higher temperatures than found elsewhere in the United States, soil bacteria are active the year around, digesting organic matter faster than plants are able to absorb the nutrients they release. As a result in practically all subtropical soils, fertilizing at least three times a year is essential. One alternative, which is good for about 18 months of feeding (but only once, when setting out new trees and shrubs), is to bury an Agriform pellet (made by Sierra Chemical Co., Milpitas, California) in the planting hole. Ordinarily, fertilizer in the hole, unless it is a slow-release product, is not advised. The new 3-M capsulated fertilizers can also be used and will continue to feed for at least 10 months.

Florida soils are deficient in practically every known nutrient element. Mixed minor element fertilizers sold through most garden centers should be used, at least when planting. Consult the county farm adviser for information on local soils and what they need most.

Florida is also an area of bright, sunny weather in winter, fine for the tourist trade but hard on trees and shrubs. Be sure of a supply of water before doing any extensive planting. Fortunately in most parts of the state, water is only a few feet down and available with little labor.

Composting and mulching are of particular importance to conserve and restore organic matter in subtropical soils. Be sure to make provisions for this.

Tropical Trees and Shrubs

Avocado

Particularly useful in the diet because, instead of storing energy as starch, the avocado stores it as fat. The fruit is also high in protein. It makes a handsome tree if pruned for landscape use and so is valuable for smaller properties.

Size and shape of the tree varies with the variety; so it is best to see it growing in a nursery before making a selection for landscape use. Homeowners can leave the fruits on the tree much longer than is safe in commercial orchards because of the loss from dropping. Most trees bear more than a family can eat; so the loss of 15 to 20 percent of the crop is unimportant when matched against the convenience of storing ripe fruit on the tree. They improve in quality with age.

In Florida avocados can be enjoyed from about late June through April, but in California they are in season (at least with enough fruits for family use) the year around. For Florida the following varieties will give a regular harvest from early July to late January: Simmonds: July to September 15; Waldin, September 15 to November 1; Lulu, October 15 thru January. Lulu is hardier than the two other varieties and is sometimes planted north of the Bradenton–Palm Beach line.

In California, Fuerte ripens in the fall-to-spring season and Hass is ready during the summer. By allowing fruits to hang on the trees as already mentioned, these two are available the year around. Both, however, are quite tender and will need to be smudged if frost threatens. Less susceptible to frost are Mexicola, Bacon, and Zutano.

Banana

Although treelike the banana plant is actually herbaceous. It is propagated from suckers that usually throw up too many shoots. Unless these are reduced to two or three stems, the plant will not produce fruit. A plant from a sucker will bear in 12 to 15 months from planting. About the only varieties grown in home gardens are Cavendish and Lady Finger. The tropical banana of commerce is unreliable and practically never planted. Cavendish or Chinese banana is the most popular because it is more resistant to cold and does not grow taller than five to seven feet. It is of little value commercially because the fruit is too tender to ship well, but it is all the better as a home garden fruit because of its superior flavor.

Of the tall varieties Lady Finger (also called Hart's Choice) is the most widely planted.

Cashew

I only mention this to warn against planting it in a home fruit collection. It belongs to the same family as poison ivy and like that plant can cause a severe rash. Harvesting the nuts is a nasty job for that reason. The smoke from burning husk and leaves is equally irritating.

Cherimoya

A tree 25-feet tall at maturity, bearing warty fruits with white, aromatic custardlike fruits. They must be eaten fresh. It survives only in southern Florida and from Santa Barbara south in California. Some authorities consider this one of the choicest of all tropical fruits, but it is too bland for my taste. Belonging to the same genus and bearing similar custardy fruits is the Sweet Sop, again highly praised by some.

Mango

Another member of the sumac family and one whose fruit is irritating to some individuals. Many are immune, however, and a ripe mango of one of the modern varieties is such a choice fruit that you should investigate before deciding not to plant it. If some member of your family is immune, he or she can wash the skin, peel the fruit, and then wash the peeled fruit. It is then safe to eat because the toxic oil is in the peel.

The mango is called the Peach of the Tropics, a name that it deserves, even though the flavor is much more complex and richer than that of the northern peach. Mangoes are very high in vitamins A and C. Because they are highly susceptible to anthracnose, they need to be sprayed with a fungicide four or five times a year.

Mangoes do not do too well in California, although an occasional tree is found growing on home properties. In Florida the following varieties will provide fruits from June to September: Irwin, Fascell, and Kent.

Mangoes are reasonably tolerant of salt spray.

Lychee

The lychee tree casts a dense shade and while attractive as a lawn specimen, grass will not grow under it. The rough, pebbly fruit is peeled like a grape, exposing a sweet, slightly acid pulp quite unlike the preserved lychee nuts served in chop-suey cafés. Does not tolerate wind or salt spray; so it should be planted in a sheltered position. Mauritius is a named variety and superior in flavor.

The fruit is in season during June and July.

Marmalade Plum

Also called sapote, this is an extremely tender tree that is grown from Miami south for its firm, sweet, but spicy, flesh used in a delicious jam or marmalade.

Otaheite Gooseberry Tree

Grown for its acid fruits used in preserves and in Florida gooseberry pie. This species has naturalized in south Florida and in the West Indies but produces more and better fruit under cultivation.

Papaya

Like the banana this is not a tree, though treelike in habit. It is seldom sold in nurseries and usually is grown from seed, flowering in between five and six months and ripening its first fruits in a year. The plant does not branch but continues to grow at the tip, producing a flower at each leaf axil. As a result it usually grows too tall and is cut down at the end of the third year. Most gardeners plant three seeds every year. Papayas are erratic in their sex life. Some flowers are perfect, some are female, and some male. To be sure fruit will be produced, the three plants are started. By the time those seeded the first year are cut down, there ought to be enough of both male and female flowers to keep the race going.

Sea Grape

This tall shrub or small tree bears clusters of purple, grapelike fruits that make one of the world's most delicious jellies.

Because of its high salt tolerance it is used for erosion control along the seashore. It does not transplant well and is usually started from seeds.

Tender Shrubs

Some of Florida's best fruits are borne on shrubs rather than trees. Although many are just as sensitive to frost as the tree fruits, they are easier to cover in case a frost is threatened. Another advantage of shrub fruits is that they occupy less space than do trees, so that a greater variety can be planted on a smaller property.

Australian Bush Cherry

Although this grows to 15 feet at maturity, it can be kept lower by pruning. It is often grown as a hedge, with its purple fruits as a bonus for making jelly.

Barbados Cherry

Its rich, red acid berries are cherrylike in appearance. They are one of the richest sources of natural vitamin C. They are delicious eaten fresh or in preserves.

Natal Plum

Although the usual height of this shrub is 18 feet, there are varieties that grow much lower. It is a superb hedge plant, spiny and bushy. The egg-shaped red berries are reminiscent of raspberries in flavor. It thrives on salt air.

Surinam Cherry

Also called Pitanga, this is a tall-growing shrub that can be trimmed in tree form, or cut back as a shrub. The ribbed crimson berries are a favorite jam and jelly fruit. Commonly used as a hedge. Will grow farther north than other shrubs in this group.

Citrus Fruits

These are being treated separately, since members of this genus differ widely in hardiness. The lime is damaged by the slightest suggestion of frost, lemons are almost as tender, most oranges and grapefruits will tolerate an occasional touch of cold, while the Satsuma and Ponkan or Chinese Honey varieties can be grown in northern Florida. What damyankees don't seem to appreciate is the extent of the citrus industry. Far more citrus fruits are grown and marketed than there are apples and pears put together.

In spite of this tremendous commercial production, there are far fewer varieties grown than of apples. Some of the most delicious varieties are all but unknown. Check with local nurserymen for these.

Lime

Lime trees are seldom found north of the Miami area because of their sensitivity to cold. The variety most commonly grown is Persian, also known as Tahiti, which is seedless and does not turn yellow as readily as do other varieties when fully ripe. In California this is known as Bearss, where it is grown to some extent. Far south in Texas and on the Florida Keys, the Key or Mexican lime is grown; it is full of seeds. A close relative of the lime, the calamondin is actually hardier than most orange varieties. It is bright orange in color, bears freely, and can be substituted for it.

Lemon

Somewhat hardier than the lime, yet less so than the orange, lemons can be grown up to the Bradenton-Palm Beach line if planted in a sheltered spot out of the wind and if given protection when temperatures below 30 degrees are predicted. The variety Meyer is "the" home garden variety in Florida. It is less acid than other lemons. South of Miami the Ponderosa is a novelty with its fruits the size of a small watermelon. In California the varieties Eureka and Lisbon are most widely grown in home plantings.

Oranges

Orange trees can survive down to 16 to 17 degrees above zero, even though at these temperatures the flower buds will be killed and there will be no crop the following summer and fall. Even if there is no crop, the trees still need the five or six feedings required by practically all fruit-bearing plants in Florida.

For trees on home properties, I feel it is a mistake to stick to commercial varieties when much superior oranges are available. Three such varieties are not only juicier, easier to peel, and finer in flavor, but are actually hardier and will survive along the Gulf Coast and produce fruit in years when temperatures do not fall lower than 25 degrees above zero. The King orange belongs to the mandarin or kid-glove group. It commands a substantial premium in price when sold commercially. The flavor is nothing short of marvelous—juicy, sweet, and delicious. It is in season from March to June. The Satsuma is also a kid-glove orange with the thick, warty, loose skin of the type that peels without effort. If grafted on trifoliate orange understock, it grows well from Ocala north. It makes a smaller tree than other varieties. The season is short, through October and November.

If you can find a tree of Ponkan or Chinese Honey, you are in luck. This is a kid-glove variety ripening in November and December. The fruit is large, soft, and so juicy it ought to be eaten while sitting in the bathtub. Its one weakness is that it must be eaten soon after ripening as it will not hang for long on the tree.

Perhaps it is heresy to downgrade the flavor of most Florida oranges, but none of the standard sorts has the rich, orangey flavor of California's favorite Navel orange. Although it ripens in November and December, it will hang on the tree until February, gaining flavor with delay.

Hybrids between the orange and the grapefruit, called tangelos, are among the best of Florida's varieties. Minneola and Seminole are among the best of these. They ripen in midwinter.

Tangors are hybrids between the orange and the tangerine, sometimes mistakenly called tangelos. The Temple variety is a superb specimen of this type.

Grapefruit

One fruit that can only be enjoyed at its perfect best when grown at home is the grapefruit. By the time it has ripened to perfection on the tree it is too soft to ship. Probably the finest specimen of citrus fruit it has even been my privilege to eat was from a tree on the property of Mr. and Mrs. Earl Webb in Bradenton. Earl (he is the engineer responsible for the design and construction of the Bay Bridge between San Francisco and Oakland—a traitor to California in his retirement in Florida) could not tell me the name of the variety, which I suspect was a superseedling and *not* a named variety. My half measured exactly seven and one-half inches across, with every segment alike. It was fully ripe and so delicious I "ate the whole thing." It had only two seeds.

A grapefruit of this quality just could not be shipped in commerce.

Since there is no great variation in maturity, probably the best variety for the home fruit garden is the Marsh Seedless, allowed to fully ripen on the tree. In California, grapefruit is grown under irrigation in desert areas. It can stand more heat than can oranges.

Calamondin

The calamondin, mentioned briefly under limes, is a citrus species worth growing if space is available. It is much hardier than the sweet orange. Intensely sour, it makes a marvelous and unusual marmalade, if the housewife can be persuaded to prepare the fruit. The individual fruits are small and seedy and dozens of them are needed for even a small batch of jam. The tree is small and can be squeezed into even a city lot. One calamondin fruit makes an elegant whiskey sour.

Kumquat

The kumquat, which resembles the calamondin in size and color, is not a member of the citrus genus but is closely related to it. It is much sweeter in flavor and can be eaten fresh, or used in preserves. Since it is much hardier than most oranges, it can be grown as far north as the south boundary of Georgia, particularly if grafted on citrus trifoliate understock.

Practically every county agent in Florida is a specialist in citrus fruit and is a good man to know when you need advice.

Other Subtropical Fruits

In areas where the true tropicals cannot be grown, there still are some delectable fruits that will thrive even on smaller home properties. Again it is important to keep in mind that all warm-climate soils eat up organic matter at a rapid pace, and that four to five applications of fertilizers must be made annually.

Figs

If I were to pick one subtropical fruit I would like to grow, it would be the fig. My idea of sybaritic living would be to have an everbearing fig tree within reach of our breakfast table. No other fruit has quite the same combination of smoothness and rich flavor, unless it be a perfect peach.

The fig is an adaptable plant, perfectly hardy outdoors as far north as Washington, D.C., along the Atlantic Coast. With protection (or if taken indoors in a tub) it is grown by fig fanciers as far north as New York City.

The Smyrna fig, which is the main type grown in California for commercial drying, is not for the home orchardist. It requires a special insect for pollination, which in turn must have a special species of fig to survive.

Instead, excellent fig varieties for California that do well for home gardeners are Oaborn's Prolific, Ronde Noire, and White Genoa. In Southeastern United States, Celeste, Brown Turkey, Brunswick, and Magnolia.

Figs are peculiarly susceptible to nematodes, particularly when grown on sandy soil. Since the ring-fungi, which actually eat nematodes, flourish in soils high in organic matter, working in all the well-decayed compost you can spare in soils where figs are grown is good practice. Mulching heavily is particularly desirable.

Persimmons

Anyone who has eaten a northern persimmon, particularly if not ripe, will shudder at the thought of deliberately planting a modern hybrid Oriental persimmon. This is unfortunate, since a well-ripened fruit of this type is a gourmet treat. This is a difficult fruit to assign to a specific region, since it is not fully hardy, yet does not thrive in hot countries. In general it will grow in about the same area as cotton thrives.

Trees have survived temperatures as low as 12 degrees above zero. Varieties that have survived near the sea in Maryland include Great Wall, Peiping, Pen, Sheng, Okame, and Delicious. Like figs they are subject to nematodes; so the same treatment with organic matter is suggested.

In the East Tane-Nashi and Fuyu are the most widely available varieties. Tane-Nashi must be allowed to fully ripen on the tree. If picked before maturity it is astringent and poor in flavor. Fuyu is nonastringent even if eaten before fully mature. In California, Hachiya and Fuyu are preferred for home planting. Fuyu is partially self-sterile and another variety is needed for good pollination.

Loquat

Also known as Japanese plum the Chinese loquat is hardy over the same range as the Chinese persimmon just mentioned. It is a beautiful, symmetrical tree that makes a handsome landscape specimen. Although the tree will survive down to 12 degrees above zero, at 26 degrees above flower buds can be injured or killed.

It blooms from October to February and the fruit ripens from February to May. There are named varieties, but they are so sparsely distributed that best practice is to consult a local nurseryman who can tell you when the variety he carries will fruit. North of Oscala, Florida, only late flowering and late fruiting trees should be planted. The fruit varies widely in quality. Once while talking to a fertilizer dealer in south Georgia, I noticed his loquat tree was in fruit. I picked one and ate it. "You cain't eat thet," he said in an alarmed tone.

He was probably right, not because it was harmful in any way, but it tasted like a raw potato. If possible check the flavor of the tree you plant before buying.

Pineapple Guava

This fruiting shrub is associated with the pineapple because of the distinct tart pineapple flavor of the greenish berries. It grows well either in the moist climate of Florida or the dry air of

California. It will survive (but may not fruit) even where temperatures drop as low as 14 degrees above zero. The fruits are delightful eaten fresh by peeling off the outer skin. It is also used in jams, jellies, and marmalades.

The purplish-white petals of the flowers make an unusual addition to salads. They open in April. The fruit ripens in August.

Pineapple

At one time Florida produced marvelous pineapples, but the development of huge ranches in Hawaii ruined the small-scale production in that state. I can recall when every pineapple-packing plant in Florida had a bin into which overripe fruit would be tossed as too ripe for shipping. These fruits were superb in flavor, far more delicious than those that were used. I would fill the back of my car with a dozen or more of these discards, cutting up one to eat as I drove. By the end of the day my mouth was raw from the enzymes in the fruit. The memory of the heavenly flavor of those "pines" remains to this day.

You can enjoy the same flavor by growing your own. You don't need to buy plants; cut off the top of any reasonably ripe pineapple picked up at a supermarket and root it in a mixture of half peat moss and half sand or vermiculite. Dipping the base in a hormone such as Rootone will speed up rooting. The pineapple prefers a deep, porous soil, not hard to find in Florida but calling for liberal feeding.

Tropical Diseases & Insects

Little has been said about the problem of disease and insect pests. Unfortunately since the Environmental Protection Agency has usurped the policing of plant protection products, materials for this purpose are in a state of confusion. Today the efficiency of control methods is not the major consideration, unless the manufacturer can all but guarantee that generations from now a product *might not* result in some mysterious malady, a product cannot be sold. Under prevailing conditions I can advise only two courses of action: Keep in touch with your State Agricultural College—and pray.

III

Materials
and Methods
in the Garden

25

Control of Insects
and Diseases

If you are to believe advertisements for plant protection products, growing vegetables is a constant, almost daily, battle against diseases and insects. This is perhaps true in the commercial production of crops for the market, where an apple with scab and marks of codling moth feeding would be rejected, but far too much is said about pests when writing for the home gardener. If a cabbage shows sign of feeding by the caterpillars of the cabbage looper on the outer leaves, that in no way spoils it as food.

I have a conviction that overemphasis on pest control has prevented thousands who would otherwise garden from doing so. A case in point is *Bacillus thuringensis,* a highly effective control for many harmful caterpillars. It is a culture of bacteria (an excellent biologic control) that, when eaten by such pests, will make them so sick they stop feeding. But to do their work the bacteria must be alive and so *Bacillus thuringensis* must be sprayed every seven to ten days on the foliage that is to be protected. A light rain won't wash it off, but if that rain is heavier than a summer shower, the bacteria will be washed away and another application will be needed.

This means that to produce the clean, unblemished cabbage you find in markets, six or seven applications might have to be made, perhaps costing as much as the value of the cabbages you save.

Personally, knowing that once cabbage begins to head, the growth is from the inside and will remain untouched by insects, I only spray until heading begins, saving myself work and money. All I do is strip off the damaged leaves when harvesting a head. This practice would be suicide for the commercial grower who must deliver an unblemished head of cabbage with outer leaves intact, but you as a home gardener can skip about 75 percent of the spraying recommended in garden magazines and on packages of sprays and dusts.

Before discussing manmade products for plant protection it might be well to make sense out of the subject of biologic controls. Millions of dollars are wasted annually in introducing lady bugs and praying mantes—not that these predatory insects fail to eat their share of harmful insects but more is expected of them than is possible.

Since most collectors of lady bugs are serving the citrus grove market in California, they collect a species that is native to Southwestern United States and that has little appetite for insects found elsewhere. For instance, if introduced into a garden in the Midwest, conditions might be unfavorable: either their food prey is not yet abundant enough to sustain them, or the lady bugs find the weather too cold or wet to feed. Another much-advertised biologic control is the praying mantis. In my experience, 95 percent of the people who introduce this predator find that it amuses the children, but as an all-over insect control, is a failure.

A common misapprehension is that scientists are deliberately refusing to employ biologic controls to protect insecticide manufacturers. This idea is stupid. Not only are scientists eager to find such controls, but over the 100 years since the first natural enemies were introduced, more than a billion dollars has been spent in trying to perfect ways to kill insects, using natural forces. These include such amazing discoveries as sex lures, sterilizing male insects so females lay nonfertile eggs, treating them with juvenile hormones so they can't grow up and breed, and tricking them into eating food that starves them to death. All these techniques are unfortunately too complex to be of any use in home gardens.

How to Program Insect and Disease Control

The Unsprayed Garden

There are three ways to plan the pest control system in a home garden. The first, and the one that costs very little, is to do nothing. Well, not exactly nothing.

To make this work the crops planted must be those that will be productive even if insects and diseases attack them. The amazing ability of tomato plants to produce fruits in spite of some 114 natural enemies has already been mentioned. Even without spraying, cabbage will head up and infested leaves can be stripped off, leaving an edible core. Carrots and beets seem to survive and produce edible roots, although the beet tops will be useless for greens. New Zealand spinach is seldom attacked; so if you want greens, this is the crop to plant.

The unsprayed garden owes much to today's plant breeders who have given us varieties of tomatoes, beans, melons, carrots, cucumbers, lettuce, peppers, peas, and squash that are either resistant or tolerant of many diseases. If you have done any vegetable gardening in the past, I am sure you have looked for many old-time favorite varieties in these pages without finding any mention of them. This has been a deliberate purpose of mine, directing attention instead to the supervegetables of today, with built-in protection against both diseases and insect pests.

Spraying as Cure Only

The unsprayed garden is today a distinct possibility, but my personal choice is a second method—wait until an infestation begins before doing any spraying. This is sheer heresy to those who advocate the third method of meeting the pest problem—regular preventive spraying such as is an absolute necessity in the commercial growers' fields.

In the past spraying after diseases occurred was not possible because they could not be cured, they could only be prevented. Today the prevention has been done for us by the plant breeder. With the introduction of varieties resistant to some of the most important diseases, you can now plant the following crops with practically all fungicidal spraying eliminated: sweet corn, tomatoes, melons, beans, cabbage, cucumbers, peppers, eggplant, zucchini, and even radishes. If disease is a problem, by all means read catalog descriptions carefully, selecting those varieties specifically mentioned as being resistant or tolerant.

Today the existence of chemicals that can treat diseases *after* they have invaded plants can help if the crop is worth the cost of spraying. Benlate (Benomyl of du Pont) is the one most widely distributed of these. Consult your garden center for information.

The extra vigor of new hybrids makes invasion by insects less of a problem than formerly, yet these pests will invade in vast numbers at times. The reluctance of organic gardeners to use chemicals puts them at a disadvantage. Although they will use pyrethrum, rotenone, sabadilla, nicotine, ryania, and similar plant-derived insect killers, what they fail to appreciate is that such sprays are not the pure substance but contain carriers and wetting agents that are purely chemical. Some, "organic" pesticides, such as nicotine sulfate, are far more poisonous than most of the chemicals used in home gardens.

I feel the home gardener should confine his efforts to low-toxic chemicals (to man) such as Diazinon (sold widely under the tradename of Spectracide), lindane, Malathion, methoxychlor (a tradename is Marlate), and Sevin, along with the standard pyrethrum and rotenone sprays.

The first basic step in using any insecticide is READ THE LABEL. An insecticide label is one of the most costly items of literature in the world. It represents perhaps three or four million dollars spent in research and testing. It is there for your protection. Smart guys and gals read labels.

As hinted elsewhere, weeds, insects, and diseases make up a troika that spells trouble for the gardener. Feeding on weeds already infected with some disease organism, insects pick up these organisms and pass them on to crop plants. Weeds also provide shelter for wintering-over pests, as well as for breeding insects all summer long. One way to prevent trouble is to clear away all unwanted growth on four sides of the vegetable garden and dig or till a dust barrier all around. This will at least stop those insects that crawl.

Spraying weeds and shrubs outside the garden area with a general insect killer, such as methoxychlor or Diazinon, soon after the petals fall from apple trees will reduce the chances of infestation while avoiding the use of sprays on the crop plants.

A new and disturbing influence in the use of plant protection products makes positive and effective recommendations all but impossible. As the result of unreasoned and emotional activity by environmentalists, regulation of such products has been taken away from agencies that have made America's food supply the safest and among the cheapest in the world and surrendered to the so-called Environmental Protection Agency. This is the equivalent of turning the custody and protection of a field of lettuce over to a committee of rabbits. As a result there is no guarantee that any chemical will be available when needed. Your only remedy is to keep in close touch with your county farm adviser or the horticultural department of your state university.

Nonchemical Controls

Plowing the garden soil after crops have been harvested in fall and leaving it rough over winter is another way to reduce insects. Not only does this expose them to freezing weather and drying out, but it allows birds to feed on them, at least until snow covers the ground.

A nonchemical insect control that should be considered by organic gardeners and by those who also use insecticides was developed by Dr. Floyd F. Smith of the U.S.D.A. Floyd is one of the great entomologists of the century who has saved American farmers and gardeners millions of dollars by his discoveries for controlling insects. When he placed clear reflective aluminum under test plants, only 19 aphids (plant lice) lit on it.

But when the same aluminum sheets were painted yellow, more than 2,000 aphids landed on them during the same period.

Aphids are particularly dangerous to many vegetables because they carry virus diseases that can reduce production to less than one-fifth of that of uninfected plants. In the case of some tomato varieties, they can completely stop production of fruits.

Out of his discovery of the repellent properties of aluminum foil has come a growing method that has been adopted by commercial growers but that has not been available to home gardeners except in do-it-yourself use. Used by commercial producers of vegetables it has increased crop yields by as much as 600 percent. The soil is prepared in the usual way and seed is sown or plants set out in rows. Strips of paper-backed aluminum foil 24 inches wide are then laid one on each side of the row, leaving about six inches of soil exposed on each side of the row.

This means that rows are three feet apart, but because production per plant is higher, crops grown in this system actually produce far more than do those in conventional 24-inch spacing.

Several companies have plans to enter the home garden market with foil strips for home gardeners within the next year or so.

The 24-inch spacing, with six inches on either side of the strips is necessary to allow the sun to reach the aluminum, which reflects ultraviolet light to repel not only aphids but a number of other flying insects, including leaf hoppers and Mexican bean beetles as well as the moth of the squash borer. Oddly the leaf miner flies and moths are attracted by ultraviolet light, but these are not serious pests in home gardens.

In commercial fields workers must wear sunglasses capable of screening out ultraviolet light to avoid eye injury, but in home gardens short exposure periods do not call for their use.

As plants spread and cover the foil, efficiency is reduced but usually older plants are more resistant to insect injury. Another effect is that foil does delay seed germination in spring by keeping the soil cool. Where this is a problem, transplants can be used instead, but except where early crops are important the delay is not a serious handicap.

If foil is not available, I have used old corrugated cartons sprayed or brushed with aluminum paint. These can be plowed under in fall and actually add humus to the soil.

26

Where Can You Garden?

Soil

An annoying practice of all too many authors of books and bulletins on food gardening is that of beginning by describing a perfect soil. They don't seem to understand that the only spot their readers will have for a garden is in their own back yards. The chances that the soil there will even approach perfection are about one in ten.

I have never known of anyone, even the most ardent gardener, buying a home with a spade in hand to check the soil on which the house stands. Most of us find out how good or how bad it is when we try to turn it over for the first time. Personally, in the 67 years I have been gardening, I have owned four homes but never once checked the soil before signing the papers. I have been luckier than most. One soil turned out to be a light sand as porous as a sieve. Another was a stiff, tight clay that took two years to condition so I could grow carrots and beets. Two, however, were deep, rich black prairie loams (one nearly four feet deep).

Because soil can be modified and improved, it need not be considered in the first decision about a site. Of the possibilities for improvement, more in a later chapter. There are, however, several important requirements for growing good vegetables that should be considered when looking at an available site for a food garden. Our English cousins make a fine art of selection (they call it "siting") and because they do such a good job of it, British cottage gardens seldom fail.

Sunlight

Perhaps the most critical element to study is that of the amount of sun that falls on the area. If you plan to grow a wide range of vegetables, including root crops such as carrots and beets, leafy "greens" and salad plants and those that produce fruits (tomatoes, peppers, and eggplant) don't do so if the spot receives less than six hours of full sunshine during the day.

Don't guess at this. Actually observe the sun and mark the time it touches the soil in the morning, as well as the time it passes off in the afternoon. Too many gardeners stand in an area at midday and think the sun will be that bright all day long. An example of how inaccurate a single observation can be is the case of a lawn problem I was once asked to solve. The owner said his Merion Bluegrass lawn, in full sun, kept dying out. Later he confessed he saw it only in the morning when he left for the office. An actual observation showed that it received less than two-and-a-half hours of sun, about one-fourth as much as bluegrass needs to thrive.

If only salad crops and "greens" such as spinach, kale, cabbage, and lettuce are grown, it is possible to produce good plants with less than six hours of sun but at least four and a half hours. Don't make the mistake of assuming that because they are closely related to cabbage and kale that cauliflower and broccoli will do well with so little light. The edible parts of these crops are modified flowers, which puts them in the class of those that bear fruits such as tomatoes and peppers, which do well only with more than six hours of sun.

Root crops also need a full six hours of sun. Herbs are a special problem. Except for parsley and mint they do well only when grown in rather dry, well-drained soil in full sun.

In checking the amount of sunshine that falls on a given area, a common mistake is to judge this in late spring, say in May. This is so close to the longest day of the year that the amount of sunshine will be greater than it will be in late summer. In Boston, for example, April 1 is 12 hours, 41 minutes long; June 23 is 15 hours, 19 minutes long; while Sept. 15 is again 12 hours, 32 minutes.

In addition to duration another "dimension" of sunshine is intensity. As the sun drops lower and lower in the sky toward the end of summer, it strikes the earth at an ever-decreasing angle. This reduces insolation (the intensity of the energy with which it strikes the soil) so that a six-hour day in September (when fall storage crops are maturing) is considerably less intense than it was in June. A spot that receives six hours of sun in June will get less than five hours of lower-strength sun in September, which slows up growth from 10 to 25 percent.

Remember that in September and October some of your most important food crops—those for winter use—are storing up starches and sugars that will improve them for winter eating.

When watching to see how much sun you have, notice whether there are any obstacles to the south, east, and west that are not in the way at the time, but might be later as the sun swings to the south. Sometimes, switching the plot just a few feet one way or the other can make an important difference in yield by giving fall crops more sun.

Air

Sunshine is a powerful disinfectant; it helps control disease by killing the spores. Another good disease control is air movement because it dries off foliage. Mildews in particular need moisture to grow. Often the only condition they need to grow is a leaf that is constantly damp for six to eight hours.

Another reason why air movement is important is that it helps feed plants. As odd as that statement may seem, plants take in air containing carbon dioxide. By a miraculous process known as photosynthesis, they extract carbon and combine it with water and food elements from the soil to make starches and sugars—energy from the sun.

Air enters the leaves through tiny openings, moved by a slight change in pressure between the surrounding air and the leaf passages. Wind blowing across these openings speeds up the exchange, supplying more "food." An airy garden will produce more than one surrounded by buildings, fences, or thick hedges.

Water

Water is another "fertilizer" that is often neglected. For every pound of dissolved minerals a plant uses for growth, it will need hundreds of pounds of water. Even in areas of America where rainfall is usually adequate, periods of drought are a constant threat. Recently I had an example of the importance of a steady supply of moisture. For several years I have gardened during five summer months on an island off the Maine Coast. With almost daily fog and frequent summer rains, my 10,000-square-foot garden has never lacked for moisture. Last summer, however, for several weeks no rain fell and fogs were light and irregular. Half of the garden could be reached with a hose but not the rest of the garden. The irrigated half produced five times the yield of the part that received no water.

If at all possible locate your garden near a hose tap or other source of water. Usually there is little choice as to drainage, but if at all possible, select a spot with a gentle slope rather than one on flat ground, unless your plot is on a light, sandy loam that drains rapidly. If that slope faces south, so much the better; it will be warmer and dry out faster in spring.

The size of a property also determines how large a garden can be. If limited in size, better stick to high-nutrition vegetables such as snap beans, tomatoes, broccoli, cabbage, bush varieties of winter squash, onions, and Swiss chard. Check the vitamin content as given in chapters on various crops to be sure you have as complete coverage as possible. If space allows, by all means include the vegetables that your family enjoys most.

The vegetable garden novice will do well to stick to a few sure-fire crops on a small plot for a year or two. All too often, beginning gardeners rush in and plant a tremendous area of vegetables that even the experts have difficulty growing.

Science has helped control diseases that formerly made difficult the growing of such crops as tomatoes, cucumbers, squash, cabbage, and snap beans. For example, three serious diseases of tomatoes—verticillium wilt, fusarium wilt, and root nematodes—have been all but conquered by VFN varieties, resistant to all three ills.

During this period of food crisis, selecting these resistant varieties is important, even if some might call for a slight sacrifice in quality. It will allow growing fewer plants of a certain crop because production will not be reduced by disease. This means that a small plot will produce as much as a larger area of nonresistant varieties.

Labor needed to produce vegetables will be less if a place to store tools, fertilizers, plant protection chemicals, and other gear can be set up next to the garden. Lugging a hose or wheelbarrow out of a basement or garage takes time, time that can be spent cultivating and weeding instead. Any simple structure will do, even a plastic tarpaulin tied over a wheelbarrow in which the tools are kept.

Planning the Crops

A small plot can be made more efficient by using succession crops, interplanting, and catch crops, which will be discussed elsewhere.

Soils, perhaps the most complex, intricate material with which man works, are discussed in depth in the chapter Soil: A Basic "Stuff" of Life.

27

Planning How Much To Plant

Deciding what to grow, how much your family will eat of what you do grow, and how to schedule your needs, are problems you should solve before you thrust a spade into the earth or start the engine on your rotary tiller.

Into these calculations should go possible variations—your family's likes and dislikes in food, sudden whims of childish appetites, and adult prejudices that run counter to popular tastes.

The following chart is not intended to tell you exactly how much of any one crop to grow, but to show you how many feet of a row should produce four servings of common garden vegetables if your family likes them. There are so many variables in gardening that most old-timers plan to grow twice as much as they expect to feed their families, with the thought of giving away surpluses or preserving for winter use.

The amounts given are for fresh use from the garden. Any additional amounts needed for storing, canning, or freezing for winter should be figured separately.

In figuring how much to grow, say of beets for fresh use, a two-foot row will produce four servings. Most families can't stand beets more than once a week, but if your family happens to be particularly fond of them and will eat them twice a week, that means you should plant four feet of row for each of the six weeks they will continue to remain in good condition, or 24 feet of row in all.

Although the chart is set up as a guide for using vegetables in the summer and early fall, it can be used for crops that are stored for winter use as well as used fresh from the garden. These are marked with an asterisk in the chart.

If your family likes winter squash, for example, you will need to plant three feet of row (one vine) to produce enough fruits to supply four adults each week from harvest until in March (about as long as winter squash can be kept in home storage). If Hubbard or other large-fruited winter squashes are planted, this will yield too much squash.

Crop	Days to Harvest	Space for 4 Servings	Length of Harvest	Remarks
Bush beans	48-75 days	4 ft.	2 weeks	Make succession plantings every 2 weeks
Pole beans	56-68 days	2 poles	8-10 weeks	
Beets (roots)	48-80 days	2 ft.	6 weeks	Replant for fall crop June 15
Beet greens	30-80 days			Use thinnings and tops for greens
Broccoli	55-85 days	2 ft.	6-8 weeks	Replant for fall crop June 15
Brussels sprouts	90-100 days	3 ft.	8-10 weeks	#
Cabbage, early	60-70 days	2 ft.	6 weeks	
Cabbage, late	95-110 days	2 ft.	6 weeks	* # Set plants June 1
Carrots	60-85 days	2 ft.	2 weeks	Replant June 1 for fall crop
Chinese cabbage	60-80 days	2 ft.	16-18 weeks	# Do not seed until July 1
Collards	60-65 days	2 ft.	10 weeks	Survives to 18° F.
Corn, sweet	60-95 days	3 ft.	1 week	Replant or use early, mid-season and late varieties
Cucumber	60 days	2 ft.	4-5 weeks	Replant July 1
Eggplant	65-80 days	1 ft.	6-8 weeks	
Endive	90 days	2 ft.	6 weeks	Curly and broadleaf

Crop	Days to Harvest	Space for 4 Servings	Length of Harvest	Remarks
Kale	60-65 days	2 ft.	8 weeks	#
Kohlrabi	55-60 days	3 ft.	2-3 weeks	One repeat planting
Leek	130 days	2 ft.	8 weeks	#
Lettuce, leaf	45-50 days	1 ft.	3 weeks	Repeat planting for fall
Lettuce, head	75-85 days	1 ft.	4 weeks	Replant July 1
Muskmelon	80-90 days	1 vine	4 weeks	
Okra	65-70 days	2 ft.	4 weeks	
Onions, sets	21-35 days	1 ft.	5-6 weeks	
Onions, seed	90-100 days	2 ft.	10 weeks	Use thinnings as green onions
Parsnip	100-130 days	2 ft.	Fall and winter	
Peas	65-80 days	4 ft.	2-4 weeks	August 1 reseeding in cooler areas
Pepper	60-85 days	1 ft.	6-8 weeks	
Radish	25-40 days	1 ft.	2-4 weeks	
Spinach	40-50 days	3 ft.	3 weeks	Sow fall second crop August 1
New Zealand spinach	55 days	2 ft.	14 weeks	

Crop	Days to Harvest	Space for 4 Servings	Length of Harvest	Remarks
Squash, summer	50-65 days	3 ft.	10 weeks	Reseed June if borers infest first planting
Squash, winter	80-105 days	†1 vine	6 weeks	* Replant June 15 for winter storage
Rutabaga	95-105 days	1 ft.	6 weeks	*
Tomato	60-85 days	2 plants	12-14 weeks	
Turnip	40-70 days	2 ft.	2-3 weeks	Replant for fall July 15

\# Indicates that use can be extended from plants that survive light freezes.

* Indicates that these varieties are also stored for winter use.

†Space for winter squash is for smaller-fruited winter varieties. Vines occupy approximately two feet in a row, but run out six feet.

28

Fertilizers: Are They "Plant Foods"?

An important fact to understand about fertilizers is that they are *not* plant foods. It is true that they are often referred to as actual foods, but in order to use them in this way, plants would have to have some way to eat them and a digestive system to break up complex organic substances into simpler forms of matter.

Instead a plant is a food factory that takes in very simple chemical materials and manufactures its own foods. In the chapter on soils we will see how important microorganisms such as bacteria and fungi are to this process.

Commercial Fertilizers

To survive, plants need 13 or more different chemical elements. Three of them make up the bulk of these elements: nitrogen, phosphorus, and potassium, usually called potash. Although the others are referred to as "minor" elements, this is not strictly true. For example, plants may use as much or more sulfur than they do phosphorus, but because sulfur is seldom lacking in soils, little importance is attached to it. Many of the other elements may be used in small amounts, often in a few parts per

276

million. This does not mean they are minor in effect.

What this means is that so-called complete fertilizers may not be truly complete. The term has become quasi-legal, since federal fertilizer regulatory agencies insist only that the "Big Three" elements—nitrogen, phosphorus, and potash—need be included to qualify for that rating.

These three elements, abbreviated as N for nitrogen, P for phosphorus, and K for potash are shown as percentages in a numerical formula on the bag. Most lawn fertilizers (the most common material sold in garden centers) are now 20-10-5 or similar in composition. This means that in a 20-pound bag, there will be four pounds of nitrogen, two of phosphorus and one of potash.

Note that this formula indicates a mixture of three sources of plant nutrients, but of the 20 pounds in the bag, only seven are indicated as actual plant foods. This does not mean that the balance is inert filler; it may include sulfur, calcium, magnesium, and other elements that plants need. Most modern fertilizers for vegetables also contain vital "minor" elements that are minor only in quantity not in their effect on plant growth.

The law does not allow a manufacturer to claim a certain mineral is in the bag unless it makes up at least one percent of the whole. Since that amount of many "minor" elements would hurt or kill plants, these are not indicated on the bags because they are safe to include only in a few parts per million. To be sure you have such elements in your soil, there is a simple answer, one I keep repeating *ad nauseam:* Add organic matter. Since plant wastes contain all the elements needed for growth, compost solves the problem nicely. I realize that I am beginning to sound like a dedicated organic gardener, but fact is fact.

There is another, more expensive way to supply minor elements—apply dried blood or fish emulsion. Although these are expensive fertilizers, they would cost no more than special mixtures of minor elements sold in fancy packages, and in addition would supply other valuable nutrients.

Commercial crop fertilizers vary with the vegetables being grown. Those that are grown for their leaves need a product high in nitrogen, those grown for their root crops should have a fertilizer higher in potash, while crops that bear fruit, such as tomatoes, need phosphorus in addition to potash. Such specialization is unnecessary in the home garden, although a fertilizer low in nitrogen and higher in phosphorus and potash will give better growth in root and fruit crops, which tend to run to foliage if given too much nitrogen.

For a mixed garden including all three types of crops, the best answer is to use a brand that is fairly well balanced between all three major elements. Formulas would be something like 20-20-20, 18-16-12, 10-12-6. Actually these are not perfect because no two soils are alike. If you were growing 50 acres of tomatoes, such formulas would be wasteful unless formulated to fit both crop and soil. On a 50- by 100-foot home garden, the amount wasted would cost less than the materials needed to make a soil analysis.

One weakness in practically all lawn fertilizers (which are all too often used on vegetable gardens) is that they are woefully weak in potash. Even on grasses, they starve them for potash while overfeeding on nitrogen. A basic rule in feeding crops is that they use as much potash as they do nitrogen. Because nitrogen is easily lost, we must feed this in excess; so sound practice calls for one pound of potash for two pounds of nitrogen in most formulas.

If forced to use a high nitrogen lawn fertilizer on the garden, add wood ashes or either muriate of potash or sulfate of potash to increase the stingy amount of this element in a 20-10-5 formula.

Sources of Nitrogen

No matter in what form you apply fertilizer, the nitrogen it contains came originally from one source—the atmosphere. In the wild, plants are supplied with it in several ways. One source is from the air, where lightning precipitates it in the form of nitrous oxide. It is also brought down in snow. Certain free-living soil bacteria are capable of fixing nitrogen directly from the air in small quantities. The principal source of natural nitrogen, however, is certain specialized bacteria that live on the roots of members of the pea family—legumes such as clover, beans, soybeans, peas, and alfalfa. The actual amounts accumulated may be small, but when crops such as snap beans, peas, and edible soybeans are grown in the garden, it is enough for growth. They draw very little nitrogen from the soil, but are hosts to bacteria that absorb nitrogen from the air. When they are plowed under, nitrogen they contain can add substantially to that element.

In the past, instead of sowing ryegrass as a cover crop after early vegetables were harvested, I have made a practice of seeding the row with leftover seeds of peas or beans, to be plowed under. Now, with seed supplies uncertain, I am keeping these for possible use later. I have gone to vetch as a cover crop since I can gather the seed I need from volunteer plants.

If seed must be purchased, alfalfa is the most efficient collector of nitrogen, adding some 250 pounds per acre. Alfalfa seed is useful to have on hand also for sprouting, as described under salad crops.

For the home gardener to try to mix his own fertilizers is a waste of time, money, and energy. The one thing to look for in commercial mixtures is the source of nitrogen. Nowadays all the advantages of the slow release of nutrients from organic matter can be had with such manmade materials as Ureaform, Nitroform, IBDU, Magamp, Green-Green, Osmocote, and others. These names are generic except for Magamp, Osmocote, and Green-Green, and will not appear as a brand name but in the formula printed on the bag.

I am in favor of slow-release nitrogen rather than quickly soluble forms, such as ammonium nitrate or ammonium sulfate, because they release nitrogen so slowly that plant roots can absorb most of it. When dissolved quickly, nitrogen is only partially used because much of it drains away. True, microorganisms in soil can hang on to some of it, but in the end nitrogen is from three to five times as effective as the slow-release types. Its chief role is in promoting healthy, green foliage.

Until recently the only mixed fertilizers containing slow release (also called timed-release) forms of nitrogen were intended for use on lawns. Although they might do for leafy vegetables such as lettuce, spinach, and cabbage, they were badly balanced for those grown for their roots or fruits.

In 1975 the introduction of special timed-release mixed fertilizers by two companies made possible the use of this type of plant food on food crops. This was a major improvement, since, today, vegetable gardeners need make only a single application in spring when preparing the soil. Once this has been plowed or dug under, the job is done for the entire season.

One of these is mentioned in the chapter on growing tomatoes—Green-Green, made by the Sierra Chemical Company, Milpitas, California 95035. This company also makes another slow-release-fertilizer line called Osmocote, used widely by greenhouse operators, with special formulas for different crops. Both Osmocote and Green-Green control the release of nutrients with a plastic coating that only allows measured amounts to pass through the coating.

Sierra also makes an unusual tree-feeding pellet called Agriform, which does not dissolve fully for two years and feeds for that length of time. The pellets are slow dissolving. (Some I had purchased ten years before turned up in the toolshed. Although in an open carton in a damp place, they had not dissolved or broken up.) Trees treated with these pellets grew much better than did those fed with a regular tree formula.

The newest additions to timed-release fertilizers are an unusual line of vegetable, rose, and flower foods, also plastic coated. The vegetable formula, a 9-12-6 product is not only well balanced but strikes a good average for all three types of vegetables—leafy, root, and fruit. This line is the product of the famous Minnesota Mining and Manufacturing Company and is marketed under their 3M brand. You can't miss it on garden center shelves; the plastic coatings are fluorescent orange (for vegetables), fluorescent chartreuse (for roses), and fluorescent yellow (for flowers).

This year in Canada, gardeners will have a new source of slow-release nitrogen that may well revolutionize the use of this type of fertilizer. Through its Canadian affiliate, International Chemicals of England will release sulfur-coated urea (sulfur-coated nitrogen). Now being manufactured by Canadian Industries, Ltd. (C.I.L.), this product has been widely tested by home gardeners, market growers, and farmers.

Its principal value is that it is cheaper to produce than other forms of slow-release nitrogen yet releases at a controlled rate. Since it is not active in dry soils, it does not become available when it could burn roots.

In 1977 a number of American fertilizer dealers plan to use this as a source of nitrogen. It is *not* a complete fertilizer, unlike some of the other slow-release plant foods just mentioned; it will be an ingredient under brand names.

Phosphorus and pH

Phosphorus is usually the biggest ingredient in vegetable fertilizer mixtures. There are two reasons for this. In the past phosphorus was the cheapest fertilizer ingredient available. Government regulations required at least 20 percent actual fertilizer units in a mixture; so it was cheaper to use phosphorus in larger amounts than the other two elements. A common formula in the past was 5-10-5. Today phosphorus is higher in price and this practice is dying out.

Another reason for using large amounts of this ingredient is that when applied to soil, most forms of phosphorus, particularly superphosphate, soon lock up in an insoluble form that plants cannot use. In order to take up what they need of this element they must absorb it quickly and store it for future use before it locks up. I have checked phosphorus, particularly in lawn soils where it had been applied for years, where the amount of insoluble phosphorus was so high that the lawn could have served as a low-grade phosphate mine, except that chemical treatment would be needed to make the phosphorus soluble.

This is one reason why pH is so important. Phosphorus is particularly sensitive to both high and low pH readings. It becomes increasingly less available as acidity drops below a reading of 6.0, and at 5.0 cannot be used by plants. On the alkaline side at 6.9, it again begins to lock up and by 7.8 turns into a glass-hard form that is again unavailable.

Need for the right pH means that the gardener should know how to measure it, and what to do if it is not right. The pH sets sold by garden centers and other dealers in horticultural supplies usually contain a chemical solution that, when dripped onto a soil sample, will alter the color of a strip of treated paper. The color of this strip can then be compared to a color chart that shows the pH of the soil sample. If the reading is between 6.0 and 6.9, consider yourself lucky. You will need to do nothing but use fertilizer. However, two weeks after you have added a highly soluble fertilizer, make a second check, as some fertilizer ingredients can change pH.

If the reading is too acid, lower than 6.0, the best way to change it is to apply ground limestone, which will supply calcium and increase the pH. How much to apply depends upon the type of soil. To raise the pH of a light, sandy loam one full point, say from 5.0 to 6.0, use 35 pounds of ground limestone on 1,000 square feet. You can use either the fine limestone chips used to top dress driveways, or regular agricultural limestone, which is even finer. On a medium loam soil, apply 50 pounds to the same area, and on a clay loam, 70 pounds.

One important point to remember: do *not* apply lime and fertilizer at the same time. Apply them at least two weeks apart. This allows the one that is applied first to react with the soil, so it will not be affected by a chemical reaction with the other. The order in which they are applied is not too critical, but usually lime is applied in fall so that by spring there is practically no interaction.

Hydrated lime is sold in bags at building material yards and is often the only form readily available. It reacts very quickly and when soil must be brought into working condition quickly, it is probably the best form to use. It is not as convenient as limestone because it is dusty, hard to spread, and cakes if it gets damp. In theory it goes farther than ground limestone, but I have had no trouble when using it at the same rate.

Acidifying Soil

There are times when soils are too sweet (alkaline) as in many places in the Southwest, or where an acid soil with a pH of 5.5 or below is wanted to grow potatoes (see chapter on potatoes for reasons). Also, where blueberries are to be grown, they need an acid soil, preferably below a pH of 5.0. The best material to acidify soil is sulfur. Although there are special forms of sulfur recommended for this purpose, the cheapest (and as good as any) is ordinary dusting sulfur. To lower pH in a sandy soil one full point (from pH 6.0 to 5.0) apply ten pounds of dusting sulfur. In medium loam soil, 15 pounds will be needed, and on clay loam, 20 pounds (all figures for 1,000 square feet).

Sulfur reacts slowly; retest in two months with a second retest in six months.

Although both calcium and sulfur are direct plant nutrients, they should not be considered as fertilizers when used for changing pH. Nor does a reading of 6.0 to 6.9 insure that plants will be well fed. The plant nutrients must be added in addition to sulfur or limestone if they are not already present.

A question often asked is whether a soil test other than for pH is necessary. In a home garden the money spent for a professional test, or for the materials for a do-it-yourself check, would be better spent for more fertilizer. Most well balanced commercial fertilizers are designed to feed garden crops for a full growing season. If applied at the rate recommended on the bag, soil fertility should be maintained even if not increased.

You should rely on my repeated advice to add organic matter for maintaining or increasing soil fertility for more than one season, not only the annual application of food needed by the current year's crop.

Effects of Various Fertilizer Elements
Nitrogen
Its principal effect is stimulation of rapid growth of stems and foliage. It gives leaves a rich, dark-green color. A lack of nitrogen is often the cause of yellowish green leaf color. In many plants too much nitrogen results in lanky, weak stems. It tends to produce watery, succulent growth, which is desirable in leafy crops such as spinach, lettuce, and celery, but undesirable in tomatoes. A classic example is the effect of chicken manure (high in nitrogen) on tomatoes, beans, and peppers. They produce soft, sappy growth but few flowers and fruits. Crops fed too much nitrogen are usually more subject to disease than are those given smaller amounts balanced with phosphorus and potash.

Phosphorus

Formerly, soil experts felt that phosphorus was used only as plants matured. True, it is an important ingredient in seeds. It is, however, so vital to young growth that if it is not available in soils as plants grow, it will be withdrawn from old foliage to supply that needed for new growth. As essential as it is, amazingly little of it is needed to promote growth. A 100 bushels to the acre of corn are produced by less than 30 pounds of phosphorus. A one-thousand-square-foot lawn gets along very well on about a teacupful. But as we have seen, to supply that teacupful, several pounds of superphosphate must be supplied.

Making phosphorus available in soil is another function of organic matter. The ferment of decay in such matter releases certain acids that make it available again, but only in small amounts that plants take up immediately.

A specialized use for phosphorus, in combination with potash is in so-called starter solutions such as Take-Hold. Low in N and high in P and K, these fertilizers are dissolved in water and used to irrigate transplants as they are set out. For some reason not wholly understood, these solutions help such transplants take hold quickly. They suffer less from the shock of transplanting.

Potash

This element is one of the most neglected in studying plant growth. Although many plants use it in relatively small amounts, actually they need more of it than they do of nitrogen. However, nitrogen must be applied in excess because it leaches away so rapidly. Agronomists recommend applying two parts of nitrogen to one part of potash. Potash is essential to starch and sugar formation during photosynthesis and production of seeds. It is also highly important in root formation, hence is used in large amounts in commercial production of root crops. Among crops producing fruits, peas and beans in particular need plenty of potash.

Since it is not harmful when present in fairly large amounts, it can be used freely without damage to plants within reason. All true soils contain some potash but usually in a form not too readily available to plants. The only organic fertilizers that contain adequate amounts of this element are unleached wood ashes. During the winter these should be saved in a dry container. They are best applied as the soil is being tilled in spring. For a short time after they are applied to soil, they can form a lye in combination with organic matter that can hurt roots, but this is soon changed into available potash.

The most common potash mineral fertilizers are sulfate of potash and muriate of potash. Like wood ashes, they are best applied before digging or tilling. In applying wood ashes the lime content and its effect on pH should be taken into consideration, since they also contain lime.

Special-Use Fertilizers

When starting plants indoors use a sand-and-peat mixture as mentioned in the chapter on tomatoes, because this contains practically no fertility whatever. If vermiculite is used instead of sand, this does contain small amounts of potash, but very little else. Even the prepared commercial mixes are low in fertility, perhaps on the theory that seedlings need practically no nutrients.

This is true, but in my tests I have never found one of these commercial mixes that did not become ineffective about a week or two before transplanting. If left in the pots without further feeding, seedlings will be set back enough to affect future growth.

For unfertilized synthetic soils, I use a good house-plant fertilizer, either liquid or dry. If dry, I dissolve it in water. The liquid house-plant fertilizers are usually diluted in water before use. Don't use these full strength; apply either type at about one-fourth the strength recommended on the package, but do use them every time you water.

Start feeding as soon as seedlings make their first true leaves. In the case of seedlings being grown in a prefertilized artificial soil, just assume they are running out of feed about two weeks before setting out-of-doors.

Stocking and Storing Fertilizers

With supplies of commercial fertilizers short and threatening to remain in short supply, don't waste unused bags or parts of bags. Today most of them will be bagged in heavy plastic. Unopened bags will not lose strength and can be stored in a reasonably dry place for a year or two. The best place for broken bags is on the compost heap. Here they will not be lost but will feed microorganisms that break down organic matter. When these organisms die, the fertilizer will remain in the pile until compost is used, except for some loss by leaching.

Saving Natural Fertilizers

One source of fertility that should not be wasted in rural areas is that which is available from the outdoor privy. Many are squeamish about this, but if peat moss is used as an absorbent, and if the peat moss is then composted over winter, the resultant mixture is superior to well-rotted cattle manure. In England the bothies (dormitories where apprentice gardeners lived) always had a urinal filled with peat. The peat from this source was always saved for propagating cuttings and seedlings in the greenhouse; it was rich in growth-stimulating hormones.

Manure from any livestock kept on a subsistence farm or large suburban property should be saved under shelter until used. Instead of the usual straw used for bedding, peat moss or ground corncobs will absorb more moisture. The addition of about a quart of superphosphate to every bushel of one of these manures will improve it for growing vegetables and also reduce odors.

Prospects for More Fertilizers

Although some authorities are predicting a more abundant supply of manmade fertilizers within two or three years, these predictions are much too optimistic. True, coal and other non-petroleum products can be used as raw materials. Unfortunately these call for costly production equipment that manufacturers are unwilling to develop. They have no assurance that once these facilities are built oil prices will not drop, leaving them with enormous capital investments in plants that could only be operated at a loss.

29

Soil: A Basic "Stuff" of Life

Those who are in a hurry to thrust a spade into the earth and start planting may want to skip much of the explanation of why soil should be treated as a living substance, but they are urged to save it for reading during the idle days of winter.

In the frenzied rush to grow food at home, millions of Americans came face to face with soil for the first time. Here was a substance with which they had had little or no experience. If they spoke of it at all, it was in disparaging words such as "cheap as dirt" or "as common as dirt under your feet."

Far from being common, simple, and a subject for contempt, soil is perhaps the most complex, the least understood substance with which man must work to survive. It has been called the "mother of us all," because from it comes the basic energy that fuels the human body. Without it there would be no green plants, the only organisms that are able to capture energy from the sun and store it as starches and sugars—sole source of energy for all living things.

If soil is such a complex substance, how is it that primitive man was able to grow crops that have sustained human life since long before recorded human history?

One of the awesome triumphs of primitive man was how he managed to manipulate soil, even though completely unaware of the intricate actions and interactions within its structure. In spite of his ignorance, he was able to force this protean stuff of life to produce the plants that enabled him to survive. Out of his conquest of soil came the foundations of civilization.

What is important to understand, however, is that he won his battle for survival at the cost of tremendous physical effort, producing only enough to feed himself and his family. Today a single farmer not only feeds himself far better than did primitive man tilling soil with a crooked stick, but he also supports 50 or more additional people in urban communities. This has been possible only because of improved knowledge of what soil is, and how it must be worked. This is knowledge that every true gardener must acquire in order to manipulate soil for superior plant growth.

During the past three or four decades there has been much confused thinking and talking about the importance of "natural gardening." The sooner this idea is dispelled the better. Growing plants for food is not a natural process. A plant in the wild has but two fates—to survive and to reproduce itself. In farming and gardening the purpose is not only to survive and reproduce but to produce a surplus to feed mankind. And to do so, the nature of soil and its manipulation are important to understand.

The Vital Microorganisms

Those who think of soil as a simple mixture of minerals devoid of life would do well to begin its study by turning over a spadeful of rich garden loam. At first the only signs of life will be a few earthworms and larger soil insects. Unseen until powerful magnification is used are millions of microorganisms, many only familiar to earth scientists—bacteria, fungi, mycorrhizae, actinomyces, protozoa, and rotifers to mention a few of the more common forms. In a clod of rich soil there can be as many invisible living organisms as there are human beings in the world. The invisible population of a single acre of tilled farmland can be so vast that it can only be numbered by the astronomer's system of numeration—the light-year and the gogol.

Small as they are, these microorganisms are far from unimportant. Without them no mixture of sand, clay, and silt deserves to be called a soil. Before it can be so named, two elements must be present—microorganisms and organic matter. About organic matter, more later. As for microorganisms a pure mineral mixture of rock debris without them is a substance in which plants will grow poorly, if at all.

These infinitesimal bits of life have a vital role to play. Without them the remains of once-living plants and animals would pile up, unchanged and unavailable. In them would be the food that once sustained them until all the nitrogen, phosphorus, and potash on earth would be stored out of the reach of organisms that survived. Fortunately for our own survival, soil organisms, principally bacteria and fungi, are capable of digesting this accumulation of organic matter and in so doing, release these elements to support other, more highly organized, plants and animals.

As vital as this process is, in their enthusiasm for so-called natural fertilizers, organic gardeners* overlook some important facts. Most important of all, green plants, those we grow for food and ornament, are completely unable to use nutrient elements directly from once-living matter in their original form. No one has ever seen a green plant munching on a hamburger or a hot dog. Roots do not *digest* anything. That is done for them by microorganisms. Crop plants actually live on a 'soup' in which are dissolved nitrogen, phosphorus, and potash, along with other simple elements they need, a liquid diet predigested for them by soil bacteria, or where mineral fertilizers are used, supplied by man.

A plant root is a highly selective filter that screens out all but soluble nutrients in near-elemental form. The way this works is

---

* I have no intention of criticizing organic gardeners in discussing the inadequacies of natural fertilizer; my only purpose is to emphasize that their methods are not fully adequate. What is badly needed is a blend of full use of organic matter with the supportive power of chemical fertilizers. The latter have their faults, as we shall see later in this chapter.

so complicated that knowledge of at least three scientific disciplines is essential to understanding it fully, but that it does work has been proved scientifically. What is significant is that the system is unable to distinguish between elements from chemicals and those from organic matter.

A case in point is urea, a chemical that can be synthesized from carbon dioxide, nitrogen, and water. It also occurs naturally in urine. Plants show no differences in growth between applications of manmade urea and that extracted from urine.

The Slow Breakdown

Important to understand is that organic breakdown is not an instantaneous process. For example, when protein from a dead animal or a soybean stalk is reduced to the simple nitrate nitrogen that crop plants need, as many as 40 different species of bacteria and fungi may take part. At first one or two species break it down to proteose, others to amino acids, then ammonia, and next to nitrite nitrogen. Plants are not yet able to absorb it in this form. Not until a final stage of breakdown converts it into nitrate nitrogen is it of any use to crop plants. Obviously all this takes time.

One reason why time is required, particularly in spring, is that the microorganisms that are vital to digesting organic matter do not work at low temperatures. They are dormant at soil readings below 40 degrees F. Between 40 and 60 degrees, they are active, but use practically every bit of what they digest for their own life processes. Not until soil temperatures warm up to 60 degrees and higher are they able to produce enough nourishing "soup" to speed up the growth of green plants. In northern New England, this increase in temperature often does not occur until mid or late June.

This means that organic fertilizers applied in early spring do no feeding. What growth early crops are able to make must depend upon scanty traces of unused nutrients that were released the year before but did not drain off. Trees grow differently; they store starches and sugars in their wood that are available for growth before energy can be drawn from the soil.

Dedicated organic gardeners, no matter how faithful they

might be to their creed later in summer, would do well to cheat a bit by using a quickly available chemical fertilizer early in spring. True, if it were available, dried blood (in which all the elements needed by plants are contained in soluble form) could be used, but this now commands so high a price for industrial uses that little or none moves through gardening channels.

The fate of bone meal, a material loved by our grandfathers as a fertilizer, is a good example why an understanding of soil is important. Its use persists in spite of evidence that it is all but useless as a plant food. At one time freshly ground raw bone *was* of value in growing crops. During Victorian days, in the potting shed of every big British estate, as well as in sheds behind humble cottages, there stood a bone grinder into which went every scrap of bone from the tables of both squires and gardeners. Bits of meat and marrow were high in nitrogen and other plant food elements. The bone itself did supply a modicum of phosphorus, but its most important contribution was calcium. Today, with our knowledge of soil action and reaction, we can supply both calcium and phosphorus at a fraction of their cost as bone meal.

The bone meal of today, sold in neat, clean packages, is a far cry from the ground raw bone of grandfather's day. Steamed to remove gelatin and other by-products, what is ground and sold is devoid of practically everything but insoluble phosphorus and a trace of lime. In fact the phosphorus it contains is so insoluble that ten pounds of superphosphate will supply more of this element to plants than will half a ton of modern bone meal.

Slow-Release Fertilizers

Old-time organic or natural fertilizers did have one advantage that has all but been destroyed by modern chemistry. They were preferred by many because they did not become available all at once but became available slowly as soil bacteria broke them down. Today pure chemical fertilizers are being made that release slowly in the same way. Actually these slow-release chemical fertilizers have one advantage over the older natural manures, since they are not dependent upon bacteria for release; they do supply nutrients to plants early in spring.

These slow-release products work on various systems. Some,

such as Osmocote and Green-Green depend on the slow movement of water through a plastic coating to release nutrients in small doses. Others, such as ureaform, IBDU, and Magamp rely on their physical or chemical makeup to release them by soil action.

The importance of slow release cannot be overemphasized. Since chemicals of this type will probably become more and more expensive (they are made largely from crude oils that are in critical supply) home gardeners would do well to lean more and more on organic materials as fertilizers. See the chapter on fertilizers for details.

Organic Matter

Another element in soil that is critical is an abundant supply of organic matter that has already undergone decomposition. As already mentioned no mixture of minerals can be called a true soil unless this element is contained in it. Here is one area where I am totally in agreement with organic gardeners. Unless you must garden on land that is high in muck or peat, it would be difficult to supply too much of this element to your garden plot. For one thing the weight of the materials needed would deter all but the huskiest gardener from moving tons of compost or well-rotted manure onto a home garden plot.

The mention of composted materials and well-rotted manure (a rare product in urban communities but one of the fringe benefits of rural living) brings to mind the reason why fresh vegetable matter should be avoided whenever possible, unless this can be buried completely so that none of it will undergo further decay on the surface of the soil. Most of the soil bacteria and fungi are benevolent, useful organisms, but they are much like the bacteria and fungi that cause plant diseases. The latter harmful forms use starches and sugars for energy and can both propagate and survive over winter on decaying vegetation. Fusarium wilt, early blight, and verticillium wilt are diseases described in the chapter on tomatoes. All three can be transmitted by infected soil splashed onto foliage by rain.

When composted, organic matter loses much of its starch content so organisms of this type can no longer propagate on them. About building a compost heap, there will be more information later.

The pH Factor

Another element enters into the complex world of soil with its ferment of microscopic life, organic matter, and food elements. That element is a reaction called pH. This sounds mysterious, but if you can read a thermometer, you can read a pH response in soil and make it work for you. It is a scale that measures how sweet or how sour a soil might be. Chemically, this would tell how alkaline or acid it is.

Grandfather called it sweet or sour because he often tested it with his tongue. He knew if it tasted slightly sour, it needed lime. Often he did not even test it; he knew that as manure decayed soil became more acid, so every three or four years he would dump a few loads of finely ground limestone on his fields. Later he learned that litmus paper would turn red if the soil was acid, blue if it were still sweet.

Litmus paper was a crude test that didn't tell how much lime was needed. Today we use other types of paper that turn different colors to show exactly how acid or how alkaline a soil is. Soil scientists use an electric bridge to measure this reaction; while much more accurate, such refinement isn't needed in a home garden. The pH kits using paper strips are sold by most good garden centers for two or three dollars and are accurate enough. .

They will give readings on a numerical scale, much as a thermometer measures temperature. This scale measures in steps from zero (the most acid) to 7.0, which is neutral, and from neutral up to 14.0, the most alkaline. The extremes are used only in chemistry. Soil readings seldom go as low as 4.0 or much higher than 8.5. Soils outside this range are unfit for growing plants and would cost too much to modify for garden use.

For practically all garden plants a reading somewhere between 6.0 and 6.9 is desirable. Within this range all the elements needed by plants are available in a soil, provided they are actually present. If not present they can be added by applying fertilizers. Potatoes are an exception to the 6.0-6.9 range.

Although they prefer sweeter soils, they are usually grown in soils as acid as 5.0 to 5.5. The reason is that they are subject to a disease called scab, an organism that cannot grow in acid soil.

In the end all gardeners should be concerned with producing a soil improved by human hands—Gardener's Loam. This is *not* a natural material such as might be found in open fields. Keep in mind that in gardening you are not trying for natural growth but for controlled and accelerated growth, which will produce healthy plants with heavier yields. What is not commonly appreciated is that even the addition of natural manures and fertilizers is only an artificial device to improve on that dear old lady, Mother Nature.

The Compost Pile

If you have read the rest of this chapter carefully, the need for some device for processing plant and animal wastes should be clear. In grandfather's day, that was the manure pile behind the barn where the motive power for the family buggy was housed. If the flies and odors did not force removal too soon, this would produce a rich, mellow substance that would improve any soil. On the farm, the housewife managed to steal a little of the manure intended for the fields to spread on her food garden.

On the farm today manure is considered a nuisance and disposing of it is a major problem. In the city and suburbs soil that cries for organic matter must be fed either with costly peat moss or dried cattle or sheep manure, or the gardener must produce this vital soil element by building a compost pile.

If he understands how soil works, he will realize that a compost pile is nothing less than a big culture of bacteria and other soil organisms feeding on table scraps, weeds, grass clippings, discarded vegetables, not to mention feathers, sawdust, hay, straw, fallen leaves, and lawn clippings, and even the remains of junior's haircut. In theory, anything that was once alive, whether animal or vegetable, will decay and can be used to make compost. The more protein it contains, such as meat scraps or spoiled dried beans, the more nitrogen it will produce and the more it is worth as compost.

A compost pile is not a thing of beauty; so try to find a spot for it that is out of sight. The site should be on well-drained soil. Start by laying down coarse material such as cornstalks, shrub trimmings, or well-washed steam cinders. The purpose of this lower layer is to allow air to penetrate under the pile. If air is driven out completely, bacteria that produce nitrites will dominate and this form of bacterial action is not good for plants. Over this bottom layer place about two or three inches of any organic matter available. In fall, dried leaves are usually available for this purpose.

Here I should point out that there has been too much idle talk about the "richness" of leaf mold, which is the form of compost that leaves will produce. They are valuable in forming a special form of compost known as humus, but their food value is low. Before a tree sheds leaves in fall, all the plant food in them is withdrawn into the trunk and branches. The shed leaf is little more than fiber. At the same time, leaves are a desirable starting material.

Over the organic matter, it is a good idea to sprinkle some good mixed fertilizer—organic if you are of that persuasion, chemical if you are not. This should go on about as thickly as you would sprinkle sugar on strawberries. Next cover the first layer with about two or three inches of good garden loam. This is to inoculate the pile with soil organisms; a compost will not work well without such organisms.

On top of the layer of soil sprinkle ground limestone (the fine size used for topping driveways) or regular agricultural limestone. In a pinch, hydrated lime from a building material yard can be used for this purpose. Don't try to save work by applying both limestone and fertilizer in the same layer. They will react and make the fertilizer ineffective. In separated layers they have a chance to be taken up by soil and organic particles before they can react.

Keep building the pile in this manner, layer by layer of organic matter, fertilizer, soil, and lime as long as organic material is available. Excessive amounts of oils, fats, or grease will slow up decomposition into humus (the material you are trying to produce from compost). Moderate amounts of fats and waxes will help rather than hurt, however. Fatty material is vital to humus development. Only when it is in excess is it harmful.

When a pile reaches a height of 18 to 24 inches, it should be turned over and mixed thoroughly so that all the material will come in contact with lime, fertilizer, soil bacteria, and fungi. Rake the top level again and build layer by layer on the lower mixed part of the pile. Often, dishing out of the top is recommended to catch rain. This is good practice, except if rains are so heavy and so frequent that the pile becomes saturated. This can be avoided if the pile is well made, and if during seasons of heavy rain, the entire pile is covered with plastic. In dry seasons, wetting down with a hose is advisable to keep the pile from drying out.

A pile much higher than three feet tends to pack down too much. If one is completed before all available organic matter is used up, start a new pile rather than build too high.

To predict the length of time needed to convert plant wastes into well-rotted compost is difficult. Dig into the pile at intervals of three to six months. If it has turned a dark brown and crumbles easily, it is ready to use.

Always screen compost through a half-inch hardware cloth screen for use. That is, a screen that has four openings to a square inch. Any material that won't go through the screen should be used as the base for a new pile.

Working Soil

The act that sets Gardener's Loam apart from soils in open fields is that it is manipulated to increase and improve the growth of plants. When and how to begin is a problem that faces the first-time gardener. If it is spring, and if the garden has been cultivated recently, the first step is to make a mud-pie test. This is done to see if it is dry enough to work. To make the test, pick up a handful of soil and squeeze it into a ball or mud pie. Now try to crumble the ball into loose soil. If it refuses to break up, it is too wet to dig or till.

If it does crumble and fall apart without too much effort, it can be worked immediately. Sometimes, spreading dry peat moss or vermiculite over a row or two where the gardener is anxious to put in early crops will absorb enough moisture to permit tilling a small area, but this is rather expensive for a larger area.

If the soil is dry and will not form a ball, it may have to be watered before working it.

Whenever possible, I prefer to turn over the soil with a spade rather than use mechanical equipment. Unless it is very light or had broad tires, a rotary tiller, for example, will pack down soil almost as much as it loosens it. Digging is much easier than it looks if you don't try to turn over the entire garden at once. Do a row or two every evening and plant the rows as you dig. If you are delayed in finishing, use the last rows for warm-weather crops.

On my 75th birthday, I dug two 50-foot rows, turning under a heavy crop of pea vines that had produced a crop earlier. It was a pleasant experience, with the odor of fresh earth and pea vines under a warm sun.

Although I do own an eight-horsepower tiller, it is not my favorite way to work up soil. It is hard to control unless you walk behind it, which means that you pack down soil you have already plowed. If used year after year to the same depth, in heavier soils it can build up a plow sole of compacted earth through which drainage is poor. I prefer plowing, followed by discing as preparation for larger plots that cannot be dug by hand.

If compost, fertilizer, or lime are to be plowed under, they should be applied at different times to avoid reaction between lime or limestone and fertilizer. Spread the lime on the surface two weeks before you plan to plow. Either compost and lime or compost and fertilizer are all right together, but applying all three at the same time is not recommended. Two weeks after lime has been applied, it will have attracted particles of clay and formed nodules or clumps that will mean looser soil. It will not react with fertilizer after this has taken place.

This is not the time to take a pH test. A reliable test can only be made in warm soil after microorganisms have been at work for some time. If lime is applied it is assumed that this was done as a result of a pH test made the summer before. In the absence of a test the presence of certain plants and weeds will tell whether lime is needed. The best of these to use as an indicator is sorrel, which is a vicious weed in acid soils, sending its white hairlike roots everywhere and sprouting at the joints.

This is true sorrel with spear-shaped leaves that taste strongly of acid if chewed. Wood sorrel, with a cloverlike leaf, is a different plant. Another weed that thrives in acid soil is smart-weed, with long pink-and-white tassellike flowers. The stems have prominent joints. Soils in which hydrangea flowers are blue are acid. If blueberries grow nearby that is also an indica-tion of acidity, as are cranberries and bunchberries.

If digging or plowing can be done a week or two before plant-ing is done, so much the better. This allows loosened soil to set-tle and fill any voids that were left when the soil was worked.

Raw land that has not been tilled for a number of years or has never been worked is more difficult to handle. Not only does it offer stiff resistance to tilling, but it calls for turning under large amounts of organic matter, which must be allowed to rot or growth of crops can be affected. If the area is not large, the best treatment is to skin off all sod and other growth, using this as the basis for a compost pile. Nothing beats compost made from a heavy sod. In the meantime, apply twice as much fertilizer as is recommended for a given area and plow this in.

Usually the beginning gardener has no source of compost, but by asking old hands some source might be turned up. If you local sewage treatment plant uses a digestion method, sludge that has been allowed to weather over winter is a perfectly good source of organic matter. If, however, your town has much heavy industry, the sludge can be loaded with heavy metals, such as lead and mercury, in which case avoid using it. The manager can usually give you an analysis. Under no circum-stances use fresh sewage sludge on a garden. Unless frozen it can carry the organism of amoebic dysentery.

Peat moss, except for a relatively small area, is too costly for use. If time permits, growing a cover crop and plowing it under is a good way to upgrade a new garden. If you get the urge to garden in August or September, winter rye seeded at that time will make tremendous growth by the following spring and can be turned under early enough to plant most crops. The seed for this is cereal winter rye, not the ryegrass used in cheap lawn mixtures.

Converting raw soil into mellow Gardener's Loam is not a

rapid process. If it is a heavy clay loam, this can limit the types of vegetables you can grow. Don't attempt carrots, parsnips, or other root crops. Although they will grow, resistance to root penetration will make roots twist and turn trying to corkscrew their way into hard soil. As a result they will be tough and tasteless.

None of the vine crops do well in clay or clay-loam soils unless they have been conditioned by the addition of liberal amounts of well-rotted organic matter. Either condition a small area for these or don't grow them. The most satisfactory crops in stiff soils are the leafy vegetables such as lettuce, spinach, cabbage, and Swiss chard.

30

Tools and Other Equipment

Good garden tools are a delight, poor ones a constant irritation. But how do you tell a good tool from a bad one? First be sure it does the work it is meant to do. A good example is two pairs of pruning shears I own. One is magnificent, with a heavy chrome plating, a Teflon-treated cutting blade and a beautifully designed lock for the blade. It is twice as heavy as the other pair. The handles are rubber covered and fit the hand perfectly. It is obviously designed by an engineer, not by a gardener. The one trouble with it is that it won't cut. To drive the blade through a branch takes exactly twice as much strength as does the lighter, cheaper pruner, which is so designed that the blade cuts with a rolling motion rather than the straight-down bite of the fancy pruner.

Hand Tools

Spades and Spading Forks

Perhaps this is a bad example to cite because usually lightweight tools are light because they lack enough metal to give them strength. A spade with a thin blade that bends when you lift a clod of soil, or a trowel you hardly dare drive into the ground, won't last long. If in doubt, and you have the strength to use it, give preference to the heavier of the two tools if they are otherwise similar.

One test of a good tool is balance. For years I struggled with the favorite tool of old-time English gardeners, the D-handled spade. The handle was short, a square end on the blade made it hard to drive into hard ground, and the balance was bad. Against my protests a shovel salesman made me a present of a long-handled diamond-pointed gardener's spade. To give it strength the blade was heavier in the center than the edges, which were thinner and penetrated soil easily. I have used no other type of spade since. I find spading with this tool is easier than running an eight-horsepower tiller.

An implement that is all but impossible to find on the American market is a really good spading fork. The ones you can buy are so flimsy that they are useless for the work they are supposed to do—turn over heavy sod or heavy clay soil. Because a fork can be thrust into soil that is difficult for a spade to penetrate, it should have thick, square tines rather than the flat, wide ones typical of American forks. Anyone who can find an English spading fork with square tines has a treasure. Otherwise put your trust in a sharp diamond-pointed spade. One manufacturer does make a fork whose tines are diamond-shaped instead of flat in cross section, but the one I have has no brand name.

An implement that is seldom found in a gardener's tool shed is a manure fork. There is no better tool for working over a compost heap or for handling weeds and harvested crop plants headed for that pile. Even dead leaves, if wet, can be picked up readily with this tool. This should be one with several tines, not only two or three (these are hay forks).

Rakes

When it comes to rakes, don't accept anything but the bow type. This is much more expensive to make than the simpler form in which the handle attaches directly to the toothed part. But because of its form, the bow type can be made lighter and for some reason, the balance is better. It has a certain spring in use that seems to take less physical effort.

One problem in selecting tools with wooden handles is length. Often cheaper tools will have handles of inferior wood, or, if of sound ash, will be too short for easy use. To tell whether a handle is long enough, hold it upright against your side. If it does not reach to the tip of your ear, it will not be as easy to use as a longer handle. Sound ash is the standard wood for handles. Beware of tools with handles that are fully painted, which usually conceals the use of poorer wood.

Hoes

A good hoe of the right balance in the hands of an experienced gardener can do a better weed-control job than most power tilling tools. If you want to confine yourself to a single type of hoe, by all means try to find an imported English scuffle hoe. This is a tool that will last a lifetime if treated well and give pleasure every time you use it. It has a sharp blade that lies flat on the ground when used and cuts as you push the handle. The blade is attached to the handle with a horseshoe-shaped socket that is set at exactly the right angle for easy working.

In using this type of hoe, you walk backward and so do not step on the soil you have just cultivated. There are American versions of the scuffle hoe, but they are a far cry from the real thing.

If you can't find an English scuffle hoe, a much easier tool to use than the conventional heavy chopping field hoe so commonly sold is what is known as an onion hoe. This has a blade about one-third the depth of the common type, which means that you pull only one-third as much weight with each stroke.

Every vegetable gardener ought to have at least one additional hoe—the type with a heart-shaped blade that has ears on the upper edge. This is called a Warren hoe and is the perfect tool for opening a trench for seeds. After the seeds are sown, earth can be pulled over them with the ears on the upper edge. Other types do a clumsy job of this operation, although an onion hoe can be used.

Gadgets

One thing to watch out for are gadgety combination tools

dreamed up by someone who is a better inventor than a gardener. My tool shed is full of weird devices combining rakes with hoes, hoes with spades, and in other ways adding weight without convenience. Most of them were given to me by some enthusiastic inventor who was sure his brainchild would set the gardening world on fire. I save them for the handles, which come in handy if I break that on some favorite tool.

Perhaps the biggest white elephant I ever had was a machine for making peat pots, given to me by a disillusioned inventor before he returned to Germany. It took me years to get up enough nerve to destroy this beautifully engineered piece of machinery, but now it is gone.

Trowels

If only some inventor would come up with a substitute for the trowel! Here is one tool that calls for stoop labor to use. Until that near miracle occurs, however, gardeners will have to use this device when setting out transplants and digging between rows where a spade would be too wide. In selecting a trowel feel its balance and check how the handle feels in the positions used in various operations. One such position used in preparing a small area is with the blade held upright in a chopping position. This is a position not thought of when buying a trowel, but the gardener winds up using a trowel in this position time after time. If the handle has too much of a curve, the trowel is almost impossible to use.

Beware of cast aluminum trowels. They start out as slick and smooth as highly polished steel, but soon after contact with damp soil they corrode worse than plain steel. I have come to use only stainless steel, which can be wiped clean and does not corrode. Among the trowels I have seen, the worst deceivers of all are those made of chrome-plated steel. The chrome plating is so thin it cannot stand contact with sand and gravel. Soon scratched, it proceeds to rust.

No Dibbles!

One device often sold to unsuspecting gardeners is the dibble, a hand tool used to punch holes for transplants. In my experience this packs the soil too firmly and the holes are hard to fill properly. Seedlings that are suspended in the hole with air spaces around the roots seldom do well. This is what happens with too many seedlings transplanted with a dibble. I find that a thin strip split from a cedar shingle does a much better job of opening the hole and closing it again.

Bamboo Rakes

A tool that might have been mentioned under rakes is the Chinese bamboo leaf rake, but since it serves a different purpose and is more of a convenience than a necessity, it really deserves a paragraph of its own. It is about the only tool that does a good job in flicking out stones from a seedbed or from between growing plants. The Midwestern gardener on deep prairie loam will have little use for it, but in the stony soils of New England, it is a great help.

Although not available in the East or South, in California the gardener can buy a very narrow version of the bamboo leaf rake, about five to six inches wide. This is perfect for raking trash and stones from between plants in the row. This is sometimes called a Japanese hand because of its flexibility.

Hand Cultivators

Most kits of small hand tools sold to beginning gardeners contain a cultivator with three to five curved teeth. The short handle consigns this to use by the young with strong backs. If you can't find the same tool with a long handle, attach one to the short stub that comes with the short-handled version. Wrapped with electrician's tape this extension will enable you to use this "back scratcher" while standing up. With a long handle it is a good tool.

Wheeled Tools

Tillers

Whether run by gasoline, electricity, or human muscle, wheeled tools have their place in cultivating the larger garden. Because it represents the largest cash outlay for power equipment, the rotary tiller should have first consideration. Although it is often recommended for cultivation between the rows, this idea saves labor only in really big gardens of an acre or more. In order to use a tiller in this way, rows have to be spaced farther apart than for hand cultivation. Even a 16-inch wide tiller cannot be operated safely in rows much narrower than 24 inches. Usually it tills much deeper than is safe for the roots of most garden crops. Most tillers are one-purpose tools—they prepare the soil for planting.

If the garden has been plowed or dug within the past two or three years, and if no heavy sod of quack grass or other weeds has developed in the meantime, a rotary tiller of not more than five horsepower will do a good job of preparing soil for planting. In my experience even an eight-horsepower unit has a tough time tearing up old sod that has not been in cultivation recently. It takes at least four trips across sod before it is in moderately good condition for planting. Even then the soil will be full of clumps of sod, roots of quack grass, and other undesirable trash.

My recommendation would be that anyone planning to garden on a plot 50 by 100 feet or more, which is on sod, should have the area custom plowed. If at all possible, this should be done in the fall and the soil allowed to lie rough all winter. In spring, again with a custom plowman doing the work, it should be disced. Commercial harrowing would save some work as an additional operation, but usually by this time the soil would be in condition so the gardener can do the rest of what is needed with a rake.

The mention of a plow (meaning a moldboard plow that cuts a slice of soil and turns it over onto the next furrow) calls to mind a weakness of this tilling device. When the purpose of plowing is to turn under a mass of organic matter, watch carefully as the slice of earth turns over the trash that is on top. The soil covers the trash first, leaning against the previously turned slice. There will be a definite separation of the two furrows. Unless the soil can be mixed together before planting so this slice is broken up, roots may have a hard time moving past this barrier.

In field practice on the farm, this is done with a disc harrow or with one with teeth, but after a small home plot is plowed, a rotary tiller does a better job. If plowed in fall, the plot can be left until spring and rototilled then. The second working over of the soil has another advantage in spring—it kills both weeds and soil insects.

If a tiller is purchased, a unit of not more than five horse-power should be big enough to turn over the soil in spring, unless the soil is a clay loam, in which case eight horsepower will be needed, at least until enough organic matter can be worked in to bring it up to the level of a good garden loam.

Where a tiller can be rented, usually it pays to use this service rather than to buy your own.

Hand-Type Cultivators

The old-fashioned wheeled cultivator pushed by hand is not ob-solete; rather it is no longer available except through mail-order houses and country supply houses catering to farm trade. If you can find one, you will find it a great convenience for running through rows in a vegetable garden. True it still does not get rid of weeds close to plants, where hand weeding will be needed.

Riding Tractors

One of the sad sights in these days of striving for status is a four-wheel riding tractor sitting in the garage of a suburban home, unused and gathering dust. In many cases it will sit alongside a power mower that was purchased to do the work that the tractor was supposed to perform. Yet when a large veg-etable garden is cultivated, as on a small subsistence farm, a small tractor can do work that is beyond the power and capacity of the biggest rotary tiller. Since it can mow the lawn, pull a cart, and plow snow as well as move earth, it does not sit in the gar-age for 11 months of the year gathering dust. Anything smaller than 10 to 16 horsepower will *not* be powerful enough to turn over heavy sod.

The important feature to look for in buying a small tractor is the capacity for using a wide variety of attachments. These are expensive and should not be purchased unless they can be used time and time again. A forklift is great if you are doing road building, moving large amounts of earth in composting or landscaping, or hoisting grain into a bin, but it is an expensive attachment. A rotary tilling attachment on a tractor is far more useful than on a hand-operated tiller, but again, unless it is used often, a luxury. For the subsistence farmer, a plow, a harrow and a disc, along with a sickle bar mower are the essential attachments.

Buy all the power you can afford. Although garden types with up to 16 horsepower motors are great conveniences, larger types, such as the International Cub, will do work beyond the capacity of the smaller units if you have several acres to plow or till.

Wheelbarrows and Carts

For the small plot a bushel basket lined with a plastic trash bag will serve most of the gardener's needs for transporting materials. Larger gardens call for some form of wheeled equipment. All too often a wheelbarrow is the choice.

Why Americans, supposedly highly sophisticated in things mechanical, have tied themselves for centuries to a Chinese device of necessity is a mystery. A wheelbarrow was the only answer to moving goods on China's narrow lanes, but to continue using that primitive vehicle today seems absurd.

What the gardener needs is a modern two-wheeled cart with big wheels and rubber tires. It will carry from five to ten times as much material with much less effort. I had its advantages brought home to me one summer when both our washing machine and our car broke down at our summer home. Living on an island has its problems. I had to be sure to have that machine on a certain ferry so it could be picked up by the repair service in Rockland. There was nothing to do but load the washer on a wheelbarrow and set off for the ferry nearly a mile away. If you have ever tried to balance a 100-pound load on one wheel, you can imagine that I reached the wharf in a state of exhaustion. When that washer came back two weeks later, you can believe I borrowed a two-wheeled cart from a friend for the trip back. That trip was almost a joy ride when I thought of the first one.

But don't be fooled into buying one of the tin saucepans with ten-inch wheels so often sold as garden carts. These are all right for the kids to use to cart sand or the family cat but are little more than toys in a garden. The one you choose should have rubber-tired wheels at least 20 inches in diameter.

Watering Equipment

Always keep in mind that most vegetables are over 90 percent water. For every pound of fertilizer taken up by roots, plants need hundreds of pounds of water, yet it is seldom mentioned when talking about fertilizers. Few areas in the United States or Canada have rainfall so well distributed that no periods of drought ever occur.

There are times when having some form of irrigation equipment available will mean the difference between near failure and a successful garden. Such periods may be short, but they can be critical.

When most beginning gardeners think of watering they think of a hose. While this flexible pipe is a highly useful device for applying water, it is far less important than it once was. We no longer think of runs of 100 feet or more, with leaks and low pressure as constant annoyances. Today it is easy to lay a one-inch plastic pipe underground for very little money, with a tap right in the garden for attaching the hose. Pressure drop in that size pipe is far less than in a hose and there are no couplings to leak.

Anyone who has tried to water a sizable garden through a hose nozzle will agree that it is a tiresome job, one that practically always is skimped because the user's arm gets tired. Nowadays, oscillating sprinklers that can be adjusted to fit a given area can work hour after hour without tiring.

In dry areas ooze hoses are available that can be laid along rows of vegetables and ooze moisture that is rapidly absorbed by the soil. Although these conserve water and so are a necessity in regions where water is scarce, the effect of moisture added to the air by conventional sprinklers is important enough to offset the loss of moisture that occurs with their use. Don't overlook the cooling effect on the air for the gardener on a hot, dry summer day: in itself this is enough to justify the loss.

Poles and Protectors

In the past, poles for supporting climbing cucumbers, pole beans, and trained tomatoes have been a nuisance to collect and even more expensive if bought at a lumber yard. A recent gadget that eliminates poles at a modest cost is the Ross Gro Net, a mesh of synthetic fiber that can be used as a support by merely stretching it between two poles.

For several years I have been using a device of this sort, but far, far heavier than it need be—a piece cut from a damaged tuna seine with individual strands strong enough to support 1,000 pounds. At the original cost of $7,000 to the fisherman whose seine was damaged, it seemed a bit luxurious, but it worked beautifully and proved that the basic principle behind the Gro Net is sound.

A device that sounds like a gimmick but that is really a useful garden tool, is the plastic cone used to protect roses over winter. It is made of a lightweight polystyrene foamed plastic. When set over some half-hardy plant in winter, heat from the soil and heat given off by the plant itself keep out frost.

This cone can be used to protect less hardy herbs from winter injury, as well as to force perennial crops such as rhubarb, sea kale and asparagus.

One rose enthusiast who uses over 200 of these on roses also gets double use out of them by protecting early sweet corn hills, planted three weeks before the normal date for that crop.

Tool Care

Today tools are expensive and will go higher. It pays to give them the best possible care, particularly over winter when they are usually thrown into one corner of a shed or garage without first being cleaned. If they are encrusted with dirt and corrosion, dip metal tools in a bucket of old crankcase oil, thinned slightly with kerosene or fuel oil. Use a wire brush to get rid of grime.

The weak point in tools with wooden handles is the place where the handle goes into a metal socket. Allow this to dry out, then soak it with boiled linseed oil. If you have some leftover polyurethane varnish or other outdoor clear varnish, this is even better than linseed oil. Oil or varnish the rest of the handle as well. If you have trouble losing tools among the garden plants, try painting with some bright color to make them more conspicuous.

Rub the tines of rotary tillers with lubricating oil to protect them from rust over winter. Be sure to drain the fuel tank, or run the engine until the tank is dry. Gasoline gets gummy over the winter if left in the engine. Grease all bearings with enough pressure to push out any dirt. If the tool shed has a dirt floor, store any metal equipment on raised platforms; soil moisture can cause rust.

Drain hose and tank sprayers. Don't close sprayers; suspend them upside down to drain.

One last precaution: If your tool shed is as jammed as mine is in winter, think of what equipment you will need first in spring. Store it nearest the door; otherwise you may have to haul out garden carts, wheelbarrows, and lawn mowers to get at the tiller you will need first.

31

Hotbeds, Cold Frames, and Cloches

Why more gardeners do not use cold frames and hotbeds to extend the gardening season is hard to understand. I recall vividly when in my youth a spring chore was tramping down manure from our old family oat burner to provide heat for a hotbed improvised from two storm windows. In urban areas today that source of heat is no more, yet that is no excuse for passing up a highly useful device for producing plants weeks ahead of normal planting time.

Hotbeds

Certainly the chance to move a messy job (growing seedlings in a sunny window) out into the open garden should be tempting. And what true gardener would not enjoy growing tiny carrots, lettuce, and beets in cold frames and hotbeds in late fall?

Heat from Decomposition

There are two ways to solve the lack of fresh manure to serve as a source of heat in hotbeds. The first solution is cheapest but not necessarily the best. It calls for making artificial manure by mixing kitchen garbage with dried leaves, straw, hay, or sawdust, adding fertilizers to feed soil bacteria while they are digesting this organic matter, and using the heat of decomposition to heat hotbed soil.

Begin by digging out the soil inside the hotbed to a depth of 18 inches. If the frame of the bed is light enough it might even be moved elsewhere while this digging is going on. A mixture of damp table scraps and dried leaves or other organic matter such as sawdust, hay, weeds, or similar wastes is laid about four inches deep in the bottom of the excavation. For an area about six by six feet, sprinkle a pound of urea (available in most garden shops) and a pound of a chemical fertilizer recommended for vegetables over the bottom layer. Add more organic matter and chemicals in layers until the bottom foot of the excavation has been filled. Wet this down with a hose until it is thoroughly moist but not sopping wet. Now fill in soil until it is level with the surface of the surrounding area. With the frame in place, cover it with a sash and allow fermentation to begin. A soil thermometer is best for checking the heat generated, which in favorable weather might begin in a week. At first it goes up rapidly, then begins to drop. When the thermometer reads less than 75 degrees, seed can be sown.

If spring weather is chilly, the fermentation process can be carried on in a warm shed or cellar by mixing the ingredients and storing in the plastic bags used for disposing of trash. Piled in an out-of-the-way place, these can be left to ferment but should be felt daily to see if heat is being generated. At the first sign of a rise in temperature, rush the bags out, empty them in the hotbed and cover with soil.

Electric Heating

A much easier way to supply heat is with electricity. This can be done in two ways, either with the weatherproof reflectorized heat lamps used to warm baby chick brooders or with electric hot-bed cables. My preference is for using lamps because they also furnish artificial light, which helps speed up growth. Light is particularly useful during cloudy spring days. It also provides extra light at night. At this stage no vegetable plants are sensitive to day length; so any extra illumination just pushes them along faster. The trick is to space four such lights over a six-foot by six-foot frame so both heat and light are distributed uniformly. Two rafters made out of two-inch by two-inch lumber with two bulbs on each works well for me.

The bulbs should be of the type with white glass, not the ones with the red glass used in chick brooders. They should be screwed into porcelain or other weatherproof sockets. All electric boxes and connectors should be outdoor type. Use three-wire cable suitable for direct burial in earth, using the third wire as a direct ground.

Although house heating thermostats are not waterproof, they can be used as controls if enclosed so that water cannot splash onto them. This is a good idea, anyway, since the enclosure can be used to protect them from direct sunshine, which can throw them off in bright, sunny weather. Special hotbed thermostats are better, available from mail-order seed houses or from larger garden centers.

When lights are used, a hotbed should be made about five to six inches deeper than normal. Although this means more shadows inside the frame, light from the heat lamps will more than compensate for this.

One gardener I knew made double use of this idea during World War II when back-yard poultry keeping was popular. As soon as he had transplanted all the seedlings, he bought a hundred baby chicks, changed the lamps to the red glass type and set the thermostat at the right temperature for brooding. With a little chopped straw spread on the soil, he had a perfect setup for raising his own egg supply and broilers for the table.

When electric hotbed cables are used, response to the demand by the thermostat for heat is much slower than when lights are used. When installing, dig out the earth to a depth of four inches, lay the cable according to directions, and cover this with hardware cloth with not less than four holes to the square inch. This will prevent a trowel or other tool from cutting into the cable. Next cover the hardware cloth with six inches of soil.

When working with electricity out-of-doors, always take precautions against shock. A good way to avoid a direct electric ground is to elevate a piece of outdoor plywood on four bricks, placed so you can stand on it when adjusting the thermostat.

Construction

Nowadays there is no need to struggle with the heavy, clumsy hotbed sash glazed with glass that made life miserable in the past. By far the best replacement is a fiberglass corrugated panel made with either rubber or redwood flashings so the panel can fit tightly. Any dealer in fiberglass can furnish the flashings and information on using them.

For a one-season panel, vinyl sheet plastic can be used, tacked to a light wooden frame. Do not use polyethylene sheet plastic, however, which is likely to rupture at any time. However, this type of plastic can be used inside a panel covered with vinyl on the top to form a double sash that will be warmer than a single covering of vinyl.

Because both vinyl and fiberglass are light in weight, they need to be held down or they will sail off with the first stiff wind. The best way to do this is by hinging them. The opposite end of the frame from the hinges should have strong hooks to fasten them down.

When using either vinyl plastic or fiberglass, you are not limited to standard sash sizes but can use any available lumber. The same is true of the sides of the frame. Two-inch-thick lumber is best for sides, but if only one-inch boards are on hand, double them with tarpaper or plastic in between for even better insulation. For permanence all wood used should be treated with pentachlorophenol, usually called Penta. It should be allowed to air for two weeks after treatment before it comes in contact with living plants. Never, never use creosoted lumber for frames or for any use where wood comes in contact with plant life. Even after years of exposure, it can still be harmful.

Cold Frames

A cold frame is made in exactly the same way as a hotbed, except that no excavation is necessary. It is used to contain plants if spring is delayed and seedlings pile up in hotbeds or seedlings started indoors. Cold frames can also be used to start plants later in spring, before danger from frosts is over but when days are warm. By covering the sash at night, plants in a cold frame can survive. A cold frame can also be used during the summer for starting transplants for succession crops. For example, cauliflower seed can be sown in a frame in late June in the North, to be transplanted in the garden following a crop of early carrots.

Many leafy vegetables such as Chinese cabbage, celery, endive, and Brussels sprouts can be dug with soil clinging to the roots and stacked into a cold frame with the sash on. The light they receive will help keep them growing at a low rate, which keeps them in better condition than in a dark cellar. The one problem is heating up on bright winter days. Either the sash must be raised slightly to let excess heat escape, or it should be shaded to keep out winter sun.

Lettuce started in either a hotbed or a cold frame can be harvested until as late as Christmas Day as far north as southern Michigan and Wisconsin. Other crops that can be grown along with lettuce are beets, parsley, mustard for salads, and American cress. For forcing, small carrots are ideal, using varieties such as Sucram, Little Finger, Baby Finger Nantes, or Tiny Sweet. If room allows try cauliflower and a midget variety of cabbage such as Morden Midget.

In the South all these vegetables can be grown in a frame all winter long in areas where outdoor temperatures are too low to permit growing them in an open garden.

In a frame in winter vegetables need much less water than they do in summer. If overwatered they are much more likely to be frozen. A good indicator of when to water is lettuce; wait until it seems just about ready to wilt before applying moisture. Try to do this on a bright, sunny day so the sash can be left slightly open to air out before the sun goes down.

One of the most important pieces of equipment in using frames is the mat used to cover sashes in zero weather and at night. It should be of waterproof material, or a sheet of plastic should be used to cover a mat that is not water resistant.

Cloches

The name *cloche* comes from the French word for bell. In fact, grandfather's name for this device was bell jar. This implied that it was made of glass, which is no longer true. Today they are of plastic, except for temporary ones made of translucent paper.

A cloche is a transparent or translucent covering used to protect plants from freezing. Some units are made for covering individual plants, others are longer covers for protecting a portion of a row. Most experienced gardeners are familiar with the waxed-paper covers called Hotkaps. These are used by the millions by commercial growers for early spring protection of tender plants. They are simple to use, not too expensive, and work very well if directions are followed. One fault, which they share with all cloches, is that in bright, sunny weather they can get so hot inside that seedlings will be cooked.

To avoid this they can be slit at the top to allow heated air to escape. The best tool for this job is a razor blade. Two cuts are made forming a cross about three inches on each bar. This does not have to be sealed; air pressure will push out the heat, but the flaps usually fall back, closing the opening as soon as the sun goes down.

My principal objection to rigid plastic cloches is that they get dirty and scratched so quickly as to reduce the amount of light they allow in. Even so, they still seem to grow good plants. These can be had both as covers for single plants or for a section of row. Most row covers are homemade. Two strips of flat fiberglass any convenient length and 15 inches wide can be laid against triangular wooden supports to cover a section of tender plants. Usually the ends of such covers are left open, so the problem of venting heat is not at all serious. If severe weather threatens these ends can be covered temporarily.

Polyethylene sheeting can also be used but deteriorates so rapidly in sunshine that it is best discarded as soon as the need for spring protection is over. Because of its lack of rigidity, it must be supported about every 30 inches by hoops or hairpins made out of stiff wire. The sheeting is drawn over the wire hairpins and held down along the row by piling earth on the edges. Like row protectors made out of rigid fiberglass, those covered with plastic sheeting are usually left open at both ends.

The cloche idea in reverse is the use of an opaque covering

such as wide boards to blanch endive, sea kale, and asparagus. I have used eight-foot lengths of exterior plywood, 18 inches wide to cover a row of curly endive and escarole. Narrower boards won't span the row when laid in teepee fashion over the plants. To keep the plants completely dark the inside face of the boards should be painted a dull black. The ends of the teepee should be closed. Because this does not provide ventilation, the boards should be painted white on the exposed face so they won't get too hot from the sun.

The Sun-Heated Pit

Unless you intend to grow a long list of vegetables in a greenhouse during the winter, a sun-heated pit is about the most elaborate structure you will need. It depends on two sources of heat. The first is the sun, which in winter enters at a very low angle, something that must be taken into consideration when planning the roof. The second is the warmth of unfrozen soil that surrounds the pit.

To be effective in the North, a pit must be at least four feet deep, dug into soil that should be well drained. In the northern tier of southern states, the pit should be as deep, but the roof and walls do not need to be insulated, a must in the North. To support the roof and glazed front, the pit is usually lined with concrete blocks or a wooden wall, which should be treated with Penta if it is to last any length of time. Any above-ground walls supporting the roof and glazed front, as well as the roof itself, should have two-by-four studs with fiberglass insulation in the stud spaces and between rafters. Although this might not be needed in the South, the saving in fuel will pay off when the pit greenhouse must be heated during unexpected near-zero temperatures.

Sometimes a skylight is let into the roof in an attempt to gain more light, but since a pit is used only in winter, this wastes more heat than the gain in light is worth.

What will pay off is to line the back wall with aluminum foil, which will act as extra insulation while at the same time reflecting light onto the plants on the side away from the glazed front.

A sun-heated pit is little more than a glorified walk-in cold frame. On a sunny day in midwinter, this is no more delightful place in the world for a dedicated gardener. With some supplemental heat such as might be furnished by an electric forced-air heater or a laundry stove, it can function as a cool greenhouse in which crops such as lettuce, radishes, carrots, parsley, and herbs can be grown. Under the benches is the perfect place to store root crops in sand, against the pit walls and out of the sun. Squashes and pumpkins store well in bins above the level of the benches but out of direct sun. If more beets were stored in fall than can be eaten, a worthwhile trick is to force them for new foliage. Bury the roots in damp sand with the top barely at ground level. As the sun rises higher and higher in the sky with the coming of spring, the increased heat will force new leaves on the beets that can be cooked like spinach but have a finer flavor than any beet greens from the open garden. The roots can still be eaten after the forced tops have been harvested.

A sun-heated pit is a good place to start transplants for the vegetable garden. Even if spring is late and the plants must be held over for several extra days, they are much better off than they would be in a cold frame or inside the house.

An important part of operating a sun-heated pit is covering the windows at night to prevent loss of heat gained during the day. Insulated shutters are excellent but awkward to handle, particularly in a long house with several windows to cover. I have seen houses where they were hinged to the window at the top and pulled up with a pulley against the roof during the day. Loose pads with waterproof covering can be used if only two or three windows need to be covered. They should go on from the inside of the window and fit tightly at the edges. If they are mounted on a frame just the size of the window and held in place with turn buttons, they are perhaps the most convenient of all coverings.

Longer pit houses are sometimes equipped with either ceiling vents or an electric ventilating fan, but usually all that is needed is to open the door on bright, sunny days.

32

The Many Reasons
for Mulching

One big difference between the way we garden in America and the way the British do things is in mulching. On this side of the Atlantic mulching is all but neglected, while on the Tight Little Isle, everybody uses a mulch at some time or another. What is unusual about America's neglect of this valuable gardening method is that mulches are much more useful in our continental climate than in England's cool, moist maritime climate.

Weed Control

Mulching doesn't sound too hard to do. It calls for covering soil with some protective material. Ask any experienced gardener who does mulch why he does so and you will get about as many different answers as there are questions. Probably the most frequent answer will be to eliminate weeding. Within limits this is true. If before applying a mulch you get rid of the first crop of annual weeds and then apply a thick covering of some weedless organic matter, chances are that such annual weeds will not bother you that year.

If, however, there are deep-rooted perennial weeds such as

Canada thistle, bindweed, and quack grass in the soil, these are not checked but grow right through the mulch. Unless these are too plentiful, they can be controlled by chemical weed killers. A trick for doing this even if crop plants are growing in the same soil is to treat each weed with some chemical such as Silvex, Amizole, Atrazine, 2,4,5-T, or Banvel D. This cannot be put on with a sprayer. Instead put a rubber glove over your hand and, over this, draw on a canvas glove. Dip the canvas-gloved hand into a solution of a weed killer recommended by your county agent. Now grasp the offending weed with the hand as close to the ground as you can and pull it slowly upward, wetting the leaves.

The chemical will enter the leaves, move down into the root, and kill the plant without injury to surrounding vegetables.

When used in this way, a mulch is applied in spring after killing off annual weeds but before soil has begun to lose all the moisture it accumulated during the winter. If applied too soon, however, it can keep the soil too cool and wet for good germination. Many gardeners plant seed first, then destroy weed seedlings and apply the mulching material, leaving space around the vegetable plants so they are not smothered.

Mulching Materials

Materials for mulching include any weed-free organic matter that will gradually rot down into a loose, fluffy matt. It should be fluffy in order to hold air. A tight, airless mulch is bad for plants and often is an incubator for plant diseases. A common material used is fallen leaves. I have found that they break down into just the right consistency if they are stored in a fairly tight bin or barrel just after a rain. The amount of moisture clinging to the leaves is enough to start decay without letting it go too far. In spring the bin or barrel will be filled with a damp, fluffy mass that is not quite leaf mold but ideal for mulching.

For small lots of leaves, plastic bags filled and tied shut will do for this operation. If leaves are not available, sawdust makes an excellent mulch. A common misconception is that decaying sawdust makes soil acid, but actually it tends to increase pH slightly. Another superstition is that sawdust from softwoods (evergreens) is bad for soil because of the rosin it contains. Since rosin is an ingredient in forming humus, rosinous wood makes a richer humus than hardwood, but the difference is too slight to consider.

What is true is that when bacteria attack sawdust being used as a mulch, they will draw so heavily on soil nitrogen that plants will suffer, unless extra nitrogen is mixed with the sawdust. However, if 10 to 15 percent more fertilizer is used in preparing the soil than is recommended for its use by the manufacturer, no additional nitrogen need be added to the sawdust. This is much easier than weighing the sawdust and adding two pounds of ammonium sulfate for every 100 pounds of sawdust.

Usually a three-inch-thick layer of sawdust is as effective as a six-inch layer of leaves.

Ground corncobs are often used as a mulch. Add extra fertilizer to the soil as recommended when mulching with sawdust.

Probably the ideal mulching material is spent mushroom manure, the growing medium in which commercial mushrooms are propagated for the market. Before use in growing mushrooms it goes through an elaborate composting process that destroys all weed seed and insect pests. At one time mushroom growers were glad to give this away, but it has become known as a valuable mulch and is usually sold, but the price is reasonable and the product unequaled as a mulch.

Wood chips are becoming more and more plentiful as landscape nurserymen and municipal arborists increase their use of chippers to dispose of tree trimmings and to grub out stumps. In my home village a pile of chips nearly a city block long is available free for residents to haul away for mulching. Wood chips have one advantage over sawdust—they decompose at a much slower rate and so do not need added nitrogen from the soil, unless that soil is a pure sand or gravel.

Because they are somewhat heavier than sawdust they pack down more and may need an occasional stirring to aerate them. There have been some protests against using chips from elms killed by Dutch elm disease, but there is no danger from this source. The fungus requires living wood to propagate, and the beetles that carry the disease will not live on dead chips.

Buckwheat hulls are not easy to find, but where they are available (usually from small country mills), they are an ideal mulch except that they are so light they must be wetted down thoroughly two or three times or they will blow away. Homesteaders who grow a crop of buckwheat to grind into pancake flour should have no trouble finding this supermulch. Because it is light, it can be used as deep as six inches if weeds are particularly troublesome. I particularly like this material for mulching strawberries and blueberries. In the South rice hulls are, if anything, better.

Spent hops from nearby breweries, if you can stand a beery smell for a couple of weeks, make an excellent mulch. They can usually be had for the hauling, but remember you are lugging nearly a ton of water to get 250 pounds of dry matter. For some reason it seems to draw rats and pigeons until after the odor is gone.

In the past, a dust mulch produced by cultivating the soil when the soil was dry was popular; unfortunately it lasted only until the next rain. In the process of working the soil to form a dust, enough moisture was lost to more than equal the amount saved. A dust mulch is good for weed control when no covering of organic matter is used but far less valuable than such a covering.

Peat moss has a couple of drawbacks, the most important of which is cost. If you have access to a peat bog, and if your back can stand the strain of lifting soggy peat, it makes an excellent mulch. Watch out for one thing, however; when it dries out during a drought, getting water through it to the soil is like trying to force water through a felt hat. It is hygroscopic and will suck water out of the soil if the mulch is not kept moist. When moisture is ample, it is an excellent mulch, but watch carefully if drought occurs.

Redwood bark and other shredded bark products are excellent mulches, but the cost of processing them and shipping costs make them uneconomical. I rate them somewhat better than wood chips.

Grass clippings from the lawn can be used for mulching, but if dumped on the garden fresh from the mower they ferment and heat up. I have noticed, too, that under conditions favorable to the growth of mildew, it propagates on grass clippings even more readily than on live foliage. Treat clippings as you would hay, drying them in the sun before using as a mulch.

In addition to buckwheat and rice hulls similar products can be used as mulches, such as peanut shells, pecan hulls, and barley chaff. Avoid walnut hulls, however, since they contain a substance that will check growth.

An old wives' tale is that coffee grounds are good for house plants. This is untrue; caffeine is a growth inhibitor. The late Dr. Sam Emsweller, who headed the research in ornamentals for the U.S.D.A., once took me through a series of experiments in which coffee grounds had been tested as a mulch. Every plant treated with this material was smaller than its untreated counterpart.

Ground sugar cane or bagasse is available in the South and makes an excellent mulch. Like sawdust it requires additional nitrogen fertilizer in the soil. My one objection to it in ornamental plantings is that it is a ghostly white in color, but this does not affect its value in the vegetable garden.

Pine needles are not sold commercially, but if you live near a pine or spruce forest, by all means gather the needles for mulching purposes. I prefer them to many other materials because they never matt down but can be fluffed up by stirring any time.

I shun tobacco stems as a mulch in the vegetable garden because they are likely to carry the tobacco mosaic virus that hurts tomatoes and many other plants. They are used widely in the South, often without damage, but why take a chance?

Coconut husk fiber, waste from making doormats, and other products made from coir, are valuable as a mulch because they contain a natural growth-promoting substance, possibly a growth hormone. Light and fluffy, they are nearly perfect.

Cocoa husks, a by-product of chocolate manufacturing, are sold commercially as a mulch. Although dry when first applied, they gradually take up water and become quite slimy and difficult to walk on. Wetting them also starts a fermentation that gives off considerable heat. If they can be had for the hauling, they are all right but must be watched for the disadvantages just mentioned.

In summer a whitish mold grows in cocoa hulls that spreads rapidly but does not seem to attack the plants. They have some fertilizing value since they contain about one percent phosphorus and nearly four percent potash, both of which become available to plants.

For rhubarb and around bush fruits I use tarpaper because it is heavy enough to stay in place once it has been beaten to the ground by rain, and it lasts two or three years without having to be replaced. It must be laid so that the paper slants down around the plants, otherwise water drains away from them. Since tarpaper is impervious to water, rain cannot reach the soil under any area it covers.

The use of aluminum foil under squash vines has already been mentioned in the chapter on vine crops. For general mulching it is too expensive, fragile, and cannot be salvaged for future use.

Black plastic sheeting is widely used in vegetable production. It has certain advantages over organic materials, such as, for instance, availability. Not everyone has a forest for gathering pine needles or a convenient mushroom cellar for spent compost. Black plastic can be bought from dealers in supplies for vegetable growers or greenhouse materials in sheets as wide as 20 feet and as long as 100 feet.

In my experience, if vegetables are grown in rows two feet apart, 48-inch wide sheets are best, cutting the roll down the middle to make two 24-inch widths. These can be laid on carefully raked soil (level soil is important when using plastic) with an inch space between them for sowing seed. This is for row crops such as carrots, beets, and lettuce. For transplants such as tomatoes and cabbage, lay the sheets solid without any openings. Cut out places for each plant as it is set out.

Working on top of plastic is tricky. Keep a piece of plywood handy to walk on when setting plants.

Do not use clear or translucent plastic under any conditions, except perhaps to heat up soil for tender crops in a late season. In the sun, soil under clear plastic will be at least 20 degrees higher than under black. Oddly enough, although black plastic is supposed to absorb heat, careful recordings with and without under identical conditions showed only one percent average difference in sunlight and none in cloudy weather.

Hay and straw are among the most widely used mulches. Both can be criticized for carrying weed seeds. One of the worst infested gardens I ever grew was covered with timothy hay as a mulch. Wheat straw, which is usually freed of all seed in threshing, is cleaner than oat straw, unless the wheat field was originally infested with other weeds. A good substitute for straw is excelsior, but because it is so light and fluffy, it must be used to a depth of about six inches.

In addition to keeping down weeds and conserving moisture, mulches of organic matter do add fertility. An interesting experiment is to cut out a soil profile (a hole that shows the different layers of soil through the subsoil) to check how far down topsoil goes. In identical soils, one which has not been mulched and the other which has been covered with an organic matter for years, the darker subsoil in the mulched area will usually be from two to six inches deeper.

Also, in heavy clays, mulched soils will be more workable and can be penetrated much faster by water after a rain.

In fall, when frosts are likely, soil under a mulch loses heat much more slowly. A difference of as much as 12 degrees has been recorded between mulched and unmulched areas. Often a mulched garden will survive a light frost that kills tender plants such as tomatoes on unmulched land.

Vegetable Garden Mulches Are Annual

Some mulches, such as those under trees and shrubs are often left in place year after year. In the vegetable garden, however, a mulch should be treated as an annual and plowed under before a new crop is seeded or set out as transplants. There was a fad a few years back that called for leaving a mulch in place and scratching through it to sow a new crop without plowing or disturbing the soil.

Those who tried this found that during the second year, both insects and diseases were much worse than the first, and each succeeding year saw more trouble. The sooner after the last fall harvest a mulch can be tilled under, the better. To feed soil bacteria, if they are active, a light sprinkling of a high nitrogen fertilizer is desirable. There are some species of bacteria that do remain active in cold soil. Plowing under a mulch year after year will increase their numbers.

At the same time the sooner plowing can be done, while the soil retains some heat, the better. It will even pay to do a piecemeal job, digging under the mulch and plant residues as soon as a crop is gathered from a row that is not to be replanted to a succession crop.

In the orchard mulching is an improvement on cultivation, at least with dwarf trees. Here coarse mulches can be used that do not decay rapidly. I make a practice of working over the mulch in late September, pulling it away from the trunk so a screen to protect against mice can be installed. After a light freeze the mulch can then be replaced for the winter. If left in place without reworking, mice are likely to move in for the winter and live on tree bark.

In mulching strawberries, blueberries, and other bush fruits, a similar treatment is desirable. In the case of strawberries, an old rule was to delay mulching with hay or straw until the soil would bear the weight of a one-horse wagon. Today the rule is to delay mulching until a temperature lower than 25 degrees above zero is predicted. Bush fruits are a problem because it is difficult to scrape out the old mulch around their stems. Here the use of mouse baits is desirable to prevent injury. The mulch on the outside of the rows should, however, be renewed annually.

33

Storing Vegetables and Fruits for Winter Use

Winter storage is one of the most neglected operations in home food gardening. Little attention is given to where vegetables and fruits are to be kept. All too often gardeners figure they can use what is left in the garden from summer crops, and preparations are left until a killing frost is threatened. Where recommendations are given for planting for storage, following these will give best results.

Unless the right space at the right temperature is available, scrubbed clean and ready to go at a moment's notice, vegetables you figured on for winter food can shrivel or rot, or spout and be ruined for the table.

Vegetable Storage

Most city and suburban gardeners will have to depend on a cellar for storage, unless they have a heated garage where the temperature is kept just above freezing. The problem with most modern basements is that the heating plant is there and keeps room temperature much too high. In some way space must be set aside where the heat can be excluded so that two temperature ranges can be maintained. One space should be kept as close

327

to freezing as possible, without actually dropping below 33 degrees. If it fluctuates upward, but not above 40 degrees, that will not be serious.

That 40-degree upper limit is significant. All root vegetables begin sprouting at 42 degrees, the temperature at which plant dormancy is broken. Most roots are storage organs that contain food in the form of starch. At any reading below 42 degrees, this turns to sugar, preparing the root for new growth. But certain natural dormancy chemicals hold back growth until readings above 42 degrees occur. By sticking to that 33-to-40-degree range for storage, you are working with natural forces, not against them. This holds true for leafy vegetables as well—cabbage, endive, Chinese cabbage, etc. All those mentioned need a fairly high humidity, say 70 percent, but not so high that moisture condenses on walls.

A big problem in storage with high humidity is that mildew will begin to grow toward the end of the season when outdoor temperatures make it difficult to keep indoor readings below 40 degrees. Scrubbing walls and shelves with water containing a chlorine bleach such as Purex or Chlorox will help prevent mildew and will destroy rot organisms that could cause trouble.

Storage of onions (also garlic, shallots, etc.) should also be done in a 33–40 degree range, but they cannot stand high humidity. If no better place can be found for them, they can be stored in trays with slatted or wire cloth bottoms, close to the ceiling of a root cellar. If a fan is used to pull in cold air, the fan can be aimed at the onion trays to keep air circulating around them.

Often a separate storeroom can be built in one corner of a modern cellar. The two walls closing it off from the rest of the cellar should be insulated, both to keep cold air from chilling the floor above, and to keep the storage space at a low temperature.

Ideally a fan system to bring in cold air should be used, both for ventilation and for cooling. A single fan is easy to operate with a thermostat that turns on the fan when temperature goes above 40 degrees and off at 33 degrees. Unfortunately house thermostats won't do; they only operate down to 55 degrees and operate in reverse to a cooling thermostat. Some garden centers sell hotbed thermostats that operate in the proper range; so do dealers in greenhouse supplies. See under florists supplies in the phone book.

The one danger in such a control system is that when the heating plant operates most of the time in sub-zero weather, the extra heat may raise temperatures in the storage space and kick on the fan. Zero air can damage some stored crops. This means that the gardener must watch to see that the fan is turned off in severe weather.

If all this seems like too much trouble, outdoor storage in a garage or other out-building is another answer. Even the area under a porch, if enclosed with plastic, will do. Root crops in sand stored next to the foundation should survive in edible condition, unless you live in an area where sub-zero weather persists for several days. In Sweden and Germany a device known in America as the Swedish barrel has been used for years with excellent results. It consists of a barrel half-buried in well-drained soil at a slant, with a fitted lid to close it. Earth is thrown over the exposed sides of the barrel and straw or hay thrown over the earth as well as the lid. A tarpaulin of plastic (in this day of plastics) keeps rain and wet snow from reducing the insulating value of the hay.

Root crops are stored in sand (although I find that the building insulation grade of vermiculite is even better). I find that when using this storage unit, root vegetables should be mixed, not stored with carrots in one layer, beets in another, and so on. Otherwise to get at one vegetable stored near the bottom, the rest would have to be removed first.

Although the Swedish barrel idea can be used for cabbages and potatoes, the capacity of the barrel is small. One ingenious adaptation of this idea I have seen was the use of a section of concrete culvert five feet in diameter buried upright to the full depth of the section. On well-drained soil with gravel underneath, it held enough cabbage for the family as well as extra heads for a flock of poultry.

Cabbage can also be stored in what the British call a clamp. This method is also called a pit in the United States, but this implies underground storage, whereas a clamp is mostly above ground. On well-drained soil there is some advantage to digging a shallow depression first. Otherwise cabbages or potatoes are simply piled over a sheet of plastic or straw to a depth of two to three feet, and covered with straw, hay, cut fern leaves, or similar material, and then with from six inches to a foot of earth, depending on the severity of winter. About every four feet, a wisp of straw is allowed to stick through the earth and acts as a ventilating chimney. Again a covering of plastic improves insulation.

Clamps can also be used for the storage of root crops, usually without burying them in sand or vermiculite; they stay moist without such protection. Clamps or pits are inconvenient and highly uncomfortable in frigid weather. One way to ease the pain is to make several small units, each containing a mixture of potatoes, root crops, and cabbage enough to supply the table for three or four weeks. A mesh bag such as used for onions will do as a container. The entire contents can then be moved to a reasonably cool spot in the house and will usually keep in good condition until eaten. For this purpose a conical clamp is best, as it exposes less surface to outside temperatures.

True pits, wholly underground, are usually in the form of a trench, covered with boards and then with straw and a plastic sheet. Celery and Chinese cabbage store reasonably well in pits, but the Chinese cabbage will not keep much longer than January.

Endive, Chinese cabbage, celery, and kohlrabi can be stored indoors under the same temperatures as root crops. Harvest them by pulling up with some soil attached to the roots, remove any damaged foliage, and pack them plant against plant on the floor. An earth floor is best, but a concrete floor will do if covered with a couple inches of clean sand. Dampen the sand before storing the plants to maintain humidity. This type of storage needs careful watching to prevent rotting. It may be necessary to move the plants, strip off any rotting leaves, and restack.

Squashes, pumpkins, and winter melons need a period of ripening at between 80 and 85 degrees, or should be held near the furnace for a week or two to harden. They should then be stored at between 50 and 60 degrees, no higher. Humidity should be less than 50 percent. Acorn squash stores poorly; don't depend on this type for longer than two months.

Always be sure that vegetables in storage are protected against rats and mice. Since the vegetables are more attractive to these pests than are dry rat baits, the only poisons effective against them are those dissolved in pans of drinking water.

Potatoes present a special problem in that they need low temperatures to keep, but temperatures much below 50 degrees will convert stored starch in the tubers into sugar. Sugar-flavored potatoes are unpalatable. Store them at 35 to 40 degrees until about two weeks before they are wanted for cooking. Them hold them at a temperature of 70 degrees until cooked. They are best stored in mesh bags at root-cellar humidity.

Where clean sand is not available, root crops can be stored in thin plastic bags. Too heavy a bag will exclude all air. The thickness used for storing food in the refrigerator is good; that of bags as heavy as those for storing turkeys or for tarpaulins is too thick. Gunnysacks, if washed clean, are satisfactory but may need light misting if roots start to dry out.

Sweet potatoes need to be "sweated" before storage. Hold at 85 to 95 degrees for ten days to three weeks, depending on humidity. Room should be ventilated to remove moisture. When no longer juicy and soft, store in open trays in a 55-degree temperature. Care in handling is important to prevent bruising.

Storing Fruits

If at all possible, do not store fruits in the same space as vegetables. They pick up unpleasant off-flavors from cabbage, onions, and other crops.

Apples will keep well if held at as close to 32 degrees as possible without actually freezing. Commercial orchards use cold storage plus an atmosphere heavy with carbon dioxide. This cuts down transpiration (loss of moisture and volatile elements) from the fruit. Although not as scientific as commercial CO_2 units, a homemade device can use the same idea.

Line a steel drum or a wooden barrel with a heavy plastic trash bag. Place the apples in this bag, taking care to see that the fruit is nearly but not fully ripe, without bruises and clean. Do not wash apples; this removes a natural wax that helps protect them. Lay a board across the top of the barrel. This should be no wider than necessary to hold a couple of candles or a tin can filled with alcohol.

If alcohol is used (it is the cleanest fuel to use), lay a rag into it to act as a wick. Light the wick or the candles and allow them to burn out completely. If candles are used, they should stand in a saucer so melting wax will not run down into the barrel. When the flames are out, remove the board and seal the plastic bag lining the barrel. The carbon dioxide given off by the flames will be heavier than air and will flow downward, surrounding the apples. Enough will accumulate to extend the storage life several weeks. If carbon dioxide is not used, don't seal the bag.

One of the difficulties in many parts of the country is that apples that are good keepers if picked late ripen so early that temperatures as low as 32 degrees will not occur for several weeks. This should be taken into consideration when planting an orchard. Nursery catalogs give the maturity dates for apple varieties; these should be about the same as the date given for the first killing frost in your area.

If a cellar is not available that can be cooled to at least 40 degrees by this date, better eat early-ripening sorts such as Golden Delicious, Red Delicious, and Stayman Winesap within three or four weeks. Rely on apples known to store well, such as York Imperial for later use.

Pears are difficult to store because they must be picked when fully mature but still firm and green. Most varieties will separate from the branch if lifted to a horizontal position when ready to pick. There is a change in color from dark green to a lighter green about this time.

If wanted for canning, keep them at 60 to 65 degrees until ripe. Can immediately as soon as ripe since pears do not keep well after ripening. Bartlett and Kieffer pears are the varieties usually canned.

Pears for later use should be picked at the mature green stage just described and held as close to 32 degrees as possible. Be sure to notice the date at which a variety is supposed to be ready for use. Don't try to store too long after this time or they will break down without ripening. To ripen for use, hold in a temperature of between 60 and 65 degrees. If ripened at too high a temperature, they will also break down without ripening.

Grapes can be stored for short periods if they are fully ripe and the storage space can be held at 32 degrees. Individual bunches should be kept in very thin food storage plastic bags because, if left open, they pick up undesirable flavors.

Cranberries may be stored the same way as pears are stored. I have kept cranberries in thin plastic bags from harvest time until March 1 without any signs of rotting in an unheated cellar that occasionally had temperatures below freezing.

None of the soft fruits can be kept for any length of time. Peaches, apricots, cherries, gooseberries, raspberries, and others of this type must be either canned or frozen.

IV

The Modern Homesteader

34

Facing Up to Modern Homesteading

There is a need to state clearly what this chapter is all about. It is neither an effort to persuade you to abandon life in the city and take up life in a remote area, nor is it intended to discourage those who have logical reasons for such a move.

Instead, I hope to present as broad a picture as possible of what such a surrender of your present life style might involve. This chapter is a condensation of talks I have had both with those who have been successful following such a move, and with those who have found their new life too difficult to face.

R.M.C.

When you are resting comfortably in a warm living room with snow beating against the windows, as radio and TV drone on endlessly about a world in chaos, retreat to some Elysian rural haven seems an idyllic way to survive in an overburdened world.

The image of a cozy farmhouse sheltered from the north by your own woodlot, a garden outside the kitchen door filled with ambrosial tomatoes and lettuce, an orchard heavy with sun-ripened red apples of heavenly flavor, and your own hens cackling about eggs of such pristine freshness as you have never before enjoyed—here is a dream within your grasp. All you need to do is act.

Before you do, consider the consequences. Each year thousands of Americans have had that dream, have thrust aside all doubts and have set out to discover their imagined paradise. True, many do find the peace of mind they sought. But about as many have learned that the Shangri-La wreathed in rosy clouds for which they hoped is instead a tough environment in which they must work hard to survive; for them the only way out was a retreat to the city. What made the difference between those who stayed in the country and those who returned to urban life?

The Reality behind the Dream

In talking with both those who are enthusiastic about their new life in spite of hardships, and with those who found it too hard to face, one fact stands out: Those who stayed were mentally prepared for their difficulties; those who gave up failed to do their homework.

Most city people know that farming, even of the limited homesteading type, does involve work. They have heard, however, that mechanization has taken the actual physical labor out of rural life. What they overlook are those everyday farming chores—slopping pigs, feeding and watering livestock, cutting wood for the stove, and the myriad other details that have no counterparts in city life. True, farming today is less arduous than it was in the early years of the 20th century, but it is by no means effortless. All too often your modern homesteader is a retiree, over the age of 65 and with no agricultural experience more extensive than raising a garden in town.

To succeed, even on a limited basis, calls for more than a willingness to work. Unfortunately the usual picture of a farmer held by city people is that of a country bumpkin chewing on a sprig of timothy as he spouts inanities punctuated with "By Gum!" Instead modern farming calls for as much executive and mechanical ability as the operation of a million-dollar business.

I do not claim to be a farmer, although I was an agriculture student and have worked with farmers for nearly half a century. As good an example of what a modern homesteader has ahead is the work I have had to do to keep our summer home in Maine operating without trouble.

When we bought our worn-out farm 20 years ago, the 120-year-old farmhouse was probably in better shape than many purchased by homesteaders. Even so it needed a new roof, the siding was in disrepair, and the window-sash mullions were worn razor-thin by weather. I was fortunate in that an old-time Maine carpenter had just finished work on two cottages on our island and was willing to work on mine. His name, Charlie Coolbroth, rang with good old Maine competence, and that's what he had. Living in the house and doing his own cooking that fall and winter, he reroofed, patched, and painted the siding but had to leave for another job before he could do the windows. He left them to my tender care.

The wavy windowpanes were as brittle as only old glass can be, but I managed to save all but three of them. Once I had dug out and replaced the century-old white lead putty and reinstalled the sash, we moved in.

The "facilities" consisted of an outhouse so primitive that I immediately built a new one with my own hands. It was a bit luxurious, with a picture window facing the Camden mountains 26 miles across the sea, an induced draft, and a tiled floor.

Eight years ago electricity came to the island, and we replaced our aged gas refrigerator with a modern electric unit. Anyone who has had to struggle with the whims of a rusting gas box will appreciate what a relief that was. Electricity also meant the end of carrying water from our shallow well, but only after someone could be found to drill 100 feet through granite for a new source of water. The next step was to dig a pit for a well house (built by my own hand this time; there was no Charlie Coolbroth on hand) and to dig a trench to the house. This in turn called for a complete water system inside, again accomplished without help. Installing two bathrooms, three sinks, and other units in a water system, I learned about the art of plumbing the hard way.

With my son-in-law, I laid out a septic field complete with tank and drains. To reach gravel soil for drainage, we had to move rocks weighing well over a ton each.

While all this was going on, I planted a 10,000-square-foot

garden and a 26-tree orchard of dwarf apples, pears, plums, peaches, and apricots.

I learned by experience that wiring an old house is far more difficult than installing a complete system in a new one, where the stud spaces are open. This work took an entire summer. Even that was easier than installing a forced-air furnace through tough eight-by-eight-inch framing!

But why go on? The point I want to make is that anyone contemplating a life away from city services and conveniences must be prepared to face problems for which no profession or desk job can prepare you.

The Energy Crisis

To mention the uproar over the Arabs tweaking our collective noses may be tiresome, yet to believe that the energy crisis is a dead issue is to ignore fact. Oil, coal, electricity, and other energy sources are finite and as time goes on will become scarcer and more costly. They are destined to run out within the lifetimes of many who are reading these lines.

How sure can you and I be that even electricity will be available for any reasonable length of time? There are so many roadblocks in the path of full atomic power that, even if these were removed today, nearly a quarter of a century would elapse before a fraction of this nation's energy needs could be met. Even short-term prospects are sometimes uncertain. On our summer island the current provided by our beat-up generators (one a WW II relic) is anything bur reliable. In spite of the amazing ingenuity and skill of island lobstermen, who make themselves available 24 hours a day for patching, there are outages that last for hours and even days.

Power failures have meant loss of food, discomfort, and even death. Anyone without an alternate source of power in a rural environment can get into trouble. Consider that you need a 5,000-watt home generator to keep an average home running normally. That will be of use only until petroleum runs out, predicted for 1985. Inventors are striving feverishly to perfect methane gas generators that can turn garbage into gas, windmills that can store energy for times when the wind does not blow, solar accumulators and other not-yet-perfected energy sources. But you will be vulnerable until these brainstorms are translated into working commercial units. And, so far, intensive search has not turned up a single practical home unit.

All of which emphasizes one aspect of homesteading that must be faced: Are you physically fit for life in a community where medical and mechanical help may only be available miles away from your home? Could you survive in a house without heat?

To show both sides of the coin, many who desert the city find their health improved. Colds are less frequent, largely because they are not exposed to infection from close contact with other people. Increased physical activity during the daily routine is a factor. Anyone pitching hay or cutting firewood has little need for jogging down a smog-filled street. Provided that the water supply has been checked carefully, farm families escape the drawbacks of chlorination and the existence of chemical contaminants that even the best treatment methods do not remove from city water systems. With wood as fuel, life could go on.

Certainly anyone who hates do-it-yourself work around the home has no business on a modern homestead. No matter how well you are fixed financially, you may not be able to find help in rural communities. It comes as a shock to many to learn that even people they look on as poor will refuse to work for money but are willing to swap labor if you have something to contribute.

If you can qualify as to physical and mechanical aptitudes, there is still one more hurdle to overcome: the psychological shock that comes with a change in life style. You will find country living a different existence from the suburban cocktail ritual. There will be no more standing on one leg and then the other to relieve the strain on your back as you swap inanities with a roomful of people who are bored to the teeth. Most farms are remote not only from other people but from what passes for entertainment in the city. TV stations are distant and reception is poor. Country radio is so drab that about all you will be able to stand will be the weather reports and farm programs.

I recall my shock on first hearing New England radio. In my

mind was the slogan so often used to identify that area, "The Athens of America." At last, I thought, here will be programs of classical music, learned discussions of science and the arts, and a pervading sense of good taste. What came out of the speaker when I turned on the set was the most raucous, tasteless racket I have ever heard over the air. Today, except for weather forecasts, our set stands mute.

For indoor recreation, be content to rely on books, magazines, records, home games, and conversation. Out-of-doors, however, the world is your oyster. The one thing we enjoy most is seeing the sun rise and set. We can see the whole panorama of the sky, unobscured by factory smoke and smog. Even the progress of a storm is a drama that few city dwellers can appreciate. Bird watching to us is far more exciting than a game of bridge. One of our daily amusements is watching a cock pheasant beat a tattoo against his reflection in our window as he threatens an imaginary invader of his territory.

At night the pageant of the heavens is awesome when you can view it from horizon to horizon. The constellations become friends, as do the moon and the planets. To walk along the road with no light other than the stars is to know the land as no city-bound human can.

If your mood is sound, even digging in a garden or cutting wood for a fire in the Franklin stove becomes fun.

Financial considerations that loom large with many are no problem for others. Although this is an area in which I claim no special competence, I can say that farm equipment, as distinguished from land, costs more than most homesteaders realize. Recently I saw figures on how much it would cost a young couple in Illinois to start farming on land they had been given. It totaled $50,000.

This does not mean it can't be done for less. I know of families that arrived on a homestead farm with less than $500 and made a go of it by substituting muscle for money.

In the South, where winters are less severe, costs are lower and life somewhat easier. It is a known fact that once a family has gone through the initial stages of getting settled, it costs less to live in the country than in town. Clothing is cheaper, they raise their own food, costly amusements and entertaining are nonexistent and taxes are lower.

Whatever you decide—to remain in the city or brave the troubles of country living—sit down and think before you make the move. Put down on paper the pros and cons. List what you must give up: the golf club, your season tickets to the symphony, old friends, the theater, and much more. On the other side of that list put down a sense of security, better health, relief from city pressures and from trying to keep up with the Joneses, lower living costs, and, perhaps, your self-respect.

Have a good life!

35

Tools and Materials
for Homesteaders

Tools

Although hand tools might not come under the definition of
food production, my experience in working at a distance from a
hardware store or other source of supply has given me an appreciation of how important to every operation in a homesteading farm the right tools can be.

Some are obviously needed: claw hammer, tack hammer,
sledge, maul, wood-splitting wedges, crowbar, long prybar, a
wrecking bar, a 100-foot steel tape, six- or eight-foot steel tape,
carpenter's level, mason's level, plumb line, slip-joint pliers,
wire-cutting pliers, open-end and socket wrenches, pipe and
monkey wrenches, putty knives, paint brushes, and all the other
hand tools needed by an all-around handyman.

The refugee from the city might, however, overlook some
that belong to the old-time farmer. These include pick-ax, mat-
tock, steel fence post driver, post hole digger, mason's trowels,
ropes (nowadays of nylon or other synthetic fiber), chains, cord-
wood saw, buck saw, winch, stoneboat, chain saw, pruning saw,
grindstone, pole trimmer, scythe, sickle, pruning shears, bush
hook, manure fork, hay fork, wooden hay rake, tilling spade,

garden spade and fork, grease gun, oilcans, and dozens of other tools and gadgets.

Power

If you are going to be truly self-reliant, an electric generator is essential even if you are on a high line. Rural power plants, which are not as reliable as a city system, can be out for a day or more at a time. This should be a gasoline- or propane-gas-driven unit with adequate reserve fuel. Notice that I say generator not alternator. Although they cost more, generators are much more reliable than alternators when called upon for continuous service following an outage that takes two or three days to repair.

If you intend to rely heavily on power tools such as a table saw, band saw, lathe, drill press, and other shop equipment, this standby generator should be big enough to run any household electrical equipment as well as one or two of these units. This will mean between 3,000 and 5,000 watts. If you can afford it, the unit should be the kind that automatically switches from line current to generator and starts the motor if an outage occurs. Even more sophisticated would be a reserve fuel supply unit with diesel power, which could draw on tanks of fuel oil for house heating.

In the South solar-heated hot-water systems are no longer an experiment. Even total house heating and cooling will soon be out of the preliminary development stage and are worth investigating. My first experience with solar-heated hot-water heating was in Florida in 1926. Even then it worked, although the roof heat exchanger was so ugly that few people were willing to install one. If you have any respect for conventional architecture, they still are not a thing of beauty.

Paint and Useful Gadgets

One item I must include in these random notes is a recipe for a paint product that will retain its color and covering power for up to 50 years. This is no miracle of modern chemistry but an old folk product that accounts for 95 percent of the old red barns you see in New England. It was the first latex paint. The basic color was an earth color, red iron oxide. Modern versions are burnt sienna and Venetian red, varying slightly in color with the degree of purity. Mixed with buttermilk, this made a crude latex paint that seemed to become a part of the wood itself and, once dry, would not wear off.

Today the red earth colors are difficult to find and may have to be ordered for you from the manufacturer. A 50-pound drum of the stuff is handy to have around for covering any wooden structure that needs dressing up. If other colors are wanted, such earth pigments as burnt umber, raw umber, and yellow ochre can be used. I once wanted to reproduce the color on some graceful wooden kitchen chairs with bamboo reeding. They were that wonderful old mandarin yellow occasionally seen on Colonial furniture. A washed French yellow ochre with just a touch of burnt sienna gave the identical color, one that glowed in sunlight.

Buttermilk paint is easy to mix: Simply stir in the pigment a little at a time until it is thick enough to keep the wood from showing through. One feature of this type of paint, which is wonderful until you want to refinish a piece of furniture painted with it, is that I know of no paint remover that will take it off. Patient sanding and scraping with broken pieces of glass is about the only solution.

Two pieces of equipment that city farmers often overlook are the wooden barrel and pottery crock. They are needed for many purposes on the farm. Making sauerkraut, storing root crops and apples, scalding hogs and chickens when slaughtering, pickling and corning meat and (in farms near the sea) salting down cod and herring for the winter, all call for crocks or barrels.

Another highly useful gadget is a fish and meat smoker. Not one of the fancy tinsmith jobs selling for fancy prices but an old refrigerator, even one from the dump. With the freezing unit ripped out, it becomes a clean metal box equipped with shelves. Cover the bottom with a sheet of asbestos board, place two bricks on the bottom and you are ready to begin. Find an old but sound heating element for an electric oven or range and set it on top of the bricks. If they are not bone-dry, lay another sheet of asbestos board on top of them. Attach wires to the heating element and put a pie tin on top of it.

Hickory or applewood chips are best, but any nonresinous wood will do. I use alder because I have tons of it. Plug in the unit and close the door over the wire. An intact rubber gasket will fit over it. Heat will generate smoke, which will all be confined in the box. Meat or fish laid on the shelves will smoke nicely. No exact timing can be given, but for the first time or two you use the smoker, examine at the end of every hour.

If electricity is not available, wood chips on charcoal can be used, but in this case a vent will have to be cut into the box to supply the charcoal with air.

Wood as Fuel

The mention of wood chips brings up another phase of home-steading—wood as fuel for heating and cooking. Most subsistence farms have plenty of wood for this purpose. An abandoned apple orchard can provide logs for a fireplace or Franklin stove that will hold a fire for hours. An old cast-iron kitchen range in good condition can serve both for heating and for cooking. If you intend to use it for cooking, one part of the stove to check carefully is the heat passage to and around the oven. In many old stoves rust causes the iron to spall or separate from the inside of castings. This debris drops down into the heat passage, blocking it completely. This does not ruin a stove as a source of heat, however. Since the oven heats only slightly, you can stick your feet inside after a cold day in the open and enjoy the warmth without burning yourself. Modern reproductions of these old woodburning stoves are available (at a price). They can be converted to burn kerosene or fuel oil (as can older stoves), but save all grates and parts for the day when fuel oil will no longer be available.

One important reason to use wood as a fuel is that it is a renewable product as well as less polluting than oil, coal, or gas. If you have a choice, the following chart, showing the rating of wood from various trees, should be helpful. Any wood, however, even punky cottonwood, has some heat value.

Wood burning central heating plants (furnaces or wood-fired boilers) are all but nonexistent today. About the only source is a heating and ventilating contractor who is removing such equipment and installing oil or gas heat. Keep in touch with two or

RATINGS FOR FIREWOOD

	Relative amount of heat	Easy to burn	Easy to split	Does it have heavy smoke?	Does it pop or throw sparks?	General rating and remarks
Hardwood Trees						
Ash, red oak, white oak, beech, birch, hickory, hard maple, pecan, dogwood	High	Yes	Yes	No	No	Excellent
Soft maple, cherry, walnut	Medium	Yes	Yes	No	No	Good
Elm, sycamore, gum	Medium	Medium	No	Medium	No	Fair
Aspen, basswood, cottonwood, yellow-poplar	Low	Yes	Yes	Medium	No	Fair—but good for kindling
Softwood Trees						
Southern yellow pine, Douglas-fir	High	Yes	Yes	Yes	No	Good but smoky
Cypress, redwood	Medium	Medium	Yes	Medium	No	Fair
White-cedar, western and eastern redcedar	Medium	Yes	Yes	Medium	Yes	Good—excellent for kindling
Eastern white pine, western white pine, sugar pine, ponderosa pine, true firs	Low	Medium	Yes	Medium	No	Fair—good kindling
Tamarack, larch	Medium	Yes	Yes	Medium	Yes	Fair
Spruce	Low	Yes	Yes	Medium	Yes	Poor—but good kindling

From U.S.D.A. Leaflet 559.

three contractors in a nearby town. Because disposing of such units can be a problem, they often are glad to sell them for a fraction of their original cost. An old unit is more difficult to install than a completely new system, since joints must be carefully sealed. Professional installation is advised.

In figuring the amount of wood needed, ask your heating contractor to estimate how many tons of coal or gallons of oil the unit would burn to heat your home. You can convert this figure into wood by counting a cord of hardwood such as ash, oak, birch, etc., as equal to a ton of coal or to 150 gallons of #2 fuel oil. If the only wood available is low in relative amounts of heat, figure at least 50 percent more, or a cord and a half for a ton of coal.

A cord measures four feet high, four feet wide, and eight feet long. Most furnace wood is cut into 16-inch lengths; when this is stacked four feet high and eight feet long, it is called a face cord, or one-third of a standard cord.

Don't think that cutting the amount of wood needed is a light task. Heating a house in the northern United States, even with some rooms shut off, might require ten cords of dry wood, 80 feet long. With a chain saw, this could take two weeks of work.

During the summer in Maine, we burn a cord or more of wood just to take the chill off in the morning and evening hours.

36

Meat Sources for
Homesteaders and Suburbanites

•

In discussing animals that can be grown as part of a
program of home food production, I wish to explain that the information needed by the inexperienced subsistence farmer or
suburban gardener is far too extensive to be covered in a single
chapter. So, I am mentioning useful ideas I have not found in
publications I have read. Do not think you can read the following lines and become an instant expert on chickens, rabbits,
quail, sheep, goats, et al. To help you chart your meat production program, send for the publications mentioned.

Most large urban communities have laws against keeping
chickens and other sources of meat that can be raised as part of a
home food production program. As a result, what follows will
apply largely to suburban towns and to homesteading farms.

There are a number of smaller animals that stand confinement well and do not present problems in preparing them for
the table. Killing of some larger animals, such as sheep, hogs,
and steers, can be a distasteful, if not traumatic, experience for
most city refugees on homestead farms. I speak from
experience.

Although as an agriculture student I had attended classes in
butchering hogs, facing a 300-pound live sow with that in mind

was another matter. It was in France, and the men in my company (practically all city boys from Chicago via Camp Grant) had by hook or crook (more likely the latter) managed to acquire the critter as the pièce de résistance of a wartime Christmas dinner. But how to turn a hog into pork?

As the only one who had ever had a hand in such an operation, to save face I was forced to take over. Imagine if you can a wrecked cottage (fortunately one that had been equipped with an ancient bathtub on legs), a nervous officer, and a cocky sergeant who had volunteered to help deal with an angry sow. Even placing the bullet was not easy; the first shot ricocheted. But a gasoline-fired army stove had been heating the water for scalding the victim, and, with the help of two husky G.I.s, that job was completed.

It was not until the ungainly carcass had been hoisted on an improvised gambrel, however, that I ran into real trouble. As the entrails came tumbling out, my noncom assistant gagged and fainted. Covered with gurry, I managed to complete the job unassisted.

I would, therefore, recommend that anyone who has not had experience in preparing meat animals for the table should confine his efforts to chickens, ducks, rabbits, and quail.

Chickens

The most practical small meat animal for the inexperienced subsistence farmer or suburbanite to raise is without question the hen, with perhaps a rooster if hatching eggs are wanted. Equipment and care are relatively simple, and structures for housing can be easily improvised by a handyman. Most old barns are much too dark for hens, but if windows can be cut in to let in sunlight they make excellent housing. Your state agricultural college or county farm adviser (usually situated at the county seat) can supply all the advice you need.

One good reason for beginning with chickens is that pullets or baby chicks are readily available anywhere, even by mail from big houses such as Sears Roebuck. Your county farm adviser can put you in touch with hatcheries that can supply both baby chicks and started pullets. The latter are not cheap, but since they are usually vaccinated against four main poultry diseases—bronchitis, Newcastle disease, laryngotracheitis, and fowl pox—and are free of parasites, they are worth the extra cost. Before you make any move, send 30 cents to Superintendent of Documents, Government Printing Office, Washington, DC 20402 and ask for Farmers' Bulletin No. 2197, *Farm Poultry Management*, 20 cents, and *The Home Chicken Flock*, Leaflet No. 497, 10 cents. These do not discuss breeds to any extent. A more extensive publication that I have found useful is *Poultry Production*, W. A. Lippincott, 8th Edition, revised by L. E. Gard.

Choosing a Breed

In considering breeds, the subsistence farmer in particular must not rely too heavily on commercial practice. The most popular of all breeds in the United States is the White Leghorn and a number of hybrid strains of it. It has been bred with egg production as its sole purpose in life.

True, one of the major advantages of chickens as a food crop is that they produce eggs, an important protein food, and Leghorns are the most important layers of white eggs. While I do not want to condemn the Great American Egg Machine to those who are primarily interested in egg production, homesteaders must also give thought to the food value of a hen after she has completed her egg-laying life. Anyone who has been faced with a choice between the carcass of a wornout Leghorn layer and a plump White Rock hen of the same age will have no difficulty in deciding which bird will be tastier in a stew with dumplings. For all practical purposes, the heavier bird will be best.

It is also best to avoid the many hybrids incorporating Leghorn blood. Some of these will seem ideal, particularly those that weigh up to five-and-one-half to six pounds. Since they are hybrids, many can only be perpetuated by making crosses annually between the two purebred parents. This means that your own flock cannot be used as a source of eggs if you plan to hatch your own chicks. Since the main idea behind homesteading is to become as self-sufficient as possible, perpetuating your flock is best done if you stick to medium or heavyweight breeds, such as New Hampshire Reds, Rhode Island Reds, White Rocks, White Wyandotes, White Orpingtons, or colored variations of the last three. Although Plymouth Rocks are popular, one trait of this breed might or might not be a drawback.

The exhibition strain of the Plymouth Rock can only be maintained by raising two separate lines, one for producing exhibition roosters and the other for hens. If this is not done the plumage does not meet show standards.

Skin and egg colors are traits that some find highly important. In a home flock where all the eggs and table fowl are consumed at home, this need not be a factor. On the market, though, this can be critical. A city refugee from Boston can learn to eat a white-shelled egg instead of the brown-shelled egg on which he was weaned. A New Yorker transplanted to the Middle West might find a white-skinned Buff Orpington just as tasty as the yellow-skinned Plymouth Rock he bought in the Eastern markets.

If, however, there is any thought of selling eggs or table fowl, local prejudices must be considered.

Feather color has some bearing on market carcasses, too. Dark-plumaged birds have dark pinfeathers, a drawback to acceptance. Another reason for preferring white-feathered breeds in the South is that they do not suffer quite as much from the heat as do those of dark colors.

Caring for Chickens

Another fact seldom mentioned in literature on poultry rearing is that chickens, not having sweat glands, can suffer severely if confined in a poorly ventilated coop in summer. They are grateful for shade in the open. Although commercial production is done almost entirely indoors with no outside runs, farm flocks and those in suburban areas should enjoy such a yard.

The ideal shade tree for this purpose is a peach or plum tree, or several if the yard is big enough. The hens will pick up insect pests, particularly the curculio, which might otherwise infest the fruit trees.

Poultry literature, in describing another difference between commercial and small farm practice, usually recommends four square feet of floor space for birds not housed in individual cages. This is not enough, in my opinion, to keep birds happy and healthy. I would suggest from five to seven square feet as reasonable insurance that diseases will not be serious. Provided that you begin with healthy stock and house your birds in a dry, well-ventilated building, you should not need to worry about poultry ills.

Although chickens cannot be said to be disease-free, millions of hens in farm flocks have never been treated for any malady and remain in robust health. Keep in mind one fact: A flock of 50 mature hens will give off two-and-a-half gallons of water a day. If this is not vented outside, that water will be absorbed in the litter, where it causes trouble. Another problem is that a flock of this size will produce a ton of manure a year, a product of increasing value in this day of shortages of fertilizers from petroleum. Much of this is voided at night while the birds are roosting. Why more roosting quarters are not fitted with pull-out trays underneath to catch this waste is difficult to understand. If a series of trays, each about three feet wide and a foot deep filled with peat moss or leaf mold, is kept under the roosts, these can be emptied regularly and the house will smell fresher. Made wider than that, they will be heavy and difficult to handle. Cover space under roosts with one-inch mesh chicken wire, the size used for baby chicks.

My preference for a litter or mulch is peat moss. Dealers in poultry supplies sell a special lumpy grade that is satisfactory and much cheaper than the finer grades sold for garden use. I have discovered another useful litter—the fallen needles that accumulate under spruce or pine trees. Their resinous odor repels insects.

Another idea, which I discovered during World War II when poultry feed was short, is a bit grisly, but economical. I prefer to kill chickens by cutting off their heads with an ax rather than the sticking method. I use ground grain or meal to catch the blood, which can then be fed to the remaining hens. At the present price of blood meal, this will add about 50 cents worth of protein as well as valuable essential elements to the feed.

A rooster is not necessary for egg production. If eggs are wanted for hatching, buy a batch of 25 male chicks of the same breed as your hen and raise them together until they begin to fight; then pick a likely candidate or two, raise them separately, and eat the rest. This will take a year before breeding begins, time to decide if you want to play mother hen to baby chicks.

You can save on feed by growing such crops as rutabagas, garden peas in the North, crowder or field peas in the South, rape, collards and cabbage, lettuce and mustard greens. Sweet corn grains make excellent poultry feed if you don't grow field corn.

An easy-to-grow substitute for wheat is Triticale (see description in special chapter).

Quail

As far-out as the idea of raising quail for food may sound, in the Orient they are reared in captivity by the millions. Maturing in six weeks into delicious table birds, they add a touch of real luxury to the diet at a cost of a few cents per bird if feed is purchased, less if you grow most of your own feed. Compared with hens, they need less than a square foot of cage space.

As egg layers they are almost equal to hens, and their eggs have a richer flavor—gourmets rave about quail eggs for breakfast, though some people find them too flavorful. It takes about three to four quail eggs to equal two hen eggs.

The quail best adapted for raising under domestication is the Coturnix species, which is descended from birds domesticated by the Japanese and Chinese as long as nine centuries ago.

For those who enjoy bird shooting, Coturnix quail are readily stocked on suitable game-bird cover. For meat and egg production in confinement, the best variety is the Pharaoh D 1 strain, which is two times the weight of an American bobwhite at maturity. It lays eggs that are equal to seven percent of its body weight, while a domestic hen lays an egg that is only three percent of its body weight. Quail start laying eggs at six weeks from hatching.

For hunters the British Range quail is a livelier, more sporting bird, a fast multiplier (it begins laying eggs at about 40 days after hatching) and gun-metal bronze or near-black in color. It is perhaps two-thirds the size of Pharaoh D 1.

For warmer climates the English White Coturnix is less sensitive to summer heat but otherwise much like the British Range variety. It is not an albino; it has dark brown eyes and can see well in daylight. As a game bird it is somewhat too conspicuous for sport. In Vietnam it is raised widely for meat and eggs and seems to survive better than darker varieties.

Perhaps the best of the game quail varieties is the Manchurian Golden, nervous and a strong, fast flyer. In spite of its nervous nature it is one of the best egg producers in captivity. The rich golden color makes it an ornament in the field or in a cage. However, this strain is not fixed as to color. About 25 percent of the chicks hatched will be the original grey-buff color of the wild Manchurian quail, obviously a throwback in the Mendelian ratio.

Under domestication any airy, clean cage with wire on four sides that provides each bird with a foot of space will do for housing. Usually two hens and one cock make a breeding trio.

Foundation stock is not expensive by livestock breeding standards, but it's not exactly cheap either. Single birds cost about eight dollars each, in lots of ten about four dollars and fifty cents each and in lots of 100, three dollars and fifty cents each. A major souce of stock and information is Marsh Farms, 14232 Brookhurst St., Garden Grove, California 92643.

My recommendation would be to go easy, with not more than ten birds. The Pharaoh D 1 strain would be first choice, unless sporting birds are wanted.

Rabbits

The domestic rabbit is a logical meat animal to raise in confinement as a change from a steady diet of poultry. In some ways the flavor is similar, but spices and sauces can give rabbit a flavor like that of veal, or an Osso Buco Italian-style sauce can make it taste something like beef.

For those conscious of their waistlines, rabbit meat is lower in fats and calories than any animal substitute.

For anyone interested in this source of food for survival, I would recommend writing to Superintendent of Documents, U.S. Government Printing Office, Washington, DC 20402 for a copy of *Commercial Rabbit Raising,* Agricultural Handbook No.

309, Stock No. 0100-1376, 30 cents. For those who want more information, *Domestic Rabbit Production*, Templeton (The Bible of rabbit raising) can be had from Countryside Publications, Route 1, Box 239, Waterloo, Wisconsin for $7.95.

One of the important steps in buying rabbits is in the selection of a breed. The size of your family is a first consideration. If you are a retired couple, a breed such as the Californian would be a waste of feed and good meat, since a dressed carcass might yield as much as seven pounds, too much for one meal. The same would be true of Checkered Giants, Flemish Giants, or New Zealands. These are all big rabbits, more appropriate for a family of four or five.

For the smaller family a breed such as the English Spot, Dutch, or the Himalayan would be more suitable. Less feed would be needed.

Again, make a small beginning, perhaps with two does or females to one buck. Housing need not be elaborate. If it's kept clean, a cage in the basement will do. For an outbuilding, such as a shed or old barn, remember that does that kindle (give birth to young) in cold weather may leave them on the wire floor of the cage, where they will die. Provision for keeping the cage warm should be made from 26 to 29 days after breeding the doe (about the time the young will be born). An infrared bulb of the type used in baby-chick incubators may be suspended above the cage. A thermometer on the floor should read about 80 degrees.

Home-Grown Foods for Rabbits

Triticale, the new grain mentioned in the next chapter, can be substituted largely for the oats recommended for most rabbit rations. Where the subsistence farmer can save the most money, however, is in crops grown especially for feeding rabbits.

Because they are more concentrated, root crops such as rutabagas, carrots, beets, mangels, and Jerusalem artichokes will reduce the need for buying grains. These are easy to store, and they retain their succulence until spring. Cabbage can be kept well into winter and is relished by rabbits.

Keep in mind that many of the suitable root crops are also

used on the table and so serve two purposes. Mangels would be too strong for this use; so why not grow rutabagas instead? Since production per square foot is lower, if space permits plant a few extra feet of row.

One of the biggest savings a rabbit raiser can effect is in hay. Where space permits, alfalfa can be sown for hay production. One advantage of growing this at home is that it can be cut young, before the stems are thick and tough. It can be dried on wire-covered frames that allow the air to circulate around the cut alfalfa. Although practically all commercial hay is allowed to air dry in the sun, actually this is poor practice. For the limited amounts needed for a few rabbits, a better practice is to spread out the alfalfa on wire screens (wooden frames covered with two-inch mesh chicken wire will do) in dry, airy shade. If an old barn is available, the hayloft is a good place for this operation.

Alfalfa dried in shade will retain more of its green color and will be higher in nutrients than that dried in the sun. Since dried alfalfa enters into practically all animal rations, it pays to use a little extra care in processing this crop.

After a winter when only dried alfalfa has been fed, start feeding fresh greens as soon as possible. Dandelions are about the first crop available. At first, feed only two or three leaves a day, gradually increasing the amount until each doe and buck can be fed an entire plant. Young plantain leaves are also good early feed.

As soon as the soil can be turned over, mixed crops, such as oats and garden peas (in the South, cowpeas or crowder peas), should be seeded and cut just before the peas blossom).

When harvesting crops for the table—such as sweet corn, peas and cabbage—instead of taking these into the kitchen first, shuck the corn ears and shell the peas in the rabbit quarters so they can be fed fresh. Do the same with any other greens used as feed. Sugar in corn husks, for example, is converted to starch in a matter of an hour or two, making it less acceptable as a source of nutrition. Particular care is needed if lawn clippings are fed. When used fresh, they should be fed before they wilt. Incidentally lawn clippings make valuable hay if dried on frames as described for alfalfa hay. However, the two-inch poultry mesh is too big; use one-inch chick wire instead. Rabbits also appreciate an apple once in a while.

Geese

To see an old gander sitting in a field of snow, apparently comfortable and happy, is to realize that here is a tough bird. Except that most families can't stand to eat goose more than two or three times a year, this would be an ideal home food source. The fact that geese do thrive under severe conditions is not an indication that this is best for them. They appreciate a roof to stand under while they view the surrounding landscape. A goose on a nest, in particular, prefers a slight mound with a waterproof roof over it, but one that is open on all sides so that she can look out for danger.

If geese are provided with a closed coop into which they can retreat, they may not use it regularly, but they will retreat there in severe weather.

Don't try to keep geese unless you can give them some pasture. Although they will pick at grain, their favorite food is grass. They are so fond of it that if turned loose in a strawberry patch overgrown with grass, they will clean it out without touching the berry plants. They are used commercially for this purpose.

About the only important requirement is unfrozen water at all times. One warning: If you have a small dog, don't let him near the gander; he might be killed. I have even seen a Doberman pinscher badly mauled by an angry gander.

Unless you plan to do considerable searching, you will probably have to be content with some breed of goose you can find nearby. If there is any choice, one that the U.S.D.A. recommends as a table fowl is a cross between a young Chinese gander and a yearling Emden goose. The cross is fast-maturing and not too big for the average family. Since geese live for many years, such a cross will not be complicated by the need for bringing in parents of both breeds annually to keep the combination going.

The following are the breeds you are most likely to find for sale:

Emden. Pure white, with adult males weighing 26 pounds and females 20 pounds, this is a lot of goose for all but a large family. Because of its white feathers, it is preferred by many. About 35 to 40 eggs are laid; if the goose cannot cover them all, they can be hatched in an incubator. Emdens are better sitters than Toulouse, which have been known to abandon their nests a few days before the eggs are ready to hatch. Most commercial raisers of geese have an incubator warmed up and ready for this possibility.

Toulouse. The same size as the Emden, it looks bigger because its feathers are looser. Gray in color, it is still preferred for plucking because the down comes away easier. Not as good a layer as the Emden as a rule.

African. The ganders are about six pounds lighter than the two breeds just mentioned, and the geese about four pounds lighter. Probably the most dashing in appearance of any breed, more up-right in carriage, with a distinct knob on the head. Plumage is a blend of ash brown and lighter tones. When swimming, it resembles a swan. As a market carcass, it is not popular because of its dark pinfeathers.

Chinese. Weighing between eight and ten pounds at maturity, Chinese geese are much more practical as table fowl for the average family. They can be had in either pure white or brown. The female lays between 40 and 50 eggs a year.

Although the literature on raising geese is limited, about all you will need to know is contained in *Raising Geese,* Farmers Bulletin No. 2251, available from the Government Printing Office for 20 cents.

Ducks

On learning that White Pekin ducks reach a weight of seven pounds in eight weeks, many home food producers become enthusiastic about this breed as a source of meat. What they fail to realize is that no other fowl has as heavy a skeleton and yields less edible meat per pound of live weight. Dressed out, that seven pounds winds up as three or four modest servings.

This by no means condemns the duck as a table fowl. Because the meat is different enough from other fowl, it is desirable for variety. For all practical purposes, homesteaders are limited to White Pekin as a breed since, in America, they have been bred for fast growth and size. The Aylesbury, a similar white duck from England, is more desirable because it is not as nervous and easily scared as the Pekin, but it is hard to find. Both are poor sitters; so their eggs must be hatched in an incubator.

Two breeds are spectacular egg layers: the Indian Runner and the Khaki Campbell. But these are so light in weight that when roasted they make a meal for only about one person. Unless there is some reason for preferring duck eggs to those of hens, there is little reason to keep either of these breeds. Incidentally any duck eggs not wanted for hatching are perfectly good for table use; only an expert can tell them from hen eggs. However, the laying season for the White Pekin breed is short, largely from February through May.

About all you will want to know about raising ducks can be found in *Raising Ducks,* Farmer's Bulletin No. 2215, available from the Government Printing Office for 25 cents.

Turkeys

Unless you want to make a career out of raising them, forget turkeys. They are without doubt the most difficult of all fowl to raise and, with poults selling for a dollar or two each, by no means cheap.

Guinea Fowl

For a really different flavor in fowl, a guinea hen is worth considering. (Somehow, the name guinea hen is accepted for both the male and female, although that usage is frowned on by purists.) The flesh is much darker and has a gamier flavor than other fowl. They are small, so that one bird per diner is usually needed. Because the rest of the carcass contains very little meat, only the breast is served. Although there are three recognized varieties, differing only in color, unless you want to exhibit at poultry shows, better buy what you can find.

Guineas are excellent watchdogs. Seeing one go after a slinking cat is often good for a laugh. Their raucous cries signal the presence of predators long before a dog would start barking.

They are also good insect killers in gardens. Since they do not scratch, they do not hurt plants, and because they are excellent fliers—unless their wings are clipped—they cannot be confined to a pen. Feathers on one wing will need to be clipped once a year. Keets (baby guinea fowl) can be pinioned by cutting off the first joint of one wing.

A government leaflet on guinea fowl is Leaflet No. 519, *Raising Guinea Fowl*, Stock No. 0100-02984, available from the Government Printing Office for 25 cents.

Sheep

For bolder souls willing to slaughter larger animals, sheep have certain advantages. Perhaps no other meat animal will stand for more neglect. On islands off the coast of Maine, where they are exposed to weather without shelter winter and summer, they survive on pasture so thin that it seems incapable of supporting life.

This does not mean that sheep can be neglected and poorly fed if they are to do well. Even on offshore islands, the lambs are usually rounded up and docked. Removing their tails keeps the wool cleaner and reduces insect damage. What is important is that sheep can make good use of grain and processed feed when grown for profit, but, for home use, they will thrive and even put on fat on good pasture alone, for most of the year, with high-quality hay for the most severe months of winter. Even on weedy pasture, they eat 90 percent of all common weeds.

Sheep require less attention than any other livestock. Although often grown without shelter, except in the extreme northern part of the United States, a rainproof roof overhead should be provided for them. On pasture the manure is widely distributed and worked into the soil by their small hoofs. If their shelter is fitted with a solid floor, even a small flock will yield enough fertilizer for most farm gardens. One ewe produces about three-quarters of a ton of manure a year.

Pasture area need not be large; a single acre, well fenced, will support two ewes and their lambs. If hay is to be cut at home, grow alfalfa, clover, or soybeans rather than timothy, as sheep do not do well on the latter.

One precaution: If you keep both sheep and goats, give them separate pastures because they can be infected by the same internal and external parasites. Do not, however, pay attention to the old superstition that cattle and sheep cannot be run on the same pasture. This is true only if the field is so small that sheep, which crop the grass closely, leave it so short that a cow cannot find enough to eat.

The best bulletin on preparing sheep for the table is a free U.S.D.A. bulletin, *Slaughtering, Cutting and Processing Lamb and Mutton on the Farm*, Farmers Bulletin No. 2152, which can be had through the Government Printing Office or perhaps from your county farm adviser.

The best book (but expensive—$15.00) is *Sheep and Wool Science*, M. E. Ensminger, Interstate Publishers, Danville, Illinois. Other helpful texts are *The Sheep Book*, John McKinney, John Wiley & Sons, New York City; *Sheep Production*, Diggins & Bundy, Prentice-Hall, Inc., Englewood Cliffs, New Jersey; and *Profitable Sheep*, S. B. Collins, Macmillan Company, New York, New York.

Goats

A doe or female goat is often recommended as a satisfactory substitute for a dairy cow. My suggestion is that before you jump in, find a good goat dairy near you and try the milk for a week. One count against goat's milk is that it is almost homogenized naturally. The fat globules, which are extremely fine, remain in an emulsion and separate from the milk in small amounts.

Many individuals prefer goat's milk to that from cows, while others find it unpleasant, perhaps because what they tasted came from a shed where both the billy and the nanny were kept.

Goats do have advantages over cows. Five of them can live in the space and on the amount of food needed for a cow in milk. Only two are needed to keep most families supplied with milk. Nannies come in heat from September to February. If two are kept, and one is bred at the early part of this period and the other toward the end, a continuous supply of milk can be maintained. However, what is often overlooked is that goats in milk cannot be left unattended for a single day; you are committed to a daily care program with *no* holidays or weekends off.

Goats can be kept entirely on pasture and hay, but feeding some grain to supplement these will mean more milk. For some reason Americans are averse to eating young goats. Actually the flesh is even more delicate and finer-flavored than lamb. Since nannies usually give birth to twins, and most families do not want to keep more than two or three milch goats at a time, at least one of these ought to wind up on the table. Except that kid meat lacks the woolly taste that sometimes occurs in lamb, there is little difference.

The male goat or billy *is* a serious drawback to keeping goats. Since he is useful only two or three times a year, his feed and care are an expense. Worst of all is his odor, about which little can be done. As a sex lure, he urinates on his legs and coat. "Smelling like a billy goat on the Fourth of July" is certainly a pungent and accurate saying. If you do contemplate keeping goats, try to locate a sire in the neighborhood that can be used for service.

If you want cream and butter, the Nubian is perhaps the best choice, since individuals of this breed usually produce slightly richer milk. The heaviest milk producers on record are Saanens, followed by Toggenburg and Nubian in that order. Toggenburgs remind me of miniature Jersey cows.

Goats have not been popular or plentiful enough in America to be given much attention by animal scientists. The one Farm Bulletin covering them is *Milk Goats*, Farmer's Bulletin No. 920, which was out of print the last time I ordered it but should be available through your county farm adviser or the Government Printing Office.

One final bit of advice: Remember that goats are *not* pets. For some reason homesteading city folk are more likely to make pets of them than of other livestock. Sheep, particularly baby lambs, are appealing, but sheep are stupid, while goats are smarter and often amusing. A good rule is never to make pets of any animals kept on a farm. If children want a pet, give them a rabbit, a cat, or dog—an animal that does not enter into the food chain. Otherwise, even a steer can become a part of the family, and it is extremely difficult to enjoy a steak when you are thinking of it as "part of Blackie."

What About Hogs?

Speaking of pets, it is difficult to keep a family from adopting a young pig. Give it half a chance to follow you around, and it will soon be as appealing as any dog or cat. Be forewarned; keep young pigs penned from the time they are weaned.

Although most of the information you will need can be found in the two books I mention, all reference works I have read make one erroneous assumption—they give directions for producing pigs with pounds and pounds of lard and other fat, on the theory that an ideal hog for slaughter should weigh about 225 pounds at the age of eight months.

Many new homesteaders, however, often slaughter their first pigs at about 180 pounds, and they are surprised at how much tastier the meat is. Hog fat is often dumped in the garbage, a waste of the food that went into its production.

Unfortunately those who want to raise only a hog or two have little choice of breeds. They must accept what is available from local hog farmers, practically always one of the lard-type breeds such as Chester White, Berkshire, Duroc, Hampshire, or Poland China. When raising a pig for meat, it doesn't pay to buy pure breeds. But if you can buy a breed sow, look for one of the following bacon-type hogs: Landrace, Tamworth, Yorkshire, Minnesota #1, or Palouse. These are long, lean hogs that produce more bacon and hams than lard.

The easy way to break into the raising of hogs for the table is to buy a weaned pig about eight to ten weeks old. Be sure it has been vaccinated; check with your county agent for advice. If it is a male, be sure it is a barrow (a castrated boar). The meat of an uncastrated mature boar has a strong, offensive taste and odor.

Cut your cost of feeding by growing rutabagas, carrots, turnips, and sugar beets to supplement any grain you must buy. The triticale mentioned elsewhere is an excellent hog feed. Because hogs grow so fast, they need mineral supplements in addition to grain and roots. Supply them with a mixture of equal parts by volume of ground agricultural limestone, salt, and steamed bone meal. A clean pasture will help reduce feeding costs.

Feeding garbage is another way to save feed costs, but it must be free from pork scraps and fat (these can pass on hog cholera if they are not from your own hogs). Although cooked potatoes, vegetables, bread, and similar feeds are acceptable, they must not be allowed to accumulate; feed them as soon as the kitchen cleanup is over. Never allow such garbage to freeze, and, of course, metal scrap, soap, and other trash should never be allowed to get mixed with garbage to be fed.

A brief, free leaflet on hogs can be had from the Government Printing Office. Entitled *Raising a Few Hogs,* it is Leaflet No. 537 of the U.S.D.A.

For more complete information, consult *Approved Practices in Swine Production* by Joergenson & Baker, $9.25, or *Swine Science* by M. E. Emsminger, $15.75, both from Countryside Publications, Route 1, Box 239, Waterloo, Wisconsin 53594.

A valuable bulletin on processing hogs into meat is *Slaughtering, Cutting and Processing Pork on the Farm,* Farmer's Bulletin No. 2138, which can be purchased for 45 cents from the Government Printing Office, Washington, DC 20402. My recommendation is that for your first attempt, you buy a suckling pig and process it instead of tackling a 180- to 225-pound mature pig. Roast suckling pig is one of the gourmet treats city folks can't enjoy, but you can.

Cows and Steers

Probably no single farm animal appeals more to the home-steader than a cow. He pictures a warm barn with a gentle bossy giving gallons of milk, a cellar with pans thick with cream and fresh-churned butter. That picture can be true, but it will call for more than passing attention. Before he rushes in and buys a cow, a good idea is to visit a general farm (not a producing dairy), where one or two cows are kept for the family's use.

The most important fact to appreciate is that a cow cannot be put out to pasture and left for a day or two while you run back to the city to see old friends. You are tied to Bossy every day she is in milk. If you are lucky, you can arrange with a friendly neighbor to take over for a short time, but, as in the case of goats, the care of a cow is a daily chore.

Selecting a cow for a family farm is not the same as buying one for a dairy herd, where production is usually the sole considera-tion. Any cow that is a reasonably good producer will probably give more milk than a family of five can consume. And if, to maintain a continuous supply, two cows are kept, there are times when you won't know what to do with it all. Of course, there are chickens and pigs to feed when two cows are fresh at the same time.

Do not figure on using milk raw. Even if your cow has had all the tuberculin and Bang's disease tests, this is unwise. Plan to buy a small home pasteurizer at the same time you buy Bossy.

If I had a choice, I would pick a Jersey or a Guernsey. Some people find Jersey milk so rich they can't drink it, but it can always be allowed to rise and some of the cream skimmed off. Jerseys are gentle, easy to care for and, if anything, too ap-pealing. By the time your cow becomes too old and must be dis-posed of to the butcher, you will find that she is a member of the family.

Guernseys are slightly larger, and, while their milk is usually yellower than that of Jerseys, it is not as rich; yet it is richer than that of other breeds. You are not likely to find an Ayrshire avail-able, but if you do she will be a good third choice. If you plan to veal her calves, she might well be a good first choice.

The subject of calves introduces another problem—that of breeding. This must be done annually. If there is a good Bang's and TB-accredited purebred bull in your neighborhood, you are lucky. No family farm should keep a bull under any circum-stances. Artificial insemination is an alternative.

Any cow you buy should not be over five years old. One of your first female calves ought to be looked over as a possible successor. A five-year-old cow has six or seven years ahead of her; after that she will have to be replaced. Too, there will be periods of six to eight weeks when a cow will be out of production—even longer if you are trying to make milking periods overlap so both won't be dry at once.

Once you have a good second cow, you might want to change your breeding practice. Instead of using a dairy bull of the same breed, use a beef breed, such as the Black Angus, Hereford, or Shorthorn, and raise the calf as a steer if a male, or as a feeder heifer if a female. Bull calves should be castrated, a job for a veterinarian if you are squeamish.

Much nonsense is written about the poor quality of meat from dairy breed calves. This idea arises because meat is graded by color. The fat in the meat of dairy breeds is a distinct yellow, actually a sign of richness that is severely discounted in market beef. The finest slice of roast beef I ever ate was in a Washington, D.C., club that has Jersey or Guernsey steers fattened on contract for its kitchen. When I expressed my opinion that this must be the finest beef in the world, my host (a national authority on cattle) replied that there was one better—from Japanese steers that were stall-fed with beer and massaged daily to tenderize the flesh! At the time this gourmet's delight was selling for the equivalent of ten dollars a *pound*.

Don't hesitate to raise dairy calves, either for veal or as baby beef. In fact, if you can buy a dairy bull calf as a feeder, it will probably be cheaper than a beef breed and make a better steer for home use.

Again, don't undertake the job of raising a steer if the prospect of slaughtering an animal of this size disturbs you. You might persuade some neighboring farmer to do the killing for you, for a share of the meat. Custom butchering is another possibility but often rather costly.

A good book for general information on the dairy cow is *Dairy Cattle and Milk Production* by Eckles, Anthony & Palmer, published by Macmillan. For home slaughtering, see Farmers Bulletin No. 2209, U.S.D.A., available from the Government Printing Office for 40 cents.

Protecting Your Animals

One of the best defenses against vandalism and theft is an alert dog of a size and breed that will discourage intruders bent on mischief. No matter what your preference, pick one that looks as though it means business. One of my pet breeds is a golden retriever, a lovely animal to have around and to use for hunting, but not too impressive as a guardian of the farmyard. Such breeds as Airedales, Doberman pinschers, police dogs (Alsatians), or Great Danes (if you can afford to feed the latter) can frighten away undesirable visitors by their appearance alone. Although you do not want a true attack dog, some schooling in defense tactics by a professional dog trainer is highly desirable. For example, teaching a dog to refuse food from strangers could prevent poisoning.

Although the idea of roadside selling is appealing, it has its dangers. The fact that a sign says *Fresh Eggs for Sale*, gives anyone the right to walk onto your property, even with no intention of buying and with an eye to later looting. If you do have extra produce to sell, arrange to dispose of it to individuals you know.

Incidentally insurance on livestock against theft and injury by vandals is not expensive. With a milking goat worth up to $100, it pays to protect her or any other valuable animals you own.

If you are feeding a steer or two and your farm is on a traveled road, use a pasture away from public view, if at all possible. At the present price of beef, rustlers are going farther and farther from big city centers to find unprotected livestock. If they can't find steers, they will settle for sheep or even chickens.

37

Triticale—
A Homesteaders' Grain

If two or three acres of tillable soil are available, homesteaders would do well to consider growing a grain that combines the ruggedness of rye and the high yield of wheat. Called Triticale, it is actually a hybrid of these two quite different grains.

Although crosses between genera are rare and are usually sterile, plant breeders have been accomplishing a near miracle with these two. Wheat belongs to the genus *triticum* and rye to the genus *Secale*.

Early hybrids between the two were promising because they combined the high protein content and productivity of wheat with the high lysine content of rye. They had serious faults, too, but these have been largely bred out of later varieties. I grew some of the earlier varieties; in spite of their shortcomings, they were quite impressive. The grain, which I ground to flour in a blender, had a flavor that resembled Bohemian and Swedish rye breads, both of which combine wheat and rye flour.

One of the most important advantages of Triticale is that it grows over a much wider range than its parents. Much of the production of this new grain was done in Mexico, where it proved adapted to tropical and subtropical highlands. At the other end of its range, it thrives on the prairies of Canada. Although it is relatively new, it is being grown on some one million acres in fifty-two countries under a wide range of climates.

One reason it can be grown so widely is that it is much more resistant to the rust that wipes out wheat in tropical and subtropical regions.

As a feed for cattle, hogs, and other meat animals, Triticale is at least the equal of wheat. As a poultry feed, certain new varieties with a high lysine content have been found so efficient that no other protein concentrates were needed.

This is not a grain that every small farm seed supply house will have. Ask your farm adviser to help you locate seed. The following facts will guide him if he has not been in touch with Triticale research. For the South the best varieties are being bred at CIMMYT, the International Maize and Wheat Improvement Center in Mexico, under the direction of Nobel Prize winner Dr. Norman E. Borlaug. The work for Northern climates is done at the University of Manitoba in Canada. One highly adapted variety for the North, called Rosner, has been released and is being sold by Canadian seed houses in the wheat belt in that country. Another source of information is the Rockefeller Foundation.

Although locating a source of Triticale may involve some effort, I have a conviction that this grain will some day equal wheat in acreage, or even exceed wheat's production in bushels.

In test plantings I have made with the earlier, primitive hybrid, production per acre was heavy enough so that two acres would produce enough grain to feed all the small animal livestock needed to supply a family of five with meat, plus flour for bread, pancake flour, tortillas, and breakfast cereals.

Perhaps the newer varieties (on which information on production per acre is not fully available) will do even better.

38

A Bible for Survival Farmers (a note on *Mother Earth News*)

Anyone who gives a passing thought to modern homesteading would do well to learn about *Mother Earth News*, a bimonthly magazine that has become the bible of dedicated back-to-yesterday survival farmers.

It is a fascinating mixture of highly sophisticated articles, obviously by writers who know what they are talking about. Although they tend to be overenthusiastic, the subjects they cover are important to anyone who would like to become at least partially self-sufficient in a civilization dedicated to spoon-feeding its members.

The value of these cogent articles is reduced somewhat by occasional letters from featherbrained individuals who would rather emote than think. No matter what you may decide about rural escapism, you will enjoy a peep into an existence of which few city dwellers are aware.

To subscribe, send $8.00 for six issues a year to the *Mother Earth News*, P. O. Box 70, Hendersonville, North Carolina 28739. At the same time, send an extra 50 cents for a catalog of *Mother's General Store*, an amazing document that offers useful devices and materials that many feel have become obsolete. (Unfortunately the massive *Whole Earth* catalog of over 400 pages is no longer available.)

Where else can you buy a right- or left-hand handle for a broadaxe if you own only the head (as I do)? In case you want to cut real Colonial shakes out of your own white cedar logs, where but in this catalog can you find a froe? A friend of mine, who was quoted a price of $110 a square for commercial shakes, cut 15 squares out of his own woods in a week, using a froe made from an old machete.

Other old-time goodies listed are soapstone griddles, kits for brewing real English ale, home knitting machines, nearly a dozen types of woodburning stoves, a sausage stuffer that doubles as a fruit or lard press, hand-operated coffee grinders, brooders for poultry, incubators that hatch quail, pheasant, duck or chicken eggs, a corn sheller, fruit presses, Pennsylvania Dutch stoneware pie plates, and hundreds of other items of the past.

A word of caution: Many of the products listed may seem expensive. Keep in mind that these are often handmade in limited quantities, not stamped out from tin or sheet metal.

Index

A

Acidity of soil, 184, 281, 282–83, 293, 297–98
Actidione, 214
Aeration
  compost pile, 295
  plant, 268–69
  stored vegetables, 328–29
Agriform, 245, 280
Alfalfa, 278, 279, 359, 363
Alfalfa sprouts, 30, 95
Alkaline soil, 281, 283, 293
Almond, 240
Aluminum foil, uses in garden
  controlling insects, 58, 263–65
  mulch, 324
  protecting tree trunks, 207
  reflecting light, 317
Aluminum sulfate, 188
Amino acids, 290
Amizole, 124, 145, 320
Ammonia, 290
Ammonium nitrate, 279
Ammonium sulfate, 186, 187, 188, 279, 321

Anasa wilt, 60
Angelica, 115
Anise, 111
Anthracnose, 72, 175, 247
Aphids, 11–12, 17, 35, 44, 53, 113, 151, 172, 263–64. See also Black aphid
Apical dominance, 226
Apple, 203–13
  budding, 220–23, illus. 221
  diseases and pests, 212–13
  dwarf trees, 203–6
  espaliers, 213
  fertilizer, 207
  grafting, 218–20, illus. 219
  June drop, 212
  pruning, 224–30, illus. 225, 226, 227
    bracing, 228, illus. 228
  rootstocks, 203–4, 204–5
  soil, 208, 212–13
  storing, 331–32
  suppliers, 211–12
  thinning fruits, 141
  varieties, 141–42, 208–11, 332

Malling stock, 204–5
weed control, 207
where to plant, 206–8
Apple mint, 118
Apricot, 190–91, 201–2
Arsenate of lead, 145, 176
Ash, 302
Ashes, used as fertilizer, 104, 278, 285
Asparagus, 123–26
Asparagus beetle, 126
Atrazine, 320
Atriplex. *See* Orach
Australian bush cherry, 249
Avocado, 245–46

B

Bacillus thuringensis, 44–45, 259–60
Bailey, Liberty Hyde, 142
Balm, 115
Banana, 246–47
Banvel D, 320
Barbados cherry, 249
Barberry, 237
Basil, 111, 121
Beach plum, 236
Bean sprouts, 31
Beans, 71–79, 273, 278–79, 284
  cowpea, or English pea, 77
  diseases and pests, 72
  fava, or English broad bean, 77
  fodder crop, 79
  herbs used in cooking, 74
  kidney, 78
  lima, 78–79
  mung, 31
  planting, 73, 273
  pole, 273
    green and wax, 73, 74–75
    lima, 79
    supports, 74–75, 309
  seed inoculation, 81
  seed propagation, 134
  shell, 77–78, 79
  snap, string, green, or bush, 1–2, 31, 71–72, 72–74, 273, 278–79
  soil, 71
  soybean, 31, 76, 79, 278–79, 363

wax, 74–75
white, 78, 79
Beaux Fruits de France, Les, 139
Beef, 110, 369
Beet, 31, 43, 95–96, 267, 271–72, 273. *See also* Swiss chard
  cooking, 43
  forcing, 318
  seed propagation, 134
  soil, 94
  storing, 95, 328, 329, 330, 331
Benlate, 8, 262. *See also* Benomyl
Benne, 111–12
Benomyl, 175, 262. *See also* Benlate
Berries, 236–38, 249. *See also* names of berries as Raspberry
Bindweed, 320
Birds as pests, 184, 198, 236, 237
Black aphid, 77, 131
Blackberry, 168, 171, 172, 173, 174, 175, 183
  diseases and pests, 175–77
Blackcap raspberry, 175–76
Black currant, 181
Black mold, 11
Black salsify. *See* Scorzonera
Black walnut, 241–42
Blanching, 317
  angelica, 115
  asparagus, 124, 126
  cauliflower, 48–49
  chicory, 34
  corn salad, 35
  dandelion, 36
  endive, 36, 37
  fennel, 50
  sea kale, 129
  shallots, 92
Blight, 241. *See also* Early blight; Fire blight
Blister rust, 179–80
Blossom end rot, 11, 22, 23
Blossom Set, 10
Blueberry, 183–89
  mulch, 188, 189, 322
  soil, 184, 186–87, 282, 298
Blueberry maggot, 188
Bone meal, 291
Books and magazines on farming herbs, 122

livestock, 353, 357–58, 361, 362, 363, 364, 365, 367, 369
Mother Earth News, 373–74
Borage, 115–16
Borer, 182, 192, 195. *See also name of borer as* Cane borer
Borlaug, Dr. Norman E., 372
Bouillabaisse, 112
Bouquet garni, 119
Boysenberry, 174, 175–77
Bramble hook, 173
Broad bean, 77
Broccoli, 31, 43–45, 267, 273
Brown rot, 201, 236
Brussels sprout, 32, 44, 45, 273
  seed propagation, 134
Buckwheat hulls, 322, 323
Bud drop, 10
Budding fruit trees, 220–23, *illus.* 221
Buffalo berry, 238
Bulb celery. *See* Fennel
Bulberry. *See* Buffalo berry
Bunyard, George, 42
Burpee Seeds, 3
Bush bean. *See* Beans
Bush cherry, 236, 249
Butler, Dr. William, 144
Buttermilk paint, 345–46
Butternut, 240, 242

C

Cabbage, 1, 31, 45–48, 267, 273
  red, 47
  Savoy, 46
  seed propagation, 134
  storing, 329–30
Cabbage butterfly, 35
Cabbage looper, 44, 259
Calamondin, 250, 252
Calcium, 282, 283
Calendula, 112
Canada thistle, 171, 320
Cane borer, 177
Cane gall, 176
Canning jars and lids, x–xi
Cantaloupe, 66, 274
Captan, 81, 156, 175, 189
Caraway, 116, 117

Caraway thyme, 120
Carbon dioxide, 268, 331–32
Carolina bean, 79
Carpathian walnut, 241
Carrot, 96–97, 267, 273
  seed propagation, 134
  soil, 94
  storing, 95, 328, 329
Casaba melon, 67
Cashew, 240, 247
Caterpillar, 259
Cattle, 367–69
Cauliflower, 31, 48–49, 267
  seed propagation, 134
Celeriac, 31, 32
Celery, 32–33, 330
  seed propagation, 134
Cellars for winter storage, 32, 127–28, 327–29, 330
Celtuce, 33
Chard, Swiss, 49–50, 115, 134
Chayote, 69–70
Cherimoya, 247
Cherry. *See also* Bush cherry; Korean cherry; Nanking cherry
  pests, 198, 237
  sour, 191, 198–99
  sweet, 191, 199–200
Chervil, 112
Chestnut, 241
Chicken, 352–56
  cooking, 109
  manure, 283, 355
Chicory, 33–34
Chinese cabbage, 34–35, 45–46, 273, 330
  seed propagation, 134
Chinese chestnut, 241
Chives, 116
  freezing, 116, 121
Chlordane, 95, 156, 176
Citrus fruits, 249–52
Clamps, 329–30
Clay soil, 299
Cleft graft, 219–20, *illus.* 219
Cloches, 315–17
Clover, 363
Club root, 48
Cobnut, 243
Cocoa husks, 323–24

Coconut, 240
Codling moth, 212, 224
Coffee grounds, 323
Coir waste as mulch, 323
Cold frames, 314–15, 318
Cole crops, 29, 44
Collards, 50, 273
Comfit, coriander, 113
Compost, 86, 165, 277, 290, 292–93,
    294–96, 297
  acid reactive, 187
  fats added, 295–96
  fertilizing, 295
  filtering, 296
Coolbroth, Charlie, 339
Copper naphthenate, 24, 232
Coriander, 113
Corn, 82–87, 273
  diseases and pests, 3, 85
  flavor, 82–83, 86
  fodder, 84, 86
  harvesting, 86
  mulch of ground cobs, 321
  pruning, 86
  seed propagation, 134
  seed started indoors, 83–84
  succession planting, 85–86
  varieties, 3, 84–85
Cornmeal, 86–87
Corn salad, 35
Cottonseed meal, 187
Cowpea, 77
Cows, 367–69
Cranberry, 235, 298, 333
Cranberry fruitworm, 188
Crenshaw melon, 67
Creosote, 232, 314
Cress, 35. *See also* Watercress
Cropper, 1, 44
Crop rotation, 48, 315
Cross-pollination, 132–35, 185, 199
Crowder pea, 77
Crown gall, 176
Cucumber, 64–65, 274
  diseases, 3
  seed started indoors, 59
  supports, 309
  varieties, 2, 65
Cucumber mosaic, 11
Cultivator, 304, 306

Cuprinol, 232
Curly endive, 36
Currant, 178–82, 207
Custard apple. *See* Sweetsop
Cypress, 206

D

Dalapon, 124
Dandelion, 36, 359
Darrow, Dr. George, 151, 174
DDT, 145
Delbard, Georges, 139
Dewberry, 173, 174
  diseases and pests, 175–77
Diazinon, 60, 95, 262, 263
Dibble, 303–4
Dill, 113
Diseases and pests, 5, 259–65, 268,
    292. *See also* Insecticides; *also
    see names of diseases, insects,
    and subhead* Diseases and
    pests *under plant name*
Dogs used for protection, 369–70
Dormant oil spray, 177
Dowpon, 145
Dried blood fertilizer, 33, 277, 291
Dryland blueberry, 189
Ducks, 361–62
Dust as mulch, 322
Dutch elm disease, 321
Dwarf fruit trees, 203–6, 214

E

Early blight, 104, 292
Earthworms, 184
Eggplant, 26–27, 274
  seed propagation, 133
Elderberry, 236–37
Electricity
  for hotbeds, 313–14
  rural, 340, 345
Emsweller, Dr. Sam, 323
Endive, 36–37, 274, 350
Endive, French. *See* Chicory
Energy crisis, 340–41
English barberry, 237
English broad bean, 77
English pea, 77

English walnut, 241
Environmental Protection Agency, 263
Equipment. *See* Tools
Escarole, 37
Espaliers, 213
Excelsior, 149, 325

F

Farmer Seed & Nursery Co., 3, 106
Farming, 337–43, 373
Farwell, Mrs. Albert D., 104
Fava bean, 77
Fennel, 50, 117
Fennel-flower, 117
Ferbam, 175
Fermate, 175
Fertilizer, 276–86. *See also types of fertilizers as* Ammonium sulfate; Bone meal; Dried blood; Wood ashes; *also see subhead* Fertilizer *under name of plant*
  acid, 188
  container growing, 22
  high nitrogen, 185
  lawn, 278, 281, 284
  mulch, 164–65, 188, 321
  organic, 33, 187, 277, 283, 284, 289, 290–91, 292–93, 298. *See also* Compost
  relation of, to lime, 282, 295, 297
  seedlings, 14–15, 285
  slow-release, x, 23, 33, 98, 124, 152, 279–81, 291–92. *See also names of slow-release fertilizers as* Green-Green
  storing, 285–86
  subtropical soil, 245
  transplants, 25, 284
Fertil-Pot, 59
Fig, 142, 253
Filbert, 243
Fire blight, 212, 214–15
Firewood, 347–50
Fish emulsion, 277
Fish smoker, 346–47
Flea beetle, 26, 27
Florence fennel. *See* Fennel
Florida fruit plants, 244–45

Flowering almond, 236
Flowering quince, 238
Fluorescent bulbs, 14, 16
Fodder, 47, 61, 79, 81, 84, 86, 97, 99, 101, 128, 241, 356, 358–59, 365, 366–67, 372
Food coloring, 114
Food crisis, vii, x–xi, 103, 109
Forcing crops, 43, 127–28, 309, 315, 318
Freezing, protection from. *See also* Hotkaps; Rose cones
  cloches, 316
  cold frames, 315
  mulches, 325
Freezing herbs, 116, 121
French endive. *See* Chicory
Fruit Testing Association, New York, 157, 161
Fruit trees and shrubs, 190–238, 245–55, 284, 290, 324, 326
Fruitworm. *See* cranberry fruitworm
Fungi
  anthracnose, 72, 175, 247
  mummy berry, 189
  mycorrhiza, 187, 188
  ring, 48, 253
  slime, 48
  soil, 289, 290, 292
  white pine rust, 179–80
Fungicides. *See* Benlate; Benomyl; Captan; Ferbam
Fusarium wilt, 9, 10, 292

G

Garden cress. *See* Cress; Watercress
Garlic, 92, 328
Geese, 360–61
Georgia Coastal Plain Experiment Station, 185
Goats, 364–65
Gooseberry, 178–82, 207
Gooseberry tree, Otaheite, 248
Grafting fruit trees, 218–20, *illus.* 219
Grafting wax, 220
Grain, 371–72

Grape, 157–67
  culture, 161–66
  fertilizer, 163
  mulch, 164–65
  planting, 164
  pruning, 162–63, 165–66, 232–34,
    illus. 232, 233
  soil, 163
  storing, 166, 333
  suppliers, 211
  trellises, 162, 163–64, 232
  varieties, 140, 158–61, 166–67
  wine grapes, 157
Grapefruit, 250, 251–52
Grass clippings, 9, 322–23, 359
Green bean. *See* Beans
Green-Green, 7, 9, 14–15, 33, 98,
    124, 152, 279, 280, 292
Greenhouses, 317–18
Grey mold, 155–56
Gro Net, 74–75, 80, 198, 309
Grub, white, 145, 156, 176
Guinea fowl, 362–63
Gynoecium, 2, 65

H

Hamburg parsley, 98
Harlequin bug, 52
Harris (Jos.) Seed Co., 3
Hastings (H. G.) Co., 4, 91
Hawthorn, 238
Hazelnut, 243
Heartnut, 242
Heptachlor, 95
Herbs, 109–22, 267
  annuals, 111–15
  books on, 122
  drying, 120–21
  dyes, 110
  freezing, 121
  perennials, 115–20, 309
  seed
    sowing, 110
    storing, 115, 121–22
  storing, 121
Hickory, 242
Hicks, Henry, 203
Highbush cranberry, 235
Hoe, 302

Hogs, 366–67
Hollandaise sauce, 63–64
Hollygrape, 238
Homesteading, viii–ix, 337–43, 373
Honeydew melon, 67
Hops, 322
Hormone for rooting, 255, 286, 323
Hormone sprays, 10
Horticultural bean, 78
Hoses, 308
Hotbeds, 311–14
Hotkaps, 17, 316
Huckleberry, 189
Hulls used as mulch, 323
Humus, 295–96, 321
Hybrid vegetables, vii, x, 1–5, 133,
    261, 262

I

IBDU, 152, 279, 292
Ichneumid fly, 11–12
Insecticides, 26, 44, 60, 95, 113–14,
    156, 175, 177, 182, 192, 201, 214,
    259–65
  organic gardens, 44–45, 113, 262,
    263–65
International Chemicals, 280
International Maize and Wheat Im-
    provement Center, 372

J

Japanese barberry, 237
Japanese persimmon, 253–54
Japanese plum, 254
Japanese walnut, 242
Jardin du Gourmet, Le, 4, 91
Jerusalem artichoke, 128
Judson, Victor, 153
Juneberry, 237–38
June drop, 212

K

Kale, 50–51, 267, 274
  seed propagation, 134
Kidney bean, 78
Kitazawa Seed Co., 4
Kohlrabi, 51–52, 274, 330

Korean cherry, 236
Kumquat, 252
Kys Kubes, 15

L

Lace bug, 26
Ladybug, 11–12, 260
Lamb's-quarters, 130–31
Lavender sachet, 118
Lawn clippings, 9, 322–23, 359
Lawn fertilizers, 278, 281, 284
Laws governing gooseberries and currants, 179–80
Leaf hopper, 172, 264
Leaf miner fly, 264
Leaf mold, 295, 320
Leaves used as mulch, 149, 165, 187, 320–21
Leek, 92–93, 274
Lemon, 250
Lemon balm, 115
Lesser peach tree borer, 192
Lethal yellowing, 240
Lettuce, 37–39, 267, 274
   seed propagation, 134
Light
   artificial, 13–14, 16–17
   flourescent, 14, 16
   hotbeds, 312–13
   sunlight, 267–68
   testing indoor, 13
   ultraviolet, 264
Lima bean, 78–79
Lime, 48, 88, 184, 282, 291, 294, 295, 297
   in ashes, 104, 285
Lime (fruit), 249, 250
Lindane, 262
Litmus paper, 293
Litter, 355
Livestock, 351–70. *See also name of animal as* Goat
   books on, 353, 357–58, 361, 362, 363, 364, 365, 367, 369
   fodder, 47, 61, 79, 81, 84, 86, 97, 99, 101, 128, 241, 356, 358–59, 365, 366–67, 372
   litter, 355
   protection of, 369–70

shelter, 79, 86, 352, 354–55, 357, 358, 360, 363
   slaughter, 351–52, 355, 369
Location of garden, 266–70
Loquat, 254
Love-in-a-mist. *See* Fennel-flower
Lychee, 248

M

Mag Amp, 124, 279, 292
Magdeburgh chicory, 34
Malathion, 44, 53, 77, 114, 151, 177, 182, 192, 262
Malling Station (England), 204
Manchurian apricot, 190–91
Mangel, 97, 267
Mango, 247
Mango squash. *See* Chayote
Manure, 146, 291, 292, 293, 294, 311
   artificial, 311–12
   cattle, 286
   chicken, 283, 355
   sheep, 363
   spent mushroom, 321
   storing, 286
Manure fork, 301
Marigold, 112
Marjoram, 113, 117
Marlate, 262. *See also* Methoxychlor
Marmalade plum, 248
Marsh Farms, 357
Meat smoker, 346–47
Melon, 59, 65–69, 330–31. *See also name of melon as* Muskmelon
   salad, 40
Merton Station (England), 205
Methoxychlor, 44, 60, 126, 156, 182, 262, 263
Mexican bean beetle, 264
Mildew, 9, 10, 328
Miller (J. E.) Nurseries, 211
Minnesota Mining and Manufacturing, 280
Mint, 117–18, 267
Mirliton. *See* Chayote
Mist flower. *See* Fennel-flower
Moth, 264
Moth borer, 58

Mother Earth News, 373–74
Mother's General Store, 373–74
Mountain spinach. *See* Orach
Mulberry, 237
Mulch, 149, 165, 187, 207, 319–26
  aluminum foil, 324
  cocoa husks, 323–24
  coffee grounds, 323
  coir waste, 323
  compost, 157, 165
  corncobs, 321
  dust, 322
  excelsior, 149, 325
  fertilizing, 164–65, 188, 321
  hops, 322
  hulls, 322, 323
  lawn clippings, 9, 322–23
  leaves, 149, 165, 187, 320–21
  mushroom manure, 321
  peat moss, 322
  pine needles, 149, 187, 323
  plastic, 9, 18, 150–51, 324–25
  plowing under, 325–26
  sawdust, 164–65, 188, 320
  straw, 9, 18, 165, 325
  sugar cane, 323
  tarpaper, 324
  wood chips and tree bark, 321,
    322
Mummy berry, 189
Mung bean, 31
Muriate of potash, 104, 278, 285
Mushroom manure, 321
Muskmelon, 66, 274
Mustard, 39, 52. *See also* Chinese
    cabbage
Mustard sprouts, 39, 95
Mycorrhiza, 187, 188

N

Nanking cherry, 191, 236
Nasturtium, 113–14
Natal plum, 249
Nectarine, 200–201
Nematode, 9–10, 47–48, 253, 254
New York State Fruit Testing Asso-
    ciation, 157, 161, 211–12, 237
New Zealand spinach, 41, 49, 53,
    261, 275
Nicotine, 262

Nicotine sulfate, 262
Night soil, 286
Nitrate nitrogen, 290
Nitrate of soda, 187
Nitrite nitrogen, 290, 295
Nitroform, 279
Nitrogen (N), 23, 152, 185, 186, 276,
    277, 278–81, 283, 284, 294
Nuts, 142–43, 239–43

O

O'Brien, Harry, 41
Oil spray, 177
Okra, 27–28, 274
Onion, 40, 88–92, 274
  fertilizer, 88
  harvesting, 90
  scallion, 40
  seed, 89, 90, 91, 135, 274
  sets, 89, 90, 274
  shallot, 40, 91–92, 328
  soil, 88
  Spanish or Bermuda, 89
  storing, 328
  varieties, 89–91
Orach (Oraches), 52
Orange, 250–51
Orange mint, 117–18
Orange rust, 176
Oregano, 117
Oregon holly grape, 238
Organic gardening
  fertilizer, 33, 187, 277, 283, 284,
    289, 290–91, 292–93, 298. *See
    also* Compost
  insect control, 44–45, 113, 262,
    263–65
Osmocote, 33, 99, 124, 279, 280, 292
Otaheite, gooseberry tree, 248

P

Paint, recipe for, 345–46
Papaya, 248
Parsley, 114, 267
  freezing, 121
  Hamburg, 98
Parsnip, 98–99, 267, 274
  seed, 135
  soil, 94

storing, 99
Pea, 71, 79–81, 274, 278–79
    culture, 79
    fodder, 81
    seed
        inoculation, 81
        propagation, 134
    soil, 71, 284
    varieties, 80, 81
Peach, 190, 191–94
    dwarf, 191, 192
    pruning, 230–31, *illus.* 231
    varieties, 193–94
Peach tree borer, 192
Peanut, 99–100, 267
Pear, 213–18
    budding, 220–23, *illus.* 221
    diseases and pests, 212, 214–15
    double-worked, 214
    dwarf, 204, 206, 214
    grafting, 218–20, *illus.* 219
    harvesting, 218
    pruning, 225–30, *illus.* 225, 226,
        227, 229
        bracing, 228, *illus.* 228
    rootstocks, 204, 214
    storage, 218, 332–33
    varieties, 142, 215–18
Pear blight, 212, 214–15
Peat moss, 298, 322, 355
Peat pots, 15, 59, 84
Pecan, 242–43
Pekin hawthorn, 238
Penta (pentachlorophenol), 24, 206,
    232, 314, 317
Peppers, 27, 274
    seed propagation, 133
Perennials, winter protection of, 70,
    309, 316, 325. *See also* Hotkaps;
    Rose cones
Persimmon, 253–54
Pests and diseases. *See* Diseases
    and pests
pH factor, 281–82, 283, 293–94, 297,
    320
Phosphorus (P), 276, 277, 278,
    281–82, 284, 291
Photosynthesis, 268
Pigs, 366–67
Pine needles
    compost, 187

mulch, 149, 187, 323
Pineapple, 255
Pineapple guava, 254–55
Pitanga, 249
Pits, storage, 317–18, 320
Plastic mulch, 9, 18, 150–51, 324–25
Plowing, 297, 298, 304–6
Plum, 191, 194–95. *See also* Beach
    plum
    varieties, 195–98
Pole bean. *See* Beans
Pollination, 132–35, 185, 199
Polyethylene sheets, 316
Popcorn, 87
Pot marigold, 112
Potash (K), 23, 98, 276, 278, 284–85
Potassium chloride (muriate of
    potash), 104, 278, 285
Potassium sulfate (sulfate of
    potash), 104, 278, 285
Potato, 103–7
    fertilizer, 104
    planting, 104–5, 106
    soil, 104, 282, 293–94
    storing, 329–30, 331
Potherbs, 29, 41–42, 43–54
Praying mantis, 11–12, 260
Proteose, 290
Prune, 194–95, 196, 197
Pruning, 224–34
    apples and pears, 225–30, *illus.*
        225, 226, 227, 228, 229
    grapes, 231–34, *illus.* 232, 233
    peaches, 230–31, *illus.* 231
    water sprouts, 228–29, *illus.* 229
Pruning shears, 300
Pumpkin, 61, 133, 318, 330–31
Purslane, 130
Pyrethrum, 60, 113, 262

Q

Quack grass, 124, 145, 171, 305, 320
Quail, 356–57

R

Rabbit, 357–60
Rabbitberry. *See* Buffalo berry
Racambole, 91, 92
Radish, 40–41, 99, 100–101, 267, 274

Rake, 301–2, 304
Raspberry, 168–73
  culture, 170–73
  diseases and pests, 172, 175–77
  planting, 171–72
  propagating, 168–69, 170–71
  pruning, 173
  staking, 172
  varieties, 169–70, 175–76
Reading material
  herbs, 122
  livestock, 353, 357–58, 361, 362, 363, 364, 365, 367, 369
  Mother Earth News, 373–74
Red cabbage, 47
Red stele disease, 146, 155
Red-necked cane borer, 177
Rhubarb, 126–28, 324
Rhubarb chard, 50
Rice hulls, 322, 323
Ring fungi, 48, 253
Robins, 184, 198
Root cellar, 32, 127–28, 327–29, 330
Root knot, 47–48
Rootone, 255
Rosa rugosa, 237
Rose cones, 117, 118, 119, 309
Rose scale, 176–77
Rosemary, 118
Rosin, 321
Ross Gro Net, 74–75, 80, 198, 309
Rotation of crops, 48, 315
Rotenone, 60, 262
Rubber tree, 244
Rugosa rose, 237
Rust, 124, 179, 237
Rutabaga, 101, 267, 275
Ryania, 262
Rye, 146, 298, 371
Ryegrass, 279

S

Sabadilla, 60, 262
Sachet, 118
Safflower, 114
Saffron, 112
Saffron, false. *See* Safflower
Saffron rice, 112
Sage, 118–19

Salad crops, 29, 30–42
Salade Lorette, 35
Salsify, 101–2, 267
Sand cherry, 236
Sausage plant. *See* Sweet marjoram
Savory. *See* Summer Savory
Savoy cabbage, 46
Sawdust, 164–65, 188, 320
Scab, 104, 294
Scale, rose, 176–77
Scallion, 40
Scallop squash, 63, 64
Scorzonera, 102, 267
Scuffle hoe, 302
Sea grape, 248–49
Sea kale, 129–30
Seed
  hotbeds, 312
  inoculation, 81
  presoaking, 114, 125
  propagating, 132–35
  soil, 14, 285
  sowing, 12–17
    indoors, 13–14, 15, 59–60, 68
  storage, 99, 115, 134–35
  suppliers, 3–4, 157, 372
Seed sprouts
  alfalfa, 30
  bean, 31
  mustard, 39
Selling produce, 370
Sesame seed (benne), 111–12
Sevin, 44, 52, 126, 182, 262
Shadblow serviceberry, 238
Shallot, 40, 91–92, 328
Shaulis, Dr. Nelson, 162
Sheep, 363–64
Shelters for animals, 79, 86, 352, 354–55, 357, 358, 360, 363
Sierra Chemical Company, 7, 20–21, 245, 280
Sieva bean, 79
Silverleaf, 238
Silvex, 320
Siting the garden, 266–70
Slate, Dr. George, 151, 153
Slime fungus, 48
Slow-release fertilizer. *See* Fertilizer

Smartweed, 298
Smith, Dr. Floyd F., 263
Smoking meat and fish, 346–47
Snap bean. *See* Beans
Soil, 287–99. *See also* Fertilizer; pH
   factor
  acidity, 184, 281, 282–83, 293,
    297–98
  alkaline, 281, 282, 293
  bacteria, 289, 290, 292
  clay, 299
  commercial mixes, 285
  commercially grown crops, 33
  fumigation, 48, 95, 175, 176, 189.
    See also Weeds, control
  microorganisms, 288–90, 297
  preparation, 9, 296–99, 304–6
  seedlings, 14, 285
  subtropical, 245
  testing, 281–82, 283, 293, 297
  transplants, 25
Solanine, 106–7
Sorrel, 52, 297–98
South Haven Experiment Station,
   193
Southmeadow Fruit Gardens, 211
Soybean, 31, 76, 79, 278–79, 363
Spade, 297, 300–301
Spading fork, 301
Spanish shallots, or Spanish garlic. *See* Racambole
Spearmint, 117
Spectracide, 262. *See also* Diazinon
Sphagnum moss, 59
Spider mite, 151
Spinach, 41, 43, 53–54, 115, 130,
   267, 275
  New Zealand, 41, 49, 53, 261, 275
Sprouting seeds for eating
  alfalfa, 30
  bean, 31
  mustard, 39
Sprout inhibitor, 229
Squash
  cross-pollination, 133
  culture, 58–60
  diseases and pests, 60
  hill planting, 59
  seed storage, 133
  soil, 58

  storage, 61, 318, 330–31
  summer, 57, 62–64, 275
    scallop, 63, 64
    vegetable marrow, 62
    zucchini, 62–63
  transplanting, 59
  winter, 55–62, 108, 272, 275
    acorn, 57, 331
    hubbard, 55–56, 57–58
    varieties, 56, 57, 58, 61, 108
Squash borer, 58, 60, 264
Squash bug, 60
Squash potato. *See* Chayote
Staking plants, 24
Stark, Paul, Sr., 208
Starlings, 184
Starter solutions, 284
Steer, 367–69
Stewart's disease, 3, 85, 134
Stokes Seeds, Inc., 4, 34
Storing crops in winter, 272, 315,
   318, 327–33. *See also name of*
   crop
  cellars, 32, 127–28, 327–29, 330
  clamp, 329–30
  pits, 317–18, 320
  root crops, 95, 328, 329, 330, 331
  Swedish barrel, 329
Straw mulch, 9, 18, 165, 325
Strawberry, 144–56
  culture, 145, 151
  diseases and pests, 146, 151, 152,
    155–56
  fertilizer, 149, 152
  mulch, 149, 322, 326
  planting systems, 144–45,
    148–50, 152
  renewing beds, 151–53
  soil, 145–46
  thinning, 152
  varieties, 146–48, 153–55
Streptomycin, 214
String bean. *See* Beans
Stunt, 189
Sugar cane or bagasse, 323
Sulfate of potash, 104, 278, 285
Sulfur, 104, 175, 184, 276, 282–83
Summer savory, 114–15
Sunlight, 267–68
Superphosphate, 281, 284, 286, 291

Suppliers
　fruit trees, 211–12
　seed, 3–4, 157, 372
Supports for climbing plants, 74–75, 309
Surinam cherry, 249
Swedish barrel, 329
Sweet basil, 111, 121
Sweet marjoram, 113
Sweet potato, 107–8
Sweetsop, 247
Swine, 366–67
Swiss chard, 49–50, 115
　seed propagation, 134

T

Take-Hold, 284
Tangors, 251
Tarpaper, 324
Tarragon, 119
Thermostat, 313, 328–29
Thompson & Morgan, Inc., 4, 21, 42, 100–101, 130
Thyme, 119–20
Ties for staking plants, 24
Tiller, 297, 304–6, 310
Time-released fertilizer. See Fertilizer
Timothy, 363
Tobacco mosaic, 8–9, 24, 323
Tomato, 6–26, 41–42, 275
　blossom end rot, 11, 22, 23
　bud drop, 10
　container grown, 7, 20–22
　　garbage can tomato tower, 7, 20–21
　diseases and pests, 8–12, 18, 23, 24, 261, 270, 292
　fertilizer, 7, 23, 278
　foliage removal, 25
　harvesting, 25–26
　insecticides, 25
　pruning, 17, 18, 24
　rooting suckers, 11
　seed
　　propagation of, 133
　　sowing, 12–17 *passim*, 285
　　sowing indoors, 13–14, 15
　soil, 7, 11, 22

　spacing plants, 23–24
　sunlight, 10
　supports, 24, 309
　　wire cages, 24–25
　temperature, 6–7, 16–17, 18, 25
　transplants, 8, 9, 11–12, 13, 15, 17, 25
　varieties, 2, 7, 10, 17–22, 42
　　southern, 10, 20
Tools, 300–10, 344–45, 374
　care of, 309–10
　hand tools, 173, 297, 300–304
　stainless steel, 303
　wheeled tools, 304–8
　wooden handles, 302
Tortoise beetle, 26
Tractor, 306–7
Transplants, 2, 25, 284, 314–15, 318
Tree pellets, 280
Triticale, 356, 358, 366, 371–72
Trowel, 303
Tukey, Dr. Harold B., 217
Turkeys, 362
Turnip, 102, 267, 275
　white, 41, 102
Twilley Seed Co., 4, 19
2,4-D, 12
2,4,5-T, 320

U

Ultraviolet light, 264
Urea, 290, 312
Ureaform, 152, 279, 292

V

Vapam, 124
Vaughan, J. C., 67
Vegetable marrow, 62
Vegetable oyster. *See* Salsify
Vegetable pear. *See* Chayote
Venison, cooking of, 119
Vermiculite, 285, 329
Verticillium wilt, 9, 10, 146, 292
Vesey Seed Ltd., 3
Vetch, 279
VF, 10, 18
VFN, 10, 18
Vinegar

dill, 113
  sweet basil, 111
  tarragon, 115
Virus disease, 151, 155, 172, 189

W

Walnut, 241–42
Warren hoe, 302
Watercress, 42
Watering plants, 269–70, 308, 315
Watermelon, 67–69
Wax bean, 74–75
Webb, Earl, 252
Weeds, 11, 124, 262–63, 297–98,
    305, 306
  control, 12, 124, 145–46, 207, 263,
    319–20
  food uses, 130–31
Western sand cherry, 236
West, Lewis J., 211
Wheat rust, 237, 372
Wheelbarrow, 307–8
White grub, 145, 156, 176
White pine blister rust, 179–80
Whole Earth Catalog, 374
Wild berries, 174, 175, 183, 189
Wild oleaster, 238
Wilt
  anasa, 60
  fusarium, 9, 10, 292
  verticillium, 9, 10, 146, 292
Winter forced crops, 43, 127–28,
    309, 315, 318
Winter protection. *See also*
  Hotkaps; Rose cones
  cloche, 316
  cold frame, 315
  mulch, 149, 325
Winter rye, 298
Wire worm, 95
Witloof chicory. *See* Chicory
Wood ashes, 104, 278, 285
Wood chips
  mulch, 321, 322
  smoking fish, 346–47
Wood sorrel, 298
Woods, 206, 320–21
  for fuel, 347–50
  for hand tools, 302

preservatives, 232, 314
Worcester Horticultural Society,
  220

Z

Zucchini, 62–63